Western Humanities AND CHRISTIAN Thought

Joshua Kira | Sandra Yang

Cedarville University

The Cover Art: Echoes From the Surface by Caleb Booth

The heart of my work stems from my faith as a Christian—the nature of which is the constant tension between what is seen and what is unseen.

I am fascinated by the inert material world and the mystery of the immaterial life that animates it. We are more than flesh and bone, blood and skin. We are also soul and spirit, conscience and emotions. I began to latch onto the metaphor of using echolocation to help describe the invisible veil between the material and immaterial realities. *Echo No. 1* is the visual interpretation of a sound wave that has made the journey to the veil and back.

I chose to paint on the nontraditional shape of a ring to reference the radial qualities of sound. I felt that using sculptural mixed media objects in conjunction with a flat painted surface would highlight the contrast between two different visual languages and parallel the two different realities. The specific imagery of the boat and the interruption of light and silhouettes of trees are evocative of our spiritual journey. I've sought to poetically describe the moment of salvation when we are reconciled to God. The various sculpted objects are a continuation of these thoughts. I connect the wind-chime to the movement of the Holy Spirit. The stone-like medallion references a primitive anchor and is inscribed with a vulture eating up the dead. This was intended to have a sobering effect, adding gravity and weight to the piece. The broken bottle is symbolic of people—broken vessels that are unable to do what they were originally designed for. In the end, these are all references to a personal narrative that I have infused into this particular artwork.

In all these things, I see the fingerprint of God, and my work allows me to wrestle with these thoughts in a meaningful way.

Cover art © Caleb Booth. Photo by Scott Huck.

Unless otherwise noted, scripture quotations are from the ESV® Bible (The Holy Bible, English Standard Version®), copyright © 2001 by Crossway, a publishing ministry of Good News Publishers. Used by permission. All rights reserved.

Kendall Hunt
publishing company

www.kendallhunt.com
Send all inquiries to:
4050 Westmark Drive
Dubuque, IA 52004-1840

Copyright © 2021 by Kendall Hunt Publishing Company

Text + Napster: 979-8-7657-1012-8
Text alone ISBN: 979-8-7657-1013-5

All rights reserved. No part of this publication may be reproduced, stored in a retrieval system, or transmitted, in any form or by any means, electronic, mechanical, photocopying, recording, or otherwise, without the prior written permission of the copyright owner.

Published in the United States of America

Contents

	Acknowledgments	v
	About the Authors	vii
	About the Editors	ix
	About the Contributors	xi
CHAPTER 1	An Introduction to the Arts: The Christian and the Art World	1
CHAPTER 2	Ancient Greece: Foundations of Western Civilization	17
CHAPTER 3	Ancient Rome: Art in Service to the State	41
CHAPTER 4	Early Christian and Medieval Eras: A New Voice in the Conversation	67
CHAPTER 5	High and Late Middle Ages: The Flowering of the Medieval Era	93
CHAPTER 6	The Renaissance: The Influence of Humanism	121
CHAPTER 7	The Baroque Era: The Divergence of Thought	159
CHAPTER 8	Enlightenment: The Age of Reason	193
CHAPTER 9	Romanticism: Nineteenth Century Part I	227
CHAPTER 10	Toward Modernism: Nineteenth Century Part II	259
CHAPTER 11	Modernism: Twentieth Century Part I	295
CHAPTER 12	Postmodernism: Twentieth Century Part II	331
CHAPTER 13	Globalization: Twenty-First Century	367

Authors' Picks	391
Timelines	395
Glossary	399
Bibliography	419
Index	427

Acknowledgments

We are very grateful for all the support along the way from conception to publication. We would like, first of all, to thank Dr. Thomas Mach, Vice President for Academics, for pushing the dream into action, and following it all the way through with advice and many helpful comments. We are also very grateful for the support of Prof. Beth Porter, Chair of the Department of Music and Worship, and Prof. Aaron Huffman, Chair of the Department of Art, Design, and Theatre for their assistance in connecting us with the excellent faculty colleagues who contributed to this book. Much thanks also to Keri Kira and Abby Rutan for proofreading many, many pages, and helping with many small details throughout the process. Thanks also to Student Research Assistants Elizabeth McAlester and Allison Zieg. Much appreciation goes to Curtis Ross and Noelle Henneman at Kendall Hunt for making this project possible with their expert guidance throughout the writing stage. Finally, our heart is full of gratitude to our Lord and Savior, Jesus Christ.

About the Authors

Joshua Kira

BA Bible, The Master's College. MDIV, The Master's College. STM, Yale Divinity School. PhD Philosophy of Religion and Theology, Claremont Graduate University

Joshua Kira is an Associate Professor of Philosophy and Theology at Cedarville University, specializing in teaching coursework on ethics, philosophy of religion, and contemporary theology. His research interests include philosophy of language, theology of revelation, the intersection of faith and reason, and, more recently, theological aesthetics. He is an advisor for the Introduction to Humanities course at Cedarville and frequently gives seminars on campus on public Christianity. He has published his dissertation on the relationship between speech, revelation, and divine activity, as well as numerous articles retrieving historical perspectives on philosophy and theology. Currently, he is writing on the effects of religions' perspectives on historical philosophers, as well as the relationship of metaphysics to hermeneutics.

Sandra S. Yang

BA Geography, MA Musicology, PhD Musicology, UCLA

Sandra Yang is a Professor of Music History at Cedarville University. She currently serves as the Course Administrator for Introduction to Humanities general education course and teaches other courses in Music History–related subjects. She is a member of the American Musicological Society and has served in its Pedagogy Study Group. She is also a member

of the Society for Ethnomusicology and College Music Society. She served as *Forums* editor of the *College Music Symposium* from 2016 to 2019 and has been the editor-in-chief of *Musical Offerings* since 2010. She has presented papers at regional and national conferences and has been published in the *Journal of Music History Pedagogy*, *College Music Symposium*, *Paul Claudel Papers*, and *Claudel Studies*. With a passion for multidisciplinary collaborations, she actively seeks opportunities to work with colleagues in other fields of study.

About the Editors

Chet Jenkins, Music Editor
BA Saxophone Performance, Cedarville University. MM Saxophone Performance, Ohio University. DMA, Saxophone Performance, The Ohio State University

Dr. Chet Jenkins is an Assistant Professor of Music at Cedarville University, and the Director of Bands, where he directs the Wind Symphony, Jazz Band, and Pep Band. He teaches courses in conducting, jazz improvisation, and jazz history and coaches various chamber ensembles. He is a member of the College Band Directors National Conference, and the North American Saxophone Alliance, where he has presented both as a performer and as a lecturer. As a supporter of new music, he has participated in the commissioning of new works for both wind ensembles and saxophone, from composers such as Gunther Schuller, David Maslanka, Steven Bryant, Julia Wolfe, and Kenneth Fuchs. Dr. Jenkins maintains an active performance schedule as both a classical and a jazz saxophonist, as well as a clinician and honor band director.

Cat Mailloux, Art and Theatre Editor
Certification in Art Education, BFA Sculpture, University of Wisconsin-Eau Claire, MFA Sculpture, The Ohio State University

Cat Mailloux is an Assistant Professor of Studio Art at Cedarville University, specializing in the areas of sculpture and ceramics. She received her MFA in Sculpture from The Ohio State in 2018 and BFA in Sculpture and Certification in Art Education from the University of Wisconsin-Eau Claire in 2014. Her visual work, which revolves around the exploration of materiality and spirituality, has been shown in various settings throughout the United States including COOP Gallery (Nashville, TN), Janet Carson Gallery (Eau Claire, WI), and Roy G. Biv Gallery (Columbus, OH). In 2019, she was a Writer-in-Residence at Vermont Studio Center (Johnson, VT) and an artist fellow at the Columbus Printed Arts Center (Columbus, OH). Her written work has been published in CIVA Voices 2020 (Christians in the Visual Arts). Her practice as a visual artist extends into community work as a teaching artist in Columbus, OH, where she teaches free sewing workshops for children and adults in the neighborhood of Milo-Grogan.

About the Contributors

Caleb Booth
BA Painting and Sculpture, Union University; MFA Painting, New York Academy of Art

Caleb Booth spent most of his formative years in Budapest, Hungary, and Alberta, Canada. After graduating from Union University with a Bachelor of Arts degree in 2011, he spent two years in Rome, Italy, as an Artist-in-Residence and later as manager of Accendere Gallery. Leaving Italy, he pursued a Master of Fine Arts degree at the New York Academy of Art, which he completed in 2016. He was selected for the Artist-in-Residence program at Byrdcliffe in Woodstock, NY, as well as the recipient of the Artist-in-Residence Teaching award at the West Nottingham Academy. He has shown work in the United States, Canada, Italy, and China. Caleb is currently an Assistant Professor of Studio Art at Cedarville University.

Phillipa Burgess
B Mus Ed, NSW State Conservatorium of Music, Sydney, Australia; MM (Conducting), California State University, Long Beach, CA; PhD Musicology, University of Kentucky

Phillipa Burgess is an Adjunct Professor at both Cedarville University and Sinclair Community College. She is passionate about exploring how humans historically have explored and expressed the creativity given to them by God.

About the Contributors

Andrew Hohman

BME in Choral Music Education Cedarville University, MM in Choral Music Education Bowling Green State University, DME in Choral Music Education Indiana University

Before coming to Cedarville University, Andrew Hohman served as Lecturer in Choral Music Education and Visiting Director of Choirs at the University of Dayton and as Associate Instructor at the Indiana University Jacobs School of Music. Andrew has been an active part of music education in Ohio, as he was previously the vocal music director at Fairborn High School in Fairborn, Ohio, and Cuyahoga Valley Christian Academy in Cuyahoga Falls, Ohio. His research interests include music teacher attrition and music performance anxiety. He is currently an Adjunct Professor at Cedarville University.

David Kauffman

BME Instrumental Music, Cedarville, MM Saxophone Performance, Wright State

David Kauffman serves as Adjunct Professor at Cedarville University and teaches K-6 General Music at Mt. Healthy South Elementary in Cincinnati. In 2012, he graduated with a BME in Instrumental Music and in 2015, earned his MM in Saxophone Performance. In addition to teaching, he serves on the Greater Cincinnati AOSA board.

Samantha Kauffman

BM Music Performance, Cedarville University, MM Music Performance, The Ohio State University

Samantha Kauffman received her BM in Music Performance from Cedarville University in 2012 and her MM in Music Performance from The Ohio State University in 2014, both with violin as her primary instrument. She served as Teaching Associate in the Ohio State violin studio alongside Dr. Kia Hui-Tan and is frequently a guest clinician in local school orchestra programs, where she is passionate about teaching students to play their instruments in a holistic, healthy way that avoids injury and promotes musicality. She is also an avid chamber musician and performs throughout Dayton and Cincinnati. She currently serves as an Adjunct Professor at Cedarville University.

Stacey Stratton

BS Speech Communication and Theatre, Murray State University; MFA Theatre-Acting, History & Literature/Theory & Criticism, University of Mississippi

Stacey Stratton is an Assistant Professor of Theatre Performance at Cedarville University where she currently teaches acting, stage combat, voice for the performer, and also directs half of the university's mainstage productions. She has been a member of the Southeastern Theatre Conference and the Society of American Fight Directors for over twenty years and has served as a dialect coach and fight director throughout Kentucky, Mississippi, and Tennessee. She is passionate about preparing young Christian artists to use their gifts in the theatre industry and the church. She is also passionate about missions and often spends her breaks working with students of all ages through performance-based workshops and activities.

Gretchen Yeh

BM Keyboard Pedagogy, Cedarville University, MM Piano Performance, Butler University

Gretchen Yeh received her MM in Piano Performance at Butler University in 2015 and her BM in Keyboard Pedagogy at Cedarville University in 2012. She currently works as an accompanist at Belmont University and serves as an accompanist at universities, churches, and high schools in the Nashville and greater Middle Tennessee area. Gretchen has also published interviews and articles in MTD Entertainment's music magazines. Gretchen is currently an Adjunct Professor at Cedarville University.

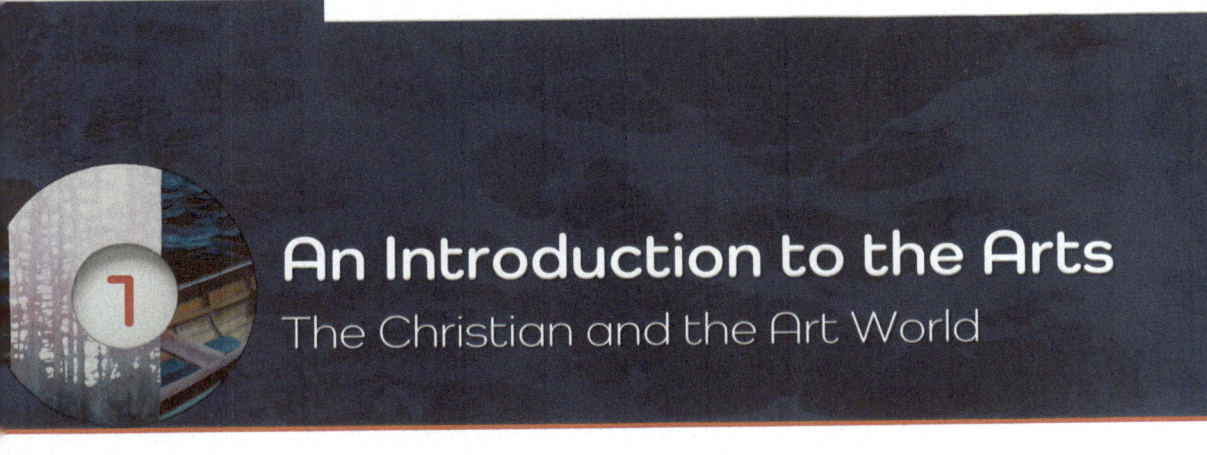

An Introduction to the Arts
The Christian and the Art World

Between Two Worlds

The Christian life is one of constant tension. There is the tension between new life in Christ and the struggle with sins of the past. There is the tension between seeking holiness and living with grace. One tension that is especially acute, however, is the believer's need to recognize that she or he is "not of the world" (John 1:19), even though she or he must live and minister within it. How one learns about the world and from the world is significant in that all Christians are called to serve well in this life. They must share the gospel (Matt 28:18-20), love their neighbor (Luke 10:27), and work heartily unto the Lord (Col 3:23). With these competing forces in the life of faith, it is easy to take an extreme position, whereby one completely shutters the world and any knowledge of it, or that one drinks deeply of the well of worldly thinking, not knowing that sometimes the well is tainted.

Christians, in the broadest sense, have struggled with this tension in relation to the arts and, sometimes, even explored this tension through art. An example of this can be seen in the **frescos**, or murals painted on wet plaster, that adorn the *Stanza della Segnatura* in the Raphael Rooms of the Vatican. Raphael (1483-1520), when commissioned to beautify the space, chose to compose two hypothetical scenes.

frescos: murals painted on wet plaster

The first of these is the *Disputation of the Holy Sacrament* (see Fig. 1.1), which visualizes what would occur if the great scholars of the Catholic Church were able to discuss the theology behind the Lord's Supper. The scene is imaginative in that many of the individuals who are speaking to one another did not live at the same time. The four seated individuals around the altar are the "Teachers of the Church," whose lives spanned the fourth to seventh centuries. Furthermore, to the right of them is Thomas Aquinas (1225-1274) and John Duns Scotus (ca. 1265-1308), both of whom are depicted with small halos. The tensity of the painting can be seen in that the individuals who are debating are being overseen by a heavenly discussion, where Christ (who is flanked by his mother and John the Baptist), is the central figure among the twelve

Chapter 1: An Introduction to the Arts

Fig. 1.1. *Disputation of the Holy Sacrament*, ca. 1510, Raphael, *Stanza della Segnatura*, The Vatican.

disciples who are also discussing sacramental theology. Interestingly, though the Holy Spirit, who is depicted as the dove in the golden halo immediately below the Christ, is descending to bring understanding to the world, the theologians and church leaders still had the responsibility to discuss. They were caught in the tension between the spiritual world that governed them and the necessity of living their lives amidst God's creation.

The second fresco is titled *The School of Athens* (see Fig. 1.2) and is Raphael's attempt to delve into the supposed discussion concerning the relationship of the physical world to the world of thought (or the spiritual world). As in the *Disputation*, there is an anachronism in that many of the figures did not have lives that overlapped. The centerpiece of the painting consists of the figures of Plato and Aristotle who are looking at one another and gesticulating as to show the differences in their understanding of the world. The same tension is found, as seen in the previous piece, yet in the secular setting of philosophy. Of importance is the placement of these two works on opposite walls, as if the church of Christ was caught between two worlds. They were caught between theology and philosophy, God and man, heaven and earth.

Chapter 1: An Introduction to the Arts   3

Fig. 1.2. *The School of Athens*, ca. 1511, Raphael, *Stanza della Segnatura,* The Vatican.

This book is an attempt to help the believer to navigate the world of art. Although the Word of God is the supreme authority for the life of the believer, Christians must understand the world in order to live in it. Moreover, art has historically encouraged an appreciation of the Lord and his gifts to humanity. With the complexity of living in two worlds, this work will attempt to be a guidebook for the believer who wants to be faithful to God, while recognizing the significance of art.

What Is Art?

To argue for the importance of art brings up the significant question of what art actually is. Though many views have been proposed, the difficulty in defining art can, in many ways, be reduced to the problem of what it is supposed to do or why one decides to produce it. With the danger of being too simple, this book will propose that the discussion be limited to fine art and define **fine art** as the intentional, creative, and contemplative expression of an idea and/or value, which frequently says something about humans, the world, and/or God.

fine art: the intentional creative, contemplative expression of an idea and/or value, which frequently says something about humans, the world, and or God

There are a few key points about this definition. First, <u>art has to do with intention</u>, specifically of the artist, since something that accidentally looks composed, beautiful, and so on, is not necessarily art. Second, art <u>often expresses something that the artist wishes to convey</u>, which is usually an idea or value, and which may intend to cause the observer of the art to react with contemplation, emotion, or desire. Last, <u>art is giving a perspective on God</u>, the world, or both, upon which the artist wants her or his audience to concentrate. An audience can be ignorant of art, but rarely does an artist expect to be ignored.

A helpful way to begin to see some of the facets of art is to understand how it is different from entertainment. An anecdote found in an early nineteenthth-century biography details how a nobleman, Lord Kinnoull, attempted to give a compliment to George Frideric Handel (1685-1759) concerning one of his musical works, *Messiah* (see Ch. 7). This piece was an oratorio, or a large-scale musical work for orchestra and voices, which was typically a narrative on a religious theme and performed without the use of costumes, scenery, or action. After the performance, Kinnoull responded by thanking Handel for the "noble entertainment" he had provided. The composer was purported to have replied, "I should be sorry if I only entertained them; I wish to make them better."[1]

oratorio: large-scale musical work for orchestra and voices, typically a narrative on a religious theme, performed without the use of costumes, scenery, or action

> ### Did you know?
>
> It is customary during the "Hallelujah Chorus," undoubtedly the most famous portion of Handel's *Messiah*, to stand and remain standing until the chorus is concluded. It is said that King George II stood during the chorus, possibly in reverence for the subject matter and the composer. Since it was polite to stand when the King stood, it meant that everyone in the audience came to their feet. Whether this story is true or not does not detract from continuing the practice to this very day.

For Handel, entertainment was not the goal, but an uplifting of the spirit as individuals contemplated the greatness of God. Unlike entertainment, art is meant to focus one's attention, typically on something that the artist finds important. In fact, entertainment might be categorized more closely to "amusement," which comes from the French word (*amuser*) and emphasizes being diverted.[2] Although one is entertained when they are distracted from the world, art's goal is to help one concentrate on ideas conveyed in the art piece.

Scripture speaks about beauty, art, and creation, but not always the way that it is often applied in the human sphere. For example, it is interesting to recognize that in Scripture, "create" terminology is never used of humans.[3] Apparently, the writers of the Bible did not want any confusion between what God does and what humans do. God creates "out of nothing" (Lat. *ex nihilo*) and makes that of which nobody has ever conceived before (Ex 34:10), whereas humans always make out of what they have received (i.e., the materials of the world) and produce art that was already in the mind of God. Thus, when humans are spoken of as being "creative," one must realize that people are using a term to point to something that is seen in Scripture, which is that the human ability to make, innovate, conceptualize, and so on, is based on God being the first and central creator. Yet, the human capacity to "create" is very different from God's.

In Scripture, beauty is most frequently talked about in relation to physical things, like people and objects in the world, while only rarely being applied in a metaphorical sense to God (Ps 27:4). That which is beautiful is always seen as an object of desire or, in other words, something that motivates one to pursue it. In this way, beauty is similar to goodness, since the Bible clearly states that those things that are good deserve our desire and motivation. It could be argued that beauty is related to the type of goodness that can be clearly perceived in the physical world. It is a good that pushes believers beyond this world to the metaphorical and transcendent beauty of God. However, beauty can become an idol when people seek that which is beautiful in order to possess or use it. When they do this, beauty ceases to attract them to the God they know Who created it and instead draws them away. The reception and use of gifts, such as art and artistic ability, is meant to compel one to focus on the Giver and not the receiver.

Why Fine Art?

As it can readily be noticed, the topic that is being discussed has begun to narrow to what is often termed "fine art." There are a few reasons for this. First, since Christians live their lives founded on a scripturally-based interpretation of the world, meaning has obvious importance to them. Moreover, Christians live their lives thinking about God's intention in Scripture, the intention of Bible writers, and the intention of believers with whom they have contact. Thus, those who follow Christ constantly relate meaning to intention. It is for this reason that art that possesses the primary goal of affecting emotions or aiding in other activities will be set aside, so that more time can be given to art that is laden with meaning and intention. Second, since fine art has been intertwined so much in the life of the church and the university, it would seem significant that believers understand the manner in which it has influenced and been influenced by institutions that Christians value. Due to the twentieth century rise of Christianity in the African continent, one can conceive of a future of studies in the humanities that will have to centralize more on Africa as the seat of the preservation of the Christian tradition. Yet, with the current effect on Protestant Christianity, emphasis will be placed on the Mediterranean, including North Africa, but will not be able to examine early spirituality in the Saharan and sub-Saharan portions of the continent. Third, since Scripture speaks of art most pointedly in relation to the artisan, believers have a vested interest in contemplating the artist. Just as one should seek to understand God through His words and works, so should one attempt to understand artists, their vision, and their concerns through their pieces. So, then, the introduction to the arts will proceed with an emphasis on fine art, which more closely relates the art to the activity and skills of the artist.

For the remainder of this book, when the term "art" is used, it can be assumed that the discussion is about fine art, especially in the Western tradition that was so influential on American society and which interacted with themes in Catholic and Protestant church history. Yet, before proceeding, it might be helpful to get a grasp of how this understanding of art contrasts with what might be termed "low art" or "folk art." Low art is termed so not because it has low value, per se, but because it is intended for a wider audience and, thus, does not require as much in terms of commitment, resources, or training to value it. The wider audience of low art relates to some of its typical characteristics, such as a focus on usefulness and functionality, as well as a simplicity that allows for easy appropriation and appreciation. High, or fine, art typically revolves around contemplation and meaning, which requires interpretive skill to understand and recognize its importance. For this reason, it tends to be complex, unique (i.e., irreproducible), and somewhat exclusive, since it requires a refinement of one's taste to understand. The value of low art can be found in seeing the way in which art is integrated into life, with the activities and rituals of humans always kept in focus, whereas high art is important for its contemplation and conveyance of complex ideas, which eventually can affect universities, societies, and

Fig. 1.3. *Campbell's Soup Cans*, 1962, Andy Warhol.

churches. Low art can immediately touch the masses, whereas fine art requires some time for its significance to be recognized, while retaining the potential to have far-reaching effects.

It should be noted that there have been times when fine art and folk art has crossed over. This is even more so in the contemporary setting. One can observe this in the pop art movement, as seen in the works of Andy Warhol (1928-1987), who attempted to subvert, or undermine, the fine art–low art distinction by portraying images that would have been familiar to a popular audience (i.e., Campbell's soup cans). In other words, he displayed low art (i.e., popular images) as high art, to show that the distinction between the two is not always so simple to maintain (see Fig. 1.3). Moreover, the change in the ways the arts are financed, with the lessening of the type of wealthy patronage found from the Renaissance through the nineteenth century, has given the fine arts a greater concern with drawing a larger audience. This type of preoccupation and crossover can be found in the National Symphony Orchestra's hiring of Ben Folds (1966-), a former alternative rock front man, to be their first artistic advisor in 2017. Yet, even with the lines blurring, it is still useful to retain the distinction for the purpose of this work. Though hints at popular art will be made, the goal is to begin the process of allowing one to appreciate fine art and its influence on humanity.

pop art: an artistic movement that did not distinguish between high and low art, often utilizing iconography from popular culture

Important Components of Fine Art

The diversity of fine art makes the task of describing it, in its totality, difficult. Perhaps, it is better to conceive of art like the philosopher Ludwig Wittgenstein (1889-1951) conceived of languages, where he spoke of them as possessing "family resemblances,"[4] even if he could not come up with characteristics that encompassed every individual tongue. Thus, the following components may be found to greater and lesser degrees in different pieces of art, but the totality of the said components will cover nearly all of what would be termed "fine art."

Fine art typically has some sort of artisanship involved. While varying heavily, depending on the message and method of the art, high art is usually characterized by great skill in its production. This can be seen in marble statues that were used in Ancient Greece and found great revival in the Renaissance. Though marble was frequently easier to use than other hard substances, the difficulty of producing individual musculature, flowing robes, and life-like hair would be hard to overstate. Thus, the sculpturers who were working with marble had skills that far surpassed the average artisan. One could also see it in the music of Frédéric Chopin, especially in a piece like *Fantasie impromptu*.

Though popular music may be pleasing to the ear, it does not usually require the same type of talent and expertise that one can see in classical music. This is not to say that it has no value, but simply that it has different characteristics.

Conceptuality is another important component of fine art, since this is a major feature that distinguishes it from other forms of craftsmanship. That art, in this sense, should be contemplated, means that the artist must be intentional with what they would like to convey. This also means, as was mentioned earlier, that fine art is laden with meaning. Humans were created by God to receive meaning, as can be seen in the creation narrative as God creates Adam and Eve in the image of God and then, immediately, begins to speak to them (Gen 1:26-30). Yet, as creation begins with a community of humans, individuals are given the ability to make meaning and convey it to one another. Language, for this reason, is a grace from God that allows men and women to begin to reveal their thoughts, desires, and emotions to one another.

> **IN THEIR OWN WORDS**
>
> "…the highest human understanding of God is this: that he knows that he does not know God, insofar as that which God is, exceeds everything he understands of Him."
>
> —Thomas Aquinas[5]

Aquinas, on recognizing that people often speak of God in analogy, believed it was important that at any point at which some sort of similarity between humanity and divinity be proposed, a greater dissimilarity must be recognized.[6] In order to prevent the pride of thinking one can easily understand God, as well as to safeguard God's transcendent holiness, He must not be seen as too similar to His creatures. God is three persons, but His personhood is somewhat different than that of humanity. He does not need human beings to be in loving community, but mankind needs Him in His triunity. God cannot have obligations imposed on Him like people can, so He is not the same type of moral being that humans are. Yet, with the great dissimilarity, it is possible to see traces of His activity in human activity. Like how it is difficult to understand what is going on in someone's head simply by seeing what they are doing, it is much more difficult to understand the mind of God by His works. Thus, to know God is to let Him speak about Himself. Moreover, to understand the work of an artist, one attempts to let her or his work speak.

The last significant aspect of fine art, though not always recognized, is that it is frequently disruptive. Since high art is emphasizing contemplation, it often attempts to encourage this by preventing a person from disregarding it. In this way, it functions similarly to miracles in Scripture. When confronted by the supernatural, an individual must recognize the presence of God and is compelled to seek what He desires. Also, the inclusion of the genre of poetry in the Old Testament performs the same function. When writing includes parallelism, a propensity for metaphor, plays on words, and so on, one must slow down to work through it. This prevents someone from quickly dismissing it. A similar idea was noticed by the philosopher Martin Heidegger (1889-1976), who discussed Van Gogh's (1853-1890) work entitled *Shoes* (see Fig. 1.4).[7]

If one were to see a dirty pair of work boots, one would simply ignore them. Yet, Van Gogh's painting is hung in a museum, whereby one is forced to ask the questions concerning it (see Ch. 10). Whose shoes are those?

Fig. 1.4. *Shoes*, Vincent Van Gogh, 1888, The Metropolitan Museum of Art.

What are those shoes for? In this way, the world of the shoes, which normally would be ignored, is forced upon the audience as the disruptive nature of the artwork prevents dismissing a dirty pair of shoes. With fine art, some of the above characteristics may be more prominent and others retreat in any given work, but the whole set of attributes presented provide some of the most important categories to use to think about art.

The Christian and the Arts

With a preliminary definition of the arts and explanation of their use in place, the question of the Christian's responsibility concerning the art world still looms. Believers are called to be involved with this world even though their citizenship is in heaven (Phil 3:20). Part of that involvement will require individuals to understand culture, so that they can steward well their gifts for the service of others unto the glory of God. Some of the readers of this work may even be called to use their artistic gifts to analyze, editorialize, and influence culture. In any case, God gives His people directives to make disciples, live peaceably in their communities, and love their neighbors. Interestingly, He does not give an exhaustive list of all the ways that these commandments can apply in differing social contexts. Thus, wisdom dictates understanding the world well, so that one can serve competently within it. Part of this, indeed, may be an understanding of the arts.

The Bible contains numerous references to creativity and the arts, none of which are obligatory for all believers. However, what is an obligation is to be lights in the world (Matt 5:14-16). Christians are called to live out their faith among unbelievers and in a world that is not Christian by nature. Thus, understanding

how people think, why they do as they do, and what their values and significant institutions are appears to be central to the way a believer can minister gospel truth in an antagonistic society. Moreover, art has had an influence on people and what they believe. One can see this just by the number of quotes from Shakespeare that are still used today, over 400 years after the Bard wrote (see Ch. 6). Thus, there appears to be good reason to be involved, in various ways, with the arts.

One question that is often broached when Christians think about art is whether devotion can be enhanced by the artistic endeavor. In some cases, this is obvious, such as the involvement of music in worship (Col 3:16). Yet, even music, with its clear uses in Scripture, was not without controversy in the early church, with some debates continuing until the present. Other areas, such as visual arts and theatre, were historically even more contentious due to them receiving lesser or no attention by the biblical authors. For example, early Protestants worried about art not only because it was so significant to Catholicism, but also because of the concerns about the possibility of idolatry with any representation of God. This is termed the "**iconoclast controversies**." Yet, their skepticism moved beyond displays of the divine persons and moved into a question of whether art could be used in any way by the believer. Another example is found in the pushback against composers during the time of the aforementioned Handel, which combined secular artistic styles with the content of Christian religious conviction. The dangers of representing religious themes, along with the very real abuses within the Catholic church in its patronage of the arts, led to a Protestant withdrawal from the artistic world.

iconoclast controversies: disputes during the Reformation on the place of visual arts in the church.

> ### IN THEIR OWN WORDS
>
> "…next to the Word of God, music deserves the highest praise. She is a mistress and governess of those human emotions—to pass over the animals—which as masters govern men or more often overwhelm them… The Holy Ghost himself honors her as an instrument for his proper work…"
> —Martin Luther (see Ch. 6)[8]

The answer to the historical neglect practiced by many Protestants toward the arts is not to overreact and to commit the very idolatry with which the early iconoclasts were so concerned. Intriguingly, there are values and practices in the Christian life that are good but are not obligatory for the believer. One would consider those things that a disciple must do, by God's command, as things that are right. Yet, there are some things that are good, as indicated by Scripture, but are not duties for the Christians. What is good might be defined as "what draws us and what deserves to draw us."[9] When individuals say something is good, they are making a judgment that it is objectively something that should be attractive and that they believe others should react the same way also. John Hare (1949-) includes "deserves to draw us" since he is well aware that often people are enticed by their own sin.

The ultimate good, as would be agreed upon by theologians as far reaching as Catholic scholasticism to Protestant Puritanism, is God (Mark 10:18). God is able, however, to use smaller goods, which He creates, to point to Himself. Everything that is right (for example, what is commanded by God) is good, but not everything that is good is right (i.e., obligatory). Right things should be our priority, since God makes it explicit that believers are to pursue them. Thus, when God tells his people to share the gospel, the good news becomes a duty to them and is therefore valued above things that Scripture does not tell them that they must do. Yet, there are some good things, which are worthy to pursue, even if God does not command it. These things can help point individuals to God, as long as one understands them through His Word and receives them with thanksgiving (1 Tim 4:4-5).

> **IN THEIR OWN WORDS**
>
> "If I find in myself a desire which no experience in this world can satisfy, the most probable explanation is that I was made for another world. If none of my earthly pleasure satisfy it, that does not prove that the universe is a fraud. Probably earthly pleasures were never meant to satisfy it, but only to arouse it, to suggest the real thing."
>
> —C. S. Lewis[10]

It would appear that beauty would be one such value. Although God never commands His followers to be beautiful or to pursue beauty as an obligation, He does appear to value it and it can be something that is a sign pointing to Him. Christians can see a beautiful sunset and marvel at their Creator, as their scriptural understanding of the world allows us to relate beauty to Him. In this way, one can recognize that art is valuable, even in God's eyes, without going so far as to argue that if one does not pursue fine art, they are failing in their duties to the Divine. Consequently, the Christian should be governed by the commendation that ". . . whatever you do, in word or deed, do everything in the name of the Lord Jesus, giving thanks to God the Father through him" (Col 3:17).

The Ability to Interact with Art

Even if one were to believe that understanding fine art could be significant to the life, worship, and ministry of the Christian, this does not mean that she or he would have the ability to interact with art such that it could perform those functions. For this reason, it appears necessary to discuss some of those skills that are necessary to appreciate art; skills that this book intends to develop.

Art, as does anything that is related to meaning and significance, requires interpretation. It is not just that fine art can encourage contemplation, but it is important to notice what the artist him or herself was intending for the audience to understand. Individuals must, therefore, ask questions like the following: What are the values that this art represents? How can one see those values as representative of the artist's contemporary social setting or as influencing such a setting? What is this piece's message? Is it consistent with what God says in the Word? What are the ways in which this art understands the world and humankind? Is what it is saying true?

It could be argued that the Christian has the ability to appreciate art in a way that those who do not believe in God could not. The theologian Eberhard Jüngel (1934-) noticed that one can learn certain things about humankind, even apart from God. In his words, "man is interesting for his own sake."[11] Yet, when individuals know God and how He relates to humans, they can reinterpret people and their world in light of God. Or, as Jüngel writes, "God can make man interesting in a new way."[12] For example, a historian can learn that Israel escaped from Egypt, but only one who knows the Lord and his relationship to the Israelites can know that "God redeemed his people." (Exod 15:13).[13] When applied to art, one could say that art can be appreciated for its meaning, but one may be able to have a deeper understanding of that meaning in light of the spiritual realities within God.

This piece is titled *Clair de lune*, which is the most famous movement of *Suite bergamasque* written by Claude Debussy (1862-1918). The title is French for "moonlight" and refers to a somewhat melancholy poem[14] that inspired the composer (see Ch. 10). If one has little knowledge, they might be able to appreciate the relaxed melody of the movement. One with more knowledge might recognize the hidden complexity of what Debussy composed and how it relates to the beauty of the night sky. Without God, one can learn from the piece according to the meaning of the artist. Though Debussy's meaning is exhausted in the moonlight and one's reaction to it, it can be the occasion for the Christian, who possesses additional understanding through Scripture, to remember or to recognize that God declared Himself to be the Creator of all things. It can, furthermore, be a reminder of the beauty of our God, Who created the night and the sky, and Who gave us eyes to see and ears to hear. In this way, art and its meaning can be something that can, when coupled with God's Word, point to a great God.

Understanding art often requires one to possess an understanding of the artist, her or his social setting, the composition of the piece itself, and the place that the piece holds in the history of art. As this book will demonstrate, the interplay between these factors will help the observer of the artwork to understand why it matters and the meaning it is attempting to convey. An example can be seen in a work of Kazimir Malevich (1878-1935), which is titled *Black Square* (see Fig. 1.5).

At first glance, this is hardly a piece of art, in that it does not require the same skill as, say, a Renaissance sculpture to produce. Yet, its place in history gives it a significance that overshadows the understated artisanship. With the rise of the camera, painters began to question their place in the art world. Surely, for them, art could not be simply about capturing reality, since a photographer with less ability could do so more ably by using technology. It is for this reason that Eduard Manet (1832-1883) pushed against historical views of what painters do and asserted the right for the artists to investigate the unusual nature of using a flat canvas to portray the world. In light of this, Malevich was making a statement about art, relating it not to the realist portrayal of subject matter, but to contemplation. As Charles Clevenger writes, "So this is not a painting *of* something, it's a painting *about* an idea—an example of blatantly *conceptual* art."[15] Thus, interpretation regularly requires an understanding of the context of the piece to appreciate its significance to art history.

Fig. 1.5. *Black Square*, Kazimir Malevich, 1915.

Not only does art require the ability to interpret, but as a Christian, appreciation of the arts requires an ability to analyze and criticize it according to Scripture. Though art, as a field, often prides itself on breaking rules and challenging norms, which is related to its aforementioned disruptive nature, a Christian who is involved in it cannot abdicate her or his responsibility before God when being involved with the art world. Nicholas Wolterstorff (1932-), an American philosopher who wrote in the area of philosophical **aesthetics**, or theory of beauty, made this very point.[16] A believer cannot choose to live like an unbeliever when seeking to appreciate the arts or when seeking to be involved with its production. Christians must understand the world, as believers who live in it, but they also must make sure that they are not "conformed to the world" (Rom 12:2). Thus, followers of Christ must think critically so as to learn from the arts, without needlessly and sinfully being influenced by it.

For this reason, not only is it incumbent upon believers to be critical in the reception of pieces of art, but it also requires them to be studied in the Scriptures so that they can evaluate according to the values and principles contained therein.

aesthetics: theory of bea

One area where this is especially critical is in the area of nudity. Pornography and erotic art should be rejected by Christians, even if the latter could technically be considered fine art, since the purpose of them is to arouse lusts that are inconsistent with God's intentions for sexual feelings. Yet, there appears to be a place for **artistic bareness**, where the intention of the artist is to convey something significant about humans through nudity and not to attempt to sexualize them in a manner inconsistent with Scriptural commendations concerning sexual relationships. For example, classical and Renaissance artists often showed unclothed figures to convey the vulnerability of humans, the closeness of humanity with the natural world, mankind as the pinnacle of creation, the beauty of innocence as seen in the creation of humanity unclothed, and so on. In each of these cases, the goal is to show a conceptual or spiritual truth, not to tempt the flesh (1 John 2:15-17). Moreover, even though there appears to be legitimacy to artistic bareness, this does not mean that it could not influence a believer to lust. Thus, even in the context of nudity that has a significant and non-erotic reason, believers must take care in knowing themselves and whether they are in danger of sin, even when observing legitimate, fine art. No art is worth the risk of sinning against God.

> **artistic bareness:** where the intention of the artist is to convey something significant about humans through nudity and not to attempt to sexualize them in a manner inconsistent with Scriptural commendations concerning sexual relationships

Conclusion

Christians are not at home in this world. They are sojourners who must be honorable among the world but abstain from its passions (1 Pet 2:11). For this reason, interacting with art is significant since, through understanding it, they gain insight into the world and its ideas. This can allow the believer to better minister to those who do not know Christ (1 Cor 9:20), better defend the faith against detractors (1 Pet 3:15), and better appreciate what God has created (Ps 19:1). This volume aims to not only explain the history of the arts but also show how believers can be involved in a fruitful dialogue with it.

Study Questions

1. What is the fundamental difference between art and entertainment?
2. How is "create" terminology used in Scripture and how does that affect the way one thinks of human creativity?
3. How can one distinguish high art from low (or folk) art?
4. What are some of the important components of fine art?
5. Why is interpretation and criticism important to Christians as the approach fine art?

Notes

1. William Forbes, *James Beattie*, 260.
2. "Amusement," OED Online.
3. It is true that some English translations will speak of humans creating, but the words that are used are typically used for "making," words that can be applied to either God or humanity. However, the Hebrew *bara'* and the Greek *ktizō*, typically translated "create," are reserved for God's activity.
4. Ludwig Wittgenstein, *Philosophical Investigations*, §67 [36-37].
5. Thomas Aquinas, *De Potentia*, q. 7, art. 5, ad. 14. Translation author's.
6. This was in line with the teaching of the Fourth Lateran Council, which occurred during the decade before Aquinas was born.
7. Martin Heidegger, *The Origin of the Work of Art*, 142-212.
8. Martin Luther, *Luther's Works*, 53:323.
9. John Hare, *God and Morality*, 253.
10. C. S. Lewis, *Mere Christianity*, 136-7.
11. Eberhard Jüngel, *God as the Mystery of the World*, 34.
12. Eberhard Jüngel, *God as the Mystery of the World*, 34.
13. See Ingolf Dalferth, *Theology and Philosophy*, 130-133.
14. The original poem was by Paul Verlaine.
15. Charles Clevenger, *Introduction to Humanities*.
16. Nicholas Wolterstorff, *Art in Action*, 88.

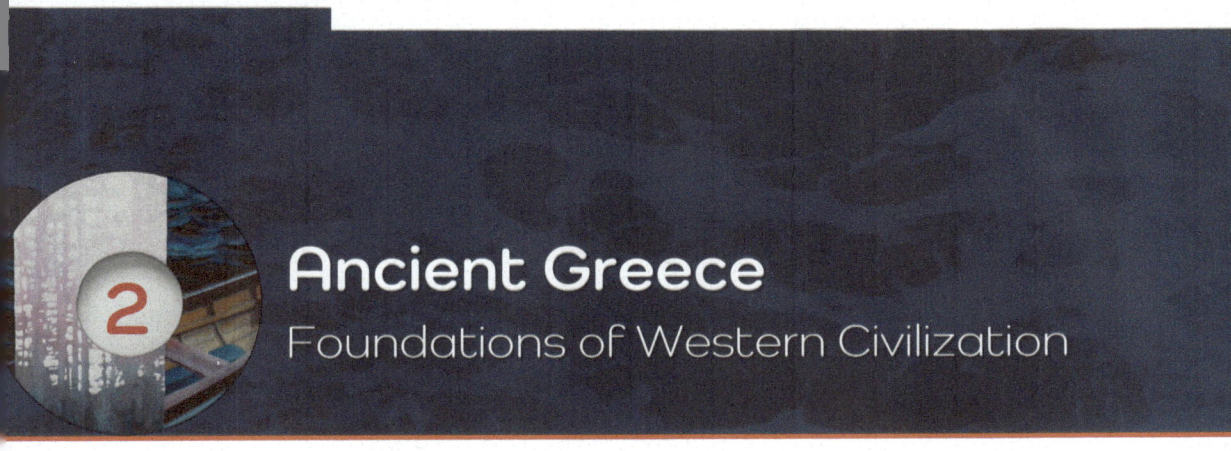

Ancient Greece
Foundations of Western Civilization

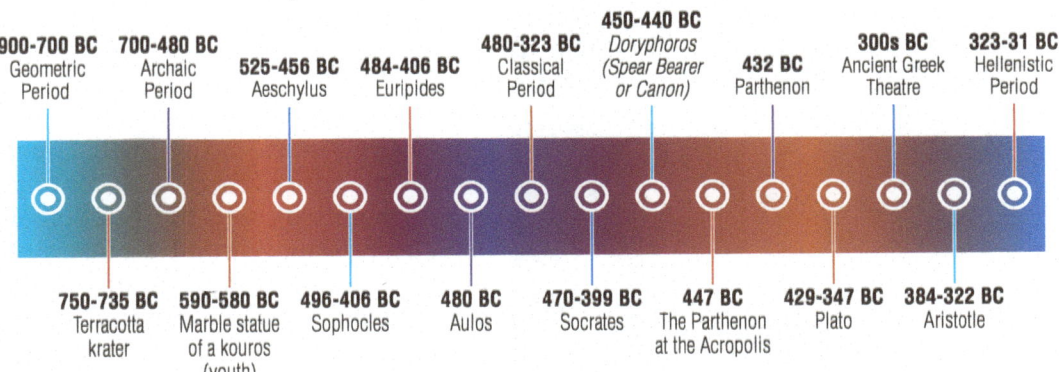

| 900-700 BC Geometric Period | 700-480 BC Archaic Period | 525-456 BC Aeschylus | 484-406 BC Euripides | 480-323 BC Classical Period | 450-440 BC *Doryphoros* (Spear Bearer or Canon) | 432 BC Parthenon | 300s BC Ancient Greek Theatre | 323-31 BC Hellenistic Period |

| 750-735 BC Terracotta krater | 590-580 BC Marble statue of a kouros (youth) | 496-406 BC Sophocles | 480 BC Aulos | 470-399 BC Socrates | 447 BC The Parthenon at the Acropolis | 429-347 BC Plato | 384-322 BC Aristotle |

Philosophy

When someone thinks of the art of ancient Greece, they often picture the pristine white curves of marble sculptures (perhaps like Fig. 2.1). Although the skill to produce them was enormous, there is a certain cool simplicity to them. They frequently had single subjects, represented with only the color of stone and possessing a focus on unity. Yet, as is often forgotten, it was not uncommon for Greek sculptors to use paint to embellish their statues. As the years have passed, the colors have faded and left unadorned limestone or marble in view. Now, the images that many people associate with the ancient Greek culture is one that has been sanitized of vibrancy and caricatured as stoic and logical. The waning of pigment color can, in many ways, be seen as an illustration of a larger misunderstanding of Hellenistic, or ancient Greek, life.

Famous atheistic philosopher Friedrich Nietzsche (1844-1900) addressed this misconception in his work *The Birth of Tragedy*,[1] whereby he attempted to retrieve an understanding of the Greeks as a people of passion and animal appetites. For him, Hellenistic culture had an Apollonian side as well as a Dionysian one. The Apollonian characteristics were named after the Greek god Apollos, who was seen as the god of truth, beauty, and logic. In other words, Nietzsche saw

Helenistic: Ancient Gree

Fig. 2.1. Marble head of a Greek general, ca. first to second century, Metropolitan Museum of Art, NY.

the Apollonian as the philosophical, which was obsessed with transcendent values, order, and ideals. However, Nietzsche was concerned that history had lost the Dionysian sense of Greek life. Dionysus was the god of wine, madness, religious ecstasy, and the theatre. Thus, the Dionysian side of Hellenism was passionate, emphasizing base instincts, natural desires, and brutish impulsiveness. For Nietzsche, the artistic endeavor relied upon the artist steering between these poles.

When Nietzsche examined Greek art, he thought of tragedy as containing elements of both the Apollonian and Dionysian. Without the restraint, logic, and ethical makeup of the former, there would be nothing tragic about what occurs. However, without the desires and passions of the latter, there would be no conflict that gives rise to tragic outcomes. Moreover, without the Dionysian, no theatrical piece would have any proximity to actual human lives. In essence, tragedy is birthed when the ideality of Apollos meets the reality of Dionysus. Interestingly, Nietzsche saw the Apollonian as more allied with the visual arts and the Dionysian with the musical ones. Since music could affect an individual without necessarily requiring much contemplation, he saw it as more direct and intuitive. The visual arts, on the other hand, require concerted thought and, therefore, were more in line with the rational and philosophical.

Nietzsche saw the death of tragedy as resulting from the rise of Socrates. The Greek philosophers, with their emphasis on the Apollonian, disavowed the type of stress on pleasure and passion that they believed were inconsistent with a rational view of the world. In this way, the vibrancy of Greek culture was suppressed for philosophical focus on the unified, the harmonious, and the ethical. Thus, the slow bleaching of marble by time is paralleled by the gradual loss of a significant aspect of Hellenistic art. The Greek people were not just contemplative philosophers, but were also passionate enthusiasts. To understand their art requires one to acknowledge the philosophical and the impassioned.

Although the rise of philosophy did suppress recognition of some important aspects of Greek culture, it also contributed strongly to the influence of Hellenism on subsequent empires and nations. The Greek philosophers were, in many ways, the West's first physicists, political scientists, psychologists, and more. They observed the world, including their own societies, and began to ask questions about the fundamental principles that governed human life and sought rational answers. In this way, they affected classical art, by emphasizing number, proportion, and symmetry.[2] The two most notable philosophers, who heavily affected every aspect of Western history, were Plato (ca. 429-347 BC) and his pupil Aristotle (384-322 BC).[3] Plato was an upper-class Athenian and student of Socrates (ca. 470-399 BC), who was inspired by his teacher to approach some of the basic questions of human life and reality. Under his tutelage, Aristotle, a Macedonian, sought to work through similar problems, though from a decidedly different perspective.

In Their Own Words

"The safest general characterization of the European philosophical tradition is that it consists of a series of footnotes to Plato."
—Alfred North Whitehead[4]

Fig. 2.2. The Thinker, ca. 1910, Auguste Rodin, Metropolitan Museum of Art, NY.

Although Plato and Aristotle's influences on Western culture are manifold, two will be worth mentioning for the purpose of this book. First, they asked questions about the relationship between ideas (or forms) and matter. For Plato, the realm of the forms was the spiritual realm, of which the physical world was merely an imperfect copy or shadow.[5] Thus, the ideals, in the realm of the forms, were far beyond the real world, with his god being impersonal and only acting indirectly on the universe. Aristotle did not see the forms as being beyond this world, but in everything in the world. Yet, he came to similar conclusions about the impersonal and somewhat abstract nature of god. Their views not only heavily affect Christian theology all the way to the present, but in broaching the question of the link between form and matter, they make explicit an issue that is frequently at the heart of the arts: what is the relationship between the transcendent and the immanent? This question guides much of art in the future, from paintings showing the gods approaching humanity, to theatrical pieces where mankind is at the mercy of the fates.

> **DID YOU KNOW?**
>
> *The Thinker* (Fig. 2.2), which has frequently been used to represent philosophy, was originally titled, *The Poet*. In this way, Rodin has continued a long history of contemplating the relationship of the arts to philosophy.[6]

mimetic: that imitates reality

anthropomorphic: man-like

catharsis: release of pent-up feelings

A second significant influence of Plato and Aristotle is in their understanding of art itself (see Fig. 2.2). Plato was skeptical of mimetic art, or art that imitated reality. He believed that poets, in their portrayal of the gods as powerful and corrupt, both lied and encouraged evil. They lied by seeing the gods as essentially powerful humans, wicked, and ruled by their passions. Plato, who continued with the trends of previous philosophers in moving away from both polytheism and anthropomorphic, or human-like, depictions of divinity,[7] thought that the poetic representations found in the theatre were deceiving the audience to believe something about god that was not true. For this reason, he saw the philosopher, who was concerned with truth, as being at odds with the artist.[8] Moreover, the poets encouraged evil by giving the young men of Athens the excuse to do every sort of immoral act by showing such acts as being perpetrated by the gods.[9] Thus, Plato both recognizes the ability of art to affect its observers, while setting off a trend of seeing the artist as one who gives a depiction of reality.[10]

Aristotle, though having some reservations about the arts, was more optimistic about its worth. Particularly, he differed with Plato on tragedy since he thought it was significant in allowing the audience to release the sorts of feelings that could be pent up. This release, which he termed *catharsis*, could occur during theatrical productions, since their audience could partake of the feelings one would possess within extreme misfortune, without having to experience tragic events.[11] In this, Aristotle promoted the idea of art as not just a depiction of what was real but also as a fictional representation that allowed observers to have an emotional response. In other words, he believed that art helped someone deal with reality. Thus, with Plato and Aristotle, one has competing stresses on both the truth-oriented nature of much art and its usefulness for human life. It is these two emphases that will underly the examples of art in the rest of this chapter.

In Their Own Words

"For the fact that in life things are really so tragic would at least account for the development of an art form—if art is not only an imitation of natural reality but a metaphysical supplement to that reality, set beside it in order to overcome it."
—Friedrich Nietzsche[12]

Art

The Cycladic, Minoan, and Mycenaean cultures of the Aegean Sea were ancient Bronze Age civilizations of the same geographical region as the Greeks, pre-dating ancient Greece between 3000 and 1100 BC (Fig. 2.3). As a legacy, they left elaborate palaces with intricately painted frescoes, legends like King Minos, labyrinths, and elaborate tombs.

Fig. 2.3. Aegean civilizations.

Ancient Greek civilization began around 1100 BC and extended until its defeat by Rome in 31 BC. Greek culture developed through four major periods, the **Geometric period** (900-700 BC), the **Archaic period** (700-480 BC), the **Classical period** (480-323 BC), and the **Hellenistic period** (323-31 BC). Throughout each period, questions of the origins of the world, the purpose of life, and conceptions of the afterlife flourished through ancient Greek stories, music, theatre, religion, and art. It is significant to see that the origins of Western art found its content with religious themes. As Augustine (AD 354-430) wrote, "you have made us for yourself, and our heart is restless until it rests in you."[13]

Geometric Era of Art

The Geometric period was characterized by its title: geometry. Decoration in this style was marked by straight and curved lines, symmetry, simple shapes, and repetition. The example pictured in Fig. 2.4 is a **terracotta** krater (vessel). The large band near the top shows a funerary scene in which a row of figures is abstracted so that they appear as patterns.

Vase Painting

Vase paintings are the most prolific surviving sources of Greek myth. In most ancient civilizations, painting on pottery was relatively unimportant. However, in Greece, especially during the Archaic and early Classical eras, the craft drew talented artisans who developed it into a significant art form. The myths of gods, goddesses, and heroes depicted in the vase paintings highlight the importance of religion in daily life and thought. **Foreground** and **background** are two important terms to keep in mind when studying vase painting. Foreground is the positive or main figure depicted. Background, or negative space, is the empty area surrounding the main figure.

Fig. 2.4. Terracotta krater, ca. 750-735 BC, Metropolitan Museum of Art, NY.

Chapter 2: Ancient Greece   23

Black-Figure Technique

In Greek vase painting, two main types of ceramic surface treatment appear. The first to manifest was called a **black-figure technique**. In this mode of making, the figures were painted with black **slip** (a mixture of clay and water that becomes glossy when fired). Interior line details were incised, defining the figures in the foreground. When fired (putting ceramic vessels under extremely high heat to change the consistency from malleable to stone-like), the unpainted background remained the reddish color of the original clay. An example of the black-figure technique (in addition to the geometric krater in Fig. 2.4) is the oil flask in Fig. 2.5.

Red-Figure Technique

The inverse of the black-figure technique is aptly called the **red-figure technique**, attributed to the famous Greek potter Andokides. In this approach, the negative space of the image is painted black and the positive figure remains in red. The red-figure technique became popular because it allowed artists greater accuracy and naturalism. The example in Fig. 2.6 depicts the hero Heracles and god Apollo struggling for possession of the Delphic tripod.

The Figure: Kouroi to Contrapposto

Although pottery was central to early Greek art, the Greeks were often more well known for their statues. The earliest large-scale, free-standing type of sculpture in the Archaic age, often used to mark the graves of wealthy aristocrats, is called a *kouros* (plural *kouroi*), which was a nude male youth (Fig. 2.7). The female version, always clothed, was called a *kore*. The males often stood with one foot

Fig. 2.5. Terracotta lekythos (oil flask), ca. 550-530 BC, attributed to the Amasis Painter, Metropolitan Museum of Art, NY. *Courtesy MET Museum, Fletcher Fund, 1931*

Fig. 2.6. Terracotta amphora (jar), ca. 530 BC, signed by Andokides, Metropolitan Museum of Art, NY. *Courtesy MET Museum, Purchase, Joseph Pulitzer Bequest, 1963*

terracotta: baked clay earthenware used for modeling

vase painting: imagery painted on Greek vases including geometric designs as well narratives of Greek myths

foreground: in visual imagery the foreground is the positive or main figure depicted

background: in visual imagery the background is the negative space of the image or the space surrounding the main figure

black-figure technique: the vase painting technique in which the figures are painted in black and the background remains the red color of the clay body

slip: a mixture of clay and water that when fired turns to a glossy sheen

red-figure technique: the vase painting technique in which the background is painted black and the figures remain the red color of the natural clay body

Fig. 2.7. Marble statue of a kouros (youth), ca. 590–580 BC, Metropolitan Museum of Art, NY.

Fig. 2.8. *Doryphoros (Spear Bearer or Canon)*, Roman marble copy of a Greek bronze, ca. 450–440 BC, Museo Archaeologico Nazionale, Naples.

forward. Influenced by Egyptian sculptures of similar design, this rigid figure was stylized and generic. The figure's slightly upturned mouth is referred to as the Archaic smile.

With the knowledge gleaned from obsessive study, the Classical Age Greeks achieved an ideal human form based on the imagined young, virile gods and heroes like Hermes and Heracles. A common pose developed in these figures is called *contrapposto* (counterpoise), demonstrated in Fig. 2.8. *Contrapposto* depicts the figure with one leg slightly bent, creating a far more relaxed and natural-looking position than the *kouroi* preceding them. It is possible that some of this movement away from the stiff styling of the Egyptians could have had to do with the previously mentioned attack by Plato on artists, since, in his view, they did not represent the world truthfully. It would have been natural for crafters, in order to defend themselves from the growing popularity of this view, to attempt to give more realistic and, therefore, more dynamic representations in their sculptures.

Architecture

As in all endeavors, Greeks were formulaic, innovative, and precise in their architectural design, developing a distinct style borrowed by the Romans and later revived in Neoclassical Architecture. The architectural styles of the Greeks are defined by their supportive structures called **order**. The Greeks moved through three main types of orders: **Doric**, **Ionic**, and **Corinthian** (Fig. 2.9). The simplest and most common was the Doric, with columns vertically patterned with lines called fluting. The Ionic order was distinguished by its scroll motif at the top of its capital and more complex fluting (Fig. 2.10). The final Corinthian order was the most ornate, topped with a floral leaf design.

order: the supportive structure of Greek architectural designs defined by its type of column and entablature

Doric: the Greek order most commonly used, defined by its simple, underrated style

Ionic: the Greek order distinguished by its scroll motif at its crown and complex fluting in the shaft

Corinthian: the most ornate of Greek orders, distinctive in its floral motif at the crown of the column and its wider, more complex base

Fig. 2.9. The Greek Orders: Doric, Ionic, and Corinthian.

Fig. 2.10. Marble column from the Temple of Artemis at Sardis, ca. 300 BC, Greek, Metropolitan Museum of Art, NY.

One of the crowning achievements of Greek architecture, built by architects Iktinos and Kallikratis, is the **Parthenon**, 432 BC (Fig. 2.11). It is a Doric-style temple dedicated to the founding goddess of Athens, Athena, and is part of the Acropolis, a "high city" built to honor the gods and celebrate the city. The Greeks believed that an ideal temple had a particular proportion of columns, where the number of columns on the length was found by taking the number of columns on the width, doubling it, and adding one. The Parthenon fits this ratio as an 8 x 17 column temple. This focus on the Pythagorean ideals of symmetry, proportion, and unity within the philosophy of beauty and art, as philosophized by Plato, eventually influenced Augustine. In his writing, *On True Religion*, Augustine noted, "By an art in this context I would have you understand not something that is observed by experience but something that is found out by reason."[14]

Music

The nature of **music** is intangible and ephemeral. It is like the wind; one cannot capture or see it, but its existence is known by observing its effects. It moves

Fig. 2.11. *The Parthenon at the Acropolis, ca. 447 BC, Athens, Greece.*

leaves and it whistles through narrow cracks. As Christ said, in his conversation with Nicodemus, "The wind blows where it wishes, and you hear its sound, but you do not know where it comes from or where it goes" (John 3:18a). When thinking of Greek music, what comes to mind may be that mysterious concept known as the Music of the Spheres. This is the idea set forth by Plato but inspired by Pythagoras (ca. 570-495 BC), that planets and stars in their proper orbit produce a harmony of sound. Although no one ever heard this music with human ears, the idea has appeared in many works of literature such as Shakespeare's *Tempest* and Milton's *Paradise Lost*. It has even inspired Christian hymns of praise of God as Creator of the world, as will be familiar in the lyrics: "This is my father's world, / And to my listening ears / All nature sings, and round me rings / the music of the spheres."[15] Plato was not a believer, but he sought to comprehend the universe. For him, music was akin to mathematical ratios (also from Pythagoras). Discoveries in fields as diverse as science and history have evidenced that Plato was right in observing an order to the universe. The cosmos was created by an omniscient and omnipotent God who set the heavenly bodies in motion in perfect balance and order (Gen 1:14-18; Ps 104:19; 136:7-9; Job 38:31-33).

Does Scripture tell of heavenly music that human ears have not heard? Job. 38:7 speaks of the morning stars singing because of God's beautiful creation. The heavenly scene in Revelation 5 says that the four living creatures and the twenty-four elders sing a new song for the freshly slain Lamb of God (Rev 5:8-9). John heard this through special revelation, but in the general revelation of God's creation, human ears cannot truly hear this. Scripture even, metaphorically, attributes singing to God (Zeph 3:17).

cithara: a large handheld lyre used especially in ancient Greece for festivals and public ceremonies

aulos: a front-blown, double-reed, double-pipe (usually) wind instrument popular in ancient Greece and Rome

Aside from the Greek concept of an unheard, yet very real, Music of the Spheres, the ephemeral nature of music that *is* heard presents problems in understanding its role in history. Its temporality requires an examination of nonmusical evidence that proves music did indeed exist. Ancient Greece yields some of its musical secrets through paintings of performers with musical instruments, writings about music philosophy and theory, myths that contain music as significant forces, fragments of Greek musical notation, and actual musical instruments. All together these artifacts are somewhat sufficient to prove that ancient Greece had a robust musical life and a deeply thoughtful understanding of musical sounds and what they meant metaphorically and rhetorically.

Paintings of Musicians

Paintings reveal how instruments were held and played, how they functioned, and what extramusical associations they conveyed. For example, Fig. 2.12 shows performance on a **cithara**, a large handheld plucked string instrument. The performer seems to be caught up in the music as seen in the position of his head lifted high in song and the imagined sway of his body. Although large, this could be performed while walking or standing, and it was used for public competitions and recitations of epic poetry. In fact, Aristotle refers to it as a professional instrument, although he does not recommend it in music education of youth, for it might make them less attentive to their studies.[16] He recognized, as Christians do, that the arts could have moral implications.

The **aulos**, a front-blown double-pipe and double-reed wind instrument, was depicted as being performed by men, women, and mythological creatures. Plutarch (ca. 45-120) noted that an early function of the aulos was an accompaniment to laments.[17] This practice is confirmed by Matthew's record of flute players gathering at the home of Jairus where his daughter had just died (Matt 9:23). In Fig. 2.13, the aulos is played by a young woman, most likely for entertainment at a drinking party. Other images confirm the later association of the aulos with licentious or drunken entertainment. Aristotle also noted that

Fig. 2.12. Man playing cithara. Terracotta red-figure amphora (jar) ca. 490 BC. Archaic era. Berlin painter. Metropolitan Museum of Art, NY.

Courtesy MET Museum, Purchase, Joseph Pulitzer Bequest, 1963

Fig. 2.13. Girl playing aulos. Terracotta red-figure lekythos (oil flask) ca. 480 BC. Archaic era. Brygos painter. Metropolitan Museum of Art, NY.

the aulos did not lead to virtue, and likewise discouraged its use in music education. He furthermore pointed out that when the aulos was being played, the performer could not sing or speak, placing an additional limitation on its function.[18]

> ### IN THEIR OWN WORDS
>
> Aristotle recounts a myth to give further evidence for the questionable value of the aulos:
>
> "And indeed, there is a reasonable foundation for the story that was told by the ancients about the auloi. The tale goes that Athena found a pair of auloi and threw them away. Now it is not a bad point in the story that the goddess did this out of annoyance because of the ugly distortion of her features; but as a matter of fact it is more likely that it was because education in aulos-music has no effect on the intelligence, whereas we attribute science and art to Athena."[19]

> **DID YOU KNOW?**
>
> Our common term *lyrics* comes from the Greek *lyre*, a smaller version of the cithara. In ancient Greece, the lyre commonly accompanied singers. For us today, lyrics are words to a song, usually referring to popular styles accompanied by contemporary stringed instruments—guitars.

Writings about Music

The most abundant evidence we have about Greek music, however, is found in writings about music. These show the depth of thought that went into understanding the nature and properties of this temporal art. One of these philosophies was known as the **doctrine of imitation**, which is a general belief that music has the power to affect *ethos* or human behavior. This doctrine arose with suspicions about music corrupting good morals and behavior. Plato believed that certain musical qualities mirrored or affected human behavior for better or worse. Because of his observations, Plato was a strong advocate for music education in building character.

doctrine of imitation: the Greek idea that music can affect ethos or human behavior

> **IN THEIR OWN WORDS**
>
> In the *Republic*, Plato expounded the influence of music on the human soul:
>
> "Education in music is most sovereign, because more than anything else rhythm and harmonia find their way to the inmost soul and take strongest hold upon it, bringing with them and imparting grace, if one is rightly trained. . . . [T]he failure of beauty in things badly made or grown would be most quickly perceived by one properly educated in music, and so, feeling distaste rightly, he would praise beautiful things and take delight in them and receive them into his soul to foster its growth and become himself beautiful and good."[20]

Another type of writing about music involved theoretical principles. Pythagoras discovered the relationship between the ratios of the sizes of sounding instruments and the pitches that they produce. Legend has it that Pythagoras heard a blacksmith pounding metal one day and noted that an anvil half the size of a larger one produced a pitch one octave higher. He noticed the same phenomenon when plucking strings of different lengths. This led to the invention of the monochord. Observe in Fig. 2.14 that a single string can be divided by the movable fulcrum below it. By dividing the string into various fractions of the whole, different pitches can be derived. In this way, every pitch in a scale can be

Fig. 2.14. Monochord.

Source: Sandra Yang

sounded by moving the fulcrum. The pitches produced by the simplest ratios were designated as the most **consonant**. For example, dividing a string in half produces a pitch exactly one octave higher; in other words, in a ratio of 1:2. Two pitches sounded simultaneously at the distance of one octave are considered the most consonant, or restful, of all **intervals**. Pitches produced with more complicated ratios were designated more **dissonant**.

Myths Surrounding Music

Greek beliefs in the power of music can be understood by their robust participation in Greek mythology. Nearly omnipresent among collections of myths, the Nine Muses personify the fine arts and science, showing the prominence of the arts in Greek society. Euterpe, the goddess representing Music, was among these, taking an equal place among her goddess sisters who represented arts such as tragedy, epic poetry, dance, and comedy.

A striking example of the influential power of music is found in Homer's *Odyssey* and the account of the Sirens. In this tale, as Odysseus and his men were sailing home, they had to pass the Island of the Sirens. These seductive creatures sang songs with such powers that any men who heard them would immediately abandon ship and swim to the island. Instead of bringing fulfillment of the promise of love, however, it brought immediate death and shipwreck. Odysseus was warned of the Sirens by the goddess Circe, who supplied him with beeswax to plug his sailors' ears and thus provide a safe solution for passing the island without hearing the intoxicating songs. Odysseus himself wanted to hear the music, however, so he asked his men to bind him to the ship's mast and not respond to his cries for release when he heard the Sirens. Thus, by taking these extreme measures, they passed safely by the island and did not succumb to the seductive power of music.

consonant: two or more musical tones that are perceived as stable, pleasant, and at rest

intervals: the distance between any two musical pitches

dissonant: two or more musical tones that are perceived as unstable and unrestful

The most famous portrayal of the power of music, however, is found in the myth of Orpheus. The tale of this demigod and his magical lyre illustrated for Greeks that music was a way to communicate with the gods. Beyond this, Orpheus could also tame wild animals and charm the world around him with his music (see Fig. 2.15).

Orpheus's marriage contains one of the most well-known tales. On their wedding day, Orpheus's bride, Eurydice, took a walk with girlfriends and was fatally bitten by a poisonous snake. Orpheus plunged into the depths of sorrow upon hearing the news but vowed to follow her into Hades and bring her back to the land of the living. His plan seemed to work, as he used his musical powers to charm the gatekeeper of Hades and convince the god of the dead to release Eurydice. There was only one condition—Orpheus could not look at his bride until both had safely arrived at the land of the living. He failed in the attempt, however, and Eurydice slipped back into death. Although the story did not end successfully for Orpheus, the reputation of Orpheus and his magical lyre have permeated the fine arts all the way to the twenty-first century. Famous composers such as Beethoven have included images of the lyre in their portraits. Operas have been written about the tragedy. Even the contemporary musical and 2019 Tony Award winner, *Hadestown*, is based on this myth (see Ch. 13).

Fig. 2.15. Orpheus taming wild animals, Table support, AD fourth century, Byzantine and Christian Museum, Athens.

The story of Orpheus draws many parallels with the biblical account of the fall and redemption of man. When Eurydice died, Orpheus pursued her into death and was able to unlock the gates of Hades by the playing of his lyre. We know that Christ entered the realm of death in His crucifixion and rose from the dead on the third day (Luke 24:7, 46; 9:22). He not only entered by His own power, He resurrected and took the keys of death and Hades with Him (Rev 1:18). Death could not hold Him. Furthermore, in His resurrection, He gave believers eternal life (1 Pet 1:3), changing their destiny from a life under the authority of darkness to the kingdom of the Son of God's love (Col 1:12-13). Orpheus, representing the broken song of the old creation, was incomplete, imperfect, and impotent in changing death into life. Christ as the perfect Song in the new creation is complete, perfect, omnipotent, and has already conquered the realm of death through his redemptive work on the cross and victory in resurrection. Thus, as one thinks about the Greeks and their view of their relationship to the pantheon of gods through the lens of music, we are reminded of the perfect redemption of Christ and that He is truly the Song of Songs. Nothing else can compare to Him.

> **DID YOU KNOW?**
>
> The apostle Paul warns of the danger of worldly philosophy when compared to the wisdom of God. In his letter to the Colossians, he wrote, "See to it that no one takes you captive by philosophy and empty deceit, according to human tradition, according to the elemental spirits of the world, and not according to Christ" (Col 2:8). Interestingly, Paul was philosophically conversant, but he had no delusions as to what human understanding, apart from the direction of God, could accomplish. Thus, when philosophy attempted to compete with a theological understanding, he encouraged his readers to "destroy arguments and every lofty opinion raised against the knowledge of God, and take every thought captive to obey Christ" (2 Cor 10:5).
>
> Ever since the false miracles of the Egyptians (Ex 7:11-12), those who rebel against God have attempted to replace his work with human activities. Yet, as is seen in the history of theology, philosophy can be helpful if used under the authority of Scripture. As Aquinas explained, all other fields are the servants, or "handmaidens," of theology.[21]

Music Notation

Music in notation is another means for understanding Greek music. Although during the Roman era and early Middle Ages there was very little evidence of a notational system for music, the Greeks did have a system for indicating melody and rhythm. Only about forty-five artifacts exist with Greek musical notation written above poetic texts or lyrics.[22] This is very important because we have a way to know how melodies and rhythms worked together to create songs. This listening example, known as the "Epitaph of Seikilos," is taken from an epitaph for a deceased person engraved on a round, marble stele from the first or second century AD. The presence of musical notation indicates that it was meant to be sung in memory of the deceased, most likely with an accompaniment on a lyre or cithara. The text makes an apropos observation about the brevity of human

epitaph: a short, often witty statement, about a deceased person

life. "As long as you live, be lighthearted. / Let nothing trouble you. / Life is only too short, / And time takes its toll."[23] This is similar to the sentiment of the Preacher in Ecclesiastes (2:24), noting the vanity of human life.

Musical Instruments

Finally, we know about ancient Greek music from instruments that have survived until now. From our understanding of instruments in use today, we can draw conclusions about how these might have been played and how they might have functioned. Fig. 2.16 shows a bell as a percussion instrument, which is an instrument that produces sound by striking or hitting. Although now missing, this bell had a clapper on the inside that would have sounded when the bell was rung. It might have been used to keep a beat or to announce time as indicated by the inscription on the bell, "I strike the time."

As evidenced by a variety of artifacts, Greeks regarded music very seriously and gave it considerable attention both in performance and in thought. Beyond a means of communicating with the gods, music could be appropriated for evil or good. Musical instruments were associated with both virtuous and vicious activities. The Sirens employed music for their own evil intentions, while Orpheus used his lyre for potential, if failed, good. Plato and Aristotle recognized the pros and cons of music in developing the character of the next generation of Greek citizens. Whereas only praise seemed to surround the unheard Music of the Spheres, the music heard by human ears tended to generate much debate and cause suspicion among the Greeks.

The Bible in like manner portrays music being appropriated both for evil and for good. Salome danced before Herod to entice him for the head of John the Baptist. David played his harp before Saul to calm him and minister as one of the first examples of music therapy. Even today, as a plurality of music is presented through a multitude of

Courtesy MET Museum, Purchase, Joseph Pulitzer Bequest, 1963

Fig. 2.16. Greek bell as a percussion instrument, the inscription in Greek on the bell states, "I strike the time," ca. third to fourth century BC, Metropolitan Museum of Art, NY.

Chapter 2: Ancient Greece   35

media, the Word of God should be the deciding factor in judging the intention of certain music. Only the Word of God is able to discern the thoughts and intents of the heart (Heb 4:12). Odysseus had the mythical warning of Circe, but the true Christ guides Christians inwardly by His Spirit, as the Word of God directs them.

> **DID YOU KNOW?**
>
> Greek musical practices and perspectives that are still with us today:
>
> - Aesthetics, ethics, and philosophy of music
> - Music theory
> - Music education
> - Wind, percussion, string, brass, even keyboard instruments
> - Music competitions, recitals
> - Fame of performers
> - Virtuosic playing
> - Instrumental music alone and song accompanied by instruments ("lyrics")
> - Music pervading all areas of life
> - Music for special functions
> - Notation; notes, intervals, scales, diatonic scales
> - Systems of tuning
> - Genres of music

Theatre

Although evidence of early ritual practices involving dance, music, and religion existed in ancient Egypt and China, most historians consider theatre to be an invention of the Ancient Greeks. The level of sophistication this art form achieved in Greek society was unparalleled in its time. Theatre developed from its beginnings in the Archaic era as a space for religious ceremonies in the worship of the Greek god Dionysus to the powerful Classical era tragedies and comedies. The **chorus**, a group of performers, participated in the Dionysian worship by singing and dancing. Over time, the chorus focused on themes that expressed emotions or acted out mythological tales. The idea of an individual actor eventually arose out of this collective acting of the chorus. According to legend, during the sixth century BC, poet Thespis introduced the idea of a single actor interacting with the chorus. With this, the theatre was born, with spoken dialogue being the distinctive feature of this new art form. During the Classical era, the number of actors increased, with more emphasis on individual human interaction. Tragedy and comedy developed primarily along two distinct paths. Tragedies

chorus: in Ancient Greece, a group of singers and/or dancers who performed in religious ceremonies and dramatic plays became dramas in which the main character suffers misfortune. The subjects were often very serious and concerned with fate and the intervention of gods in the lives of humans. In contrast to this, comedies had happy endings for the main characters and often contained humor that satirized contemporary society in a lighthearted manner.

> **DID YOU KNOW?**
>
> The common English word, *thespian*, traces its origin to Thespis. The word came into use in the seventeenth century and is used both as a noun—an actor—and as an adjective, for anything related to the dramatic arts. The word itself, however, means "inspired by the gods."

Greek Masks

Greek drama emphasized the general character types of greed, anger, sorrow, and happiness, rather than focusing on individual personalities within stories. To reinforce this idea, actors wore masks with stereotypical gestures when they portrayed their characters. There were very few actors in any one drama, so they had to play multiple characters, with the masks helping the audience to understand the distinct roles. Additionally, the mask likely helped to amplify their voices to crowds of up to 15,000 spectators. Unfortunately, no masks remain today, most likely because they were constructed of stiffened linen or wood. They were larger than the physical proportions of the actors in order to match the enlarged space and distance of the theatre, and probably were worn over the head like helmets. Evidence that they were used in Greek theatre, however, exists in terracotta statuettes that might have been offered to gods, in **bas-reliefs** depicting dramatic scenes, and in images of masks that were attached to medallions common from this period. Fig. 2.17 depicts an actor wearing a mask showing what appears to be agonizing contemplation.

bas-reliefs: a type of relief with less depth; the faces of the statues have been carved proportionately; relief being a type of sculpture that is attached to its original material as a background

Tragic Drama

Several early Greek playwrights who defined Greek tragedy and comedy were Aeschylus (525-456 BC), Sophocles (496-406 BC), Euripides (484-406 BC), and Aristophanes (450-385 BC). Among these, the playwright Sophocles is credited with creating the play that serves as a classic example of Greek tragic drama, *Oedipus Rex*. In it, Sophocles's characters are set up in a dramatic and futile battle against fate. Aristotle, in his theoretical treatise entitled *Poetics*, used *Oedipus Rex* to illustrate the elements of tragic drama (plot, character, thought, diction, music, and spectacle). In accordance with Aristotle's three unities—time, place, and action—*Oedipus Rex* took place in a single day in Thebes, unfolded the reaction of King Oedipus as he discovered that he had, through his own unwitting and rash actions, killed his own father and married his mother. Since the play aligned with these unities so well, Aristotle considered it to be a perfect example of great tragic drama.

Throughout the play, classic themes of Greek drama were performed on stage. The character of Oedipus reflected the nature of hubris, a tragic pride that ultimately leads to one's downfall. With poetic acuity, Sophocles weaved the metaphors of sight and blindness throughout the play. He emphasized the "second sight" of oracles who prophesy, the blindness of arrogance, the "seeing" of self-awareness, physical blindness, and the ultimate blindness of death.

Fig. 2.17. Terracotta statuette of an actor; his statuette is an example of a standardized character type common in Greek plays using masks with stereotypical expressions, ca. fifth to fourth century BC, Metropolitan Museum of Art, NY.

Courtesy MET Museum, Rogers Fund, 1913

hubris: a trag pride that ult mately leads one's downfa

DID YOU KNOW?

The metaphorical use of sight and blindness continues as a theme in artistic endeavors to this day. One example, in popular culture, can be seen in the Academy Award–nominated science fiction film *Minority Report*, which starred Tom Cruise, was directed by Steven Spielberg, and scored by John Williams. In it, the audience becomes aware that the main character, who is blinded in one eye, "sees" the truth better than those around him. More pointedly, the only completely blind character talks with a nearly omniscient understanding of what is occurring around him.

Tragically, the play ends in the suicide of Oedipus's mother-wife and the self-blinding of Oedipus himself. The play also illustrates dramatic irony, the idea that the deeds and decisions made in the play have the opposite

dramatic iro the idea that the deeds an decisions ma in the play h the opposite consequence of the desire effect consequences of the desired effect. The tragic hero Oedipus fulfills his own fate by trying to escape it. Parallels of this reversal fortune is a constant theme in the book of Esther, with its culmination in Esther 9:1 "…on the very day when the enemies of the Jews hoped to gain the mastery over them, the reverse occurred: the Jews gained mastery over those who hated them."

In early Greek theatre, an altar was frequently located at the level where the action of the play took place (see Fig. 2.18), where a priest would preside and sacrifice an animal. Eventually, the physical sacrifice was symbolically replaced by the metaphorical sacrifice of a central character of a play at their downfall, such as Oedipus, to restore order to society. *Oedipus Rex* is an example of how drama was used as a device to speak universal truths that instruct listeners about life. Fate was unavoidable and there was no free will. Gods, not individuals, determine the destiny of humanity. Practically, it also served as a grim public service announcement against incest.

> **DID YOU KNOW?**
>
> The influence of *Oedipus Rex* is far-reaching. Sigmund Freud coined the phrase "Oedipus complex" to describe one of his psychoanalytic theories in the human developmental process, mirroring the fraught parent–child relationships seen in the legend of Oedipus. It seems the Greeks recognized the depravity of humanity, as reflected in the troubled story. As Scripture says, "The heart is deceitful above all things, and desperately sick, who can understand it?" (Jer 17:9).

Fig. 2.18. Ancient Greek Theatre (ca. fourth century BC). Epidauros, Greece.

After examining the art of the ancient Greeks, some common threads emerge. First, most of their artistic expressions in art, music, and theatre included portrayals of man's relationship with the gods and why that mattered to humanity. Second, their art conveyed something beyond the media that the artists used. The art meant something both metaphorically and rhetorically, making it worth contemplating. Third, the art tells us that ancient Greeks had a regard for what existed beyond or behind the physical universe that could be perceived with the five senses. And fourth, for the ancient Greeks, art and artistic expressions were regarded as a special category of cultural artifact. They were human-produced items, but they were distinct from other products such as furniture, tools, or weapons. Although some art could also serve as practical, functional items, these items as *art* communicated something deeper than their practical use.

Christians can relate to the Greek view of the arts. David encouraged believers in Psalm 8 to contemplate God's purpose in creating man: "What is man that you are mindful of him, and the son of man that you care for him? Yet you have made him a little lower than the heavenly beings and crowned him with glory and honor. You have given him dominion over the works of your hands; you have put all things under his feet." (Ps 8: 4-6; cf. Gen 1:26). Furthermore, Ecclesiastes tells us that the Creator, in His wisdom, has placed eternity in man's heart that man could have a sense of what is beyond the temporal world (Eccl 3:11). Consequently, Christians have a way to understand, through the special revelation of Christ, the "mystery of His will" (Eph 1:9), "hidden for ages in God, who created all things." (Eph 3:9).

Study Questions

1. What main stylistic shift is seen in the development of the figure in Greek art?
2. What are examples of how art and life intersected in ancient Greece?
3. How did Greek philosophical ideas influence stylistic choices made in art and architecture?
4. How have Greek musical practices and theory influenced the way we practice and think about music today?
5. Describe the elements of Greek tragic drama. What were the goals of this art form? Use at least one example to explain.

Notes

1. Friedrich Nietzsche, *The Birth of Tragedy*. There is an irony in that this work allowed Nietzsche to become the youngest ever Chair of Classical Philology at University of Basel, while being questionable in its philological conclusions. It

is with his philosophical interpretation of history where Nietzsche's greatest contribution lies.
2. This is especially so under the influence of Pythagoras and his mystical understanding of mathematics.
3. It should readily be recognized that Socrates is also of note in Greek philosophy. However, since he did not write and nearly all of what has been learned about him is mediated through the works of his student, Plato, the focus of philosophy has typically been on the pupil. It has led to many controversies in the interpretation of Platonic dialogues as to who should be given credit for the novel thought contained therein. Should it be Socrates or should it be Plato?
4. Alfred North Whitehead, *Process and Reality*, 39.
5. Plato, *Republic*, 514a-520a.
6. http://www.musee-rodin.fr/en/collections/sculptures/thinker-0.
7. For an example, see Xenophanes of Colophan, *Fragments*, 25.
8. Plato, *Republic*, 607b.
9. Plato, *Republic*, 391e.
10. Plato, *Republic*, 598c, 602d.
11. Aristotle, *Poetics*, 1449b.
12. Friedrich Nietzsche, *The Birth of Tragedy*.
13. Augustine, *Confessions*, 1.1.
14. Augustine "Of True Religion" *Augustine: Earlier Writings*, xxx, 54.
15. Sheppard, no. 58.
16. Aristotle, *Politics* 8, in Strunk, V. 1, 31.
17. Mathiesen, 132-133.
18. Aristotle, *Politics* 8, in Strunk, V.1, 31.
19. Aristotle, *Politics* 8, in Strunk, V.1, 32.
20. Plato, *Republic* 3.12, in Strunk, V.1, 14.
21. Aquinas, *Summa Theologica*, 1.1.5.
22. Burkholder, 10th ed., 17.
23. Burkholder, 10th ed., 17.

Ancient Rome
Art in Service to the State

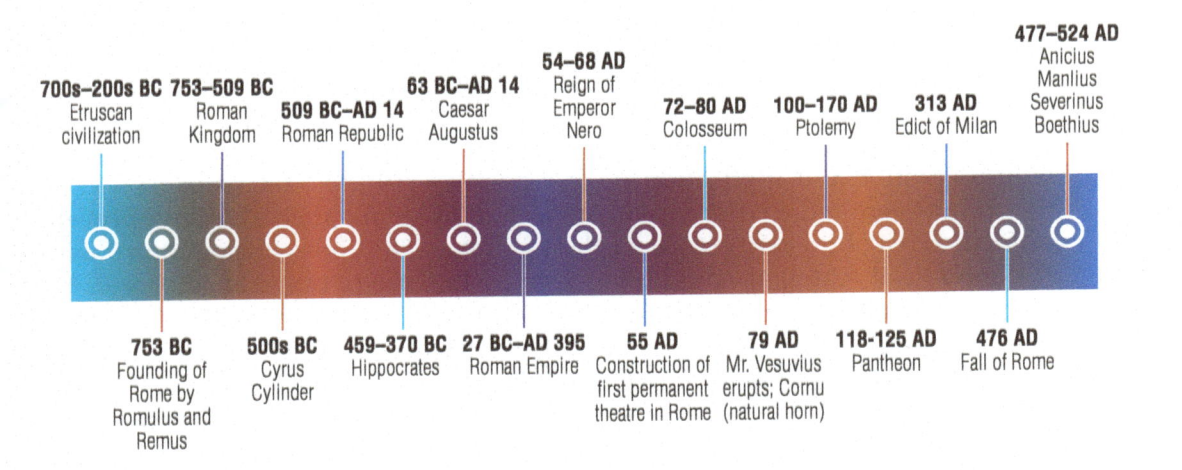

3

700s–200s BC Etruscan civilization
753–509 BC Roman Kingdom
509 BC–AD 14 Roman Republic
63 BC–AD 14 Caesar Augustus
54–68 AD Reign of Emperor Nero
72–80 AD Colosseum
100–170 AD Ptolemy
313 AD Edict of Milan
477–524 AD Anicius Manlius Severinus Boethius

753 BC Founding of Rome by Romulus and Remus
500s BC Cyrus Cylinder
459–370 BC Hippocrates
27 BC–AD 395 Roman Empire
55 AD Construction of first permanent theatre in Rome
79 AD Mr. Vesuvius erupts; Cornu (natural horn)
118–125 AD Pantheon
476 AD Fall of Rome

Philosophy

The movement from the Greek to the Roman eras was, in many ways, a change in the way one managed an empire. The characteristics that were necessary to conquer vast domains were not necessarily the same as those necessary to keep control of such lands. The fall of the Hellenistic Empire was a product of their success in empire building and their failure in administering their power over the people in their various territories. The accomplishments of the Roman Empire (27 BC-AD 476), ironically, start with its humble beginnings. As a people who were under foreign (i.e., Etruscan) authority, they rose in power by being *pragmatic*. They did not have the same lofty ideals as found in Greece, which caused Alexander the Great the pride of seeing the Greek Empire as the epitome of intellectual and political greatness.[1] It is, in many ways, for this reason that Alexander reverted to an earlier style of empire building in attempting to force a singular culture on all of the lands he controlled. He felt that if the entire Empire was *Hellenized*, or forced to live out Greek culture, then it would be easier for him to control. This, coupled with the lack of institutions and structures to make sure that the Greek Empire could

pragmatic: focusing on what works

Hellenized: be compelled live out Gree culture

41

govern smaller and distant districts, meant that without Alexander's hand, the Empire was headed for ruin. Once the Great one died, so did the future of Greek dominance.

> **DID YOU KNOW?**
>
> With lands that stretched from Europe to India, the Greek Empire was one of the largest domains in human history. Yet, in spite of its size, Alexander was only in his early 30s when he finished his conquering. Also significant is the fact that, if his troops had not mutinied because they wanted to go home, he could have continued expanding his territory indefinitely.

jurisprudence: theory of law

The Roman Empire's expertise was not innovation, as most historians note, but in the adaptation and application of other peoples' cultures. Yet, one area where they did provide large contributions, which allowed for their stunning power, was in the area of **jurisprudence**, or theory of law. The Greeks had a high value for the political realm, as could be seen in Plato's use of political categories to organize his famous work, *The Republic*,[2] and Aristotle following up his main ethical writing[3] with *Politics*.[4] In both of these works, Aristotle drew a strong connection between the moral realm and the political one. The Romans, however, coupled the recognition of the significance of politics with a more complex view of law and how to use it. They were not concerned with the ethics as much as how law could be a tool to get what they wanted. Thus, when they controlled lands, they ensured they would stay in control by having hierarchical power structures that stretched down to the smallest areas. They were experts at making sure that authority flowed down from the emperor and developed currency (see Fig. 3.1) so that they could ensure that money flowed up from the various people groups. Thus, they could finance a massive army that could enforce their will.

Obviously, the Roman Empire was very diverse in terms of languages, ethnicities, and ideologies. They completely surrounded the Mediterranean and thus had peoples from North Africa, the Middle East, Europe, and Asia. In light of that, rule of law was not enough to guarantee the continuity

Courtesy MET Museum, Gift of Joseph H. Durkee, 1899

Fig. 3.1. Gold aureus of Julius Caesar, 46 BC, Metropolitan Museum of Art, NY.

of their power. Thus, they employed two additional practices that they adapted from previous empires, both of which are illustrated in the biblical narrative. First, they did not attempt to force Roman culture on the various parts of their Empire. They allowed different areas relative autonomy to determine their language, economy, and religion. As long as they paid taxes and did not revolt, the Romans were relatively *laissez-faire*, meaning that they exhibited a pattern of nonintervention. This is similar to what we see in the Medo-Persian Empire, where Cyrus allowed the Israelite people to repatriate their land and worship their own God (2 Chr 36:22-23; Ezek 1:1-4). A sixth-century inscription, dubbed the Cyrus Cylinder, has been found that confirms this account (Fig. 3.2). Second, knowing that such religious differences could lead to dangers of internal strife if there was no sense of unity, the Romans employed the venerable practice of divinizing the emperor and treating him as an object of worship. Thus, even if the various peoples of the land could practice their own religions and worship their own deities, they also had to pay homage to the emperor. This mirrors the centralizing of worship on Nebuchadnezzar in the Babylonian Empire (Dan 3). The Romans sought unity without uniformity.

laissez-faire: exhibiting a pattern of nonintervention

The Roman Empire's diversity, focus on the pragmatic (including law), and attempts to influence religion for political reasons are just a few of the significant ways that it influenced Christianity and the arts during its reign. From a theological perspective, the New Testament arose out of the context of a powerful Roman government. Thus, it had to navigate the Israelite's desire for a political king to cast off the Romans, with the scriptural teaching concerning the Messiah's spiritual work. In Christ, the authors of the Bible describe a Messiah who

Fig. 3.2. Cyrus Cylinder, 6th century BC, The British Museum, London.

was concerned first about sin and only subsequently about the powers that be. The authors of the New Testament also had to address the issue of how to approach a Roman government that encouraged the worship of the emperor (Matt 22:15-22; Mark 12:13-27; Luke 20:19-26; Rom 13:1-7). Furthermore, the Empire provided the language and setting that helped couch the biblical writings as well as the theological explanations of the early church. It is likely that the setting of the Roman courts and government provided an impetus for the Apostle Paul to use legal terminology to explain the work of Christ. For example, he used the Greek term which is usually translated "justify" in English ("dikaioō"; Gr. δικαιόω), to describe being declared righteous before God.[5] That declarative sense, at home in Roman courts, became influential in early theology. Thus, though the language was Greek, the setting for its use was Roman.

> **DID YOU KNOW?**
>
> The most influential theologian after the completion of Scripture was an African scholar named Augustine. Augustine was born and ministered in what is now modern-day Algeria. He was a seminal influence in the works of Thomas Aquinas, John Duns Scotus, Martin Luther, and John Calvin.

The pragmatism of the Romans and the diversity of its Empire also had necessary effects on art. Roman artists were no strangers to aesthetics, but there was a greater emphasis on the usefulness of art during their time period. Thus, they continued to develop architecture, visual arts to propagate the message of the Empire, idols for worship, and so on. Moreover, as will be seen as the chapter continues, the Roman arts, whether it be visual, musical, or theatrical, would draw from heavily varied influences related to the multiplicity of peoples who were conquered. Many ideals were drawn from those who preceded them and who they conquered, but those ideals were adapted for the service of the Roman Empire (Fig. 3.3).

Art

According to legend, Rome was founded by the twin brothers Romulus and Remus in 753 BC. In its early days, Rome was a **monarchy** (ruled by a king) and was subjugated by a small people of Northern Italy called the **Etruscans**. As mentioned, the Romans were a practical people and, thus, by the time they had freed themselves in 509 BC to establish a republic, they were well-equipped with knowledge gleaned from their former rulers, including skills in commerce and architecture, to begin the growth of an empire. Importantly, the tombs of the Etruscans influenced the advancement of the Roman arch and dome.

monarchy: ed by a single g

Etruscans: small people up in Northern Italy who ojugated Romans he early ys of Roman ilization

Fig. 3.3. Ancient Rome at its height of power, AD 117.

In addition, Etruscan or "Tuscan" columns (Doric columns with bases) were later incorporated into Roman architecture, such as in the Colosseum.

> **DID YOU KNOW?**
>
> The myth of the founding of Rome traces the twin brothers Romulus and Remus, who were left to die on the banks of the river Tiber. Legend tells that they were suckled by a she-wolf until rescued by a shepherd. Once the twins grew, they established a city on Palatine Hill, the site where they had been saved as infants. The brothers fought with each other for the power of the city, and Romulus killed his brother Remus. Thus, the city was named Rome. Because of this origin story, the she-wolf has become iconographic of Rome's origin story (Fig. 3.4).

Art of the Etruscans

Although little is known about the Etruscans, they are recognized as a progressive culture and were masterful at working in metal, stone, and painted

Fig. 3.4. *She-Wolf*, bronze with glass-paste eyes, ca. 50–480 BC.

terra-cotta. A sculpture that exemplifies the Etruscan style is *Apollo of Veii* (Fig. 3.5). In Etruscan temple design, the life-sized terra-cotta statue of Apollo would have been placed on the ridge of the temple roof along with his counterparts. Set against the sky as a backdrop, the mythic scene would play out in a frozen tableau on the rooftop. Like the *kouroi* of the Greeks, *Apollo of Veii* has highly stylized features. Unlike the *kouroi*, Apollo strides forward with energy and verve. This forward-moving, dynamic stance predates the active *contrapposto* pose of the classical Greeks. On Apollo's face, one even sees the all-knowing Archaic smile.

Much like the Egyptians, Etruscans believed that an individual could take objects and possessions with them to the afterlife. This, obviously, contrasts what Jesus taught in Matthew 6, as he warned against earthly treasures that are eventually lost or destroyed. Paul reinforced this in his letter to Timothy, where believers were encouraged to pursue heavenly treasures that were "rich in good works" (1 Tim 6:17-18). Evidence

Fig. 3.5. *Apollo of Veii*, Painted terra-cotta, early fifth century BC, Museo Nazionale di Villa Giulia, Rome.

Fig. 3.6. *Sarcophagus of the Spouses*, painted terra-cotta, found in Banditaccia necropolis, Cerverti, ca. 520 BC, Museo Nazionale di Villa Giulia, Rome.

of the Etruscans' beliefs about the afterlife is seen in the surviving **sarcophagi** (sculpted or carved elaborate coffins). In the *Sarcophagus of the Spouses* (Fig. 3.6), two elongated, reclined figures, presumably a husband and wife, recline on cushions at what would have been a dinner party in the afterlife. This pose, of a man and a woman drinking and eating together, reflects the elevated status of women in Etruscan culture, for that would not have occurred in the early Mediterranean cultures of Greece and Rome.

sarcophagi: elaborately sculpted or carved coffins

Portraiture as Propaganda

Although the Roman civilization was considered by many to be the greatest Western empire, its rule, from kings during the monarchy, to patricians in the Republic, to emperors of the empire, was fraught with power struggles and division. In this context, art, such as public portraiture, was often used to convey the attitude of the ruling power.

With the onset of the Roman Republic (509 BC-27 BC), in which citizens were represented in government by elected officials, a **veristic**, or true to life, style of portraiture emerged. A typical bust, like the *Republican Portrait of a Man* in Fig. 3.7, is a startlingly honest representation of the patrician leader. In the upheavals of shifting power in the late Republic, this patrician looks old, gritty, and wise in a way that would likely have been perceived as reliable and confident in an ever-changing political landscape. He even has wrinkles, drooping skin, and a receding hairline.

veristic: a true to life, or realistic, style

This style of verism contrasted sharply with the idealistic style that was introduced at the beginning of the Roman Empire or Imperial Rome. Octavian

Chapter 3: Ancient Rome

Fig. 3.7. *Portrait of a man in the Republican style*, marble copy of the original, first century AD or later, Museum of Art, Rhode Island School of Design, Providence, Rhode Island.

Fig. 3.8. *Augustus of Prima Porta*, first century AD, Vatican Museums, Rome.

(ca.63 BC-AD 14), renamed Caesar Augustus, came to power after a series of civil wars and a duel for power between Marc Antony and Julius Caesar. A statue of Augustus (Fig. 3.8) depicted a heroic, ever-youthful version of the ruler. To the people of Rome, this reinforced Augustus's assertion that as an emperor he should be worshiped as a god. Although contrasting, both verism and idealism were used as a propagandic tool by those in power who sought to reassure their citizens that they were in good hands.

Are you curious about what the city landscape was like in the Roman Empire? Take a virtual tour of Imperial Rome.

Architectural Revolution

Rome's impressive success in urban architecture and city planning came down to one material: concrete. The Romans did not invent it but were one of the earliest civilizations to successfully capitalize on its structural potentials. They improved the product of mortar by mixing it with lime, sand, and small rocks.

The basic building block that allowed Romans to achieve such architectural feats such as amphitheatres, bridges, aqueducts, public baths, and temples was the arch (Fig. 3.9). The arch is a semicircular structure made from a

Chapter 3: Ancient Rome   49

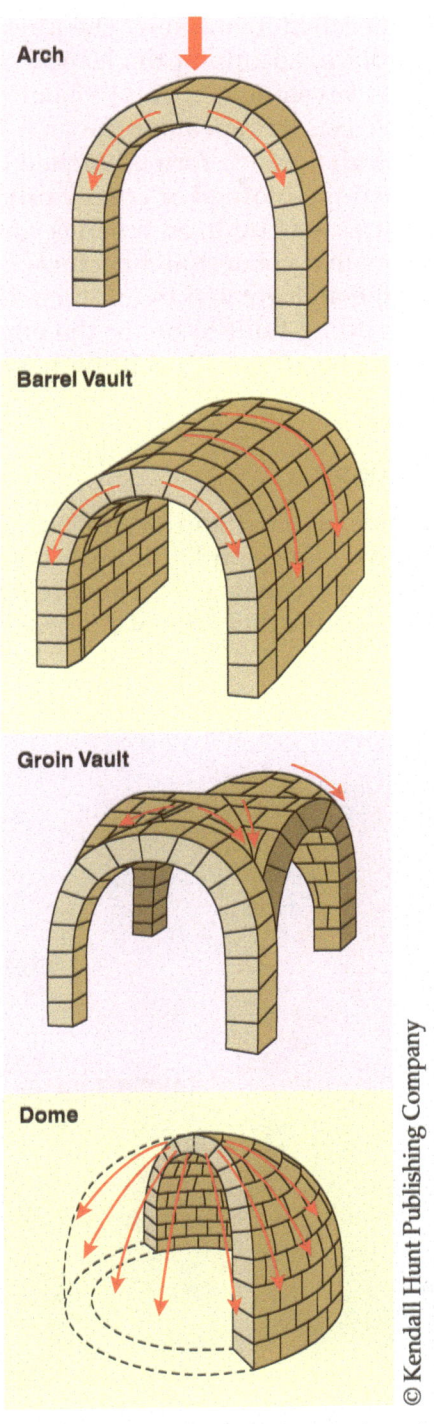

Fig. 3.9. Structures of Roman architecture: arch, barrel vault, cross vault, dome.

Chapter 3: Ancient Rome

voussoir: the wedge-shaped unit that formed the elements of an arch

keystone: the voussoir at the center of an arch that anchored the support of shape

barrel vault: the repeated form of an arch to form a ceiling or hallway

groined: (also cross vault) the intersection of two barrel vaults

cross vault: (also groined), the intersection of two barrel vaults

dome: the architectural achievement using the arch rotated in a full circle to create a ceiling in the shape of a hemisphere

oculus: an architectural element of a cut open circle in the crown of a dome

basic wedge-shaped stone called a voussoir. The keystone, at the center of the arch, locked the arch in place, absorbing the leaning pressure from both sides of stacked voussoirs. This keystone is a vivid visual of Christ the cornerstone spoken of by Paul (Eph 2:19). By repeating the arch in subsequent order, the Romans created barrel vaults, which formed arched ceilings. The intersection of two-barrel vaults created the groined or cross vault. The Colosseum, Rome's most famous amphitheatre, was built on a series of barrel vaults (Fig. 3.10). The dome, one of the Roman's greatest architectural contributions, was the architectural evolution of the arch rotated in a full circle in space, as seen in the Pantheon (Fig. 3.11); a building built to honor the emperor Hadrian. The Pantheon boasts a dazzling oculus (Fig. 3.12) at its highest point, a circular opening framing the sky.

Illusionary Wall Paintings

In AD 79, Mount Vesuvius erupted and decimated the cities of Pompeii and Herculaneum. The massive explosion left a thick layer of ash upon the cities, preserving them for modern archeologists. These remains are some of the richest sources of information on the daily life of a Roman city.

Fig. 3.10. Colosseum, ca. AD 72-80, Rome.

Chapter 3: Ancient Rome   51

Fig. 3.11. Pantheon, outer view, ca. AD 118–125, Rome.

Fig. 3.12. Pantheon, inner view, ca. AD 118–125, Rome.

Chapter 3: Ancient Rome

In Their Own Words

The Roman Author Pliny the Younger was a firsthand witness to the dramatic eruption of Mount Vesuvius, and even had an uncle who perished in rescue efforts. In a letter to Tacitus, Pliny describes the eruption of Mount Vesuvius.

"A cloud, from which mountain was uncertain, at this distance (but it was found afterwards to come from Mount Vesuvius), was ascending, the appearance of which I cannot give you a more exact description of than by likening it to that of a pine tree, for it shot up to a great height in the form of a very tall trunk, which spread itself out at the top into a sort of branches…it appeared sometimes bright and sometimes dark and spotted, according as it was either more or less impregnated with earth and cinders."[6]

murals: a large wall painting

tromp l'oeil: meaning "to fool the eye," a style of illusionistic painting

Underneath the ash, Roman wall paintings or murals were uncovered in villas, public buildings, and temples. The earliest wall paintings were meant to imitate marble-colored slabs, creating an expensive-looking faux wall. As styles progressed, wall paintings became even more focused on realism, eventually creating illusions that transformed a flat wall into a scene that was strikingly real (Fig. 3.13). This style is known as *tromp l'oeil* ("to fool the eye"). The illusion of depth increased the sense of the spaciousness of the room.

Fig. 3.13. Wall paintings in the villa at Oplontis, ca. 40 BC.

DID YOU KNOW?

Roman religion was deeply affected by the beliefs of neighboring and conquered peoples, particularly the Greeks. The Romans adopted the Greek deities into their own divinities. You might know the deities by both the Greek and Roman names.

Roman	Greek
Jupiter	Zeus
Juno	Hera
Neptune	Poseidon
Pluto	Hades
Vesta	Hestia
Apollo	Apollo
Diana	Artemis
Mars	Ares
Venus	Aphrodite
Vulcan	Hephaestus
Minerva	Athena
Mercury	Hermes

Music

Remains concerning music in Ancient Rome indicate that it was often imported from conquered countries and displayed modifications from their mother culture. These borrowed characteristics appear in various functions of musical activities, in the remains of musical instruments, and in music theory. More than with Greece, however, music in Ancient Rome served the state directly. Furthermore, there is a scarcity of music in notation during this period, so it is hard to reconstruct the melodies and rhythms of Roman music. This could be due to the acquisition of performers and musicians and slaves from those who were conquered. In a sense, they were subcontracting or outsourcing their culture to the conquered peoples. Consequently, it is rather challenging to distinguish what is original Roman music.

Despite this difficulty, it is recognized that the Roman perspective on music was intrinsically different from that of the Greeks. Whereas the former shared the latter's view that music had magical powers and facilitated communication with the gods, thus making it a suitable artistic expression for worship, the Romans differed in their aforementioned pragmatic approach to the arts. They also saw music's function in either subduing or exciting public gatherings rather than shaping the character of individual citizens. During the Roman Republic,

Liberal Arts: the medieval studies comprising the trivium and quadrivium

Trivium: consisted of the language arts of rhetoric, logic, and grammar

Quadrivium: consisted of the mathematical arts of arithmetic, geometry, astronomy, and music

tibia: a reed flute-like instrument often associated with religious gatherings in Roman religion

music and the arts ultimately existed to serve the state. Only after the conquest of Greece in 31 BC did Hellenistic education change the view of music and the arts from practical tools of the state to more intellectual and conceptual expressions of humanity. Indeed, the study of what came to be known as the humanities spread throughout the Roman Republic and later Empire. These disciplines were also known as the **Liberal Arts** and were themselves divided into two groups. The **Trivium** consisted of the foundational language and philosophical arts of rhetoric, logic, and grammar, while the **Quadrivium** consisted of the mathematical arts of Arithmetic, Geometry, Astronomy, and Music. Pythagoras's legacy of the study of the proportions of musical sounds established music as part of the Quadrivium.

Musical Activity

Like Ancient Greece, music played a significant role in special events such as religious rites, funerals, military operations, and music competitions. Music also became part of work and everyday life. Existing artifacts such as paintings and sculptures depict people playing musical instruments or singing. The **tibia** (see Fig. 3.14), a reed flute-like instrument, was often associated with religious

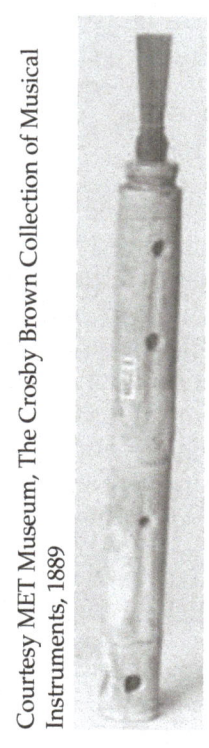

Courtesy MET Museum, The Crosby Brown Collection of Musical Instruments, 1889

Fig. 3.14. Tibia, bone and cement, double reed, Roman, ca. 100 BC–ca. AD 200, Metropolitan Museum of Art, NY.

gatherings. During sacrificial rites, tibia players served to render inaudible any harsh or unwelcome noises, banish evil spirits, and summon beneficial deities. The tibia became so prominent that it was regarded as the national ritual instrument of the Romans, either in its single-reed pipe form or its double-reed pipe form like the aulos. There were even guilds of tibia players. In addition to the tibia players, priestly guilds of trumpeters and choruses of boys and girls served the state religion and government-sponsored public ceremonies. The existence of such organizations implies that there was significant training and support for specialized groups of performers.

Before Christianity was legalized by Constantine in the Edict of Milan in AD 313 and subsequently became the official state religion by Theodosius I in the Edict of Thessalonica in 380, many religions existed, although the religious practices of the most powerful classes gave them an official aura. As more and more countries were conquered by the Romans, the Empire was filled with diversifying ideas. The concept of the separation of state and church did not exist, as high offices in both religious and state offices could be held by the same individual. Therefore, the practice of government support for religious activities was fairly common by the time Christianity began to spread in the Roman Empire. Ch. 4 will discuss the challenges of art and music in various stages of the church's relationship with the Empire.

The biblical view of the acceptable use of music related to worship differed from the Roman pragmatism. Although there are several lines of musical activity recorded in the Bible, they can be divided between those examples related to idol worship and those related to the proper worship of God. Scripture acknowledges that music can be an aid in leading man either away from God or toward God. The Roman worship of deities was not unlike the former category.

Two striking examples of the division are recorded in the Old Testament. When Moses was on Mt. Sinai for forty days with God receiving the tablets of stone and instructions for building the tabernacle, his delay tempted the children of Israel to turn from God and build a golden calf. In their worship, they offered sacrifices to the calf, ate and drank, and "rose up to play" (Exod 32:6). God saw what they were doing and expressed his grave displeasure to Moses. When Moses returned from the mountain, he asked Joshua what the sound was. Joshua replied that it was the noise of war. Moses responded that it was actually the "sound of singing that I hear" (Exod 32:18). The rising up to play must have included singing, for it was a sound of many people that could be heard from afar at the foot of the mountain—even before Moses could see what was going on. That singing was used to instigate the Israelites into the frenzy of the moment. Most of the people were guilty of this participation, and Moses condemned the incident as a "great sin" (Exod 32:21, 30).

Another example of a pragmatic misappropriation of music is during the captivity of the children of Israel in Babylon. Nebuchadnezzar built a large golden image and commanded all the people to bow down to it. The signal to bow down was the sound of music. "You are commanded, O peoples, nations, and languages, that when you hear the sound of the horn, pipe, lyre, trigon, harp, bagpipe, and every kind of music, you are to fall down and worship the golden image that King Nebuchadnezzar has set up. And whoever does not fall down and worship shall immediately be cast into a burning fiery furnace" (Dan 3:4b-6). Nebuchadnezzar was practical. He knew that there were many languages in his kingdom, so he used the universal sentiments of music to cue the people to worship. Thus, at least in these two examples, it is clear that music and idol worship was a common practice among the peoples of the Mediterranean.

In contrast to this, the proper use of music in worship should always lead a believer God-ward, away from the distractions of the flesh and sin. Ch. 4 explores in more detail how the early church fathers conceived of such music with this desired effect. Two striking examples are recorded in the Old Testament. Both are related to the proper worship of God. In I Chronicles 15 and 16, David arranged to return the Ark of the Covenant to Jerusalem. In preparation for this, he carefully planned detailed musical accompaniment on a variety of instruments, all of which could be handled only by the Levites designated for priestly service. Realizing that this required precise coordination, he instructed Chenaniah to be the music director, for he was the "leader of the Levites in music" and "he understood it" (I Chr 15:22). As the procession approached Jerusalem, David "commanded the chiefs of the Levites to appoint their brothers as the singers who should play loudly on musical instruments, on harps and lyres and cymbals, to raise sounds of joy" (I Chr 15:16). After the Ark reached its destination, David "appointed that thanksgiving be sung to the Lord." (I Chr 16:7). The passage that follows (I Chr 16:8-36) is the song of thanks that David wrote for them to sing. At the end of the song, "all the people said, 'Amen!' and praised the Lord." (I Chr 16:36b). Surely, this is music that leads to the acceptable worship of God.

A second example comes from Nehemiah at the time of the dedication of the rebuilt wall of Jerusalem after the return of the Israelites from captivity in Babylon. During the time of exile, the Levites who had formerly been in charge of the music for worship came to Jerusalem with musical instruments they had kept secure from the time of David. The same harps, lyres, and cymbals are mentioned, along with choirs who sang songs of thanksgiving. It seems that nothing of the former practices was lost. "For long ago in the days of David and Asaph there were directors of the singers, and there were songs of praise and thanksgiving of God" (Neh 12:46). These examples are echoed in the New Testament where Paul encouraged believers within the church to encourage one another through music (Eph 5:19; Col 3:16). In both contexts, the apostle sought for the people to worship God in thanks (Eph 5:20; Col 3:17).

In summary, two things should be noted. First, the Roman practice of music in worship was not unlike the surrounding peoples that they had conquered. This is in line with the fact that much art and music found in the Roman era was imported and had its roots in earlier civilizations. Second, it is highly possible that the Roman religious rites were influenced not only by Greeks, but by Babylonians and other nations living around the Mediterranean Sea.

In addition to religious appropriations of music, the secular sector offered equally robust opportunities for music. As with the Greeks, music competitions abounded. These events, as with today, were vehicles for encouraging the highest levels of virtuosic performance. Just such a competition is shown in a bas-relief found on a Roman sarcophagus (see Fig. 3.15). Presiding over the competition at the far left are the gods Athena, Zeus, and Hera, noted by their scepters and absence of musical instruments. The competition is between the Muses and the Sirens. The Muses represent the ideal in art, such as Euterpe's representation of the Music of the Spheres. The Sirens represent that music that can seduce and destroy, such as seen in the story of Odysseus's encounter with them (see Ch. 2). Note, in the bas-relief, that the more intellectual Muses are defeating the Sirens, as seen in their being forced to the ground. This indicates that the philosophical views of music maintained some influence in the Roman Empire and that there was both a lively practice of music competitions and high ideals for their value in society.

Fig. 3.15. Marble sarcophagus showing a musical competition, Roman, third century AD, Metropolitan Museum of Art, NY.

Did you know?

The legend of Emperor Nero (r. AD 54-68) "fiddling" as Rome burned may have some truth to it. We do know that Nero was drawn to public musical competitions imported from conquered Greece. As a child, he studied the cithara with a famous teacher. After six years of study, he participated in a public competition. He later made appearances as a performer outside of Rome, including a trip to Greece. In addition to playing the cithara, he acted out parts of tragedies in full costume and mask. His extravagant performances may have given rise to the rumor that during the great fire of Rome in AD 64, Nero was playing music. Was he playing the fiddle? No, this bowed instrument had not yet developed into the fiddle (or violin) as we know it today, but he might well have been playing the cithara.

But there is a much darker side to Nero. Nero blamed the great fire on Christians and in his cruelty, he initiated the first major persecution of the church. His musical entertainment was a sadistic mask to unconscionable crimes against humanity that he simultaneously carried out. A striking contrast to this is David's appropriation of music when hearing of King Saul's death in 2 Sam 1:11-27. Although Saul had tried to kill David in the past, David acknowledged that Saul was his king, and thus he properly and honorably mourned him and the many Israelites who died in battle. David turned to the arts by writing a poem in vv. 19-27 that was most likely a song that he would have sung as a lament, accompanying himself on his harp. Unlike Nero's cruel, hard heart, David had a contrite, repentant heart. It was the heart of the performer that made all the difference.

Musical Instruments

Musical instruments themselves add to the story of a lively, although somewhat hidden, history and practice of music in the Roman era. Not only were they frequently themselves imported or at least made from imported metals, but they were also often played by slaves coming from conquest. Skilled labor rose in prominence under the Roman Empire, as pragmatism introduced new materials and artisanal techniques.

The **cornu**, or natural horn, was an instrument most likely used by the military, showing the practical attitude of the Romans toward music. The one shown in Fig. 3.16 is a 19th-century replica of one found in the ruins of Pompeii after AD 79.

Chapter 3: Ancient Rome 59

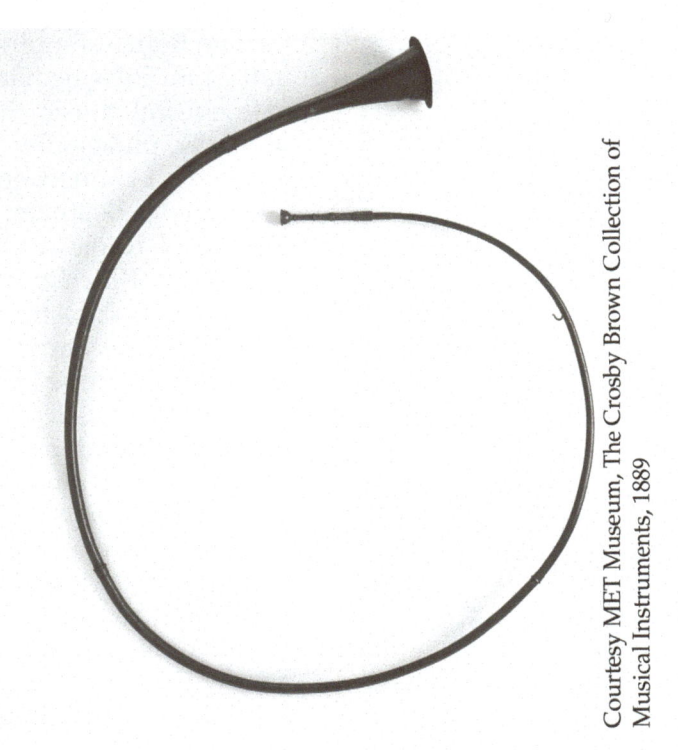

Courtesy MET Museum, The Crosby Brown Collection of Musical Instruments, 1889

Fig. 3.16. Cornu (Natural horn), metal and wood, late 19th-century replica of one found in the ruins of Pompeii after AD 79, Metropolitan Museum of Art, NY.

> **DID YOU KNOW?**
>
> In Greek and Roman thought, a *musician* was one who knew the philosophy and mathematical science of music and was considered to be of the highest status among those who dealt with things musical. Others were *poets*, who wrote songs, indicating that poems were considered lyrical and at least song-like, if not meant to be entirely sung. *Performers* were those who played instruments. Today, many in the English-speaking world and, indeed, the West at large would consider the musician and performer as synonymous, while a poet deals with words and not songs. It is worth considering, however, how philosophy, science, music, and poetry are related, both in the past and in the contemporary setting.

Music Theory

Anicius Manlius Severinus Boethius (ca. 477-524), commonly known as Boethius, is considered the most important writer, if not the only writer, on music theory in

Fig. 3.17. Manuscript illumination depicting *musica mundana, musica humana, and musica instrumentalis*, 13th century AD

the late Roman Empire. He was important as an intermediary because much of medieval music theory was based on Greek philosophy, but without Boethius, that connection might not have been made. Boethius, born right after the fall of Rome in 476, also bridged the world of the Roman Empire in the status of a statesman in the former class structure and of a consul to the conquering Gothic king Theodoric. He later was accused of treason and was imprisoned and executed. Boethius's writings about music are found in his *De institutione musica* (Fundamentals of Music), written as one of four works to serve the curricula of the Quadrivium. Boethius's work fell out of favor between the sixth and the ninth centuries, after which it was revived during Charlemagne's reign (r. 800-814). It became one of the most widespread music theory treatises during the medieval era.

Boethius based his *De institutione musica* on earlier Greek treatises, primarily one by Nicomachus (60-120) and the first book of *Harmonics* by Ptolemy (100-170). One of his most influential models of music is the concept that related the ideal, unheard Music of the Spheres, the idea of music representing a harmony seen in humans as part of God's creation, and the sounded, aurally perceived sounds that are typically called music. Boethius calls these *musica mundana, musica humana*, and *musica instrumentalis*. In the illuminated manuscript shown in Fig. 3.17., the top right image symbolizes *musica mundana*. It depicts the stars and solar system with the four known physical elements: fire, air, water, and earth all existing in harmony. The middle right image depicts *musica humana*, symbolizing man in balance with the four known bodily humors or temperaments: black bile, yellow bile, phlegm, and blood. These bodily substances were related to personality traits, and it was believed that when these substances were in balanced proportions, the human body and mind functioned well and in harmony. Finally, in the lower right of the illumination is a depiction of *musica instrumentalis*, showing a performer playing on one of a variety of available musical instruments. While the first two *musicae* are divine, the third, *musica instrumentalis*, shows man in his creativity using God-created elements to mirror His natural order.

The common thread of these three *musicae* is a perfect balance that causes each part to work together to create a beautiful whole. Scripture reveals God as the Intelligent Designer Who alone could do such detailed work, holding everything together. Boethius could not tell how, but Scripture does complete the picture. "God upholds the universe by the Word of His power" (Heb 1:3), all things hold together in Him (Col 1:17), and the Word of God even frames the entire universe (Heb 11:3).

Did you know?

Hippocrates (ca. 459-370 BC) developed the idea of the four bodily humors (substances) and how they affect human personality. He was one of the first physicians to explore the relationship of the body to the soul. Although his theories were not scientifically grounded, many consider Hippocrates as the father of human psychology.

- Black bile—melancholic personality (characterized by pensive sadness, depression)
- Yellow bile—choleric personality (characterized by irritability, anger)
- Phlegm—phlegmatic personality (characterized by lack of emotions, calmness)
- Blood—sanguine personality (characterized by optimism and cheerfulness)

These categories are furthermore associated with seasons, physical elements, and planets. Check it out here.

How does music fit in this picture? A later idea (see Ch. 7) known as the Doctrine of the Affections, which somewhat mirrors the Greek Doctrine of Imitation, promoted the idea that music of various types could help to balance the bodily humors by reinforcing a perceived lack by means of music. For example, upbeat cheerful music in a major key could balance someone with too much black bile. These theories together contributed to the field of music therapy, now proven to be an effective means of medical treatment for certain conditions. Something similar can be seen in David's use of the lyre to refresh Saul (1 Samuel 16:23).

In their own words

In his *De institutione musica*, Boethius describes the ideal, most worthy pursuit of music.

"It should be borne in mind that every art, and every discipline as well, has by nature a more honorable character than a handicraft, which is produced by the hand and labor of a craftsman. For it is far greater and noble to know what someone does than to accomplish oneself what someone else knows, for physical skill obeys like a handmaid while reason rules like a mistress. And unless the hand does what the mind sanctions, it acts in vain. How much more admirable, then, is the science of music in apprehending by reason than in accomplishing by work and deed! It is as much nobler as the body is surpassed by the mind because the person destitute of reason lives in servitude. But reason reigns and leads to what is right; and unless its rule is obeyed, a work thus deprived of reason will falter. It follows, then, that reason's contemplation of working does not need the deed, while the works of our hands are nothing unless guided by reason."[7]

Theatre

As with other art forms found in the Roman era, the roots of theatre trace back to outsiders or conquered peoples. Although most archeological remains of theatre show that there was a thriving practice during the republican and imperial eras, at least one site, a theatre at Ostia Antica, may indicate that the Etruscans influenced theatre among the earliest Romans. Ostia Antica was an early Roman colony built at the mouth of the Tiber River in the seventh century BC, not far from the future capital of Rome. This settlement is one of the earliest evidence of Roman activity independent of Etruscan control. Fig. 3.18 shows a decorative mask atop a column, indicating the presence of dramatic performances and suggests a practice that included masked actors.

Greek culture spread throughout the Mediterranean region starting from at least the eighth century BC, long before the rise of the Roman Republic; archeological remains of Greek theatre artifacts, especially in the buried seaside city of Pompeii, strongly suggest a thriving practice of dramatic performances. Here also is evidence that Greek masks were featured prominently, with large-scale proportions and exaggerated facial gestures. As seen in Figs. 3.19 and 3.20, two mosaics preserved in Pompeii's ruins depict examples of such facades. Although it is difficult to ascertain the date the mosaics were made, it is known that this type of theatre existed well before the destruction of Pompeii in AD 79.

Chapter 3: Ancient Rome 63

Fig. 3.18. Mask decoration in amphitheatre, stone, Ostia Antica, Roman colony, seventh century BC.

Fig. 3.19. House of the Tragic Poet, mosaic showing various masks, before AD 79, Pompeii.

64 Chapter 3: Ancient Rome

Fig. 3.20. Mosaic of mask, before AD 79, Pompeii.

DID YOU KNOW?

The Latin word for mask, such as used by characters in a drama, is *persona*. This term is believed to be the origin of the use of a *person* to describe the Divine Trinity, found as early as the third century in the writings of Tertullian.[8]

The Romans enjoyed scripted drama, in addition to mime, acrobatics, music, and dance. During most of the Republican era, theatres were small, wooden, temporary buildings constructed for specific seasons, productions, or purposes. Greek-style tragedy and comedy were popular until about the first century BC, when they were overshadowed by a taste for large-scale lavish spectacles, often sponsored by the Republic and later by emperors.

With the transition from Republic to Empire, the function of theatre became more and more an expression of imperial command along with the public taste for spectacle (see Colosseum Fig. 3.8). The construction of the first permanent theatre in Rome in AD 55 by the highly successful general, Pompey the Great, suggests a number of characteristics and attitudes toward theatre in Imperial Rome. First, as with the Greeks, music and religion remained strongly associated with theatre. Greek terms such as "orchestra," "hymn," and "chorus"—which

Fig. 3.21. Imagined Reconstruction of Pompey's theatre.

implied musical practices, as they remain so today—were also present in Pompey's theatre. Religion was an important emphasis as well. The theatre was built to feature a temple to Venus Victrix at the top of the seating area, showing the preeminent function of worship. The seating area could be viewed as steps descending to a lower area where games honoring the gods would be conducted. In this way, the theatre was arguably a temple (see the imagined reconstruction in Fig. 3.21).

Seating capacity in the Roman amphitheatre surpassed those of the Greeks, with space for 20,000 spectators and a stage width of approximately 300 feet. This allowed for mass communication of public information and imperial proclamations. For six centuries, this edifice was one of the most prominent cultural and political structures. Parts of the structure remain in the Largo di Torre Argentina Square in Rome (see Fig. 3.22.).

The transition of the theatre from scripted dramatic performances with lessons in morality to large-scale spectacles that emphasized both imperial power and pagan religion became problematic for early Christians. Additionally, during the time of intense persecution, Christian leaders encouraged believers to avoid public games in theatres. With the legalization and official sanctioning of Christianity (described earlier in this chapter), public theatre with its pagan associations began to decline, in part due to Christian condemnation of the entertainment. With the fall of the Empire in 476, political support for theatre ended, and the last recorded events in Rome were in 549.[9]

Fig. 3.22. Site of remains of Pompey's theatre, Largo di Torre Argentina Square, Rome.

Study Questions

1. How can you explain the shift from realism to idealism in portraiture during the Roman Empire?
2. Why was Boethius important for his writings about music?
3. How and why did theatre transform from sophisticated Greek drama to large, mindless, and gross spectacles at the height of the Roman Empire?

Notes

1. This was also influenced, undoubtedly, by the choice of Philip of Macedon, Alexander's father, to employ Aristotle to tutor his young son.
2. Plato, *Republic*.
3. Aristotle, *Nichomachean Ethics*.
4. Aristotle, *Politics*.
5. For the early usage of the term in a legal sense, see Aristotle, *Rhetoric*, 1, 1366b, 9. For a description of early Greek usage and its development during the Roman times, see Gottlob Schrenk, "Δίκη, Δίκαιος, Δικαιοσύνη, Δικαιόω, Δικαίωμα, Δικαίωσις, Δικαιοκρισία," 193-95.
6. Pliny the Younger, LXV.
7. Boethius, in Strunk, V. 2, 32.
8. Oxford English Dictionary, "Person."
9. Kennedy, V.2, 1151.

4

Early Christian and Medieval Eras
A New Voice in the Conversation

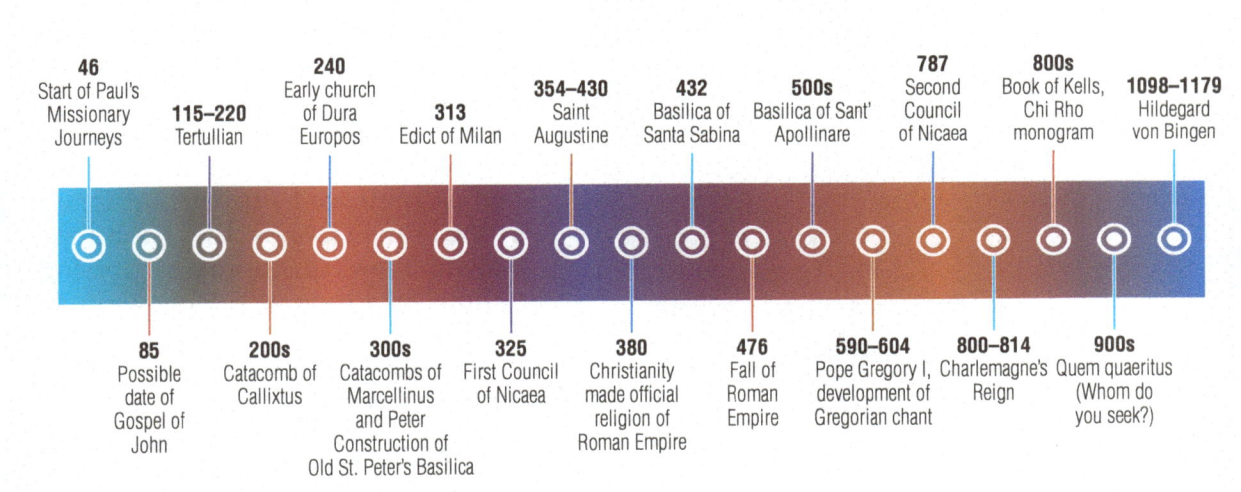

46 Start of Paul's Missionary Journeys
115–220 Tertullian
240 Early church of Dura Europos
313 Edict of Milan
354–430 Saint Augustine
432 Basilica of Santa Sabina
500s Basilica of Sant' Apollinare
787 Second Council of Nicaea
800s Book of Kells, Chi Rho monogram
1098–1179 Hildegard von Bingen

85 Possible date of Gospel of John
200s Catacomb of Callixtus
300s Catacombs of Marcellinus and Peter Construction of Old St. Peter's Basilica
325 First Council of Nicaea
380 Christianity made official religion of Roman Empire
476 Fall of Roman Empire
590–604 Pope Gregory I, development of Gregorian chant
800–814 Charlemagne's Reign
900s Quem quaeritus (Whom do you seek?)

Philosophy

If one were to characterize artists by their relationship to art, one might be able to separate them into two categories. The first would be artists who choose to produce pieces because they can and they want to. The second would be those individuals who produce art because they feel like they must. Art to some is the joyous exercise of creativity, but to others it is the painful process of self-expression. One can see this difference in the book of Psalms, if one were to contrast the praise Psalms to those that exemplify lament. Such a distinction one can also perceive in the history of the early church. With the close of the canon and the passing of the Apostles from their lives of ministry in the first century, the church was in a time of turmoil. Christians realized that theirs was an Easter religion, defined by the hope of the resurrection certifying the truth of salvation in the death of Christ. And yet, the persecution that they began to endure was more akin to the life of the cross than the victory of the risen Savior, as seen in an early *intaglio*, or engraved design, depicting the moments before martyrdom (Fig. 4.1). Thus, the ever-present dichotomy of the church was once

intaglio: engraved design

Fig. 4.1. Intaglio, ca. third to fourth centuries, Metropolitan Museum of Art, NY.

Courtesy MET Museum, Gift of John Taylor Johnston, 1881

again presented. The people of God were pulled between this world and the next, between suffering and hope, between a murdered man and a risen King.

It was within this setting that Christian interaction with the arts began. As will be demonstrated throughout the rest of this chapter, the many uses of art can be seen in the various ways that believers in the persecuted church attempted to involve art in their worship. As the church moved into prominence by being sanctioned by the Roman Empire, they continued this multifaceted approach to using various art forms. Art, then, was one way that the early church coped with the circumstances while they waited for the Second Coming of Christ. Various art forms gave believers the outlet to remember the work of the cross and then think theologically about their own lives. Furthermore, in being a reaction to the situation of the day, this art was reflective of believers' current concerns, as will be seen in the pronounced change in how early art depicted Jesus.

The pragmatic approach to the arts was not just a function of the external pressures of the church but also an outcome of its internal constitution. The Body of Christ, ironically, mirrored the beginnings and approach of the Roman Empire that persecuted them. As the Empire grew, it began to control a highly diverse population with contrasting languages, rituals, and ideas. Thus, the Romans had a tendency to appropriate the practices of various people groups, modifying them as necessary to serve their political ends. Similarly, the explosion of Christianity in size, from the early evangelistic movements of the book of Acts to the first few centuries of the post-apostolic church, created a worshipping body that was intrinsically multicultural. Whereas the Old Testament was clear that the Gentiles would be saved (Isa 42; 56:6-8), it was less clear that the Gentiles and Jews would inhabit one institution. Thus, Paul describes it as a "mystery" that those who were outside of the nation of Israel would be part of "same body" as the Israelites (Eph 3:6). Such diversity is illustrated with the beginning of the church at Pentecost (Acts 2), where "devout men from every nation under heaven" (Acts 2:5) heard the gospel and many were saved.

> **DID YOU KNOW?**
>
> The church started in Jerusalem, but quickly moved throughout Judea and Samaria, and to the "ends of the earth" (Acts 1:8). Thus, by the time the Middle Ages began to dawn, it encompassed areas of Europe, North Africa, the Middle East, and Asia. This diversity can be seen in the fact that though the church started in Israel, it eventually had the strongest support in Europe and the strongest influence from Africa (by means of the theologian Augustine).

Diversity was one of the ways in which the church was fundamentally different from Judaism. While both centralized on religious features of their beliefs, the Israelite people were more homogenous based on the instructions of the law and God's decision to constitute them as a nation (Exod 19:4-6). The Israelites had the same language, lived in the same place, ate the same types of foods, and so on. With the coming of the church, there was now a Christian body whose only shared culture was based on the unity found in being saved by Christ (Gal 3:25-29). Thus, to deal with the diversity of their members, churches, in a manner similar to the Romans, adopted the art forms and uses of art from the various cultures that had become part of their communities. This also led, in some cases, to the misuse of external culture, as can be seen in the work of Gregory the Great, who attempted to keep as much of the pagan religions as possible of unbelievers, so that they might be able to worship in ways similar to their unbelieving past.

> **IN THEIR OWN WORDS**
>
> "Let blessed water be prepared, and sprinkled in these temples, and altars constructed, and relics deposited, since, if these same temples are well built, it is needful that they should be transferred from the worship of idols to the service of the true God; that, when the people themselves see that these temples are not destroyed, they may put away error from their heart, and, knowing and adoring the true God, may have recourse with the more familiarity to the places they have been accustomed to."
> —Gregory the Great[1]

early church fathers: those significant Christian theologians and leaders in the first six centuries of the church

How the early Christian church related to art was profoundly influenced by the thought of the early church fathers or those significant Christian theologians and leaders in the first six centuries of the church. On the one side was Tertullian (155-220), who had a high amount of skepticism to non-Christian thought. On the other side was Origen (ca. 184-ca. 253), who was too accepting, at times, in his approach to external ideas. In this way, two streams of reactions can be traced, even to this day. There are those who react to the arts as something that is often (or only!) in opposition to Christian thought and practice. Then there are those who do not critically appraise the activities of believers and unbelievers in the art world.

Neo-Platonism: the term given for the school of thought deriving from the work of Plotinus; characterized by the attempt to incorporate Aristotelian philosophy into a Platonic framework

One church father who was especially influential in his understanding and in whom both of these streams can be seen was Augustine. He was influenced philosophically by Neo-Platonism, or the term given for the school of thought deriving from the work of Plotinus (ca. 204-270). Neo-Platonism was characterized by the attempt to incorporate Aristotelian philosophy into a Platonic framework. Thus, Augustine had a penchant for being distrustful toward certain art forms, in line with Plato's aforementioned cynicism about the arts. This can be seen in the *Confessions*, where he voices displeasure with fiction in the educational setting,[2] as well as with the theatre which he loved before he was saved.[3] However, in line with Plato and his understanding of Scripture's commands concerning worship, he had a high view of music. Thus, Augustine becomes a microcosm of what was occurring in the church at large. He was a Christian struggling to grapple with the arts while being faithful to the calling of Christ.

Art

In AD 46, the Apostle Paul followed Christ's mandate to "go therefore and make disciples of all nations" (Matt 28:18) and embarked on the first of his three missionary journeys, jumpstarting the spread of Christianity to the Greco-Roman world (see Fig. 4.2). Paul traveled to Mediterranean cities like Ephesus, Corinth, Thessalonica, and Rome to share the gospel. As evidenced in previous chapters, these regions were steeped in pagan religious practices that guided their worship and influenced their art and architecture.

Distinctly Christian art does not appear until the end of the second century and the beginning of the third century. This can be explained in a few ways. In Judaism and the early church, there was a tradition of avoiding religious imagery that might be considered an idol. In the Ten Commandments of Mt. Sinai, God explicitly forbade the making of any graven image (Exod 2:20). Christians, viewing themselves as an extension of the Israelites, had reverence for this commandment. The absence of Christian art in the first century might also be explained by the Christian pursuit of heavenly treasures rather than earthly luxuries. It is also important to note that early Christians were

Chapter 4: Early Christian and Medieval Eras   71

Fig. 4.2. Journeys of the Apostle Paul.

of a very modest social status and did not have the means to commission expensively crafted work. In spite of their social and political status, Christian images and carvings are evidenced in early **catacombs** (underground tombs) and sarcophagi.

The most significant change in the status of Christians was the Edict of Milan (313), in which the emperor Constantine legalized Christianity after his personal conversion. This conversion was conspicuously timed in an empire that faced political upheaval and a rising challenge of the Ottoman Empire of the East. Constantine needed a means of unification in his empire and national religion offered such an opportunity. Less than a century after the Edict of Milan, in AD 380, Theodosius made Christianity the official state religion.

The dramatic change in Christianity from humble origins to being backed by the power and wealth of an empire is strikingly illustrated in the dramatic shifts seen in early Christian art. It is helpful to look at such art in pre-Constantine and post-Constantine stages. These changes demonstrate how the early Christians engaged with dominant culture, sometimes

catacombs: systems of underground tombs

conforming to it, sometimes transforming it, and most often doing both, a pattern that still resonates today.

Pre-Constantine Art

The most common remains of early Christian art are from the environments of Roman and early funerary settings. Exceptions to this are sculptures from Asia Minor, relief carvings from Gaul, and wall frescoes from Dura-Europos (modern-day Syria, see Fig. 4.13). The imagery found supported the devotional, evangelical, and theological interests of early Christians.

Adapted Pagan Imagery

As Christianity was heavily steeped in converts and settings of established pagan religious traditions, the earliest imagery borrows from the pagan religious world but is adapted to serve Christian teachings. Common figures were the Good Shepherd (Fig. 4.3), a fisherman of men, the philosopher or teacher, the **orant** (praying figure), and even Christ in the guise of Orpheus or Apollo, such as in the Catacomb of Domitilla (Fig. 4.4.).

Some adopted symbols were less figurative and more decorative, yet could still be recognizably Christian, like doves, peacocks, twining vines and grapes, lambs, and olive or palm trees. Each had potentially Christian interpretations, such as baptism, resurrection, the bread and wine of the sacraments, Christ, or even the cross. They often had layers of meaning, as in grapevines that could remind one of Jesus the "true vine" or the wine of the Eucharist. Bread served as a reminder of Jesus the "bread of life" (John 6:35), the miracle of the loaves and fishes, or the bread of the last supper (Fig. 4.5). All leaned heavily on symbolism. For instance, the peacock was a pagan symbol adopted to represent resurrection, because the birds lose their tail feathers every summer and regrow them by winter.

orant: a praying figure, often seen in early Christian catacomb paintings and sarcophagi reliefs

Narrative and Biblical Stories

A later category of catacomb paintings broadened into narrative-based images drawn from biblical stories and the life of Christ. Common stories were of Abraham, Isaac, Jonah, the baptism of Jesus, and his healing and miracles. In these biblical

Fig. 4.3. The Good Shepherd, third century, Catacomb of Callixtus, Rome.

Chapter 4: Early Christian and Medieval Eras 73

Fig. 4.4. Orpheus, fourth century, Catacomb of Domitilla, Rome, Italy.

Fig. 4.5. Fish and Loaves, third century, Catacomb of Callixtus, Rome, Italy.

Fig. 4.6. Three Youths in Fiery Furnace, late second century to early fourth century, Catacomb of Priscilla, Via Salaria, Rome, Italy.

typology: the use of foreshadowing of events in the Old Testament for events in the New Testament

accounts, **typology** occurred, with the foreshadowing of events from the Old Testament to the New Testament, such as the story of Abraham sacrificing Isaac being seen as a parallel to God's sacrifice of his Son. Other narratives were influenced by the persecution Christians faced at the end of the second century and the beginning of the third century. By using imagery from scriptural stories like Shadrach, Meshach, and Abednego in the furnace (Dan 3; Fig. 4.6), or Noah and the ark (Gen 6-9), they referenced characters in need of deliverance that corresponded to their own plight of suffering.

Stylistic Shifts

The style and quality of early Christian catacomb paintings contrast sharply with the Roman equivalents. Unlike the highly illusionistic style of wall art found in places like Herculaneum and Pompeii, catacomb paintings look rudimentary. They are unconcerned with composition, setting, shading, or the conventions of perspective. Perhaps the relaxed approach can be attributed to the lack of access of early Christians to professional artisans. Yet, despite their haphazard qualities, the paintings are highly expressive, suggesting that the images were meant to move beyond pure decoration in order to elevate the message. In the humble and sketchy execution, the symbolism of the images weighs heavy with urgency and reverence, as in the catacomb painting of Jonah being cast into the sea (Fig. 4.7).

Chapter 4: Early Christian and Medieval Eras   75

Fig. 4.7. Jonah Cast into the Sea, fourth century, Catacombs of Peter and Marcellinus, Rome, Italy.

There is a higher level of craftsmanship in the **reliefs** (carved forms not fully in the round) of sarcophagi. Generally, relief imagery was carved on the three exposed sides of the lid and the base of the sarcophagus. Since this kind of burial was expensive, only the wealthiest Christians could afford the skilled craftsman that would be required to complete this work. The carving on various sarcophagi ranges from high relief to low relief.

High relief (Fig. 4.8) carving has a deep range of dimensionality, and **low relief** (Fig. 4.9) is shallowly carved. Although the skill of relief carving is more sophisticated than the catacomb wall paintings, the relief carvings on the sarcophagi are still haphazard in their composition and setting, with little thought for **visual hierarchy** (an organization of visual elements to show their importance). One can describe the scenes as crowded, with similar imagery to the catacombs that brim with symbolism. For example, the sarcophagus of "the three shepherds" in Fig. 4.9 depicts a grape harvest, doves, and the Good Shepherd figure, all referring back to biblical imagery or the life of Christ. The "Ram's head sarcophagus" (Fig. 4.8) pictures the shepherd, philosopher, listeners, and the harvest in a tangled and busy design.

Post-Constantine

After Christianity was legalized, believers were given a new status and resources. Shortly after Constantine's conversion, he embarked on a far-reaching

reliefs: carved forms attached to a flat base, not fully "in the round" sculpture

high relief: a type of relief carving in which the carving stands out strongly against the background

low relief: a type of relief carving in which the carving is shallow

visual hierarchy: an organization of visual elements to show their importance

76 Chapter 4: Early Christian and Medieval Eras

Fig. 4.8. *Ram's head sarcophagus* from the Via Salaria, Vatican Museo Pio Cristiano, ca. 250-275.

Fig. 4.9. *Grape Harvest with Good Shepherd* (Sarcophagus of "the three shepherds"), Vatican Museo Pio Cristiano.

building project to support the new state religion in cities like Rome, Jerusalem, and Constantinople. This encouraged Christians, through royal patronage, to expand the quality and quantity of religious art displayed on the walls and floors of local churches, adorning them with beautiful mosaics, objects of ivory, precious gems, gold, silver, and glass.

Christ and the Saints

Around and after the time of Constantine (extending from the third century to the fourth century), the range of Christian iconography increased to include episodes from the nativity and passion, Jesus as lawgiver and king of heaven, and images of the saints, with emphasis on Peter and Paul. Throughout the fourth century, Christian iconography shifted from scenes that portrayed Christ as a healer, miracle worker, and teacher to themes that focused on his divinity as God incarnate, like his transcendence, resurrection, judgment, and heavenly reign. For instance, the mosaic from the Basilica of Sant'Apollinare (Fig. 4.10) depicts Jesus as a judge, flanked on either side by angels, separating the sheep from goats. At the Basilica of Santa Pudenziana (Fig. 4.11), Christ is shown on the throne in heaven, surrounded by the apostles. One reason for this transition was the controversy that arose with Arius (AD 256-336) and his

Fig. 4.10. Good Shepherd separating the sheep from the goats, sixth century, Sant'Apollinare Nuovo, Ravenna, Italy.

Fig. 4.11. Jesus enthroned with the apostles in the heavenly Jerusalem, ca. 400, Apse of the Basilica of Santa Pudenziana, Rome, Italy.

teaching which argued that Christ was the first and supreme created being. This theological conflict led to the first ecumenical council (Nicaea, AD 325), where **Arianism**, which denied the divinity of Christ, was condemned and the biblical teaching concerning Christ being the Son of God was defended. This heresy was not entirely new, as the apostle John, centuries earlier, focused on Christ's deity in his gospel in response to early opposition.

Arianism: a fourth century influential heresy denying the divinity of Christ, originated by Alexandrian priest Arius (c. 250-c.)

Conflict of Image and Idol

Throughout early Christian art, there was a strong debate between the use of imagery in religious spaces and the folly of idols. As was mentioned earlier, Tertullian was doubtful of any idea that had its origins outside of the church. However, his distrust extended to cultural artifacts that came from pagan contexts. In "On Idolatry" Tertullian posited that since illusionary art had the potential to be worshiped as an idol, artists should simply be craftsmen. In his writing "Soliloquies," Augustine (354-430) made the argument that because images were illusions of reality, they were lies, claiming a false identity. This idea, as was mentioned in Ch. 2, could be seen in the work of Plato, who strongly informed his view. Thus, in deference to the popular theological perspective of Augustine and early Platonic Christians, religious images changed from the realism of Greco-Romans to depictions that were more abstract. Artists moved away from shading, modeling, and perspective. Flat representations of people, animals, and objects were preferred (see Fig. 4.12). This approach was intensified in the Byzantine Empire and dominated thought until Charlemagne (747-814) and the Carolingian Renaissance. In the Second Council of Nicaea in 787, the church ruled in favor of realistic images.

Fig. 4.12. Christ curing the man born blind, sixth century, Sant'Apollinare Nuovo, Ravenna, Italy.

Did you know?

Although there is a strong presence of narrative scenes depicting Jesus as healer, teacher, and miracle worker, as well as images that portray Christ's transcendence and triumph over death, there are rare examples of the suffering Christ in early Christian art. Today, the image of Christ on the cross is the most recognizable Christian image, but it did not become a staple of Christian iconography until the seventh century. It might be that early Christians, being relatively close to the time of Christ's crucifixion, wanted to avoid the gruesome details of his suffering. Artists may have also been wary to try to depict an event so drenched in mystery and holiness. Socially speaking, crucifixion bore the stigma of punishment for low-class criminals, slaves, and foreigners. Thus, it is also possible that early Christians wanted to avoid being persecuted for its negative stigma. Theologically speaking, another reason might be that some early Christians were still struggling with the idea of Christ's true humanity, which would be evidenced in a portrayal of death. The First Council of Nicea (325) affirmed Christ as fully man and fully God, while the Second Council of Nicea (787) clarified the idea of the trinity and the crucifixion.

Early Christian Worship

Before the Edict of Milan, Christian worship occurred in homes, at gravesites of saints and loved ones, and even outdoors. Since many early Christians were

Fig. 4.13. *Isometric rendering* of the Christian building at Dura-Europos in ca. 240, 1932-34, Henry Pearson.

Jewish, they continued the worship practices from the Temple and synagogue, while incorporating new Christian practices. This included the chanting of the Psalms, reading of creeds, the singing of hymns, prayers, the reading of the Septuagint, teaching, shared meals, and baptism.

One of the earliest Christian churches is found at Dura-Europos (Fig. 4.13), a Roman outpost in Syria. The building is based on the layout of a typical Roman home, square with a courtyard at the center. There is a larger hall for teaching and celebration of the Eucharist. It includes a baptistery and some of the earliest surviving Christian frescoes.

In response to the growing need in Christianity for larger gatherings of people and more standardized liturgical rituals, the Roman **basilica** was adopted as the form for church buildings (see Fig. 4.14). The basilica was a design used most commonly for civic structures. Its design included a long rectangular portion with a central nave and two aisles ending in a semicircle base (or **apse**) where the magistrate would sit. Appropriately, the design distanced itself from Greek or Roman temples and offered natural, set apart space in the apse for the altar. The basilica formed the basic floor plan for later medieval cathedrals.

---

silica: a type of Roman civic building including a rectangular portion ending in a semicircular apse, adopted by Christians as a floor plan for early churches

apse: the semicircular architectural element of a basilica

Fig. 4.14. Exterior view of the apse, Basilica of Santa Sabina, ca. 432, Rome, Italy.

Holy Text: Illuminated Manuscripts

Medieval Christians, like believers today, held the Word of God in the highest regard, viewing it as God's principal communication with mankind. Scribes and artisans meticulously recorded Scripture in illuminated manuscripts, handwritten and hand-drawn texts augmented by initials, borders, and miniature drawings. Because the mission was to *illuminate*, or enlighten and explain the content, the relationship between image and text was symbiotic, one strengthening the other. For example, the Utrecht Psalter, a book of Psalms, used enlarged and ornamented initials to give organization, creating visual hierarchy among paragraphs of text (Fig. 4.15). *The Book of Kells* is an example of the elaborate marking and patterning of illuminated

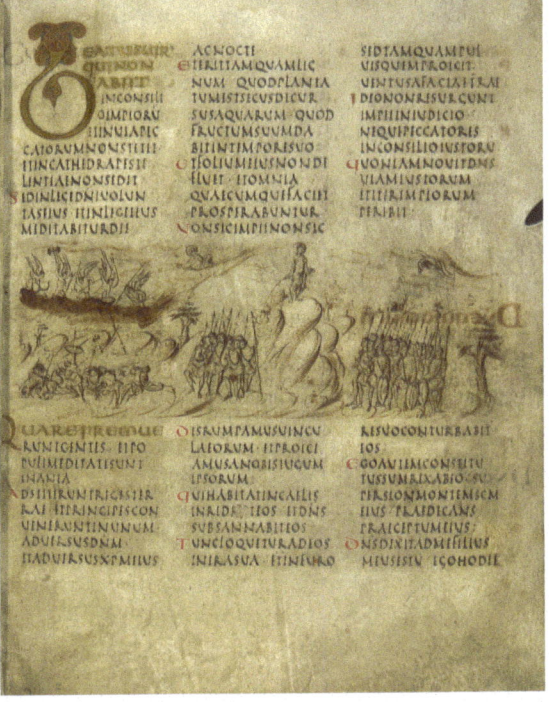

Fig. 4.15. Utrecht Psalter, Psalm 1, ninth century, Netherlands.

Fig. 4.16. Folio 34r from Book of Kells, Chi Rho monogram, ninth century.

manuscripts. Pictured in Fig. 4.16 are the Greek letters *chi* and *rho*, the first two letters of the word *Christ*. Painstakingly and laboriously decorated, the initials took on a sumptuous graphic presence.

The manuscripts were circulated according to content. The books of the Pentateuch and the Four Gospels were stitched together in a **codex** (pages bound in book form) to signify their unity, while the Psalms and the Book of Revelation circulated as their own entities. Illuminations were made on **vellum**, parchment made from animal skin that was bleached white through a preparation process. These manuscripts, having been made from the skin of animals, were seen metaphorically as the Word becoming flesh (Jn 1:1). The idiosyncrasies, or peculiarities of the previous life of the skin, were sometimes intentionally embellished, as when drawn patterning around a natural scar drew attention to the nature of the writing medium.

codex: pages bound in book form

vellum: parchment made from animal skin, bleached white through a preparation process

Music

Early Christian Era

While the Old Testament abounds in references to and prescriptions for music related to temple worship, the rest of Scripture is much more subtle concerning music in worship. Although there are no instructions regarding melody, instruments, or styles, the New Testament clearly indicates that music played a significant role in Christian worship. Early Jewish believers continued to sing psalms, a practice they brought from their Jewish background. The singing of these psalms might have been accompanied by the psaltery, a type of zither with plucked strings attached to a flat wooden sound box (see Fig. 4.17). Two sister verses in the New Testament, Col 3:16 and Eph 5:19, confirm that music for Christian worship always included text, and consisted of at least three categories: psalms, hymns, and spiritual songs.

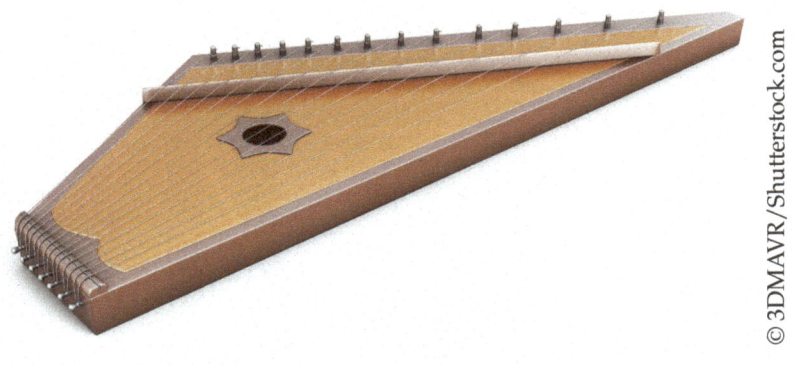

Fig. 4.17. Psaltery.

> **IN THEIR OWN WORDS**
>
> In his foundational work, *History of the Christian Church*, Philip Schaff notes:
>
> "The psalter...springs from the deep fountains of the human heart in its secret communion with God, and gives classic expression to the religious experience of all men in every age and tongue. Nothing like it can be found in all the poetry of heathendom."[4]

Hymns were most likely inspired by Greek *hymnos* or songs of praise to the Greek gods. The earliest hymns were probably founded on scripture and composed in the poetic form associated with Greek hymns. An early Latin Christian hymn, *Pange lingua gloriosi,* may indicate the poetic emphasis of rhymed lines of equal length. This text, loosely based on Psalm 45:1,[5] maintains the poetic sentiment of the psalmist. Other New Testament passages recounting the birth of the Savior, such as the angels' *Gloria in excelsis* (Luke 2:14), have become well-known Christian hymns.

Whereas the nature of psalms and hymns are relatively unambiguous, it is less clear with "spiritual songs." The original Greek for the Colossians and Ephesians reference is *ode*, generic for any type of song. Thus, to distinguish music for Christian worship from its secular counterparts, the term *spiritual* was added. A possible example of this would be the song in I Tim 3:16: "He was manifested in the flesh / Vindicated by the Spirit, / Seen by angels, / Proclaimed among the nations, / Believed on in the world, / Taken up in glory."

With the spread of Christianity, singing accompanied believers' gatherings across the Roman Empire. It complemented Scripture reading, preaching, and prayer in worship settings. As the basilica (Fig. 4.18) became a central

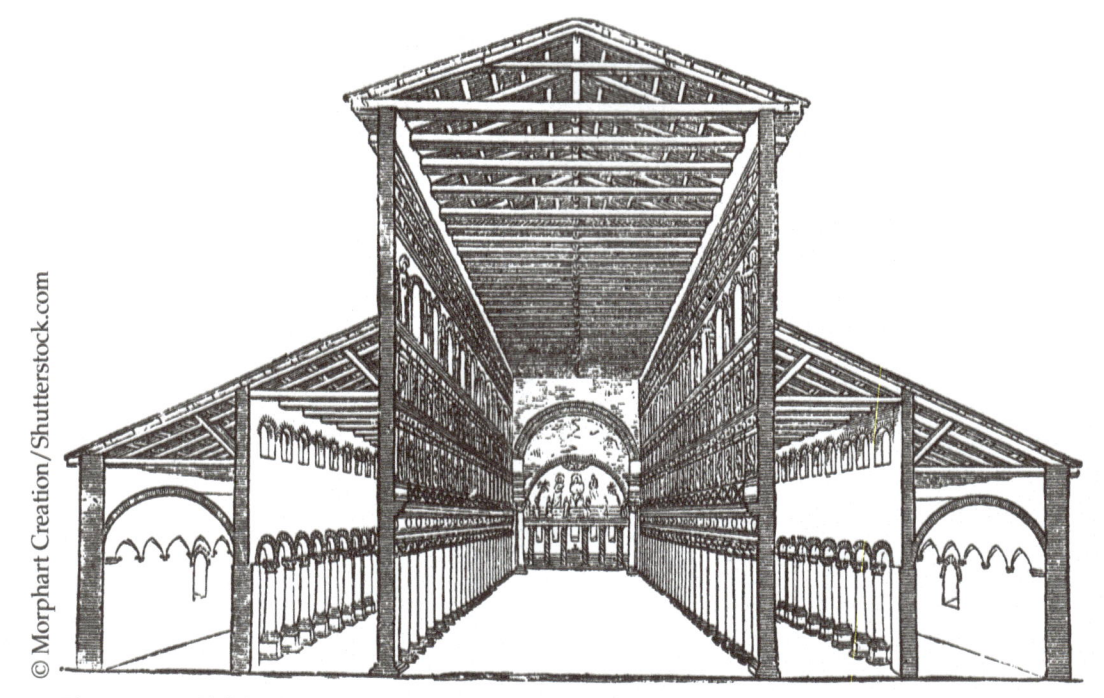

Fig. 4.18. Old St. Peter's Basilica, cross-section interior drawing.

location of worship activities, the music of the church found natural amplification. Music grew into a role of calling believers to worship, identifying believers from unbelievers, and creating a sense of community in the Body of Christ. It also served to support the ministry of the Word by echoing its truths. The connection of melody and words in human memory became a powerful tool of the gospel that the church utilized early in its growth.

Early Church Fathers on Music

Along with music's ability to reinforce memorization, early believers also noted that music could affect emotions, both to turn the heart toward God and to turn it to worldly matters, frequently sinfully so. It was not long before music became the subject of many debates concerning what constituted appropriate musical worship. One such debate concerned the use of instruments in church services. While the lyre and psaltery continued to accompany personal and home devotions, instruments for public worship became suspect due to their associations with pagan festivals and immoral activities. Thus, for more than 1,000 years, music for Christian worship was *a cappella*, simple, monophonic, and without dancing or other worldly accompaniments. Augustine noted that while music was an active agent in calling a believer's heart to worship, there was also an inherent danger if the music itself drew the believer's attention away from worship (see text box below). Thus, "worship wars" are not a contemporary phenomenon; the debates have been going on nearly as long as the church has existed.

> **IN THEIR OWN WORDS**
>
> In his *Confessions*, Augustine describes his dilemma with music and worship.
>
> "When I recall the tears which I shed at the song of the Church in the first days of my recovered faith, and even now as I am moved not by the song but by the things which are sung, when sung with fluent voice and music that is most appropriate, I acknowledge again the great benefit of this practice. Thus I vacillate between the peril of pleasure and the value of the experience, and I am led more. . .to endorse the custom of singing in church so that by the pleasure of hearing the weaker soul might be elevated to an attitude of devotion. Yet when it happens to me that the song moves me more than the thing which is sung, I confess I have sinned blamefully and then prefer not to hear the singer. Look at my condition!"[6]

Development of Gregorian Chant

By the time the Roman Empire ended in 476, the Roman Catholic Church was well established throughout its territories. Although political Rome fell, religious Rome with its established papacy at the head, continued as the most stable institution in Western Europe until the rise of Charlemagne in 800. The pope believed that maintaining a strong organization with a well-defined hierarchy of power was critical to the church's continuation. One of the moves that Pope Gregory I (r. 590-604) made was to standardize the music for worship, or **liturgical music**, in the churches. The legend that Pope Gregory received this music directly from the Holy Spirit gave rise to the general name for this music, Gregorian chant (see Fig. 4.19).

The spread of Gregorian chant was accomplished through oral transmission. Choir directors in Rome were trained to teach the standard liturgy in every church, which was no small feat. Without written notation at the time, transmission took place by meticulous listening, singing, and the memorization of both the words and the melodies. They repeated the process over and over until the choir directors were confident that the music was perfectly duplicated. The music was a single melody, or monophonic, with small stepwise movements that connected the tune in a memorable trajectory of notes.

liturgical music: worship music in the early Roman Catholic Chu standardized Pope Gregor generally cal Gregorian ch

syllabic: a melodic style with one note per syllable

melismatic: a melodic style with many notes per syllable

responsorial: call and response manner between soloist and choir

antiphonal: call and response manner between choirs

It could be sung with one note per syllable, known as **syllabic** singing, or with many notes per syllable, known as **melismatic** singing. It was most likely vocalized in a smooth manner with notes of even length that did not evoke strong rhythmic movement. Rather, it provided a calm repose from the everyday chaos and uncertainty outside the church building or cathedral. Its purpose was to turn believers from earthly cares to their hope in Christ. Chant was sung in a call and response manner between soloist and choir (**responsorial**) or by choirs singing alternately (**antiphonal**).

For the most important service of every day, the Mass, in which the Eucharist was celebrated, five particular chants became standard. These became known as the Ordinary, for they were sung every time Mass was conducted. Four of these are in Latin and one, *Kyrie Eleison*,[7] is in Greek. They were interspersed throughout the service and function as prayers, supplications, praises, and statements of faith. The order in which they appeared in Mass is as follows:

Kyrie Eleison (Lord, have mercy—a plea for mercy)

Though ***Kyrie Eleison*** had very few words, it could have a long duration. "Kyrie Eleison" (Lord, have mercy) was sung three times, "Christe Eleison" (Christ, have mercy) was then sung three times, and finally "Kyrie Eleison" was sung three times again. Note the emphasis on three, which was representative of the Trinity. Additionally, this chant was usually sung melismatically, which stretched out the syllables over a longer period of time.

Listen for the repetition of the words and the melismatic style of singing of the ***Kyrie***.

Gloria (Glory to God in the highest—a praise to the Triune God)

Credo (I believe in One God—a long statement of faith)

This began with the choir director setting the pitch by chanting, "Credo in unum Deum" (I believe in one God). The choir then entered and sang mostly syllabically for the rest of this chant. It was usually less

Fig. 4.19. *St. Gregory I*, with dove depicting the Holy Spirit, fresco in neo-mannerist style, ca. 1866, Cesare Mariani, Chiesa di Santa Maria in Aquiro, Rome, Italy.

melodic and more in a reciting tone, eventually pronouncing an extended statement of faith.

Listen for the opening "Credo in unum Deum" and then a mostly syllabic delivery of the words.

Think about how the *Credo* contrasts in style with the *Kyrie*. Note on the recordings: These alternate between men's and women's choirs, which would not have been allowed in the early medieval church. Only men were permitted to sing in choirs. Later, boys were allowed, after which time the octave became a permitted harmonic interval by necessity.

Sanctus (Holy, holy, holy—a chorus of praise)

Agnus Dei (Lamb of God—a plea for mercy and peace)

Did you know?

Not only did monks and priests need to sing Gregorian chant for the Ordinary of the Mass daily, but they had to memorize music for eight other daily services, known as the Offices. In addition, over the course of one week, they sang all 150 Psalms. Memorizing music was more than a full-time job! Over time, musical notation was developed to aid the singers. One ingenious monk even developed a system to remember the intervals of a scale. Guido of Arezzo (ca. 991-ca. 1033) invented *solmization*, where each note is associated with a particular syllable. This practice is still used today in teaching children to sing, as is illustrated in Maria's famous "Do-re-mi" lesson in *The Sound of Music*.

Music Theory

The medieval view of music was greatly influenced by the mathematical findings of Pythagoras (see Ch. 2), the application of Greek music theory in the Quadrivium by Boethius (see Ch. 3), and the integration of these principles in Christian music. The synthesis of these ideas informed the development of Gregorian chant as appropriate music for worship.

With the growth of the Christian faith, the Music of the Spheres was also understood as reflecting the perfect order in the Empirium, where God existed. Along with the understanding of a cosmological view of music, the Quadrivium's association of music with mathematical sciences and astronomy reinforced an objective, measurable, orderly, and quantifiable understanding of music. The hierarchy of musical notes, intervals, and scales generated by Pythagorean processes, however, took on new associative meanings for the early church. The simplest ratios in the Pythagorean system that were called perfect intervals became known to early Christians as the intervals believed to be the most representative of God. The octave, for example, created by pitches in a ratio of 1:2, was seen as the most perfect of intervals and thus, most reflective of God. The next most perfect interval was the **Perfect Fifth** (P5), produced by a ratio of 2:3. This was followed by the **Perfect Fourth** (P4), created by ratios of 3:4. These three intervals, still referred to as "Perfect" intervals today, were the principal consonances allowed in musical worship.

Early Gregorian chant was monophonic, and thus avoided different pitches sounding together. With the development of polyphony, however, **consonance** and **dissonance** become an issue. The earliest examples of polyphony emphasize octaves, P5s and P4s, in keeping with perceived degrees of perfection. Until nearly 1400 with the beginning of the Renaissance and the influence of humanism, these three intervals remained the only ones in the "consonant" or acceptable categories. As intervals increased in perceived complexity due to the ratios of the sizes of the sounding instruments, they were perceived to be more dissonant. While consonance was associated with God and the heavenly realm, dissonance was associated with Satan and the devilish realm of hell. The most dissonant of all intervals, the **tritone**, was nicknamed the "diabolus in musica," or the Devil in Music. Ironically, this interval occurs acoustically in the space between two of the most consonant intervals, the P4 and the P5. In medieval church music, this interval was to be avoided at all costs. Why? The answer is found not only in the association with the Devil but practically in the acoustics. The simpler intervals tended to reinforce sound by the syncing of their sound waves in such a way that they could create natural amplification in large cathedrals. The tritone was so complex in its acoustics that the lower and upper pitches of the interval actually canceled out each other, causing the sound to decay quickly and in keeping with the spiritual analogy, fall to the ground rather than rise to heaven. It was not difficult to imagine this interval representing Satan, the fallen angel. Practically speaking, then, music written with an emphasis on the perfect intervals resonated in cavernous halls was clearly heard in its text declamation and served worshippers much better. Cacophonous or dissonant music did not accomplish the goal of music for worship in sounding forth the message of scripture, of creating a sense of community among worshippers singing together, and of creating a sense of calmness and order in the presence of God.

Theatre

Although Roman-type spectacles had died out after the end of the Roman Empire, evidence of theatrical productions on smaller scales, both in the public sphere and in churches, continued and even grew. During times of relative peace, secular drama came with traveling minstrels who brought variety shows featuring music, dancing, and acting along with acts of tumbling, bear-leading, juggling, and puppetry. Among these were **troubadours** and **jongleurs**, early professionals seeking work for hire (see Ch. 5).

Christians most likely enjoyed both secular and sacred theatre, and at least one church father explained his dilemma with secular drama. In his *Confessions*, Augustine describes the temptation he felt in allowing theatre to affect him emotionally. His comments indicate that he most likely watched tragedy, and the effects of the vicarious feelings of suffering and empathy toward the characters were viewed as undesirable. Perhaps like Paul, he realized that he was unable to overcome the law of sin that dwelled in his members (Rom 7:23).

IN THEIR OWN WORDS

In Book III of his *Confessions*, a later reflection on his life at 17-19 years old, Augustine writes about his negative view of secular theatre.

"Stage-plays also carried me away, full of images of my miseries, and of fuel to my fire. Why is it that man desires to be made sad, beholding doleful and tragical things, which he himself would by no means want to suffer? Yet he desires as a spectator to feel sorrow at them, and this very sorrow is his pleasure. What is this but a miserable sorrow?"[8]

Sacred medieval drama naturally flowed out of the rich tradition of the Christian liturgy and most of the existing artifacts reinforce the spread of the gospel through reenactments of Bible stories, prominent Christian figures, and lessons in morality. Several types developed as the church established itself in monasteries, basilicas, and cathedrals (see Figs. 4.14 and 5.5).

Biblical plays developed as early as the ninth century as a response to the growing disconnect between church services and congregations who were not only illiterate but also could not understand the classical Latin spoken in Mass. This caused both a decline in attendance and interest, so one solution was a more dramatic enactment of the celebration of Mass. This proved to be popular and led to other dramatic enactments of biblical stories and topics.[9]

Liturgical drama reinforced the liturgy, especially surrounding the high points of the liturgical year: Christmas and Easter. These dramas included monophonic **plainchant** in Latin, with music serving as an integral part of the play. One of the earliest, and definitely the most famous, is *Quem quaeritus* ("Whom do you seek?"), an Easter dialogue involving the Angel guarding Jesus's empty tomb and the women who were present, which Catholicism typically identifies as the three Marys. This dialogue originally found in the tenth century was technically called a **trope**, an extension of new words or music to an already established part of the liturgy. Tropes were not viewed as foreign elements to the

---

troubadours: traveling musicians and entertainers as called in Southern France

jongleurs: traveling musicians and entertainers

Biblical plays dramatic enactment of the Mass; developed as early as the ninth century as a response to the growing disconnect between church services and congregations who were not only illiterate but also could not understand the classical Latin spoken in Mass

liturgical drama: play that included monophonic plainchant in Latin, with music serving as an integral part to reinforce the liturgy

plainchant: generic term for monophonic medieval church music, often referred to as Gregorian chant

trope: an extension of new words or music to an already established part of the liturgy in the tenth century

liturgy, but rather as natural outgrowths that further developed or explained the truth. This was similar to the **scholastic** practice of **glossing** a text. The short dialogue (in translation) is as follows, with the respective voices in parentheses:

Whom do you seek, O followers of Christ? (*Angel*)

The crucified Jesus of Nazareth, O celestial one (*Women*)

He is not here. He has risen as he had foretold. Go, announce that he has risen (*Angel*)

Alleluia (*All*)

[Stage direction: The Angel remaining at the tomb announces that Christ has risen]

Behold, that is fulfilled which he himself formerly said through the prophet, speaking thus to the Father: I have risen. . . [continues with the established Introit of the Liturgy][10]

Morality plays were dramatic enactments using allegorical characters usually representing forces of good versus evil, virtue versus vice, or God versus Satan. Unlike liturgical drama, these were independent of liturgical function and served to edify and warn believers. Although music was not an integral part of this genre, some prominent examples exist which were highly musical. One of these was *Ordo virtutum* (The Way of the Virtues) written by Hildegard von Bingen (1098-1179), founder and abbess of the convent in Rupertsberg, Germany (see Fig. 4.20).

Sidebar definitions:

scholastic: related to the system of philosophy and theology taught in Medieval universities

glossing: comment on a text; addition of a footnote

morality plays: dramatic enactments using allegorical characters usually representing forces of good versus evil, virtue versus vice, or God versus Satan

Fig. 4.20. Eibingen Abbey founded by Hildegard von Bingen, near Rüdesheim am Rhein, Germany.

> **IN THEIR OWN WORDS**
>
> Hildegard of Bingen was a versatile scholar whose advice was sought out by royalty and church leaders. In addition to detailed accounts of her mystical visions from God, she authored works on medicine, theology, liturgical poetry set to music, along with *Ordo virtutum*, the only existing musical morality play from the medieval era with a known composer. In the following account from *Epistle 47: To the Prelates of Rome*, she describes why the Devil could not sing:
>
> "When. . .the Devil, heard what man had begun to sing by the inspiration of God, and that man was invited by this to recall the sweetness of the songs of heaven, seeing that his cunning machinations had gone awry, he was so frightened that he was greatly tormented, and he continually busied himself in scheming and in selecting from the multifarious falsehoods of his iniquity, so that he did not cease to disrupt that affirmation and beauty of divine praise and spiritual hymnody, withdrawing it not only from the heart of man by evil suggestions, unclean thoughts, and various distractions, but even (wherever possible) from the heart of the Church, though dissension, scandal, and unjust oppression."[11]

The characters in this play include Patriarchs, Prophets, sixteen female Virtues (such as Chastity, Innocence, Obedience), a Happy Soul, an Unhappy Soul, a Penitent Soul, and the Devil. All of the characters have singing parts (monophonic chant style) except for the Devil. Because the Devil is denied any "divine harmony," he can only speak, shout, and utter threats. This drama, performed traditionally on a staircase with characters in colored costumes ascending and descending according to their degree of temptation by the Devil, provided exciting visual and aural entertainment for audiences, while conveying the gospel message of sin, repentance, confession, and forgiveness.

View a performance of this play.

Study Questions

1. What are some examples of "adaptions" early Christians made from the iconography of pagan culture? What were their reasons for doing so?
2. What are some of the possible reasons for the absence of the depiction of the crucifixion in early Christian imagery?
3. What political event brought about the most significant shifts in the social and cultural status of early Christians? How would you imagine the history of Christianity without this event? Do you think this event was good or bad for the church?

4. In what ways do you see early Christians engaging with dominant culture?
5. Describe the conflict in early Christian art between image and idol?
6. How can believers distinguish between the acceptable use of music for worship and misappropriation of music that Christians cannot affirm?

Notes

1. Gregory the Great, *Letter to Mellitus*, 85.
2. Augustine, *Confessions*, 1.22.
3. Augustine, *Confessions*, 3.2-4.
4. Schaff, V. I, 104-105.
5. "My heart overflows with a pleasing theme; I address my verses to the king; my tongue is like the pen of a ready scribe." Ps 45:1.
6. Augustine, *Confessions* X, xxxiii, in McKinnon, 155.
7. It should be noted that *Kyrie Eleison* is a Latin transliteration of the original Greek (Matt 17:15), which would usually be transliterated in English with *kurie eleēson*.
8. Augustine, *Confessions*, III.2, 59.
9. Kennedy, V. 2, 826-7.
10. Fuller, *European Musical Heritage* 800-1750, 4.
11. Hildegard of Bingen, *Epistle 47*, in Strunk, V.2, 75.

5

High and Late Middle Ages
The Flowering of the Medieval Era

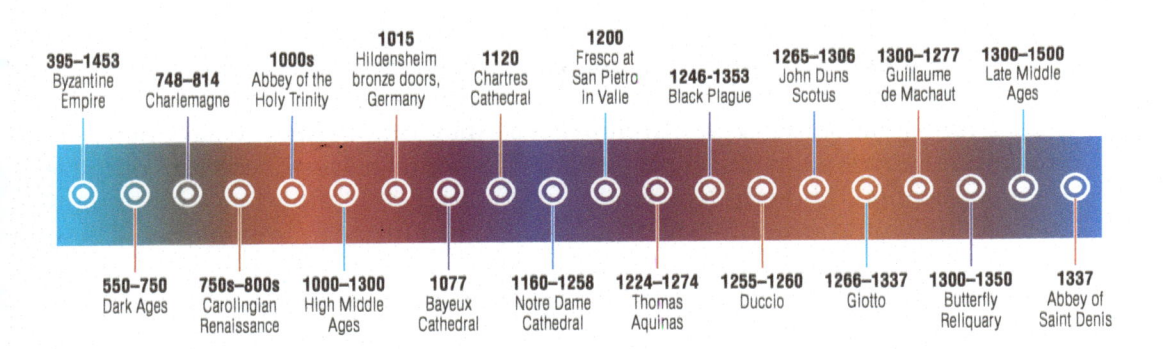

395–1453 Byzantine Empire
748–814 Charlemagne
1000s Abbey of the Holy Trinity
1015 Hildensheim bronze doors, Germany
1120 Chartres Cathedral
1200 Fresco at San Pietro in Valle
1246-1353 Black Plague
1265–1306 John Duns Scotus
1300–1277 Guillaume de Machaut
1300–1500 Late Middle Ages

550–750 Dark Ages
750s–800s Carolingian Renaissance
1000–1300 High Middle Ages
1077 Bayeux Cathedral
1160–1258 Notre Dame Cathedral
1224–1274 Thomas Aquinas
1255–1260 Duccio
1266–1337 Giotto
1300–1350 Butterfly Reliquary
1337 Abbey of Saint Denis

Philosophy

The way in which multifarious fields of study think about the movement of history is often different. For example, the eras and transitions that a scientist sees would look very different than those perceived by a scholar of religious studies. It is no different when one looks at the arts and its relationship to theology and philosophy. When envisioning the relationship between Christianity and the humanities, most will gravitate to the Renaissance and they would do so with good reason. Thus, the Middle Ages, which immediately precedes the Renaissance, will often be interpreted as a transition from the classical period to the rise of the Renaissance masters. Yet, in theology, the High Middle Ages were not transitional. They were considered to be a significant moment where many factors, both internal and external to Christianity, led to great strides in theological thinking. Moreover, to Protestants, the Renaissance was the transitional period, where the rise of **humanism**, or the retrieval of ideas and values from classical (i.e., Greek and Roman) sources, influenced Luther and Calvin's (1509-1564) emphasis on returning to the ancient scriptural text. Thus, the High Middle Ages could be depicted variously, from the high point

humanism: an intellectual movement originating in the Renaissance which focuses on the retrieval of ideas and values from classical sources

of Catholic theology to the period, which, though providing great strides in art itself, was in many ways the precursor to the Renaissance.

It would be difficult to overstate the significance of the rise of Charlemagne (748-814) for the progression of the humanities. As Charlemagne unified the Germanic peoples and, eventually, conquered the Saxons, he ruled a kingdom that incorporated much of Western Europe. Such centralization of power had some significant effects on the High Middle Ages. First, it led to rapid changes in economies, entrenching **feudalism** with a movement toward the centralizing of power in cities. During the period, as well as the centuries that followed, powerful urban areas helped lead to the rise of nations. It is this effect that would eventually allow for the types of trades and industries that concentrated wealth in the hands of the nobility. Furthermore, it was this prosperity that, for better or for worse, allowed for the patronage, or sponsoring, necessary for Renaissance artists to flourish as they did. Second, Charlemagne's concern for citizenry, both for political and religious reasons, led to an emphasis on education. Though he was not fully literate, the importance of thought to civic life would eventually lead to the rise of European universities. These universities arose first and foremost for ministerial training, but also grew to incorporate various trades. It was the rise of these types of educational structures that provided the backdrop for the intense movements of theology during the High Middle Ages, as well as for the return to classical humanism in the Renaissance.

Unusually, the greatest influence in philosophy and theology during the Middle Ages was found in the same person, Thomas Aquinas (1225-1274). It was the first time such a convergence occurred since Augustine…and the last time it would occur as philosophy began to distance itself from its partnership with Christianity. Aquinas was a Franciscan monk, whose work became definitive for all Catholic theology that followed. For a long period following the rise of the Greek Empire, the works of Aristotle remained relatively uninfluential in the West, primarily being preserved in Arabic and Islamic philosophy. Thus, early Christian theology was developed in dialogue with Platonism. With the Crusades, increasing trade, and Muslim incursions into Europe, the globalizing forces in the Near East led to the reintroduction of Aristotle to the Mediterranean. Thus, theology in the Middle Ages can be envisioned as an attempt to relieve the tension between Plato, Aristotle, and the work of Augustine. Not only did Plato and Aristotle have contrasting views, with the former focusing on the transcendent and the latter focusing on the immanent, but they also both contrasted with the Bishop of Hippo. Ancient Greek philosophers knew that humans had a faculty for thought, which they called the mind. However, they did not possess concept of a faculty for choice. As Augustine began to think through various theological topics,

feudalism: a system in medieval Europe in which peasants lived on land owned by nobles and paid homage to them through service

especially the issue of grace as being God's free choice to love His creatures beyond their worth, he started using the idea of the will (Lat. *voluntas*) to speak of the faculty that God, angels, and humans have that is the foundation for choosing. Thus, the tension arose. Greek philosophers with their nearly sole emphasis on mind, in contrast to Augustinian theologians with their rising focus on the will.

Aquinas was a master at synthesis, deftly working between the worlds of philosophy and theology. This is the reason he was depicted as the central figure in *The Apotheosis of Thomas Aquinas* (Fig. 5.1). The four seated individuals that flank him are the four *doctores* (teachers) of the early church, Gregory, Ambrose, Jerome, and Augustine.

Fig. 5.1. *The Apotheosis of Thomas Aquinas*, Francisco de Zurbarán, 1631, Museum of Fine Arts of Seville.

They are considered, by Catholics, to be the greatest theologians of the early church. Yet, Zurbarán (1598-1664) depicted Aquinas as the "*apotheosis* of theology," employing a theological term that has to do with someone ascending to become like God or a god themselves. In other words, Zurbarán treated Aquinas as the pinnacle of thought, so much greater than all preceding and following him that he was more like God in his understanding than merely a man. Such a high view was largely due to his ability to mediate between competing and, often, conflicting theological perspectives.

One of his significant contributions was in clarifying and expanding on the idea of revelation, whereby knowledge of God came not by human discovery, but by divine activity in approaching humans. Aquinas, though believing that humans could know some things about divine being by looking at nature (i.e., natural theology), he placed an emphasis on Scripture as the primary way one was to know God.

> **IN THEIR OWN WORDS**
>
> From Thomas Aquinas, *Summa theologica*: "Even for those things about God that can be investigated by humans, it was necessary for humans to be instructed by divine revelation. For the truth about God that is investigated by reason, comes forth for only a small number of people, only after a long time and with an admixture of much error..."[1]

Furthermore, his usage of light as a metaphor for revelation became significant for further development of the doctrine.[2] Not only was Scripture to be understood as God's speech to humanity, but it could only be recognized when something sheds light on it. Just like one could have the presence of something, but not recognize it is there since one is in the dark, so Scripture requires some sort of illumination. It is this the idea that became central to Calvin's stress on the work of the Holy Spirit such that one can be receptive to Scripture. Ironically, the Swiss Reformer used this doctrine to combat the notion that the Catholic church was necessary because it alone could give the authoritative interpretation of the Bible.

Another idea of Aquinas deserves mention, especially in view of the current discussion of the arts. During the Middle Ages, aesthetics was not a major field of study. Likewise, art forms were practiced, but art as a topic was only rarely discussed. Though Aquinas, himself, only infrequently touched on the topic, he did make a connection that became significant in how philosophers and theologians after him have thought about the artistic endeavor. As was discussed earlier (Ch. 1), Scripture is clear to separate the activity of God as creator from the human work of making. Thus, there is a disjunction between divine and human creativity. Yet, Aquinas drew the analogy between them in writing that "all natural things…may be called God's works of art."[3] Thus, he begins a trend of comparison between human and divine activities that has led to some unhelpful consequences. Where Aquinas was careful, whenever drawing analogy between God's activity and that of humans, to emphasize the dissimilarity even over the similarity, Christian artists have often been so focused on the resemblance that they claim a mandate from God for their artistic works. As has been mentioned, art is a good thing, but care must be taken not to attempt to assert divine authority for its production.

Another scholar of significance during the Middle Ages, especially as he is often seen as a foil for the work of Aquinas, was John Duns Scotus (ca.1265-1306). Scotus was a Dominican monk who carried on the Augustinian tradition of focusing on God's will and choice. This caused him to have a different view of the theology, the afterlife, and divine activity when compared to Aquinas. Scotus's emphasis on God's freedom to choose as He pleased had many effects, some beneficial and some detrimental. His view of will ended up being significant for the Reformers in their development of *sola gratia* ("grace alone"), or the view that one can only be saved by God's grace apart from any merit of works. Martin Luther (1483-1546), who was educated at Erfuhrt, a school steeped in the Scotian tradition, believed that God was free to save and free not to save. Calvin agreed and extended this type of thinking. Yet, there were some dangers, as the emphasis on freedom that was an attempt to push against the Catholic church, would be the same view of freedom that was used during the Enlightenment to push against all Christianity. It would also be a perspective that led to the quick turn in how people viewed the relationship of Christianity to the arts. During the Renaissance, for example, the Catholic church was seen, in Europe, as the greatest patron of the arts. By the end of the Enlightenment, Christianity, in general, was often seen as the enemy of the artist.

sola gratia: Latin for "gra alone"

> ### DID YOU KNOW?
>
> By the early part of the sixteenth century, the theology of Duns Scotus had fallen greatly out of favor, since it was seen as being too traditional and not open to some of the more novel ideas developed during the Reformation. For that reason, calling someone a follower of Scotus was essentially a derogatory way to speak of someone being unintelligent. Thus, the term "dunce," from Duns Scotus, came to be an offensive term to attack someone's intellect.

Art

As was mentioned earlier, the Middle Ages, also called the Medieval Era, was the time period that connected the world of Rome in antiquity to Europe that emerged in the Renaissance. This span of about one thousand years is typically divided into three periods. The early Middle Ages (550-1000) began with the fall of the Roman Empire to Germanic tribes of the north (Fig. 5.2). The traditions and influence of Germanic kingdoms replaced the set of political, social, and cultural structures of Roman Imperialism. Within this period, 550-750 are referred to as the "Dark Ages" because there is so little documentation recording the activities of the time. As the population of Europe was gradually Christianized, monasticism grew in strength. Prominent leaders like Charlemagne, "king of the Franks," crowned himself the "holy Roman Emperor" and ushered in a revival of art and culture known as the Carolingian Renaissance.

The High Middle Ages (1000-1300) underwent even more dramatic changes. This period manifested population growth, territorial expansion, and economic development. The religious wars of the Crusades, led by Europeans under the

Crusades: rel gious wars le by Europeans under the gui ance of the ne papal monarchy, launched against the ri ing power of Islamic Calip ate in Palestir to recover the Holy Land

Fig. 5.2. Barbaric kingdoms after the fall of the Roman Empire, ca. AD 500.

guidance of the new papal monarchy, was launched to recover the Holy Land from the rising power of the Islamic Caliphate in Palestine. The base violence of the Crusades was in stark contrast to the intellectual advancements occurring at the European universities.

In the Late Middle Ages (1300-1500) the **Black Plague** decimated between one-quarter and one-half of the population of Europe, the number of deaths estimated to be nearly twenty-five million. War, famine, and pestilence atrophied Europe like leprosy and the advances of the High Middle Ages swung on a pendulum the opposite way. Nonetheless, the underlying political, cultural, and social structures codified in the Middle Ages were revived in the Renaissance of the fourteenth and fifteenth centuries.

Art of this era was wrapped up in the presence of Christianity, the worship of the faithful, and the activities of the church. All these were significantly influenced by the pagan practices of the Germanic tribes, which held polytheistic religions that revered both the physical properties of the earth as well as the supernatural. The art of the time reflected a redirection of pagan religious practices toward Christian spirituality. Medieval art was obsessed with a reverence for materials

Black Plague: a global epidemic the bubonic plague that devastated Europe and Asia in the early 1300s

and images, channeling them as embodied metaphors between the physical and the spiritual, the worldly and the heavenly. Though they often did this incorrectly, by uncritically appropriating pagan practices or by thinking that the world revealed God, there is a parallel idea in 1 Tim 4:1-5. There Paul wrote of how all created things were good if they directed one in thanksgiving toward God. This belief that the physical world could facilitate a heavenly experience is evidenced in the architecture of cathedrals, their interior design, the documents of sacred texts, and objects used in worship by clergy and parishioners. Moving from the outside to the inside, one can see how artwork enhanced and distinguished the secular and the sacred, transitioning the physical to the celestial.

Cathedrals

The need for a church building grew from the expansion of Christianity, codification of liturgy and clergy practice, and the growth of the papal state. With the rise in popularity of pilgrimages to abbeys, a church design that allowed for pilgrims to move around the monks as they performed daily rituals was needed. The design of the church building in the Middle Ages, eventually becoming known as a **cathedral**, borrowed from the floor plan of the Roman basilica (see Ch. 4). It was based on a rectangle ending in a semi-circle with bisecting arms, or **transept**, that created a cross shape. The adapted floor plan consisted of a narthex, nave, aisle, choir, transept, and ambulatory (see an example floor plan in Fig. 5.5). This design style became known as **Romanesque**, such as the Abbey of the Holy Trinity in Fig. 5.3. This style utilized the **complex rib vault**, an intersecting pattern of groin vaults that allowed for high ceilings and ample room for the entrance of sunlight (Fig. 5.4).

cathedral: large church building in the Middle Ages

transept: bisecting arms on a basilica that create a cross shape

Romanesque: design style of cathedrals of the Middle Ages that used an adapted floor plan consisting of a narthex, nave, aisle, choir, transept and ambulatory

complex rib vault: an intersecting pattern of groin vaults that allowed for high ceilings and the pouring in of sunlight

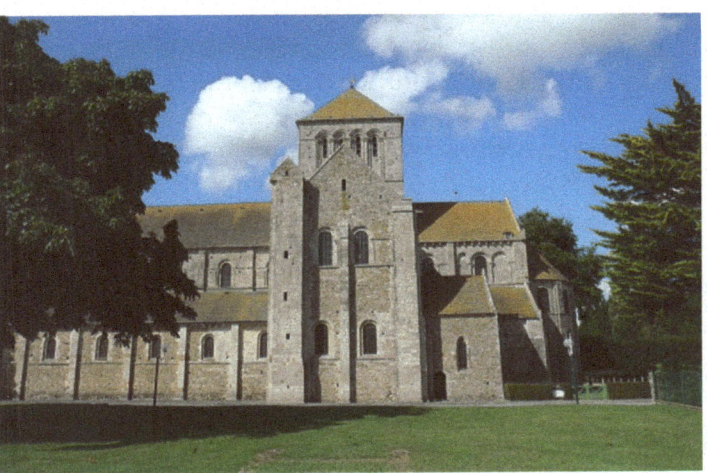

Andia / Contributor / Universal Images Group / Getty Images

Fig. 5.3. Abbey of the Holy Trinity, eleventh century, Normandy.

The floor plan of cathedrals has several levels of symbolism. One was body symbolism, where the **sanctuary** (the area around the altar containing ambulatory, chevette, and choir) serves as head, the transept as arms, the nave as torso, and the **narthex** (entryway) as feet. It was in the sanctuary, or head, where the altar was placed and the Eucharist was celebrated, the altar being an adaption of the bema seat from the Jewish synagogue. In that sense, the physical transitions in the church also mirrored the journey from the world (narthex) to kingdom of God (nave) to kingdom of heaven (altar area).

The impressive exteriors of cathedrals dramatized the distinction between the earthly and the spiritual, as one can imagine the effect of soaring medieval structures set on hilltops against an otherwise bleak landscape. This complex exterior was brought to new, literal heights in the development of the **Gothic** style, originating in the Ile-de-France region. The style was considered new and modern, originally tagged "Gothic" as a derogatory name in its abandonments of classical traditions as the Goths took power. Gothic style had an extreme emphasis on vertical space, articulated by large stained-glass windows, pointed arches, **flying buttresses** (exterior supports), and thin walls. Credited with this new style was Abbot Suger (1081-1151), whose work at the Abbey Saint-Denis (Figs. 5.6-7) exhibited the soaring qualities of these sky-scrapers, magnified in the interior by substantial stained-glass windows that allowed for the otherworldly filtering of light. Another stunning example of Gothic architecture is the Chartres Cathedral (Fig. 5.8).

Fig. 5.4. Complex rib vault in interior of Bayeux Cathedral, began ca. 1077, Normandy.

sanctuary: area in a cathedral around an altar

narthex: the entryway of a cathedral

Gothic style: considered new and modern, originally tagged "Gothic" as a derogatory name in its abandonments of classical traditions as the Goths took power; extreme emphasis on vertical space, articulated by large stained-glass windows, pointed arches, flying buttresses, and thin walls

flying buttresses: exterior supports of building in the Gothic style

Entryways

The Cathedral of Hildesheim was fitted with sixteen-foot-tall bronze doors (Fig 5.9). On the surface, cast bronze relief images depicted the Biblical accounts of Creation and the Fall to the death and resurrection of Christ. In entering

Chapter 5: High and Late Middle Ages 101

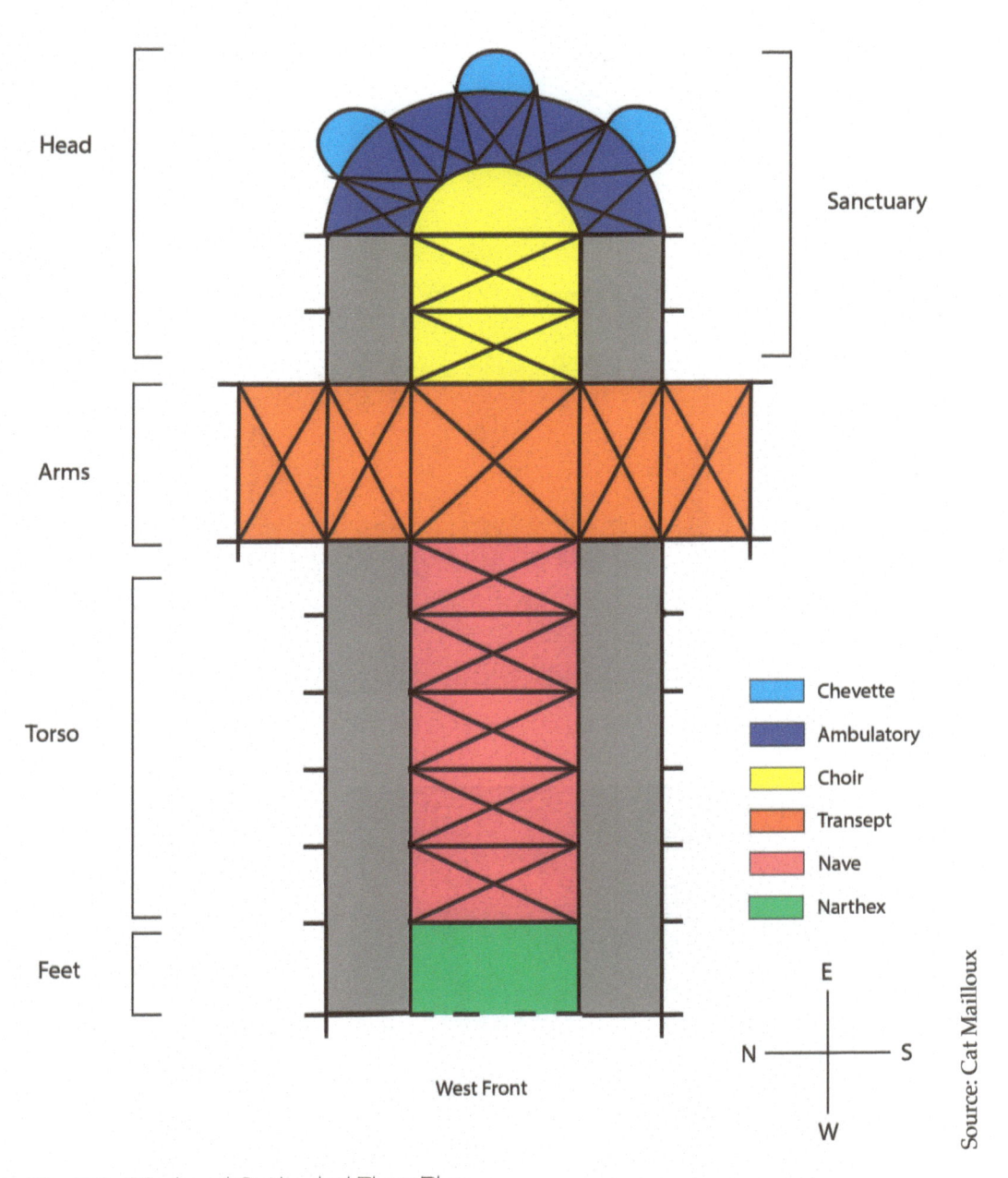

Fig. 5.5. Medieval Cathedral Floor Plan.

Fig. 5.6. Exterior of Abbey Saint-Denis, began in 1337, Paris, France.

Fig. 5.7. Interior of Abbey Saint-Denis, began ca. 1137, Paris, France.

Chapter 5: High and Late Middle Ages 103

Fig. 5.8. Chartres Cathedral, ca. 1220, Chartres, France

Fig. 5.9. Hildesheim bronze doors, ca. 1015, Germany.

Fig. 5.10. *Last Judgement,* west tympanum (portal arch), ca. 1050–1130, Church Sainte-Foy, Conques, France.

through the church door, one was met with the fullness of Scripture. Typology was deftly wielded to draw visual and narrative parallels between the Old and the New Testaments. The Tree of Life in Genesis was depicted horizontally across from Christ on the Cross. Likewise, Eve holding Cain was placed across from Mary, who cradled Jesus.

The symbolism of a door as a spiritual passageway is reinforced in the west tympanum of *Last Judgment* at the Church of Sainte-Foy at Conques (Fig. 5.10). The **tympanum**, the semi-circular portal above a door, is filled with images of the final judgment. The relief carving is divided into two parts, one with heaven's angels greeting believers and one with demons ushering the unrepentant to hell. As parishioners walked under the arch, they were graphically reminded of two paths they could choose.

tympanum: the semicircular portal above a door

Interiors

The interiors of medieval abbeys and cathedrals were carefully considered to create a sacred environment and elevate the worship experience. This was accomplished through elements of stained glass, murals, and small tempera paintings.

Stained Glass—There was perhaps no greater emphasis on the interiors of cathedrals as the attention that was given to stained glass. One can imagine the beauty of high stained-glass windows that erased the muck and dirt of daily life to direct one's attention heavenward. At Chartres Cathedral, brilliant arched domes of light stream through the opulent stained-glass windows (Fig. 5.11).

Chapter 5: High and Late Middle Ages 105

Light was a physical reminder of the divine Christ, "light of the world" (John 8:12), who was God's way of communicating with humanity.

Stained glass was both architecture and image, reinforced with stone to form the wall of the cathedral while depicting Biblical narratives and iconography of saints. Arched stone latticework bracing the windows, called *tracery*, amplified the size of windows to allow for maximum light while remaining structurally sound. The *rose window*, also called a wheel window, was a common stained-glass device placed high in a *façade* (the main, frontal facing wall of a building) (Fig. 5.12). The rose window developed out of the circular shape of the oculus. Contained in a round opening, small rings of petals, or spokes, moved outward in a *radial design* (visual symmetry rotating around a central axis).

Fig. 5.11. Stained glass at Chartres Cathedral, ca. 1220, Chartres, France.

© Ivan Soto Cobos/Shutterstock.com

IN THEIR OWN WORDS

In writing on stained glass, medieval architect Pierre de Roissy, reflects that works of stained glass were: "divine writings…that throw the light of the true sun, that is to say the light of God, into the interior of churches, that is, into the hearts of the faithful by filling them with light."[4]

Murals—Mural paintings emphasized the nature of the church as a sacred and metaphorical space by depicting scenes that highlighted the earthly and the heavenly. Artists used the technique of *fresco painting*, mural painting that combined pigment with wet lime plaster where, when dry, the image became embedded in the wall. At San Pietro in Valle, a Romanesque Abbey in Ferentillo, Italy, a mural symbolizing the relationship between earth and heaven covers the walls (Fig. 5.13). In the mural, images of fish symbolize the earthly realm, while iconography of birds and griffins reflect the heavenly. In entering the interior

tracery: arched stone latticework bracing the windows

rose window: also called wheel window, was a common stained-glass device placed high in a façade

façade: the principal front face of a building

radial design: visual symmetry rotating around a central axis

fresco painting: mural painting that combined pigment with wet lime plaster that when dry the image becomes embedded in the wall

Fig. 5.12. Rose window at Notre-Dame, ca. 1163–1345, Paris, France.

Fig. 5.13. Fresco at San Pietro in Valle, ca. 1200, Ferentillo, Italy.

space and walking along the wall, the faithful would be reminded of their heavenly citizenship (Phil 3:20).

Tempera Paintings—Three pre-eminent painters of the Middle Ages were Cimabue (ca.1240-1302), Duccio (ca.1255-ca.1319), and Giotto (ca.1266-1337). They created their works on **tempera panels** (gesso covered, engraved, and painted wood) and wall frescoes. Thematically, their paintings highlighted the role of Mary as a warm, compassionate mother figure of Christ. In Duccio's portrait of *Madonna and Child*, (Fig. 5.14), Mary looks at Christ both adoringly and sorrowfully, suggesting that she foresees his later suffering and crucifixion. Stylistically, the proportional relationship between Mary and Christ is exaggerated. The bottom of the frame is burned, which suggests it was hung near an altar where candles were regularly lit in ritual practices of the church.

Fig. 5.14. *Madonna and Child*, Duccio, ca. 1290-1300, Metropolitan Museum of Art, NY.

Courtesy MET Museum, Purchase, Rogers Fund, Walter and Leonore Annenberg and The Annenberg Foundation Gift, Lila Acheson Wallace Gift, Annette de la Renta Gift, Harris Brisbane Dick, Fletcher, Louis V. Bell, and Dodge Funds, Joseph Pulitzer Bequest, several members of The Chairman's Council Gifts, Elaine L. Rosenberg and Stephenson Family Foundation Gifts, 2003 Benefit Fund, and other gifts and funds

Objects

After having considered the exterior and interior of cathedrals, one arrives at the small objects of pilgrimage and worship of medieval art. These included **relics**, pilgrimage souvenirs, and liturgical implements that were often worn or displayed on or within the altars in sanctuaries. In these objects, materials played symbolic roles. The materials used were both precious (gold, silver, gems, ivory, stained glass) as well as bodily (bones, dirt, blood, sweat).

Silver and gold were valued to represent wisdom and were often a reference to the immutability of the Word of God. Psalm 12:6 states that the words of the Lord are pure, "like silver refined in a furnace on the ground, purified seven times." Stone frequently symbolized Christ, the cornerstone, and was compared to the rock from which Moses drew water in the desert (1 Cor 10:4). Ivory connoted purity and chastity. Precious gems symbolized the pre-fallen stated in the Garden of Eden (Ezek 28:13)

tempera pane gesso covered, engraved, and painted wood

relics: sacred earthy objects from Christ's passion and death, like thorns from hi crown, woode shards from th cross, his bloo sweat, and scraps from hi burial shroud

Fig. 5.15. Butterfly Reliquary, silver, gilt, and enamel, ca. 1300–1350, Cathedral Museum, Regensburg.

and the New Jerusalem described in Revelation (Rev 21:19).

Early Christians believed that at Christ's ascension, his whole body was taken up, but that he left behind sacred earthy objects from his passion and death, like thorns from his crown, wooden shards from the cross, his blood, sweat, and scraps from his burial shroud. Such relics were often encased in **reliquaries**, containers of metal, enamel, and gems, elevating earthly matter to the holiness of the New Jerusalem. Likewise, dirt from the holy land and bodily elements from revered saints were treated similarly. The veneration of such relics was often on the border of idolatry, which set the stage for the iconoclast controversies of the Reformation. The *Butterfly Reliquary* (Fig. 5.15) is a small, enameled locket in the shape of a butterfly with the crucifix at the center. This doubled imagery symbolizes transformation and new life. Such a locket would have been worn around the neck for its purported, protective powers.

Badges such as the *Badge with Saint Leonard* (Fig. 5.16) were sold as souvenirs at pilgrimage sites of commemorated saints. The souvenirs were a major source of income for religious institutions. Humble materials like lead, tin, and pewter, were used for such modest objects, representing the virtue of humility.

Liturgical objects from the **Byzantine Empire** (the eastern half of the Roman Empire that lasted a thousand years after the western Roman Empire fell) serve as key visuals for the elements used in the **Eucharist**, in which Christians received consecrated bread and wine in commemoration of the Last Supper and Christ's death. This set (Fig. 5.17) includes chalices, censers, a strainer, and a representation of the Holy Spirit as a dove. Many of the objects were offered from wealthy citizens of the affluent merchant town.

Music

Development of Polyphony

As chant continued largely unaltered from the codification and spread of Gregorian chant after 800, outside factors began to influence it. Europe's economy

Chapter 5: High and Late Middle Ages   109

Courtesy MET Museum, The Cloisters Collection, 1986

Fig. 5.16. Pilgrim's *Badge with Saint Leonard*, fifteenth century, Metropolitan Museum of Art, NY.

Courtesy MET Museum, Purchase, Rogers Fund and Henry J. and Drue E. Heinz Foundation, Norbert Schimmel and Lila Acheson Wallace Gifts, 1986

Fig. 5.17. The Attarouthi Treasure, ca. 500–650, Byzantine, Metropolitan Museum of Art, NY.

Fig. 5.18. Parallel voices singing in note-against-note style. Arr. Elizabeth McAlester.

polyphony: the sounding of two or more melodic lines at the same time

organum: an early term found in manuscripts for two or more voices singing different notes together in acceptable intervals

principal voice: original liturgical chant

organal voice: added voice to liturgical chant

prospered in the eleventh and twelfth centuries and the long-term political stability resulting from Charlemagne's influence caused the church to fare well and grow. With the rise of the Romanesque and Gothic styles that influenced the construction of large urban cathedrals throughout Western Europe, chant began to adapt to a new environment. Larger, more elaborate sounds—yet still under the constraint of simple consonant intervals—developed to match the space (see Figs. 5.4 and 5.7). This new development was known as *polyphony*. Simply put, polyphony is the sounding of two or more melodic lines at the same time. The earliest polyphony was not written down, but existed as a performance practice, whereby a second singer added another layer of melody to an existing chant. This was done in the same spirit as tropes, which did not alter existing liturgical chant, but rather added to it. Unlike *Quem quaeritus* (see Ch. 4), which added dialogue *before* the chant was sung, polyphony added layers of music above or below the chant *while* it was being sung. Some of the earliest polyphony is known as *organum*, an early term found in manuscripts for two or more voices singing different notes together in acceptable intervals, such as the P5 or P4. The original liturgical chant was known as the *principal voice* and the added voice was called the *organal voice*. In a simplistic adaptation in Fig. 5.18, one voice sings the higher line of melody, and the other voice sings the lower line. They maintain a distance of a P5. The lower voice is the principal voice. This familiar tune may be recognizable from the shape of its melody.

At first, organum was sung note-against-note, or in a ratio of 1:1. As layers of architecture took structures higher and higher, the idea of layering in different ratios likewise mirrored the buildings. With Gothic architectures' largest and bulkiest structures at the bottom, transitioning to the lighter, smaller structures above, music similarly developed with a lengthened chant in long durations and a low range anchoring additional quicker, lighter, more agile voices in upper ranges.

In the image of the interior of Notre Dame Cathedral in Paris (built ca.1160-1258), note that the larger, heavier, wider arches are at the bottom (see Fig. 5.19). Looking upward, notice that the arches and windows decrease in size, yet increase in number or frequency when compared with the lower, foundational structures. Sacred polyphony maintained the idea of unaltered chant, although with a growing number of variations built above and around it. This seemed to satisfy church authorities' demands for a codified music; yet grew with the evolving taste of urban centers for more elaborate displays. Of course, they were met

Chapter 5: High and Late Middle Ages   111

Fig. 5.19. Notre Dame Cathedral, interior, built ca. 1160–1258, Paris, France.

Fig. 5.20. Excerpt from *Magnus liber organi*, ca. 1175, 2-voice organum, the upper notes (with black noteheads) are sounded at a much faster rate than the long-held note below them (open square stemless note).[5]

Source: *Magnus liber organi*, 1175

with opposition at every turn, but that is the ongoing story of what is known today as **worship wars**.

It comes as no surprise, therefore, that Notre Dame Cathedral is associated with one of the most extensive collections of early polyphony. Located on the Île-de-France, across a short bridge from famed Left Bank where university life flourished, Notre Dame became an important disseminator of new music. Choir directors developed an innovative musical notation that included rhythm along with pitch, facilitating a more accurate spread of this new music. The architectural features mentioned above can be clearly seen in the polyphony contained in the *Magnus liber organi*, a collection of the earliest polyphonic chant that clearly contain indications for rhythm (see Fig. 5.20).

Not only does the rhythm indicate how the voices relate to one another in speed, the rhythm is also an innovation that reveals what pitches are sounded together to create harmonies. This is still of utmost importance because the three most important intervals in terms of theology: the octave, P4, and P5 must be

worship wars: the ongoing conflict of musical taste between the church authorities and congregations

emphasized, and anything of dissonance and especially the tritone (*diabolus in musica*) had to be avoided.

Listen for the ratio of the speed of the upper voices to the lowest voice in this example from [Magnus liber organi](#).

Further departures from chant led to the **motet**. Derived from the French *mot*, meaning *word*, the motet is a polyphonic vocal work that began as a part of chant, and then added lines and words to extend the meaning until it was no longer considered suitable for sacred use. In the thirteenth century, the motet began with a section of original chant laid out in long notes in the lowest voice of a polyphonic piece. The original Latin or Greek, in the case of the *Kyrie Eleison*, was maintained. Subsequent upper voices were added, with the highest voices being the most rapid and containing the most words. Often the upper voices maintained a thread of meaning that tied it to the tenor line. Those voices could also be in Latin and on a sacred subject, or they could be in different languages and about completely secular topics—or they would have double meanings that walked the line between the sacred and the profane. These became very popular and lasted long through the Renaissance era. Although during the High Middle Ages the motet virtually left the Cathedral and took up residence on the streets as secular music, it returned to its sacred roots during the Renaissance (see Ch. 6).

Secular Music and Culture

Beginning in the early medieval period with traveling musicians and entertainers known as **jongleurs** and **minstrels**, secular music became popular and spread both by oral tradition and by the apprentice system. As interest grew, many parts of Western Europe during the High Middle Ages experienced a lively culture of musical entertainment by poet-musicians, who over time found permanent employment. Depending on the geographic location, they were known as **bards** (England); **troubadours** (southern France), **trouvères** (northern France), and **minnesingers** (Germany). The most well-known among these held permanent positions in aristocratic courts and had the opportunity to preserve their music in written collections. Secular music was quick to adopt the innovations of the Church, including music notation to maintain uniformity, the employment of polyphony, and the expansion of motet. While the lyrics of secular and sacred music remained distinct, the music in both arenas began to sound more and more similar. As the popularity of secular music grew, the idea of the professional musician developed, and performers followed the practice of the time to group themselves into guilds in order to build and protect their craft. This might be seen as the forerunners of today's highly successful entertainment industry with its complex web of professional unions, agencies, and media companies.

One such leader of the fourteenth century music "industry" was Guillaume de [Machaut](#) (ca.1300-1377). He had the foresight to collect all of his works—equally versatile in the secular and the sacred genres—into manuscripts. This was a sign that the composer's status in society was increasing. Machaut's collection, which is an expensive production with beautiful hand-painted illuminations (see Fig. 5.21), tells us that he had a strong sense of his self-worth as a composer and cared deeply about preserving his work for the future. It obviously worked, because Machaut is recognized as one of the most famous composers from the High Middle Ages.

Machaut's secular works include the most popular song forms of the day and both monophonic songs and polyphonic works. None of them include instrumental accompaniment but it is believed that singing was accompanied by a plucked or bowed instrument, such as the lute or the **vielle**.

Listen to a **rondeau** by Machaut, *Puis qu'en oubli* or *Since I Am Forgotten*.

The form of the rondeau is ABaAabAB, in which "A" and "a" are set to the same music, but the lower-case "a" has different words. Likewise is the case with B and b. Use the guide below to listen more closely. Listen for the repeats of the capital A and B sections. They provide a framing structure for the rondeau while reinforcing the message of someone who has been forgotten in love.

minnesingers: German traveling musicians and entertain[ers]

vielle: medie[val] fiddle

rondeau: a memorably simple tune t[hat] repeats a two part melody throughout

Section	Text
A	Puis qu'en oubli [Since I am forgotten]
B	Vie amoureuse [Life, love, and joy I leave to God]
a	
A	Puis qu'en oubli
a	
b	
A	Puis qu'en oubli
B	Vie amoureuse

Eye Music

With the growth of music and more aristocratic support, skills in music preservation elevated to the level of fine art. Once a mere means of communication and pedagogy, musical scores were purchased as artifacts in themselves. Advances in musical notation and increased skill in reading and performing music in score led to a style known as eye music. This was music written in the shape of objects and was often brightly colored. Although very hard to read with its curving, complex staves, the notes were actually performable and if the performers could do it, would produce a worthy work of music in the style of

Fig. 5.21. Manuscript illumination, monks singing in the letter D, Psalter, Girolamo dai libri, Metropolitan Museum of Art, NY.

the late fourteenth century known as *Ars subtilior* (subtle arts). More than that, however, it was meant to be enjoyed visually, as a work of fine art. Stripped of its practical function, this "eye music" was an early example of what the nineteenth century would refer to as "art for art's sake." In Fig. 5.22 the musical staves artistically create the shape of a heart.

Theatre

Sacred Drama

Theatrical performances, with and without music, continued in popularity during the High Middle Ages. Not only did religious plays abound during the Easter and Christmas seasons, but throughout the rest of the year morality (see Ch. 4), **miracle**, and **mystery plays** continued sacred messages that served to educate and correct believers as well as spread the gospel to unbelievers. Miracle plays dramatized the lives and miracles of past saints in the Roman Catholic church. Mystery plays were often a sequence of short plays or scenes that depicted Bible

Chapter 5: High and Late Middle Ages   115

Fig. 5.22. *Belle, bonne,* an example of *Ars subtilior,* musical notation in heart shape, ca 1400, Baude Cordier (ca. 1380–1440), Museum at Château de Chantilly, Oise.

stories or enacted the work of Christ that led to humanity's salvation. These were performed in churches or public places, like town squares.

The **Passion play** is a drama focusing on the days leading up to the crucifixion of Christ. Although there may have been enactments of these events as early as the fourth century, they rose to prominence in the twelfth and thirteenth centuries, especially in German lands. Although many were written in Latin, indicating their liturgical origins, some from this period appeared in the vernacular (i.e., the common language of the people).

Several of these are found in *Carmina burana,* an unusual collection of secular songs (*carmina*) written in Latin. They were named for the monastery in which the manuscript was found: Benedicktbeuren (*burana*) in Bavaria (today's southern Germany). These are unusual because they were written by **goliards**, wandering students who wrote satirical literature and songs. The content of some of these portray a youthful and humorous parody of society. Within the collection, however, are four plays: one on Christmas, one on Easter, and two Passion plays, one of which includes a significant portion in German. These include

passion play: a drama focusing on the day leading up to the crucifixion of Christ

goliards: wandering (often clerical) students of the twelfth and thirteenth century who wrote satirical literature in Latin

specific stage directions that indicate that they may not have been permitted to be performed in a church, although their content is liturgical.

The Passion play continues to be popular in the German lands even until today. It grew into the German oratorio (see Ch. 7), especially the well-known *St. Matthew* and *St. John Passions* by Johann Sebastian Bach (see also Ch. 13). Beyond Bach's works for the Lutheran Church, Passion plays grew into very large public events lasting many days and attracting thousands of visitors. Today there is a continuation of the tradition at the beginning of every decade in Oberammergau in Bavaria, lasting all day, every day between May and September. [6]

> ### DID YOU KNOW?
>
> As a whole collection, *Carmina burana* is well known today for its musical setting by the twentieth century composer, Carl Orff. Orff selected 25 of the songs and created a modern-day cantata. The opening (and closing) song, "O fortuna," is the most famous of these and has circulated all over the world, appearing in television commercials and films, as well as being used at public events. It depicts a common theme of the High Middle Ages, that of the rise and fall of kings being subject to Lady Luck and her inevitable Wheel of Fortune (see Fig. 5.23).
>
> Listen to "O fortuna."

Secular Drama

In the midst of a thriving culture of court-employed troubadours and trouvères, urban minstrels, and the rise of professional musicians in the High Middle Ages, the popularity of secular musical plays should not come as a surprise. Although most of the annotated music comes from musicians employed by aristocrats who desired the music to be preserved, by no means does it indicate that there was an absence of a culture of secular entertainment outside the court. Poetry, music, and plays were performed regularly by traveling musicians without permanent employment. As was mentioned earlier, this music was taught orally, which is why most of the music from this tradition has been lost.

Musical plays thrived in this culture and there seemed to be no lack of excellent musicians to perform and certainly no lack of interested audiences. One such trouvère, Adam de la Halle (ca.1240-ca.1288; see Fig. 5.24), composed what is believed to be the earliest musical comedy, containing an abundance of singing and dancing, not unlike today's Broadway musical. *The Play of Robin and Marion* is also considered a pastoral drama because of its setting in the country with rural characters. In this play, Marion, a shepherdess, resists the advances of a knight, and remains faithful to her shepherd lover, Robin/Robert. This play was

---

cantata: a medium-length narrative piece of music for voices with instrumental accompaniment, typically with solos, chorus, and orchestra. A chamber cantata often used one soloist and basso continuo on a secular topic. Larger works were often sacred and performed in church buildings

pastoral drama: a drama set in the country that focuses on pastoral characters

Chapter 5: High and Late Middle Ages 117

Fig. 5.23. Lady Fortune atop her Wheel of Fortune. German postage stamp honoring Carl Orff and his famous work, *Carmina burana*, 1995.

likely written to honor a patron, Robert II of Artois and Robert's uncle, Charles of Anjou. Adam himself staged the play, and most likely arranged for improvised instrumental accompaniment to support the singing and dancing. The opening song is a rondeau (see Music, this Ch.) sung in the voice of the female lead.

Section	Text
A*	Robin loves me, Robin has me.
B	Robin asked me if he can have me.
a	Robin bought me a skirt
a	Of scarlet, good and pretty
b	A bodice and a belt. Hurray!
A	Robin loves me, Robin has me.
B	Robin asked me if he can have me

* The capital letters indicate a repeat of the same words with the same music. The lower-case letters indicate the same music as its capital letter, but with different words.

Fig. 5.24. Adam de la Halle from the Chansonnier d'Arras, a songbook that includes some of his songs.

Listen for the repeated A and B music.

Adam de la Halle wrote at least one other secular play, *The Play of the Feuillée*, the French term possibly meaning "folie" or "leafy bower." This one is a satirical drama on colorful characters in his hometown of Arras, France.

Study Questions

1. What impact did the presence of Germanic tribes in the medieval ages have on Christian worship practices?
2. What are some examples of ways that the art of the medieval ages was meant to facilitate a spiritual experience?
3. Describe the stages in the development of polyphonic music.

Notes

1. Aquinas, *Summa Theologica*, I.1.1.
2. Aquinas, *Summa Theologica*, I.1.2,5,6; I–II.109.1.
3. Aquinas, *Summa Theologica*, I.91.3.
4. Pastan, 11.
5. Davison, 24.
6. Unfortunately the 2020 event was cancelled due to the COVID-19 pandemic.

6 The Renaissance
The Influence of Humanism

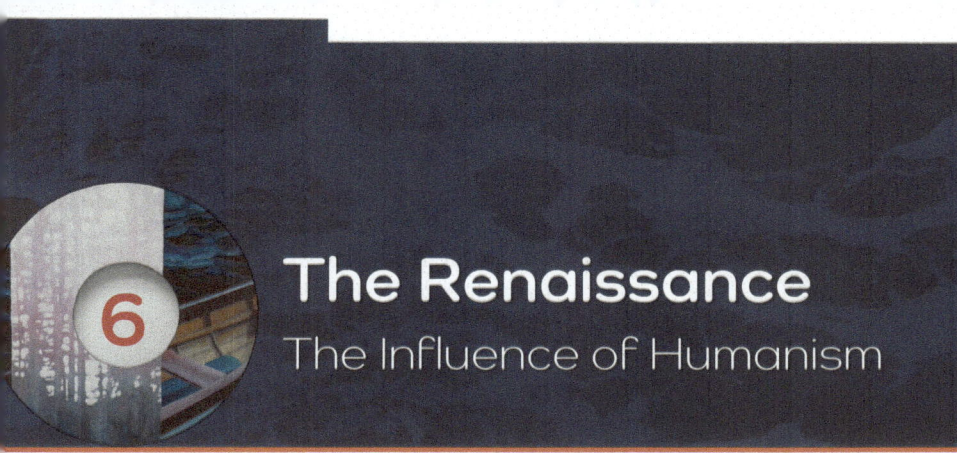

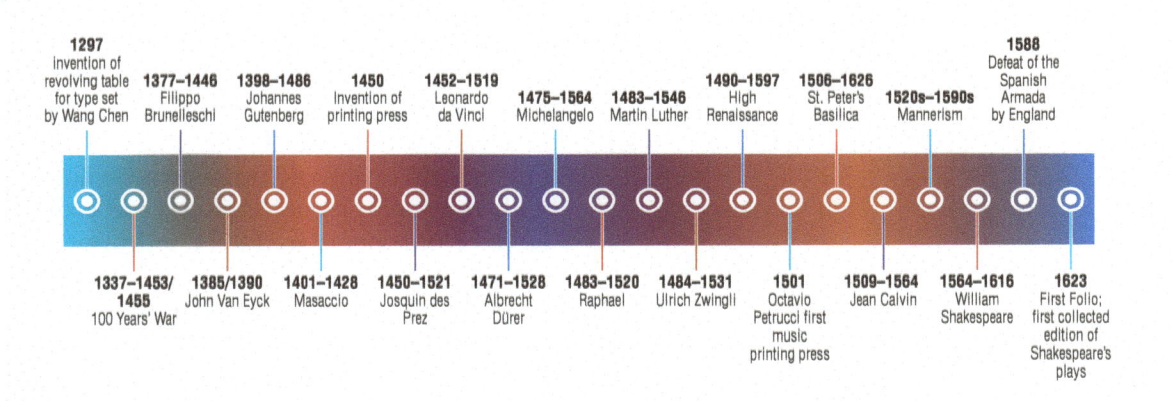

1297 invention of revolving table for type set by Wang Chen
1377–1446 Filippo Brunelleschi
1398–1486 Johannes Gutenberg
1450 Invention of printing press
1452–1519 Leonardo da Vinci
1475–1564 Michelangelo
1483–1546 Martin Luther
1490–1597 High Renaissance
1506–1626 St. Peter's Basilica
1520s–1590s Mannerism
1588 Defeat of the Spanish Armada by England

1337–1453/1455 100 Years' War
1385/1390 John Van Eyck
1401–1428 Masaccio
1450–1521 Josquin des Prez
1471–1528 Albrecht Dürer
1483–1520 Raphael
1484–1531 Ulrich Zwingli
1501 Octavio Petrucci first music printing press
1509–1564 Jean Calvin
1564–1616 William Shakespeare
1623 First Folio; first collected edition of Shakespeare's plays

Philosophy

The ebb and flow of different fields of study are complex. Though philosophy has been around for over two millennia, at times different areas of the field have had greater emphasis. From metaphysics to epistemology, from ethics to the philosophy of language, philosophers have moved with the times and in reaction to the philosophical forces that preceded them. Similarly, art has had movements, where different art forms have had greater emphasis, advancement, and popularity. It is this fact that makes the Renaissance so unique. Rarely do golden ages coincide, but during the fifteenth and sixteenth centuries, artisans in the West produced music, paintings, theatrical productions, and architectural masterpieces of nearly unparalleled genius. Yet, not only was the Renaissance a significant moment for art, but it was so for theology as well. The rise in strength of the Catholic Church, along with the centralization of merchant wealth, allowed for the patronage of Renaissance masters, while also giving rise to discontentment among individuals who believed that the papacy was immoral, opulent, and promoting unbiblical doctrine.

The most prominent unifying element to the Renaissance was its return to the classical era. The artists of the period saw their work as a recovery of the past.

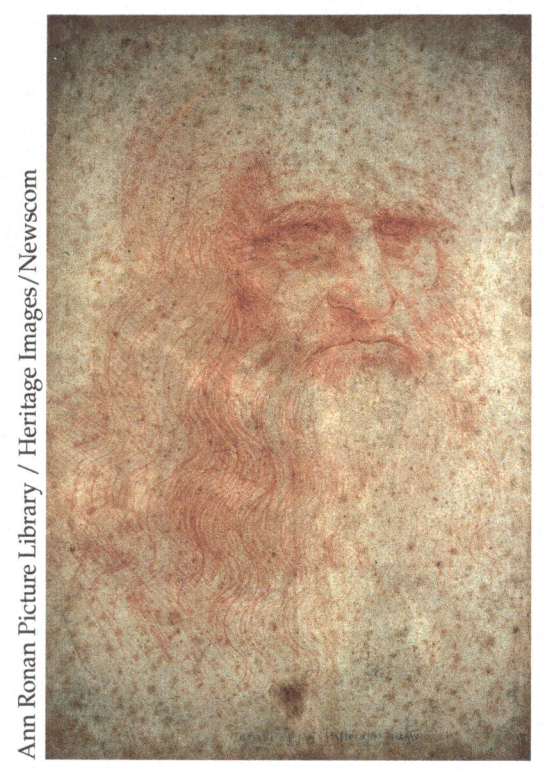

Fig. 6.1. *Portrait of a Man in Red Chalk*, presumed self-portrait, ca. 1512, Leonardo Da Vinci, Royal Library of Turin.

They looked to the Greeks and, to a lesser degree, the Romans to provide foundational techniques, ideas, and subject matter that related to their art forms. This retrieval could also be seen in the philosophy of the day. If one were to look at a list of Renaissance philosophers, it would have very few names that are widely recognizable. One reason this is the case is that their thinking was not as novel as it was applicational. Acknowledging the centrality of the nation-state to the Greek philosophers, especially to Plato and Aristotle, they tended toward political philosophy and were not as concerned with the metaphysical issues, some of which were considered to be unimportant or overly specialized, that characterized the scholastics. Moreover, the scholars and artists at the time tended to be highly interdisciplinary, in many ways characterizing the older philosophers who attempted to delve into all areas of life and thought. It was this inclination that is exemplified in the idea of the "Renaissance man" or the individual who was highly accomplished in various areas of art and study. As seen further in this chapter, Leonard da Vinci (1452-1519) would be considered a central example of such a **polymath**, or individual of varied learning (Fig. 6.1).

polymath: individual of varied learning

The retrieval of classical elements had two important effects related to theology. First, in appropriating Greek ideas, Renaissance masters often also accepted certain non-Christian values, one such value being the centrality of humanity to the world. Renaissance artists did not look to Greek philosophers for a view of the world, but to the artists and purveyors of myth in the ancient Mediterranean. Greek mythology pictured the gods as glorified humans, a view that found strong opposition in Xenophanes (ca. sixth to fifth centuries BC) and Plato. Both of the thinkers thought that the idea of divinity and indeed the greatness of God was attacked by making him like humans. Yet, it was common in the popular culture of the day and was mimicked in the composition and content of Renaissance art, specifically in its portrayal of God as a human. One need to look no further than the Sistine Chapel (Fig. 6.19) or the *Disputa* (Fig. 1.1) to see instances of the Father depicted in a way that more closely mirrored early depictions of Zeus than they reflected biblical material concerning the idea that only Christ was revealed in flesh (John 1:14,18).

The second significant aspect of retrieval was the recovery of the significance of the humanities. Emphasis was given to the importance of ancient literature and the close textual study that paid attention to the original languages. It was this practice, perhaps more than any other, that influenced the **Reformation**. As Martin Luther (1483-1546; Fig. 6.2) studied Scripture, particularly the book of Romans, he began to recognize that the Catholic church was holding views and supporting practices that were contrary to the teaching of the Bible. Most consequential of these were the doctrines that salvation was by grace and works and that the Catholic Church had authority on earth. Luther believed these views attacked Christ's role in saving individuals by his own work and using Scripture to extend his authority on earth. Accordingly, Luther's publication of the Ninety-Five Theses in 1517 emphasized the freedom that humanity had from the authority of the church and indeed their freedom from sin, because of what Jesus had done. Jean Calvin (1509-1564) extended these arguments and focused on the importance of approaching Scripture as the revelation of God's plan, promises, and intention. In doing so, he followed Luther in highlighting the importance of returning to the biblical text.

Fig. 6.2. *Martin Luther*, 1529, Lucas Cranach the Elder, St. Anne's Church, Augsburg.

Reformation: a movement that marked the splintering of the Protestant Church from the Catholic Church

The effect of the Reformation on art is evidenced in many ways. To see the stamp of the Reformers, one only needs to observe the rise in skepticism of the importance of the arts to the church in the early sixteenth century. Since the Catholic church had misused money taken from its parishioners and had treated art with a reverence that bordered on (if not was) idolatry, early Protestants questioned the place of artistic pieces in worship. Though Luther was not as antagonistic as some, the Swiss scholars, such as Ulrich Zwingli (1484-1531) and Calvin attacked the adorning of places of worship with artwork. Such a resistance is called **iconoclasm**, which refers to the destruction of symbols or representations. An example of the effects of this can be seen in the *Interior of St. Bavo's Church in Haarlem*

iconoclasm: the destruction of symbols or representation

Fig. 6.3. *Interior of St. Bavo's Church in Haarlem*, 1636, Pieter Jansz Saenredam, Rijksmuseum.

(Fig. 6.3), which is striking not because of the grandeur of the building portrayed, but due to the unadorned whiteness of its walls. The church had been touched by the reactionary nature of the Reformation against art in church buildings. This suspicion, though based on very real abuses within Catholicism, did not pay attention to the possibilities of art given in Scripture itself. Yet, to this day, there are many Evangelical churches that are suspicious of anything that would be considered part of the art world.

One last way in which the Reformation would affect art was in its dealing with the freedom of humanity. Luther and Calvin always engaged with free choice theologically, as a function of one's relationship with God and constrained by the fact that humans were created and therefore under divine authority. Freedom was never meant to be unqualified, but it was lived out in accordance with the commands of God found in the word of God. However, philosophers who were influenced by the Reformers and their philosophical predecessors in the Middle Ages, began to combine the Renaissance concentration on the importance of humanity and a modified version of the Reformers' stress on human freedom to attack the idea that humans were under any transcendent authority, even that of God. This would have a deleterious effect on further eras of art. Though Christians should recognize their freedom from sin and death in Christ, they should not believe that they have the unbridled freedom to live apart from divine instruction (Rom 6:1-2). Freedom, in the theological sense, is not freedom from God, but the freedom found in God to live for Him. It is freedom that takes responsibility.

Art

The term *Renaissance* comes from French word "naissance," which means birth. Thus, the Renaissance (spanning from the fourteenth centuries to the seventeenth centuries) was a "re-birth" of culture. Coming out of the Middle Ages and the recent devastation of the Black Plague, Europe was ready for a re-emergence and

Fig. 6.4. Florence Cathedral, ca. 1436, Brunelleschi, Florence, Italy.

new identity. As was mentioned, the Renaissance was sparked by a rediscovery and excitement around the ideas of antiquity from ancient Greece and Rome that had been lost in medieval times. Classical manuscripts were scrutinized for philosophy, aesthetics, and ideas of human life. With this, humanism encouraged a greater focus on the individual. Explorations in travel, scientific innovations, literature, Reformation in the church, and advancements in art were fueled by a desire to re-awaken the remarkable culture of the Greco-Roman world that had fallen with the Roman empire. The influence of humanism spurred the attempt in the arts to marry knowledge and religion, as well as the ideas of Greek and Roman authors with Christian beliefs.

Politically and socially speaking, old feudal structures were broken up and replaced by city-states throughout Italy, which were either governed by rulers or took the form of small republics. Amongst these, the city-state of Florence, a hub of banking and trade, became the center for cultural rebirth. In the early Renaissance (1280-1400), guilds of merchants, bankers, and artisans, which were inherited from the Middle Ages, were politically powerful and controlled the economy. As individuals and families amassed wealth through trade, they invested in religious and secular artwork, with commissioned art arising as a symbol of social status. The emerging use of **tempera paint** (pigment that is suspended in egg yolk) and oil paint on panels allowed paintings to be moved, which allowed for their entrance into a larger market.

By the time of the **High Renaissance** (1490-1597) artists of the academy were supported by wealthy individual patrons rather than guilds. During this time, the economic system of capitalism emerged, as well as an exceptional flourishing in

tempera pain pigment suspended in egg yolk

High Renaissance: time period of 1490-1597 tha marked the peak flourishing of the Renaissance the arts defined by towering figures like Leonardo da Vinci, Michelangelo, and Raphael. At roughly the same time, cultures to the north in France, Germany, and England experienced the **Northern Renaissance**, invigorated by the Italian Renaissance. Interestingly, at the end of the Renaissance, after artists had believed that they had achieved artistic perfection, styles often turned to **Mannerism**, which exaggerated and distorted figures and objects for the sake of expressiveness.

The visual arts were influenced by the remains of ancient Rome, still present throughout Italy in fragments of architectural structures, sarcophagi, sculptures, and coins. Advancements or, more properly, *re-discoveries* from antiquity spanned innovations in naturalism, free-standing sculpture, oil painting, printmaking, and architecture.

Naturalism and Realism

Renaissance artists pursued **naturalism** rather than **realism**. Both attempt a faithful representation of the visible world, but naturalism is an idealized representation while realism attempts to be as close as possible to what was observed. Italian renaissance artists were similar to their Greek and Roman predecessors in their interest in stylized beauty. **Linear perspective**, the practice of preliminary drawings, and the return to *contrapposto* were all techniques used by these artists to achieve naturalism.

Linear Perspective

In ancient Greece, painting was not included in the liberal arts. While the Greeks celebrated philosophical, mathematical, and scientific practices, painting was considered a mere form of imitation. Painters of the Renaissance revolted against Plato's derision of representational art (see Ch. 2). With their highly illusionistic, complex compositions and pointed subject matter, artists of the era proved painting to be an intelligent mode of thinking, well deserving of being considered in the liberal arts. Artistic **illusionism** is the employment of techniques of composition and perspective to make the audience feel like they are sharing space with the subjects of artwork. Its success can be attributed to the discovery of linear perspective, which, unusually, was not clearly evidenced in Greco-Roman times.

In medieval imagery, artists were not concerned with creating a convincing illusionistic earthly setting, perhaps because of their religious emphasis on a heavenly realm. Figures remained flat and little information of setting was given (often figures were placed on solid or decorative backgrounds). Differences in scale denoted a hierarchy of authority, the relative size of a figure indicated its importance.

Filippo Brunelleschi (1377-1446) was a metal worker and architect. As a young man, he had traveled to Rome to study Greek and Roman objects of antiquity that were highly considerate of analytical and mathematical techniques.

Chapter 6: The Renaissance 127

Vanishing Point   **Vanishing Point**

Fig. 6.5. Linear perspective at Florence Baptistry.

Fig. 6.6. *The Tribute Money*, Masaccio, 1425, fresco, Brancacci Chapel, Santa Maria del Carmine, Florence, Italy.

In a famous experiment, Brunelleschi made a drawing of the Florence Baptistry that proved his idea of linear perspective, the drawing convention that uses vanishing points and **orthogonal lines** on the horizon line to give the illusion of three-dimensionality to two-dimensional art (Fig. 6.5). In this system, the orthogonal lines are horizontal parallel lines that appear to converge in vanishing points on the horizon line to the human eye.

Linear perspective affected the way artists approached painting. In his work *The Tribute Money*, (Fig. 6.6), the artist Masaccio (1401-1428) used linear perspective

illusionism: a style of painting in which the image is highly accurate and representative of real physical space

orthogonal lines: horizontal parallel lines that appear to converge in vanishing points on the horizon line to the human eye

Chapter 6: The Renaissance

Fig. 6.7. *Last Supper*, tempera and oil on plaster, 1498, Leonardo da Vinci, Santa Maria della Grazie, Milan.

foreshortening: creating the illusion of object receding in space through size and placement

atmospheric perspective: the effect of objects or subject matter appearing to lighten in value as they recede in space

and **foreshortening** (creating the illusion of an object receding in space) to create a setting of stark depth. He accomplished this by employing orthogonal lines within the architecture that converge at a vanishing point, uses of variation in scale to show depth (figures that were closer were larger, figures further away were smaller), and **atmospheric perspective** in the depictions of the mountains (objects lightening in value as they recede in space).

Artists were able to use linear perspective to heighten the drama of a scene and the complexity of the composition. For example, in Leonardo da Vinci's *Last Supper*, all orthogonal lines converge on Christ, the center of the composition (Fig. 6.7). The implied diagonal lines of the architecture lead the viewer's eye directly to Christ. In contrast to the very real, panicked reactions of the disciples to his announcement, Christ's serenity is emphasized by his placement.

Return of Contrapposto

The Renaissance brought on the return of the free-standing, nude sculpted figure. It marks an interesting blend of classical and Christian thought. In many ways, the bronze and marble statues of the Renaissance mimicked Greek sculptures of gods and goddesses. Because of Christian influence, the free-standing sculpture was revived with Biblical subject matter. Michelangelo (1475-1564) sculpted *David* (Fig. 6.8) out of marble, a figure that bore striking resemblance to Greek and Roman figures (see Figs. 2.8 and 3.8) with an ideal, athletic body, and unblemished face that effuses eternal youth and beauty. One leg bends casually, tilting his pose into the classic *contrapposto* of antiquity. The Biblical account of David and Goliath was interpreted as a metaphor for Christ's triumph over Satan.

The Practice of Drawing

In the High Renaissance, the artists Leonardo da Vinci, Michelangelo, and Raphael formed a triad of artistic mastery. Proficient in painting and sculpture, each artist relied heavily on the practice of drawing, both as exercises in seeing and as preliminary designs for their finished works.

Leonardo da Vinci, a true Renaissance man as a painter, sculptor, scientist, and inventor, created precise, anatomical drawings of the body in his sketchbooks (Fig. 6.9) as well as studies of the nuances of light and shadow on folding cloth (Fig. 6.10). A series of gesture drawings of *Madonna and Child* by Raphael show quick, experimental mark making (the different lines, marks, patterns, or textures created in drawing) to capture realistic movement (Fig. 6.11). Full-sized, to scale renderings of final works, called cartoons, were made first on paper before being transferred to the final, permanent surface, such as in Raphael's cartoon for *School of Athens* (Fig. 6.12, see Fig. 1.2 for the finished fresco).

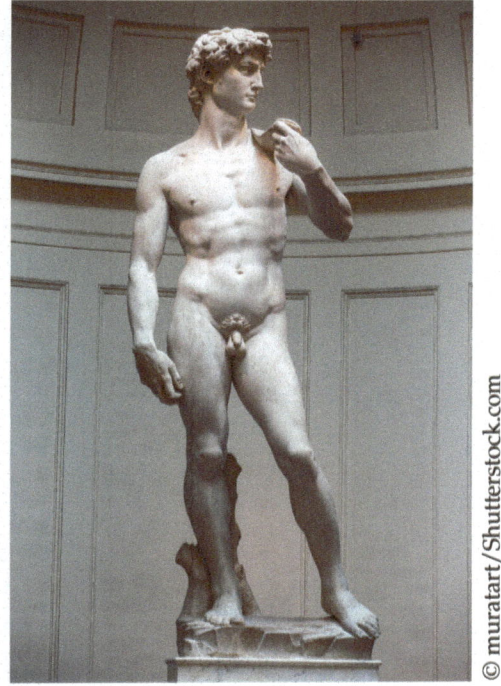

Fig. 6.8. *David*, 1501-1504, Michelangelo, Galleria dell'Accademia, Florence.

Northern Renaissance

Parallel to the Italian Renaissance, the Northern Renaissance took place in modern day France, Germany, and England. Though influenced by the rebirth of ideas migrating north from thinkers in Italy, they did not have access to the works of antiquity that demonstrated mathematical ideals of proportion and beauty. Rather, they drew from the imagery of illuminated manuscripts; thus, their human figures were slightly elongated. Jan Van Eyck (ca. 1390-1441), a Netherlandish painter, pioneered oil painting (painting with pigment suspended in linseed oil) on wooden panels. His work was meticulous, more interested in realism than the naturalism of his Italian counterparts. *The Arnolfini Marriage* (Fig. 6.13) is rich in texture and color. In the center of the composition, behind the figures on the wall, is a small mirror reflecting the scene with the addition of a third figure, standing presumably outside of the picture plane.

gesture drawing: quick, experimental sketches that seek to capture the energy of movement

mark making: the different lines, marks, patterns, or textures created in drawing

cartoon: to scale preliminary drawing made on paper before being transferred to wall murals or panels

oil paint: pigment suspended in linseed oil

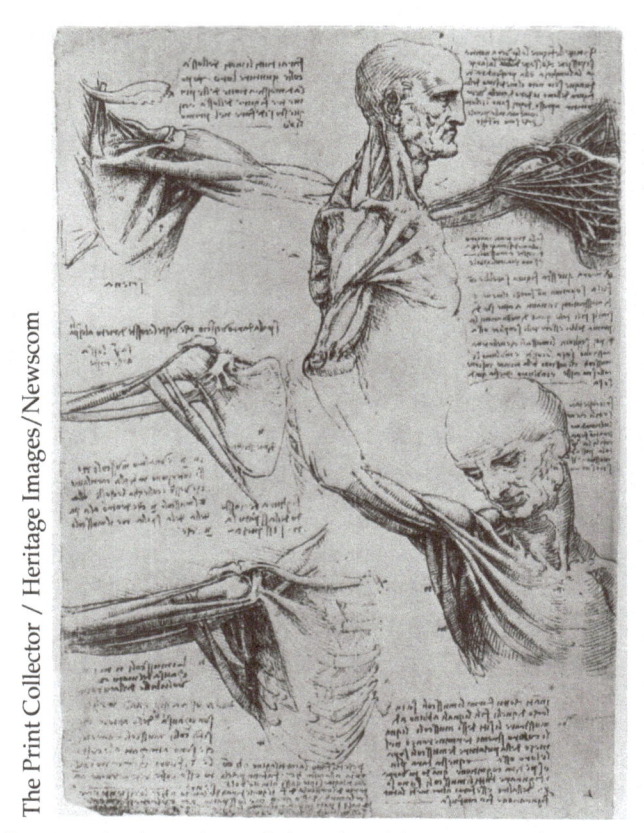

Fig. 6.9. *Anatomical studies of the shoulder,* Leonardo da Vinci, ca. 1510.

Fig. 6.10. *Drapery for a seated figure,* brush and tempera, 1470, Leonardo Da Vinci, The Louvre, Paris.

Chapter 6: The Renaissance 131

Fig. 6.11. Madonna Studies, 1511–1513, Raphael, Palais des Beaux-Arts de Lille, Lille, France.

Fig. 6.12. *Cartoon of School of Athens*, Raphael.

Albrecht Dürer (1471-1528), a German painter, traveled to Italy and made friends with Raphael, after which he incorporated Italian and Northern techniques into his woodcut prints (Fig. 6.14), successfully integrating the elaborately detailed northern style with the ideals of balance and coherence of the Italian Renaissance. Dürer became one of the most influential artists of **printmaking** (transferring images from a matrix onto another surface), elevating it to an art form.

printmaking: transferring images from a matrix onto another surface

132   Chapter 6: The Renaissance

Fig. 6.13. *The Arnolfini Marriage*, 1434, Jan van Eyck, National Gallery, London.

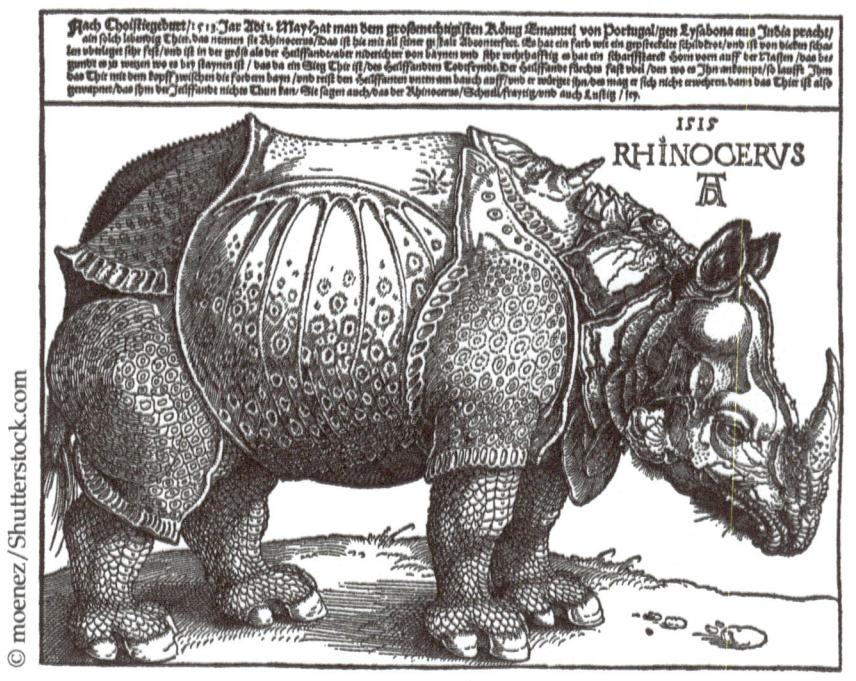

Fig. 6.14. Woodcut, 1515, Albrecht Dürer, British Museum, London, UK.

Fig. 6.15. Saint Peter's Basilica, 1506–1626, Vatican City, Rome.

Architecture

Prominent architecture of the Renaissance borrowed classical proportions, Roman orders, arches, and decorations from antiquity. Renaissance scholars and architects gleaned information from the writings of the ancient Roman architect Vitruvius (ca. 75-15 BC) and fragments of architecture from Roman ruins such as the Pantheon and Colosseum (see Ch. 3). For example, the design of Saint Peter's Basilica borrows the Roman dome and Greek orders in its design (Fig. 6.15).

Brunelleschi, the creator of linear perspective, successfully engineered a dome for Florence Cathedral (Fig. 6.4) that was the same size as the dome of the Pantheon without the support of flying buttresses, which was common to Gothic cathedrals. In his floor plan for the Basilica of San Lorenzo (Fig. 6.16) Brunelleschi used **space block planning** (planning based on a single geometric unit). This type of planning reflected a Greco-Roman influence of the mathematical principles of sequence and proportion, while also integrating in the Christian architectural tradition of a cross floor plan.

Fig. 6.16. Basilica of San Lorenzo, *floor plan sketch* from 'Taccuino senese,' ca. 1480, Giuliano da Sangallo, source: Biblioteca Comunale, Siena.

space block planning: architectural planning based on a single geometric unit

Did you know?

The first printing presses were developed by the Chinese, using hand-carved woodblocks in reverse. In 1297, Wang Chen (1271-1368) invented a revolving table for typesetters. During the Renaissance, over 150 years later, Johannes Gutenberg (1398-1468) used metal to create movable type, using brass plates in reverse. Using brass movable type, Gutenberg printed the Gutenberg Bible. This invention allowed for the mass production of books for the populace.

Mannerism

After the death of master artists like da Vinci, Michelangelo, and Raphael, artists rejected the values of the High Renaissance with a more heightened, or "mannered" approach, witnessed at the end of the Renaissance. After the height of naturalism was reached, it broached the issue of what the artist could do next. Mannerism answered this question with painting that was no less technically proficient than its predecessors but emphasized exaggeration, visual complexity, unnatural compositions, and dramatic light. An example can be seen in Italian painter Tintoretto's (1518-1594) interpretation of *The Last Supper* (Fig. 6.17) in comparison with da Vinci's of the same name (Fig. 6.7). Tintoretto's composition is unbalanced rather than symmetrical. The tension is increased through imposing light and forced, exaggerated perspective. The scene is not calm and serene like da Vinci's, but bristles with activity and drama.

Fig. 6.17. *The Last Supper*, 1592-1594, Tintoretto, San Giorgio Maggiore, Venice.

Chapter 6: The Renaissance   135

> **DID YOU KNOW?**
>
> At age 23, Michelangelo was commissioned by a French cardinal to carve the *Pietà* (Fig. 6.18), a freestanding sculpture of a serene Mary holding the broken body of Christ in her lap, which can be found at St. Peter's Basilica in Rome. At its unveiling to the public, someone in the crowd commented that it must have been made by a fellow countryman. Infuriated, Michelangelo stole back to the church and carved his signature "MICHELANGELO BUONAROTUS FLORENT FACIEBAT," or loosely translated "Michelangelo Buonarroti, *Florentine*, made this." It is the only signature that appears on any of Michelangelo's works.

Tension of the Sacred and the Secular

Throughout the art of the Renaissance there was an obvious tension between Christian ideology and humanism and the secular pursuit of knowledge. Medieval values that elevated spirituality and denounced the flesh were challenged by Renaissance values of individualism and independent reason. Like Michelangelo's fusion of classical beauty with Biblical figures in the work of *David*,

Fig. 6.18. *Pietà*, Michelangelo, 1498–1499, St. Peter's Basilica, Vatican.

Fig. 6.19. *Creation of Adam*, Sistine Chapel Ceiling, 1510, Michelangelo, Sistine Chapel, Vatican.

artists, however sincerely or insincerely, found ways to merge Christian values with the emerging secular culture. This is powerfully provoked in the portion of Michelangelo's Sistine Chapel Ceiling commonly called the *Creation of Adam* (Fig. 6.19). In Renaissance fashion, complex compositions and idealized figures meet in the scene of God descending to Adam. The fabric that surrounds God's descent is part womb and part brain, embodying creation and knowledge. The reaching culminates in a moment of emptiness, the space between outstretched arms and flexed fingers marked by tension and mystery.

Music

Shifting Perceptions

One of the biggest changes that affected music around 1400 was a turning away from the scientific concept of math-based music and a turn to what simply pleased the ear. While the sounds produced by the perfect harmonies remained the most desirable, people began to favor the sound of a more complex harmony, the triad. The third, a sound produced by two pitches that are separated by another pitch (for example, C and E), had a sweet, modern sound to many ears. Music in England had used this sound long before anyone on the European continent and prior to its incorporation by composers associated with sacred music. However, the pleasant effect it had on hearers caused it to soon appear in abundance in polyphonic vocal music in France and Italy. This sound was known as the "English appearance," or *contenance angloise*. Chant was modernized with triads, similar to the parallel organum discussed in Ch. 5 (see Fig. 6.20).

Fig. 6.20. A simplistic comparison of parallel organum and triads. The first measure shows parallel organum; the second triads. This is the same recognizable tune found in Fig. 5.18. Arr. Allison Zieg.

Dissonances—the remaining intervals that were even more complex: 2nds, 7ths, and the tritone—were still very much avoided, although not as much because they were closer to the Devil's music, but because they were not as pleasurable to the ears.

A partial underlying reason for the shift in music from a mathematical to an anthropological conception was the development of humanism. What man perceived as pleasing eventually trumped what the math stated was true and thus, perception became the measure of music. Until this time, the belief in the music of the spheres and the mathematical relationships that produce music created a *cosmological* view of music's source. The Music of the Spheres was the ideal and earthly tones could, at best, be copies. In the early Renaissance era, with the growth of humanism, the idea of music being an art produced by man grew in prominence; that is, the idea that music was *anthropological* in its source. This shift has some truth, as the definition of music, for present purposes, is the art of combining vocal and/or instrumental sounds, organized through time to produce an intentional human expression. Additionally, since most music at this time was vocal music that required underlying text, musical production shifted from being related to math or science to being related to the language arts. Music began to be seen as being "expressive," being able to "say something." This caused a shift in the placement of the discipline of Music in the Seven Liberal Arts. Whereas Music had always been part of the Quadrivium along with Arithmetic, Geometry, and Astronomy, its association gradually shifted toward the Trivium, and was perceived as being more closely related to Logic, Grammar, and Rhetoric. Music was becoming a language art, or at least a language-like art. The Renaissance marked the era whereby Music joined the ranks of the humanities, or human-produced disciplines, rather than the sciences. In the painting in Fig. 6.21, Music is placed exactly in the middle of the "Hill of Knowledge." This may reflect widespread change in the perception of music's relationship to other fields.

The 100 Years' War raged in France during the cultural transition from the High Middle Ages to the Renaissance, from approximately 1337-1453. As England and France battled, the transmission of music across the Channel took place

Fig. 6.21. *Allegory of the Liberal Arts*, 1446-1508, Biagio d'Antonio da Firenze.

and expanded the influence of English artistry. A significant political development in France toward the end of the war saw the rise in power of Burgundy, the lands flanking the eastern and northern reaches of France, which created a continuous arc that ran from Belgium (Flanders) in the north to Provence in Southern France, bordering on Italy. Fortuitously, for the sake of artistic development, this rich network of connected, powerful nobles famously supported music for court and private chapels. The Burgundians' taste for music—which included lovely new harmonies from England—demanded new developments in composition, allowed for permanent, well-paid positions for performers and musicians to grow in their skills, and facilitated borderless travel from the north all the way to Italy. This was a prime situation for musical innovations.

Meanwhile, Florence, under the influence of the Medici family, experienced a similar growth in the arts, including music. With so much money poured into the arts by the Burgundians and Medicis, the direction of the age changed; so much so, that most scholars recognize the fifteenth century as very different from the fourteenth century in terms of artistic expression, to the point of labeling it as part of a new cultural era. This was especially so in the musical arts.

Several technological advances also affected musical development. The first was the invention of the printing press around 1450, which led to the widespread availability of the printed word and sparked a rise in literacy over the next few centuries. This greatly contributed to the importance of language studies and literature, as well as a new independent means of communicating directly in the vernacular of the people. On the heels of this development, Octavio Petrucci (1466-1539) created the first music printing press in 1501, and likewise changed the course of musical production forever. Musical scores became a commercial business and music in print broadened the access to new styles throughout Europe, similar to today's availability of nearly infinite styles of music immediately accessible to any listener worldwide with a smart phone. Over time, as with its literary counterpart, the music printing press sparked a desire for music literacy and produced a market of amateur performers who wanted to learn to perform. This likewise brought musical activities that had been the privilege of the upper classes into the hands of lower classes. Both sacred and secular music in print grew in variety, prevalence, and in popularity.

A Cappella Vocal Music

Sacred

While the Renaissance experienced a major shift in thinking about and consuming of music, there remained some strong continuities. On the eve of the Reformation, Roman Catholic music was innovative, exciting, and even spectacular. The Church continued to support the Mass cycles with elaborate and complex polyphony. The motet grew as well and reached a pinnacle of beauty and expression in the work of Josquin des Prez (1450-1521), a Flemish composer who found ample support throughout the Burgundian lands and in Italy (see Fig. 6.22). He was at the right place at the right time, for his career coincided

Fig. 6.22. *Josquin des Prez*, Woodcut, The only image for this composer of the Renaissance.

with Petrucci's printing press. Josquin had the privilege of being the first composer to have his work published on said press, giving him an advantage in the dissemination of his music throughout Europe.

Not only did he have fortuitous circumstances, but his music was also of such a high quality that the music matched what the words conveyed in a convincing example of musical text expression. In one of his most famous motets, *Ave Maria virgo serena*, he begins by having each of the four voices (**soprano, alto, tenor, bass**) stagger their entries but with the same music and same words. This became known as **points of imitation** and served to beautifully reinforce the message. If one missed "Ave Maria" the first time, there were three more opportunities in rapid succession! In the example below, listen carefully to how the voices mimic one another's entries, almost like an echo. Listen also for places where the voices line up for their entries. The table below should help you navigate through the first four minutes. If you listen carefully, Josquin varies the vocal entries, texture, and meter to compose constant variety within a unity of sound.

Listen to Josquin des Prez, *Ave Maria virgo serena*:

Time	Description
0:00	Ave Maria..., in 4 successive points of imitation. **Duple meter**
0:16	Gratia plena..., in 4 successive points of imitation
0:34	Dominus..., in 4 successive points of imitation
1:06	Ave cuius...soprano and alto enter as a pair in **homophony**
1:14	Ave cuius...tenor and bass enter in same fashion
1:25	Solmni...all 4 voices enter in homophony; returns and alternates with points of imitation and paired entries
3:20	Ave, vera...all 4 voices enter in homophony. **Triple meter** and quickened pace

Catholic church music reached a pinnacle in the **polychoral** works written for the famous double choir lofts of St. Mark's Church in Venice during the late sixteenth centuries (see Fig. 6.23). The glorious sounds of one choir answering to the other across the cavernous space, would most likely be heard by the congregation sitting below as a reflection of something divine. The polychoral motet spread throughout Europe and reached such a sophistication in England that one gifted composer, Thomas Tallis (ca. 1505-1585), wrote *Spem in alium*, a polychoral motet for no less than eight separate choirs singing together, all with different music, but harmonizing in some of the grandest and most glorious sounds that the Renaissance had to offer.

Chapter 6: The Renaissance 141

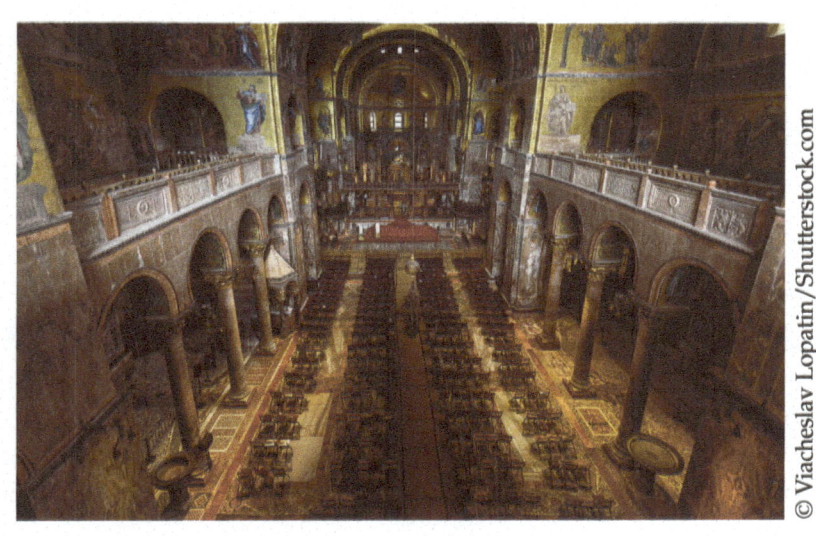

Fig. 6.23. St. Mark's Church, interior, Venice, Italy.

homophony: musical textu[re] in which one main melody [is] supported by other subord[i]nate voices th[at] move togethe[r] in the same rhythms and the same spe[ed]

triple meter: grouping of notes into me[a]sures of three beats

polychoral: musical work involving mo[re] than one cho[ir]

Did you know?

During the pandemic of 2020-2021, *Spem in alium* was performed with appropriate social distancing. Getting 40 people together in one room properly spaced is one thing; getting them to sing as one voice is quite another. Executing this professional, beautiful concert was no small feat. The work was performed in a large hall in the Tate Modern in London (see Ch. 13), not far from where *Spem in alium* was written 450 years earlier. This performance was streamed live on Sept. 16, 2020, reaching virtually an audience the world over. Its message, "In No Other Is My Hope" is a most fitting one to encourage the world that, while it seems that people are in desperation at times, ultimately believers find their hope in Christ Jesus through faith in Him. As you listen, do not worry about understanding the words, but rather try to get a sense of the beautiful moving harmonies and how the overall sound of the music fills the hall. Every voice is different from every other, yet together they produce a glorious, unified message of hope.

Listen to *Spem in alium*.

Much of the music for the Roman Catholic church was elaborate, matching the wealth of the church, which could be seen in its architecture. Conversely, the Protestant Reformation produced music that developed along a very different line. The two main streams of the Reformation, Calvinism and Lutheranism, made drastic changes to music based more on theological principles than on tradition, architecture, or wealth. Calvin held music in some suspicion and recommended that only Psalms be sung in church meetings. He, furthermore, limited the style of music to regular rhythms and meters with simple tunes and no instrumental accompaniment. This became known as **metrical psalmody**. One of the most famous of these, still heard today in churches, is nicknamed "Old Hundredth," and is based on Psalm 100.

Listen to the simplicity of the metrical psalm, "Old Hundredth."

> ### In their own words
>
> Jean Calvin (Fig. 6.24) advocated a more reserved approach to music in the church, warning that the aesthetic qualities of music could be a distraction from the spiritual message. In "The Epistle to the Reader" of *The Geneva Psalter* (1542), Calvin wrote:
>
> "Now among the other things proper to recreate man and give him pleasure, music is either the first or one of the principal, and we must think that it is a gift of God deputed to that purpose. For which reason we must be the more careful not to abuse it, for fear of soiling and contaminating it, converting it to our condemnation when it has been dedicated to our profit and welfare."[1]

Martin Luther, however, saw music as a gift from God and as something that could be used to communicate truth to God's people. He instituted congregational singing in the Lutheran church, with his development of the **chorale**, a

metrical psalmody: a type of sacred music limited to regular rhythms and meters with simple tunes written as psalms and no instrumental accompaniment

chorale: a German hymn

Fig. 6.24. Jean Calvin, bust, Targu-Mures, Romania.

German hymn. Luther's most famous chorale is *Ein feste Burg*, or "A Mighty Fortress [Is Our God]," also heard frequently today in churches. Luther took advantage of existing songs and re-set a number of secular tunes with scriptural references, thus sanctifying them for the church.[2] Were church goers bothered when they heard re-purposed secular music in church? Possibly. The same type of vertiginous feeling with the introduction of something new is experienced today with contemporary styles. Now, most are not bothered by any profane associations with Lutheran chorales, since those connotations had long since disappeared by the coming of the twenty-first century.

Listen to the simplicity of a chorale.

In Their Own Words

Martin Luther (Fig. 6.25) was an unashamed apologist for the role of music in worship. In the 1538 Preface of Georg Rhau's *Symphoniae Iucundae*, Luther wrote:

"Next to the Word of God, music deserves the highest praise. . . . After all, the gift of language combined with the gift of song was only given to man to let him know that he should praise God with both word and music; namely, by proclaiming [the Word of God] through music and by providing sweet melodies with words."[3]

Fig. 6.25. Martin Luther, monument, Dresden, Germany.

Secular

If the motet and mass cycle developed to the same breathtaking heights as the walls of the Gothic cathedrals, the secular sphere experienced equally astounding developments in the Italian madrigal. This genre had existed in the High Middle Ages, then was forgotten, but returned with a vengeance in the Renaissance period, dominating much of the sixteenth century. One of the most significant developments in this genre was that it drew from the language of the people. While only a few privileged individuals, mostly upper-class Italians, could appreciate the word–music relationship of Latin motets, everyone could understand the witty Italian madrigals. The poetry was colorful, symbolic, and, most importantly, lent itself easily to the imaginations of composers, who developed a high level of skill in word painting, or depicting in music what the words meant. This instigated something of an obsession, as both audiences and performers highly esteemed the accessible and inventive music. The Italian madrigal eventually made its way to England and, with the same emphasis on word painting, the English public soon enjoyed the genre as much as their counterparts in Italy.

word painting: musical depiction of a word's meaning

Thomas Weelkes's English madrigal, *As Vesta Was from Latmos Hill Descending*, provides some wonderful and distinct examples of word painting. With a little help from a few cues in the table below, let the imagination picture the words in their aural analogues.

Time	Description
0:07	Descending—Music goes down
0:24	Ascending—Music goes up
0:40	Attended on by all—All voices in homophony
1:06	Running down a-main—Fast notes running down like scales
1:27	Two by Two—Two voices sing together
1:31	Three by Three—Three voices sing together
1:45	All alone—One voice sings
	Got the idea?

Listen for word painting in As Vesta Was.

The Search for a New Aesthetic in Music

Just as new thoughts about the importance of man and new ways of perceiving music with man at the center affected the course of music in the fifteenth and sixteenth centuries, new ideas about the dramatic effects of music became a focus of inquiry in the decades leading to 1600. Throughout the Renaissance, the search for ancient Greek primary source materials led to the recovery or re-birth of ancient arts and practices. In Florence by this time, after nearly 200 years of flourishing arts and a thriving economy, groups of scholarly men began meeting in the interest of the pursuit of knowledge. These informal groups became known collectively as the **Florentine Camerata**, so named for the small private rooms, or chambers, in which they regularly met. One of the expansive topics of inquiry was the role that music may have played in ancient Greek drama. After a certain amount of study of primary sources, many of these scholars believed that the reason that these dramas were so highly effective was that they were entirely sung. Not only did the traditional Greek "chorus" sing collective commentaries on the action, but individual actors were thought to have delivered powerful speeches and dialogues through a kind of speech-singing known as **recitative**. These were considered to be so moving, that actors could easily elicit the responses of lament or joy through means of music. Judging the popular music of that day in Italy against this new criteria left these styles wanting in terms of dramatic delivery. The three prevalent vocal genres in the mid- to late-sixteenth century required multiple voices and were all interwoven lines of polyphony. This made the dramatic delivery of a soloist unconvincing in terms of expression and believability. The complex polyphony, with its imitative entries and lines that had been so prized for the past two centuries, became a problem nearly overnight for the new aesthetic with its evolving artistic goal.

As the Florentine Camerata studied, discussed, and experimented, a solution emerged, which would be known as **monody**. It was a completely new texture for song (see Fig. 6.26). It stripped the number of voices down to one and supported that with a sparse bass accompaniment known as **basso continuo**. The basso continuo, which means "continuous bass," was formed by a constantly sounding low instrument, like the modern-day cello or string bass, and another instrument that played chords at key points of emphasis in the vocal delivery. The basso continuo would follow the singer and go faster or slower to match the speed of the song. In this way, the ensemble could play as a unit, metaphorically as one mind and one heart, led by the singer. The singer was now free in this texture to deliver quick lines of dialogue in a declamatory style known as recitative or take more time to explore one emotion more deeply, such as a lament or a confession of love, the latter of which became known as an **aria**. At

Fig. 6.26. Simplistic example of monody using same tune as Figs. 5.18 and 6.20. Arr. Allison Zieg.

Florentine Camerata: groups of scholarly men around 1600 who met in pursuit of knowledge; named for the small private rooms or chambers, in which they regularly met one of the big topics of inquiry was the role that music may have played in ancient Greek drama, leading to the development of recitative and early origins of opera

recitative: the traditional Greek delivery of actors' powerful speeches and dialogues through a kind of speech-singing

monody: solo singing accompanied by basso continuo in the early baroque period

basso continuo: a continuous sounded bass line, usually requiring two performers. The bass includes a continuous sounded bass line and chords. Associated with the early baroque period

first these two styles were fairly similar, but over time, they developed their own distinctiveness and became a familiar formula of recitative-plus-aria in early performances. Soon this manner of singing convincingly supported characters in a drama and, thus, **opera** was born . Although this word simply means "works" in Latin, it denoted a genre of music and drama in which all the words are sung. There is instrumental accompaniment and there may be choruses and ensembles singing in addition to the soloists, but there is no spoken dialogue. The seventeenth century would become known as the century that saw the development of opera from its humble beginnings to large-scale lucrative works for public theatre performed in many cities throughout Italy and, then, spreading to France, Germany, England, and Spain.

a: an elabo- solo song ally within opera, orato- or cantata

ra: com- tely sung ma; a dra- tic stage rk that is irely sung er than ken

ios: the col- ed, printed, l published rks of Shake- are compiled r his death

arto edi- s: separated, lier printed tions of kespeare's ys, separate n the Folios l smaller in

Theatre

Though Italy, France, and Spain experienced their own renaissances in theatre, the legacy and innovation of the Elizabethan theatrical tradition dominated the era of the European Renaissance. The star of Elizabethan theatre was playwright William Shakespeare (1564-1616), also known as "the Bard of Avon," or more simply "the Bard." During his lifetime, Shakespeare wrote 39 plays, 154 sonnets, and three longer narrative poems. Little is known about the playwright other than what is contained in public records, his birth, baptism, marriage, and death certificate. None of his own manuscripts survived the time, but after his death, his works were compiled and published in four **Folios**. The first collected edition of Shakespeare's plays, the First Folio (Fig. 6.27), was published in 1623, twelve years after the first edition of the King James translation of the Bible was published in London. Previously, 18 of the 36 plays published in the First Folio were published in separate editions known as **Quarto editions.** As folios were bulky, quartos were more convenient as they were half the size.

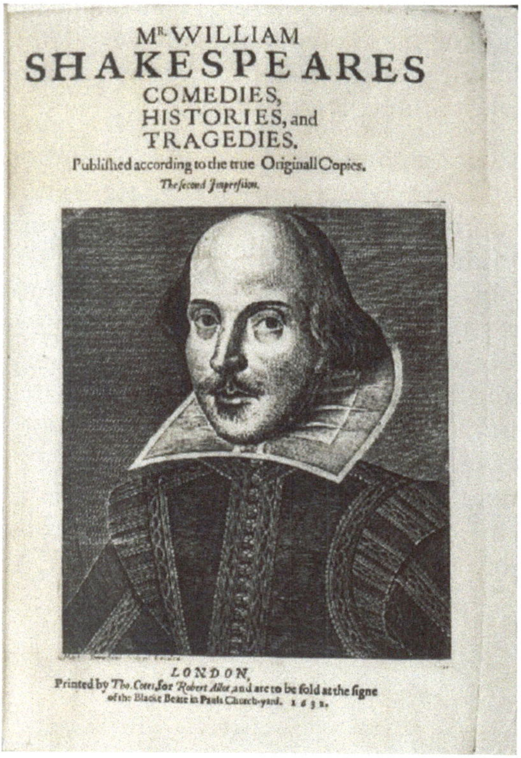

Yale University Library

Fig. 6.27. Title page of the First Folio, 1623, copper engraving of Shakespeare by Martin Droeshout.

Chapter 6: The Renaissance   147

> **DID YOU KNOW?**
>
> In 2020, one of 235 known surviving copies of Shakespeare's first compilation sold for $10 million.

The Renaissance brought the formalizing of theatre buildings to house sets, stages, audiences, and performers. The first theatre was aptly christened, "The Theatre," and was followed by the construction of the Curtain, the Rose, the Fortune, the Globe, and the Hope. Most of Shakespeare's plays were produced at the Globe, which subsequently became the most famous Elizabethan theatre. None of the original theatres survived the time, but remains of the Rose theatre and drawings of the Globe theatre have led to conjectural reconstructions (as in Fig. 6.28), and in some cases, physical reconstructions.

Shakespeare is noted for writing in **iambic pentameter**, the use of ten syllables per line and syllables alternating between unstressed and stress beats. For example, from *A Midsummer Night's Dream*: "And I do love thee. Therefore go with

iambic pentameter: the use of ten syllables per line and syllables alternating between unstressed and stress beats in the pattern of "de/DUM de/DUM de/DUM de/DUM de/DUM"

Fig. 6.28. Conjectural reconstruction of the Globe theatre by Joseph Quincy Adams and Henry Roenne.

me. / I'll give thee fairies to attend on thee, / And they shall fetch thee jewels from the deep / And sing while thou on pressed flowers dost sleep." (Act III, Scene I). Shakespeare often used iambic pentameter when high-status characters spoke. Lower-status characters often spoke in prose. He was a genius with language structure and would often vary the iambic pentameter verse in tense or unraveling scenes into non-rhyming, non-metered, erratic rhythms that signaled the ensuing chaos.

Shakespeare's plays are typically grouped into three main categories: **tragedy**, **history**, and **comedy**. Tragedies, like Greek tragedies referenced in Ch. 2, concerned a main character brought to ruin as a consequence of a tragic flaw. History plays dramatized historical narratives. Comedies were written to amuse and entertain, and were filled with witty remarks, unusual characters, and strange circumstances that highlighted human frailty and vanity.

Sixteenth- and seventeenth-century England was culturally saturated with the Bible. Young William Shakespeare would have been exposed to the Bible in grammar-school curricula that encouraged much scriptural reading and would have experienced morality plays as a child. It is also surmised that Shakespeare must have spent time reading the Bible on his own time since many of the biblical passages cited in his plays were outside of the typical passages used in liturgy and recitations in the church. Additionally, during the Renaissance, the Bible was treated as an ancient text for humanistic scholarship. Though it is unclear how reverently or irreverently Shakespeare regarded Scripture personally, larger biblical themes were often reflected in his plays.

Shakespeare might have imitated scriptural models, mimicking complex plots and storytelling techniques of the passages in the Bible, such as contrasts between incidents and the use of recurring symbols and motifs. One can see that the Bible could be considered to overlap with literary genres of Shakespeare: Exodus through Kings functioning as history, Job as a kind of tragedy, and Ruth or Esther as, perhaps, comic romance.

Tragedy

Shakespeare's imagination might have been inspired by the book of Job in his tragedy *King Lear*. In his old age, King Lear of Briton decides to divide his kingdom between his three daughters, Goneril, Regan, and Cornelia, based solely on flattery. His youngest daughter, Cornelia, who truly loves him, refuses to proclaim her love when it is demanded for an inheritance, unlike her older sisters. King Lear is enraged by her response, casts her off, and divides his wealth and lands between Goneril and Regan. Eventually, King Lear realizes the deceit of Goneril and Regan, who do not care for him. He reconciles with his daughter Cornelia, but it is too late, and the play ends after the death of all three of his daughters. King Lear is left in despair and destitution.

Both Job and King Lear appear in the narrative in a land that is vague and undefined, Job from the "land of Uz" and King Lear from a pre-historic Briton. Both have a great reversal in fortune, from wealth and prosperity to extreme loss. Both have a moment of great recognition. Job recognizes that the righteous and wicked do not always get what they appear to deserve, but righteousness is still worth pursuing. This can be observed in his claim that "I have heard of you by the hearing of the ear, but now my eye sees you; therefore I despise myself, and repent in dust and ashes" (Job 42:5-6).

King Lear's great recognition is realizing the foolishness in believing flatterers, and briefly, his health, sanity, and dignity is returned to him by nurturing reunion with his daughter. The story of Job is theocentric: God is present, and the ending is restorative, when Job receives ten-fold of his losses. Shakespeare's King Lear is anthropocentric: God is silent and matters are left in the character's hands. In the First Quarto version of *King Lear*, there is a possibly hopeful ending of Lear being reunited with Cornelia in the final lines of the play, "Do you see this? Look on her. Look, her lips. / Look there, look there."[4]

Did you know?

Shakespeare coined some of the most commonly spoken idioms in English, such as:

- "Heart of gold" (Henry V, Act IV, Scene I)
- "Kill with kindness" (The Taming of the Shrew, Act IV)
- "Laughingstock" (Merry Wives of Windsor, Act III, Scene I)
- "Wild-goose chase" (Romeo and Juliet, Act II, Scene IV)
- "Lie low" (Much Ado About Nothing, Act V, Scene I)
- "Faint-hearted" (Henry VI, Part I, Act I, Scene III)
- "Apple of my eye" (A Midsummer Night's Dream, Act III, Scene II)
- "Wear your heart on your sleeve" (Othello, Act I, Scene I)
- "Green-eyed monster" (Othello, Act III, Scene III)
- "Seen better days" (As You Like It, Act II, Scene VII)
- "Good riddance" (Troilus and Cressida, Act II, Scene I)
- "It's Greek to me" (Julius Caesar, Act I, Scene II)
- "Love is blind" (The Merchant of Venice, Act II, Scene VI)
- "Break the ice" (The Taming of the Shrew, Act I, Scene II)
- "Knock, knock! Who's there?" (Macbeth, Act II, Scene III)

He also had a penchant for inventing words, due to the desire to rhyme or make them fit in iambic pentameter. He transformed nouns into verbs or adjectives or vice versa, combined words together to make new words, added prefixes and suffixes to existing words, and invented entirely new words.

History

During the Elizabethan era, writings about history and historical plays became very popular, especially concerning British history. In 1599, Shakespeare presented his *Henry V* and used it to both portray history and to support British loyalty to the Crown. England had grown strong under the Tudor reign and especially flourished under Elizabeth I's reign. She had defeated the Spanish Armada just 11 years before in 1588 and put an end to internal enemies such as her rival, Mary Queen of Scots. In addition to her power, the Queen was the spiritual head of the Church of England. In 1599, England faced another crisis, a rebellion in Ireland that had to be addressed.[5] In the context of this milieu of politics, war, and power struggles, Shakespeare crafted the character of Henry V as a hero-king. The historical Henry V, though a young, impetuous king, had courageously taken his troops across the English Channel during the Hundred Years' War and fought for England's claim to land in France at the Battle of Agincourt (1415). He did this with a small army that faced the French on their own territory with an army five-fold greater in number.

Shakespeare used the art of the spoken word—the weapon of theatre—to convey both the power and spiritual headship of the monarchy in the most famous monologue from the play (Act IV, Scene III). Henry's troops are just minutes from facing the French in battle, as Henry inspires them with courage and hope. The speech ends with this reminder to look beyond the momentary lightness of their affliction.

> But we in it shall be remembered—
> We few, we happy few, we band of brothers;
> For he today that sheds his blood with me
> Shall be my brother; be he ne'er so vile,
> This day shall gentle his condition;
> And gentlemen in England, now a-bed,
> Shall think themselves accurs'd they were not here;
> And hold their manhoods cheap whiles any speaks
> That fought with us upon Saint Crispin's day.[6]

At the beginning of this speech, Henry reminded his men that England would be celebrating St. Crispin on this day, and he offered to send anyone home who did not want to stay and fight. Needless to say, by the end of his speech, no one withdrew as all rallied around their King.

Similar to the way in which Henry V emboldened his army with his words, Shakespeare used the English language with great effect in empowering theatre. In some ways, theatre, itself, is a mirror of the means by which God reveals

Himself—through His word. Not only did the Word, Jesus Christ, become "flesh" and "dwell" among humanity (John 1:14), but only in Him is the Father seen (John 1:18). Thus, the power of words comes with their ability to express and reveal what is unseen.

Although against all odds, the battle ended in victory for the English. In the 1989 film version of *Henry V*, under the direction of Kenneth Branaugh, who also played the lead role, Branaugh included the singing of a Latin chant as the few fallen English soldiers were carried from the battlefield. The chant, *Non nobis Domine*, quotes Ps 115:1, "Not to us, O Lord, but to Your name be the glory." Although the music swells from a single line of chant sung by one soldier to a grand chorus with orchestra at the end of the scene, in full film-score style (music by Patrick Doyle), the opening in monophonic Latin recalls Gregorian chant and all the associations with solemnity and tranquility of medieval Christian worship (see Ch. 4). In the following example, imagine being transported from a bloody battlefield to the serenity and safety of the presence of God.

Listen to Non nobis Domine.

Concerning this particular scene in the play, and knowing the Bible as he likely did, Shakespeare made intentional parallels with and references to Scripture. The most obvious one is the young David standing up against Goliath. Henry V, as the spiritual head of England, defied France "in the name of the Lord of hosts, the God of the armies of Israel" (I Sam 17:45). Another direct reference, which includes the life-giving power of the Word, is found in John 6:67, after Jesus revealed that He was the bread of life. Many of his disciples couldn't take such a radical thought and turned away. Jesus asked the remaining twelve if they also would go away. Simon Peter spoke up, showing that he understood what the Word could do. "Lord, to whom shall we go? You have the words of eternal life."

Did you know?

The term "band of brothers" may be more familiar to you as the title of the 2001 war drama miniseries, *Band of Brothers*. This miniseries was based on a 1992 non-fiction work of the same name by historian Stephen E. Ambrose. The titles for both are based on this phrase found in Henry V's speech. The book contains a quote from the speech and one of the characters in the drama speaks it. Shakespeare's legacy is alive and well in the twenty-first century, more than 400 years after the Bard's ingenious artistry with language!

Comedy

Most of Shakespeare's comedies continue to be performed in high schools and universities, as well as summer outdoor Shakespeare festivals. Many students are familiar with such titles as *The Merchant of Venice*, *A Midsummer Night's Dream*, *Much Ado about Nothing*, and *All's Well That Ends Well*. Although couched in good humor and lots of laughter, Shakespeare's comedies provide an oft-needed respite from humanity's everyday burdens. As with the tragedy and history, comedy sets up a mirror through which the audience can see a reflection of themselves. Humor disarms an audience, allowing them to put down defenses and look inwardly. In facilitating introspection, Shakespeare might agree that laughter was the best medicine.

In their own words

Rebekah Priebe, Associate Professor of Theatre at Cedarville University, is responsible for designing costumes for all of the University main-stage plays. She offers keen insight into Shakespearean comedy from this unique vantage point. Below she describes the research, planning, and decisions for outfitting a recent production of Shakespeare's *Comedy of Errors*:

"When designing costumes for a Shakespearean play, one of the first aspects to consider is the time period. Whether that is the time period that the play is set in/written in or a different period that the director has chosen, this will greatly inform the costume designer of the director's approach and where to begin research. A designer must also consider if specific clothing pieces, such as doublets or jerkins, are mentioned and how those will be addressed, particularly if the play is not set in the Elizabethan period. Another important consideration is if the play includes any well-known or historical characters and how those will be incorporated into the costume designs.

In the case of the Cedarville University production of *The Comedy of Errors*, I also had an additional set of considerations. Our production was set in Ephesus in the 1960s with influences of the commedia dell'arte style of theatre, and this all informed my research and design choices. The commedia dell'arte style of theatre uses stock characters with stylized movement and physical characteristics and defines certain types of characters by the use of masks and specific

commedia dell'arte: a form of popular theatre with masked, stock characters in predictable roles

costumes. While we did not utilize the traditional commedia dell'arte masks, the mask styles did somewhat influence the makeup design for certain characters. Many commedia dell'arte characters are also associated with certain colors or styles of costumes, so I used these colors and styles as inspiration for certain characters.

The commedia dell'arte influence was used in different ways for different characters. Two examples would be the character of Egeon and the twin Dromio characters. The character of Egeon is an older merchant who had enough similarities to the commedia character of Pantalone that I drew inspiration from Pantalone's typical costume of a red doublet/jacket and black breeches/trousers as well as his typical beard (Figs. 6.29, 6.32). I chose Egeon's style to be more from the 1950s because as an older man he probably would not be following the mod fashions of the mid-1960s seen on many of the other characters, including his sons. The Dromio characters (Fig. 6.30), who are servants, were influenced by the commedia character of Arlecchino, who is also a servant often depicted in a diamond patterned costume made up of a doublet/jacket and breeches/trousers. These characters in our production were played by females, so I chose cropped women's suits that were popular in the mid-1960s as a nice equivalent to the traditional Arlecchino costume (Fig. 6.31). Since the Dromio characters are supposed to be long-lost twins that are confused for each other, each Dromio wore a matching green diamond patterned suit and diamond patterned hat with different accents of red and yellow.

In addition to these aforementioned characters, each of the other characters was tied to a specific commedia character, or a combination of characters, that then influenced the design of each costume piece, including styles, colors, and patterns. Most of the costumes were actual vintage pieces or vintage-inspired clothing purchased online, with some additional pieces pulled from our costume stock and some pieces constructed. All of these pieces, whether constructed, purchased, or pulled, were combined together to create a cohesive costume design that reflected the mod styles of the 1960s influenced by the stock characters of commedia dell'arte."

Fig. 6.29. Egeon, from Cedarville University's production of *A Comedy of Errors*, 2019.

Fig. 6.30. The Dromio Twins, from Cedarville University's production of *A Comedy of Errors*, 2019.

Chapter 6: The Renaissance   155

Fig. 6.31. Costume design concept for Dromio of Syracuse, by Rebekah Priebe, 2019.

Fig. 6.32. Costume design concept, by Rebekah Priebe, 2019.

Study Questions

1. In what ways do humanism and Christianity conflict?
2. How do you see tension manifested in the visual artistic work in the Renaissance between Christian traditions and humanistic thought?
3. How did humanism influence music during the Renaissance?
4. Why is Shakespeare one of the most important figures in theatre history?

Notes

1. Jean Calvin, "Epistle to the Reader," *The Geneva Psalter* (1542), in Strunk, V.3, 88.
2. There is no evidence, however, that *Ein feste Burg* was not an original composition by Luther himself. In fact, the tune appears in *Luther's Works*, V. 53.
3. Luther, 323-324.
4. Marx, 78.
5. Shakespeare, *King Henry the Fifth*, Folger Library, n.d., vii.
6. Shakespeare, *Riverside Shakespeare*, 960.

7

The Baroque Era
The Divergence of Thought

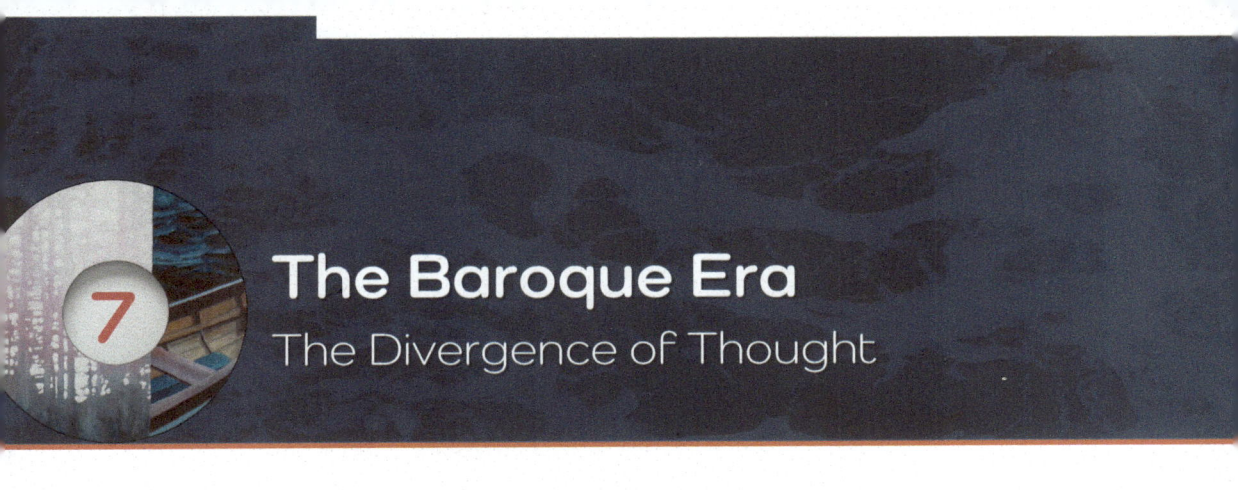

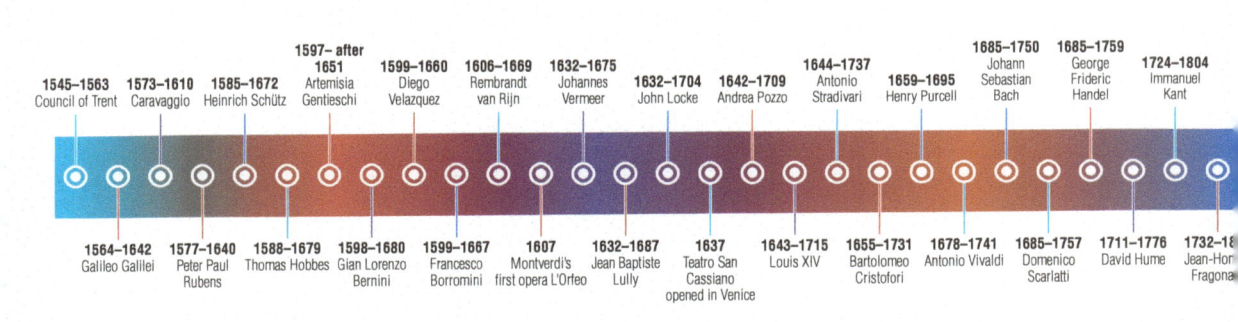

Timeline:
- 1545–1563 Council of Trent
- 1564–1642 Galileo Galilei
- 1573–1610 Caravaggio
- 1577–1640 Peter Paul Rubens
- 1585–1672 Heinrich Schütz
- 1588–1679 Thomas Hobbes
- 1597–after 1651 Artemisia Gentieschi
- 1598–1680 Gian Lorenzo Bernini
- 1599–1660 Diego Velazquez
- 1599–1667 Francesco Borromini
- 1606–1669 Rembrandt van Rijn
- 1607 Montverdi's first opera L'Orfeo
- 1632–1675 Johannes Vermeer
- 1632–1687 Jean Baptiste Lully
- 1632–1704 John Locke
- 1637 Teatro San Cassiano opened in Venice
- 1642–1709 Andrea Pozzo
- 1643–1715 Louis XIV
- 1644–1737 Antonio Stradivari
- 1655–1731 Bartolomeo Cristofori
- 1659–1695 Henry Purcell
- 1678–1741 Antonio Vivaldi
- 1685–1750 Johann Sebastian Bach
- 1685–1757 Domenico Scarlatti
- 1685–1759 George Frideric Handel
- 1711–1776 David Hume
- 1724–1804 Immanuel Kant
- 1732–18 Jean-Hon Fragona

Philosophy

The life of Galileo Galilei (1564-1642) is, in many ways, a parable of the Baroque period (Fig. 7.1). As the natural sciences grew into their own, they occasionally came into conflict with religious beliefs, particularly with those of the Catholic Church. His claim that the earth was part of a system that was heliocentric, or revolving around the sun, was in tension with the perspective of the scholastics, who felt that Scripture pointed to a geocentric, or earth-centered system. Eventually, conflicts arose, and Galileo was forced to recant under the persecution of Catholicism. As scholars began to agree with the Italian astronomer, skepticism arose as to the ability of Christianity and its Scriptures to provide a true account of the world. The Baroque period was a time in which the divergence between the sacred and the secular began to become more acute. Thus, the optimism bred by the successes of science to predict events in the universe led to the dubious belief that humans may be able to solve their own problems without the aid of the Bible, a trend that continues to this day. Such confidence, in light of the scriptural depiction of sin's effect on the human mind (Rom 1:18-23), was obviously unfounded. Furthermore, science, which had historically been a

Fig. 7.1. Portrait of Galileo Galilei, 1623, Francesco Villamena, Metropolitan Museum of Art, NY.

subsection of philosophy, began to break free and was more frequently treated as an independent discipline.

> ### IN THEIR OWN WORDS
>
> "It strikes me as gruesome and comical that in our culture we have an expectation that man can always solve his problems. There is that implication that if you just have a little more energy, a little more fight, the problem can always be solved. This is so untrue that it makes me want to cry-or laugh."
> — Kurt Vonnegut (1922-2007)[1]

Counter-Reformation: time of resurgence in the Catholic Church in response to the Protestant Reformation

Just as the Reformation was reactionary, so was the **Counter-Reformation**, which was the attempt of the Catholic church to stem the tide of the rising popularity of Protestantism. It began with the Council of Trent (1545-1563), a set of

Fig. 7.2. *Speculum Romanae Magnificentiae: Council of Trent*, 1565, Anonymous, Metropolitan Museum of Art, NY.

meetings that put forth the official standpoint of Catholicism in contrast to the Reformers (Fig. 7.2). Along with other beliefs, the Council condemned anybody who believed in the central Reformed view that salvation was by grace alone, through faith alone, and by Christ alone. One of the peripheral issues affected by the dispute between Protestantism and Catholicism was the development of the style of the Baroque period. As was mentioned in the previous chapter, the iconoclasm of the Reformers tended to attack the art developed by the Catholic Church to adorn its buildings. In reaction, Catholicism and the artists it financed, developed a highly ornate style, leading to an opulence that had not even been seen under the Medicis during the Renaissance. Art was more elaborate and, in the case of architecture and theatre, more grandiose.

The philosophy of the Baroque period and its successor the Enlightenment had a profound impact not only on the art of its period, but also on subsequent eras, all the way to the present. The skepticism that had begun under the rise of the sciences was given philosophical rigor under the atheist scholar David Hume (1711-1776). His attacks against belief in God and religion not only emboldened further opposition to Christianity, but also precipitated the work of the most important philosopher since the Middle Ages, Immanuel Kant (1724-1804). Such suspicion of the Christian faith led to an increasing belief in the independence of the arts from all theistic perspectives, which would eventually culminate in the twentieth-century denial of any relationship of values to the artistic endeavor. Such a divorce was further supported by the rise of British **empiricism**, or the view that all knowledge is derived from the senses. By separating truth and knowing

empiricism: the view that all knowledge is derived from the senses

from anything that was beyond what one could see and hear, the ability to deal with ideas like "right" or "good" was heavily undermined.

> **IN THEIR OWN WORDS**
>
> "If we take in our hand any volume of divinity or school metaphysics, for instance, let us ask, Does it contain any abstract reasoning concerning quantity or number? No. Does it contain any experimental reasoning concerning matter of fact and existence? No. Commit it then to the flames: for it can contain nothing but sophistry and illusion." David Hume [2]

conventions: agreed-upon rules

social contract theory: view that individuals should enter into relationships whereby all parties involved give up certain practices in order to secure certain protections and freedoms for themselves

The assault on values caused individuals like Thomas Hobbes (1588-1679) to develop theories that relied heavily on **conventions**, or agreed-upon rules, to deal with morality. For example, Hobbes developed **social contract theory**, which argued that rather than holding to standards of rightness that were immutable and beyond this world (e.g., divine moral laws), individuals should enter into relationships with others whereby all parties involved give up certain practices in order to secure certain protections and freedoms for themselves. In essence, one entered into social contracts with others that placed restrictive obligations on everyone, but also gave rights to everyone. Thus, morality was separated from eternal value and placed under the power of the arbitrary will of humans. In this way, movements toward conventions were continued in art, which saw the artist less and less as a moral creature who should obey his God, and more of a creator of his own values. In this way, the movement of Western art away from its use within the Christian faith was nearly complete. The question of what should be done was replaced with the question of what could be done.

Art

Baroque Era: period from 1600 to 1750; was a counter-response to the Reformation; is defined by its elaborate and dramatic style

Like the term *Gothic*, *Baroque* began as a derogatory term coined by eighteenth century thinkers to describe the ornamental artistic style following the Renaissance, the period between 1600 and 1750. The **Baroque Era** was a counter response to the Protestant Reformation and its frequent call for simplicity in the decorations within churches. In a concerted effort to draw back Catholics converted to Protestantism, the Catholic church increased the production of elaborate church architecture and decoration. Thus, the Baroque was born, a term that describes the theatrical sculpture and architecture of the era as well as the painting produced during the time. As Protestantism gained hold in the eighteenth century, religious art became rarer and was eventually phased out and outpaced by portraiture, **genre painting**, landscapes, and **still lifes**.

In some ways, Baroque can be described as the fusion of the lofty principles of the High Renaissance (symmetry, composition, balance, naturalism) with the struggles and emotional expressiveness of Mannerism. The product of such a combination was technically excellent, wild, and full of drama.

An example that embodies this marriage of ideals is the rendition of *David* (Fig. 7.3) by sculptor and architect Gian Lorenzo Bernini (1598-1680). In the previous chapter, Michelangelo's *David* (Fig. 6.8) signaled the idealized realism achieved during the Renaissance. In comparison with Bernini's *David*, Michelangelo's *David*, though natural looking, is visually stagnant. Bernini sculpted David in tense, implied movement. David's mouth is fixed determinedly, his muscles are flexed, and his arm is frozen in backswing, about to fling his stone. Bernini brought the calm and composure of the Renaissance style into full dynamic and active movement.

genre painting: a style of painting depicting scenes from ordinary, everyday life

still lifes: visual studies of inanimate objects

Fig. 7.3. *David*, 1623-24, Bernini, Galleria Borghese, Rome, Italy.

Baroque Architecture

Baroque architecture segmented, twisted, decorated, and curved traditional architectural elements. The style is **staccato** and eye-catching, with an emphasis on ornament, such as the Church of San Carlo alle Quattro Fontane (Fig. 7.4), in which the façade curves inward and outward in an undulating rhythm. Italian architects led in designing fountains, palaces, and churches. Most influential was the pioneer Bernini and his contemporary, Francesco Borromini (1599-1667).

staccato: short and detached

Bernini was both an architect and a sculptor. In his design *Gloria and Chair of Saint Peter* (Fig. 7.5) in Saint Peter's Basilica, the decorative chair of Saint Peter is practically hidden by the mass of writhing figures and dramatic sculptural forms. Rays of stained glass radiate outward from the image of a dove. The rays morph into three-dimensional bronze rays of sculpture, then tangle with bronze

Fig. 7.4. Church of San Carlo alle Quattro Fontane, 1638-46, Borromini, Rome.

Fig. 7.5. *Gloria and Chair of St. Peter*, St. Peter's Basilica, 1657-1666, Bernini, Rome, Italy.

Chapter 7: The Baroque Era 165

figures and floating clouds. The hybrid sculpture–architecture spills out of the enclave in excess and energy.

Interiors of the Baroque style were intended to combine media to create visual and emotional excitement. In such examples, the viewer can hardly discern what is painting, what is sculpture, and what is architecture. Andrea Pozzo (1642-1709) created the ceiling of the nave of the Church of Saint Ignazio, called *The Triumph of St. Ignatius* (Fig. 7.6). He uses techniques of quadratura (illusionistic ceiling

quadratura: illusionistic ceiling painting architectural elements like columns and arches

Fig. 7.6. *The Triumph of St. Ignatius*, Andrea Pozzo, 1688-94, Rome, Italy.

painting of architectural elements), including trompe l'oeil, exaggerated linear perspective, and atmospheric perspective to increase the sense of height in the ceiling and dramatize the scene.

Baroque by Region

In the Baroque era, Europe was cementing regions and monarchial governments into the countries that are recognizable today. During the period, there were clear similarities and differences both in the way that countries welcomed the arts, but also in the timing in which they peaked in any particular art form.

Italy: Caravaggio and the Carracci School

Italian artists, having been saturated with the achievements of the Renaissance, were determined and inspired to create art that exceeded their predecessors. Michelangelo Merisi (1573-1610), known as Caravaggio, was among the earliest and most influential painters in the Baroque movement. He was adept in the technique of *chiaroscuro*, the painterly technique of using light and shadow to show three-dimensional form. Caravaggio's work was critiqued for its unashamed realism, particularly in his religious subjects.

Such is Caravaggio's painting *The Incredulity of Saint Thomas* (Fig. 7.7). The piece utilizes **tenebrism** (the dramatic use of light as a compositional technique) to divide the picture plane in near half. Light illuminates the figure of the risen

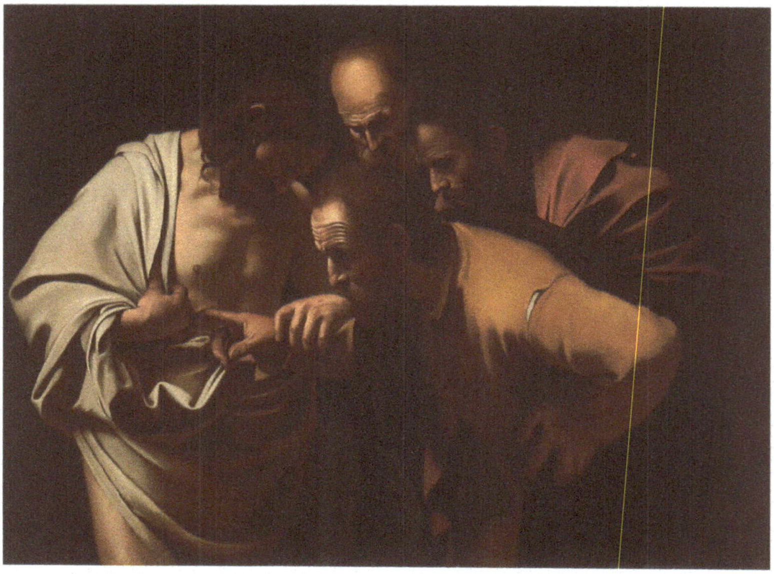

chiaroscuro: painterly technique of shading to show three-dimensional form

tenebrism: the dramatic use of light as a compositional technique

Fig. 7.7. *The Incredulity of Saint Thomas*, 1601-1602, Caravaggio, Sanssouci, Potsdam, Germany.

Christ, whose corporeality is emphasized in the absence of a halo. Eyebrows raised and forehead furrowed, "Doubting" Thomas probes his finger into the flesh of Jesus's side. Christ, with patient countenance, guides Thomas's hand to his wound.

Caravaggio's dramatic use of dark and light influenced later Italian painters, including the Carraccis, Lodovico (1555-1619) and his cousins, brothers Agostino (1557-1602) and Annibale (1560-1609). The Carraccis founded a teaching academy in Bologna with a mission to return to the principles of Renaissance painting: balance, directness, and depth of space. *Christ and the Woman of Samaria* (Fig. 7.8) by Annibale Carracci has a symmetrical composition and treatment of illusionistic space that is similar to da Vinci's *The Last Supper* (Fig. 6.7) or Raphael's *School of Athens* (Fig. 1.2). Interestingly, the halo over Christ has reappeared.

> **DID YOU KNOW?**
>
> In a world and trade dominated by men, Artemisia Gentileschi (1597-ca. 1656), daughter of court painter Orazio Gentileschi (1563-1638), made a name for herself in the style of Caravaggio. In her famous painting *Judith Slaying Holofernes* (Fig. 7.9), Gentileschi mirrors the gruesome violence of another one of her paintings which portrayed Jael slaying Sisera in the book of Judges. Gentileschi's own personal life was permeated with abuse and victimization, including rape by one of her father's associates. Her paintings highlighted female strength and offered metaphorical justice.

Spain

Within Europe, Spain was the most deeply religious country with the strongest ties to the church of Rome. Much of its painting, sculpture, and architecture was concerned with biblical subjects and used for the decoration of the church. It

Fig. 7.8. *Christ and the Woman of Samaria at the Well*, ca. 1604-1605, Annibale Carracci, Kunsthistorisches Museum, Vienna, Austria.

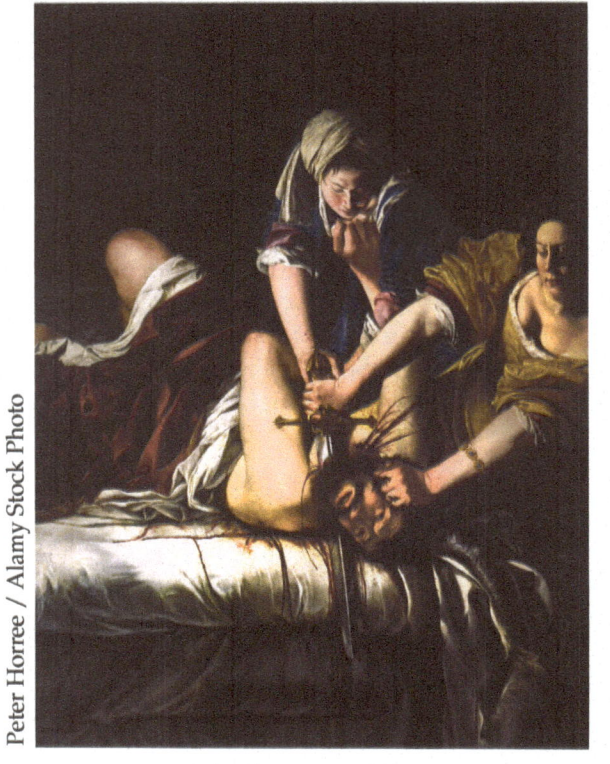

Fig. 7.9. *Judith Slaying Holofernes*, ca. 1611-1613, Artemisia Gentileschi, Museo di Capodimonte, Napoli.

is interesting then, that the most famous painter to emerge from Spain was Diego Velazquez (1599-1660), who rose to prominence as a painter of court portraits and genre paintings (illustrations of everyday popular life). He decided to be a genre painter rather than tackle more ambitious subjects like the masters of the Renaissance, stating, "I would rather be the first in this coarse stuff than second in nicety."[3] So he did, becoming a court painter to Philip IV. In *Las Meninas* (Fig. 7.10), Velasquez painted a disarming scene, which appears to be the interruption or intermission of a portrait sitting. The subject, Infanta Doña Margarita, is centered with her entourage of companions, with her parents appearing only in a reflection in the background. In a most unconventional approach to portraiture, the painting captures the typical, absurd dynamics of royal family life.

Did you know?

In *Las Meninas* (Fig. 7.10), Velasquez actually included himself in the painting. The figure in the shadows to the left, with paintbrush in hand, was the portraitist. The phenomenon of an artist inserting themselves into their own work, sometimes termed meta-reference, is used to this very day in diverse types of media. Vermeer's *The Painter in His Studio* (Fig. 7.11) may also be an instance. Notable recent examples would be the comic book character of Deadpool's recognition that he is a comic book character while referencing his artist, Charlie Kaufmann's penning a screenplay about himself adapting a screenplay in *Adaptation*, and Stephen King's insertion of himself into the later novels of his *Dark Tower* saga.

Fig. 7.10. *Las Meninas*, 1656-57, Diego Velazquez, Museo del Prado, Madrid, Spain.

The Netherlands

The Dutch excelled in the simplicity of painting the ordinary. Early masters of the Baroque era like Peter Paul Rubens (1577-1640) established Flemish traditions of movement, color, and richness of surface. As time went on and Protestantism became more influential, wealthy merchants rather than religious institutions became patrons of the arts. They wanted paintings of the scenes that were dear to them—familiar natural landscapes, portraits of family, and quiet still lifes (visual studies of inanimate objects). Even when artists painted biblical scenes, they were set in ordinary life in contemporary costume. The goal of Dutch painting was to tell a story and be descriptive. Craft, rather than intellectual ideals, was prioritized.

One such example of Dutch style painting is Johannes Vermeer (1632-1675), who painted genre scenes with a focus on light and texture. With photographic

Fig. 7.11. *The Painter in his Studio*, 1666-68, Johannes Vermeer, Kunsthistorisches Museum, Austria, Vienna.

precision, Vermeer created interiors with quiet, composed figures (Fig. 7.11). The textures are immaculate, from the heavy drapery to the marble floor and brass chandelier. Subsequent artists in the Netherlands and Germany slowly drifted to the "impression" of texture, which came into greater influence in later movements.

Immediately prior to the Baroque period, Dutch painting was considered very provincial. By the time of Rembrandt van Rijn (1606-1669), Caravaggio's shadows and dramatic effects had reached Holland. Rembrandt began as a portrait painter and was dedicated to drawing and etching. Unlike his contemporaries, he had a deep interest in moral history and depicted mythology and scenes from the Bible, in which he used family and friends as models. Rembrandt was not as concerned with the number of details, but the deeper realities and emotions

Fig. 7.12. *The Supper at Emmaus*, Rembrandt, 1648, Louvre Museum, Paris, France.

within the subject matter. In *The Supper at Emmaus*, (Fig. 7.12), Rembrandt paints the resurrected Christ having supper with his disciples. The treatment of light leans heavily into the technique of **sfumato** (the painting technique of fading colors gradually into one another to produce hazy forms) creating a simple luminescence around Christ that is both revelatory of his divine nature and full of peace.

sfumato: the painting technique of fading colors gradua into one anoth to produce ha forms

France

In the Baroque era, France, under the reign of Louis XIV (r.1643-1715) the "Sun King," was distinguished by frivolity and excess. During his rule, an academy was set up for the promotion of the visual arts, including manufacturing organizations entirely devoted to furnishing his personal chateau, the **Palace of Versailles**. The ensuing style was highly crafted, though not necessarily highly innovative.

Architect Louis Le Vau (1612-1670) was the first designer to work on the Palace of Versailles, the primary residence of Louis XIV and the center of court life. The

Palace of Versailles: King Louis XIV's lavish palace that served as the principal royal residenc of France from Louis XIV's reign to the French revolution

design of the exterior is detailed and ornate. The landscaping consists of neatly cut hedges, parks laid out in geometrical and symmetrical designs, elaborate fountains, and pools (Fig. 7.13).

Jules Hardouin Mansart (1598-1666) rose to replace Le Vau as lead architect. Mansart is responsible for the Galerie des Glaces, a hallway covered nearly entirely with mirrors composed on several panels (Fig. 7.14). In addition to the gilded architecture, painted ceiling, and ornamented marble details, the mirrors, with their constantly moving reflections, make for a distorted and striking chamber.

Fig. 7.13. Palace of Versailles, exterior, Versailles, France.

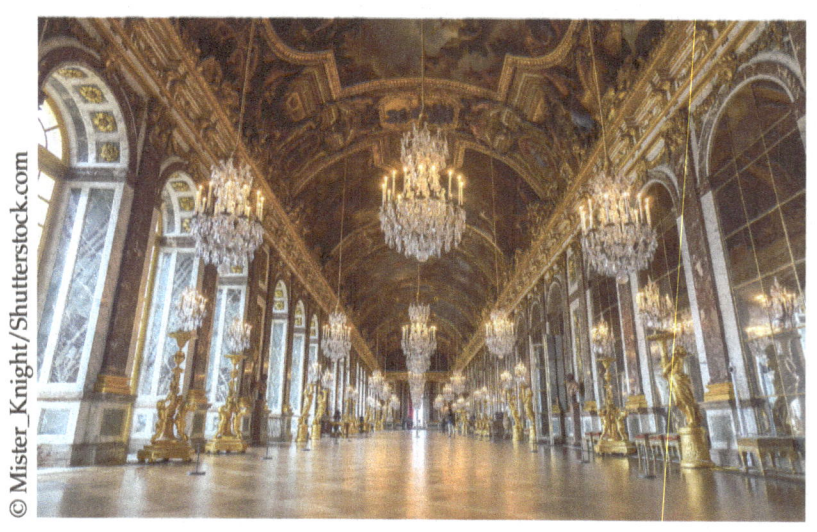

Fig. 7.14. *Galerie des Glaces*, Palace of Versailles, Versailles, France.

Louis XIV held court at the Palace of Versailles, for it was large enough to accommodate the entire aristocracy and give him direct contact so that he could force compliance to his decisions. Although the French monarchy was politically unsuccessful in the end, France was the cultural center of the universe. French was the most spoken language in Europe, French dance was disseminated abroad, the architecture of Versailles was imitated around Europe, and French painters were commissioned by foreign royals, princes, and kings.

The style of French painting that developed is best described as frivolous. Jean-Honoré Fragonard (1732-1806), an establisher of the Rococo style (the most ornamental and theatrical expression of the late Baroque) painted *The Swing* (Fig. 7.15), the visual equivalent of the dictum that is often attributed to Marie Antoinette, "Let them eat cake,"[4] with its pastels and lighthearted subject matter.

Rococo: the late Baroque style most ornamental and theatrical

Once again, in the Baroque era, the European mind was beset with inner and outward conflicts; between contemplation and expressiveness or piousness and indulgence, as seen in the artwork that reflected on biblical moments, the everyday, and royal life. Nearing the end of Baroque, the era was awakened to a consciousness that was self-driven rather than God-centered, following in the philosophy of Descartes who surmised, *"Cogito, ergo sum"* ("I think, therefore I am").

Fig. 7.15. *The Swing*, Fragonard, 1767, Wallace Collection, London, England.

Music

Stylistic Considerations

stile moderno: new Baroque musical sound that had the text dominate over the music

homophonic texture: displays a prominent melody in the top voice while having the continuation and development of the basso continuo (or supporting harmonies) in the bottom voice

At the beginning of the Baroque, there was a novel sound emerging. As opposed to the typical Renaissance style (known as *stile antico*) the new sound was called *stile moderno* with the text dominating over the music. Emphasis continued to be placed upon the understandability of the words. The **homophonic texture** found in much of its music displayed a prominent melody in the top voice while having the continuation and development of the basso continuo in the bottom voice (see Fig. 6.26). This is not to say *stile antico* completely disappeared. Rather, they coexisted throughout the Baroque and influenced one another.

As was noted from the Renaissance, a revival in the interest of ancient Greek thought had occurred. This was no exception for Baroque music. Just as the ancients believed that music could alter the mood and influence behavior, Baroque composers sought to bring about strong affections for the listener. Common **affects** for Baroque music included joy, sadness, love, hope, desire, and humility. These passions were brought into a more positive light, with the consequence that they were no longer viewed as something to be avoided.[5] In this new compositional style, harmonies were becoming more chromatic, using notes not found in the familiar major or minor scales. Pieces that were played one after another would frequently have contrasting moods for the sake of balance.[6]

Listen to Henry Purcell's (1659-1695) "Hear My Prayer" and hear the connection between the two styles and dissonances to display the affect.

What a listener knows today as large **crescendos** and **diminuendos** leading to overall volume changes were not commonplace in this era. Instead, a concept called **terraced dynamics** was used. In this form, a section of music would be played at a particular volume and immediately change to another.

While listening to "Spring" from Antonio Vivaldi's (1678-1741) *The Four Seasons*, imagine what affection this represents and how terraced dynamics would have influenced this.

Although much variation exists within Baroque music, a substantial portion can be characterized as music with long flowing melodies, embellished passages, and much ornamentation. Just as Baroque architecture has many aggrandizements, music and art found a parallel with one another.

Listen to Sonata in D minor (K. 141) by Domenico Scarlatti (1685-1757) to hear the embellishment and ornamentation common in many pieces present of the Baroque.

The presence of **counterpoint** in music was becoming more prominent. Literally meaning note against note, counterpoint was able to take a melody and contrast other melodies against it using rules proposed during this era. Along with counterpoint, improvisation was an important prerequisite for every musician.[7]

Listen for the improvisatory nature of the toccata at the beginning and the fugal counterpoint following in J. S. Bach's (1685-1750) Toccata and Fugue in D minor (BWV 565).

Time	Description
0:01	Introduction to a famous theme
0:19	Tension is created through dissonance, then resolved through briefly held major chord
0:29	Faster ideas begin being explored in the toccata, quickly migrating from one to the next, interrupted by held chords that define a cadence
2:26	Fugue begins. The melody of the fugue, called the subject, is created by a note followed quickly by a note below, back to the higher repeated note, and down again. Listen for the melody line created in the lower, non-repeated pitch. You will be able to hear this idea repeated throughout.
3:20	You can hear the subject repeated clearly in the bass pedals in the lowest register
5:41	The subject appears in the upper voices, followed by the lowest voice ten seconds later
6:30	The subject appears for the last time in the middle voice
6:44	The improvisatory nature of the opening toccata returns through to the end

affects: static emotional state

crescendo: growing gradually louder

diminuendo: becoming softer in volume (of sound)

terraced dynamics: a section of music would be played at a particular volume and immediately change to another

counterpoint: literally meaning note against note; take a melody and contrast other melodies against it using rules proposed during the Baroque era

IN THEIR OWN WORDS

John J. Mortensen is a leading figure in the mastery of historic improvisation, especially of the eighteenth century. In his latest publication, *A Pianist's Guide to Historic Improvisation*, he explains Bach's skills in light of expected musical training of the time:

"I love the legends of the improvisational powers of the masters: Bach creating elaborate fugues on the spot. . . . The stories implied that these abilities were instances of inexplicable genius which we could admire in slack-jawed wonder but never emulate. But that isn't right. Bach could improvise fugues not because he was unique but because almost any properly trained keyboard player in his day could. Even mediocre talents could improvise mediocre fugues. Bach was exceptionally good at something that pretty much everyone could do at a passable level."[8]

figured bass: a bass line for an instrumentalist with numbers written above (or below) the notes; if the numbers notated were 6/4, the musician would play the given note along with a 6th and a 4th above in order to realize the harmony

As previously hinted in Ch. 6, **figured bass** was becoming a part of music at the end of the Renaissance. Its influence only grew during the Baroque. As seen in Fig. 7.16, a bass line was written for an instrumentalist with numbers above the notes. If the numbers notated were 6/4, for example, the musician would play the given note along with a 6th and a 4th above in order to realize the harmony.

As in most eras, musicians faced societal challenges. Many musicians were reliant on patronage from cities, churches, and royals.[9] To this end, composers were not always free to choose their own styles, topics, or how much work they performed. Unlike current musical productions that can run for decades, the music of the Baroque was not as popular over time. Most works were not performed longer than a few years, meaning composers had to keep composing for multiple occasions.[10] The views of society on the importance of music and musicians seems to be a consistently swinging pendulum. One generation valued the arts greatly only to be replaced by a non-empathetic populace.

> ### IN THEIR OWN WORDS
>
> John Locke (1632-1704) downplays the value of music in education in *Some Thoughts Concerning Education*.
>
> "Musick is thought to have some affinity with dancing, and a good hand upon some instruments is by many people mightily valued. But it wastes so much of a young man's time to gain but a moderate skill in it; and engages often in such odd company, that many think it much better spared: and I have amongst men of parts and business so seldom heard any one commended or esteemed for having an excellency in musick, that amongst all those things that ever came into the list of accomplishments, I think I may give it the last place."[11]

Composers and Forms

The Italian composer Claudio Monteverdi (see Fig. 7.17), maestro di cappella at St. Mark's in Venice (see Fig. 6.23), was able to bridge the gap between the Renaissance and the Baroque.[12] In his *Vespers of 1610*, he combined the reverent sound of the Renaissance with the embellished sound of the Baroque. Monteverdi grounded his musical style in the Platonic idea (see Ch. 2) that words come before sounds and rhythm.[13]

Hear the connective sounds from what was previously heard in the Renaissance with *stile antico* and the new *stile moderno*. Listen to Track 1.

Chapter 7: The Baroque Era   177

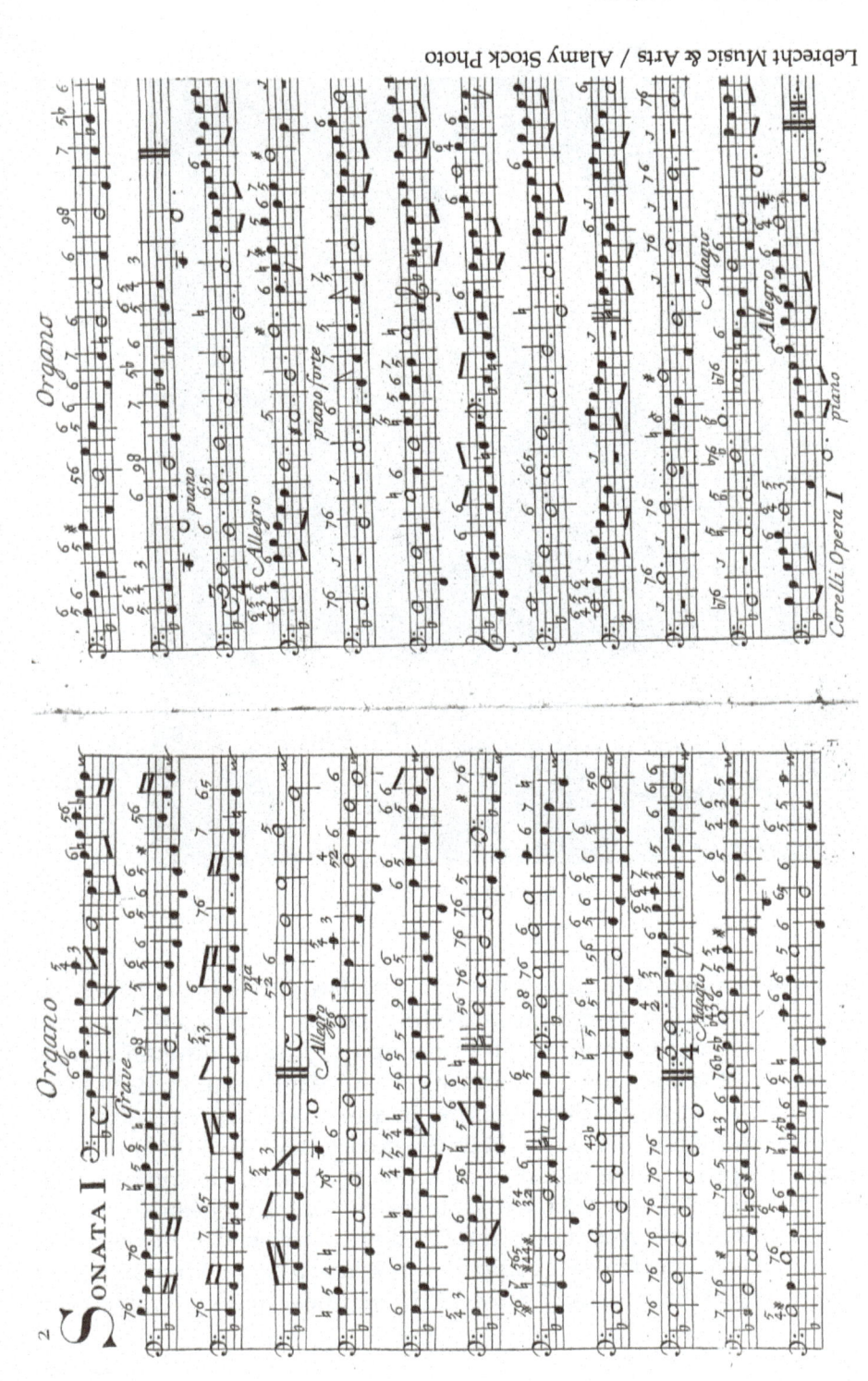

Fig. 7.16. Music from Arcangelo Corelli (1653–1713) with figured bass.

Fig. 7.17. Claudio Monteverdi (1567-1643).

Perhaps the most important figure of the musical Baroque, Johann Sebastian Bach (see Fig. 7.18) was a German composer who is now widely regarded as one of the greatest in history. Although Bach was employed as a Lutheran church musician, he was best known in his lifetime as an excellent organist. Bach's genius was not recognized in his own lifetime. It was not until a revival of his works during the Romantic period by Felix Mendelssohn (1809-1847) that his work was given its place in the canon of musical composers. He composed in each common genre except for opera, with solo instrumental, orchestral, and vocal works.[14] One of his most important contributions to music was his work on the **fugue**. A fugue is a contrapuntal composition where a subject (main theme) is stated in one musical line and then passed to other lines. To the untrained ear,

Chapter 7: The Baroque Era   179

Fig. 7.18. Johann Sebastian Bach (1685-1750).

passion: a musical depiction of the story of Christ's crucifixion with orchestra, chorus, and soloists

a fugue may sound like an elaborate piece similar to a round, but it is indeed far more complex. Bach wrote two volumes called *Well-Tempered Clavier*, which includes 24 preludes and fugues in every major and minor key. These stand as a premier example of the form.

Listen to one of the more recognizable fugues ("Fugue No. 2 in C minor" from *WTC I*) and hear the subject being passed from one part to others.

Another important form that developed in the Baroque is that of the **passion**. Revolving around the events of Holy Week, the passion musically depicts the story of Christ's crucifixion with orchestra, chorus, and soloists. Keeping his ideas consistent with the Protestant Reformation, the language of the vernacular was used instead of Latin to communicate the truth of Scripture. Congregants were now able to embrace truth from music in their own language, making a worship experience much easier.

Listen to the hauntingly beautiful alto aria "Erbarme dich" from Bach's *St. Matthew Passion*.

Also important to Bach was the form of the cantata. The Lutheran cantata was designed for use in church services. It was based upon Biblical, liturgical, and chorale texts with orchestral, vocal, and recitative arias to reinforce the Gospel reading.[14]

Listen to an excerpt from Cantata No. 140, Wachet auf, ruft uns die Stimme.

J. S. Bach was not regarded as the premier composer of the Baroque. In Germany, this distinction would be awarded to Heinrich Schütz (1585-1672).[15] His work with madrigals, motets, requiems, passions, and other secular works was able to elevate the Germanic music scene to primary importance.

DID YOU KNOW?

At the end of compositions, Bach would write the initials SDG. This was short for the Latin phrase, *Soli Deo Gloria*, which is translated, "For the glory of God alone." Bach wanted little recognition for his compositions and dedicated them to his Creator. He exemplifies the Scripture of I Cor 10:31 which states, "So, whether you eat or drink, or whatever you do, do all to the glory of God."

Listen to an example of Schütz's choral work, So fahr ich hin zu Jesu Christ.

In England, George Frideric Handel found great success with the English oratorio. (For more on his operas, see Theatre, this Ch.) Like the passion, the oratorio was a sacred (usually) form, although not limited to the story of Christ's crucifixion. Oratorio acted as a type of religious opera, but without the costumes and dramatic action on the stage.[16] Topics for the oratorio ranged from *Samson* to *Messiah*, the latter of which contains the famed "Hallelujah Chorus" (see Ch. 1). In this excerpt from Handel's *Israel in Egypt*, the music uses the theme of the Egyptian plagues mixed with word painting and the new embellishments of the Baroque.

Listen for the word painting as the chorus sings, "He Gave Them Hailstones for Rain."

Time	Description
0:01	Lightly scored introduction of woodwinds, high strings, and keyboard.
0:30	Brass (trumpets and trombones) and timpani enter, emphasizing the text "He gave them hail-stones for rain" sung by the first choir, and echoed by the second choir, providing a sense of darkness and power, creating the pounding of the hailstones.
0:38	As the second choir ends the opening phrase with "rain", the first choir sings the next line, "Fire, mingled with the hail." The same moment they sing "hail" the second choir sings this phrase, "Fire, mingled with hail." As it is sung back and forth between the two choirs, "hail" and "fire" are literally being sung at the same time, as they are "mingled" together in this example of text painting.
0:43	The melody wanders up and down on the line, "Ran a long upon the ground" and is again shared between the two choirs.
1:25	As the basses sing a long melodic line on the word "rain" the rest of the choir interjects with the words "hail" and "fire."
1:53	The musical ideas here are similar to the introduction; however, the presence of the brass and timpani change the texture of the scoring to sound much more powerful and triumphant.

cantata: a medium-length narrative piece of music for voices with instrumental accompaniment typically with solos, chorus, and orchestra. A chamber cantata often uses one soloist and basso continuo on a secular topic. Larger works were often sacred and performed in church buildings

requiem: a mass for the dead, a funeral mass

Musical education in Italy often came from an unlikely source. *Oespedali* were institutions that took care of orphaned girls and provided a quality musical education. Antonio Vivaldi (see Fig. 7.19) was the full-time maestro di cappella at one of these institutions and wrote music to suit their needs.[17] Other composers such as Monteverdi took part in the education of these students as well.[18] Although he was a composer that worked in many Baroque forms, Vivaldi was known best for his work with **concertos**. The following are the types of concertos within the Baroque: solo concerto (one instrument playing in opposition to a large ensemble), concerto grosso (small ensemble in opposition to a large ensemble), and orchestral concerto.[19]

Instrumental Development in the Baroque

Orchestras during the Baroque became more common as the development and manufacturing of stringed instruments grew. Being led by such craftsmen as Antonio Stradivari, violin making saw an increase in quality and productivity (see Fig. 7.20). His violins are still sought today, fetching prices well in excess of several million dollars for a single instrument. Contemporary piano makers still seek out the forests in the Italian Alps from which he harvested the wood for his instruments.

concerto: an instrumental ensemble featuring one or more soloists in opposition to a large ensemble: solo concerto (one soloist playing in opposition to a large ensemble), concerto grosso (small ensemble in opposition to large ensemble

Fig. 7.19. Antonio Vivaldi (1648-1741).

<small>**hestra:** large rumental emble with a e of stringed ruments</small>

The French were the first to form large stringed instrument ensembles, which became the basis for the modern **orchestra**. The present-day idea of a conductor with a baton standing in front of an ensemble directing their play and singing would be foreign to a Baroque musician. In order to keep everyone together, the concertmaster would often bring everyone in together and assure everyone cut off at the precise moment. In order to further aid synchronicity within the ensemble, the famed Baroque composer Jean Baptiste Lully (1632-1687) was recorded as beating a long stick on the ground so the musicians could hear the beat. However, while conducting an ensemble, he inadvertently hit his foot and it became infected. Lully would eventually succumb to his injury. A modern baton would soon take the place in the hands of the conductor.

The piano as it is known today did not exist in the early Baroque. Rather, keyboard works were generally written for the clavichord (see Fig. 7.21) and

Chapter 7: The Baroque Era   183

Fig. 7.20. Antonio Stradivari (1644–1737).

harpsichord (see Fig. 7.22) along with a few other keyboard instruments such as the clavicytherium. Pieces written for these were quasi-improvisational, suites, or theme and variations.[20] Emphasis on these compositions was not on dynamic range as these instruments were only capable of playing one volume. Toward the end of the Baroque, Bartolomeo Cristofori (1655–1731) developed several instruments that eventually became what he called the **fortepiano**.[21] It was so named because of its capability of playing both loud (*forte*) and soft (*piano*). After the Baroque, the fortepiano overtook other keyboard instruments in popularity.[22] Composers would favor the fortepiano and eventually the modern day piano due to its flexibility of sound and volume and its stability of holding pitch.

fortepiano: an early form of the modern piano, differing from similar keyboard instruments in that the force of the hand playing altered the volume of the notes played

Fig. 7.21. Clavichord of the Baroque era.

Fig. 7.22. Harpsichord of the late seventeenth century.

Theatre

By definition, opera as completely *sung drama*, took its position in the Baroque era as an alternative art form to completely *spoken drama*. The most lavish Baroque opera houses were capable of sets and stage machinery that were able to win over theatre-loving audiences. During Monteverdi's lengthy career as an opera composer, he experienced the transition from private, court-supported operas to the public performances in newly constructed theatres. The first opera house, Teatro San Cassiano opened in 1637 in Venice. This had significant implications because opera became the servant to a paying public and from that time on, had to respond to the tastes of the audience. Although there were still significant donations by wealthy patrons, the income from subscriptions and general ticket sales established a financial model that continues today. From Monteverdi's first opera *L'Orfeo*, privately funded by the nobility in Mantua, Italy in 1607, to his last opera, *L'incoronazione di Poppea*, publicly produced in Venice in 1643, the changing social structure foreshadowed the age of European revolutions more than a century before they occurred. Thus, rather than being a reflection of society, art—in this case, opera—was a harbinger of the future.

Teatro San Cassiano was the first of nine public opera houses in Venice built by the end of the seventeenth century. Finding great success there, theatre companies toured to other cities, which in turn spurred the construction of permanent opera houses in Naples, Florence, Paris, Vienna, and additional urban centers throughout Europe (see Fig. 7.23). Thus, the establishment of Italian opera as a

Fig. 7.23. Teatro di San Carlo, the oldest opera house with continuous performances since its construction, 1737, Naples, Italy.

leader in the genre became a hallmark of the Baroque era, which then became a continuing trend.

Opera seria

Opera grew quickly during the seventeenth century. In addition to steady and generous financial support, it required many players in a complicated system to succeed. Opera is often the most expensive and extravagant art form both then and now. Highly skilled professionals included the **impresario**, or producer, the composer, the librettist who wrote the **libretto**, or words, for all the music, costume designers, set designers who were expected to create spectacular stage effects, and, finally, the singers themselves. The best singers became stars, with **divas** and **prima donnas** making their fortune and fame on the opera stage. During the seventeenth century, the story was not as important as the singers, with audiences returning night after night to hear them.

In this style of opera, the lead male singer was likely a **castrato**, a male who had been castrated before puberty in order to retain a high voice and develop a powerful vocal range. Usually this was a decision made by the family who hoped for their son's success and financial gain. It often came at the recommendation of a singing master who found promise in the young boy's voice. Schools developed for castrati especially in Rome, where they found employment both in opera and in church service. In early opera productions there, castrati sang the role of female characters because the Church prohibited men and women together on the stage. In Venice and other cities, however, the castrati sang primarily male roles, for there was no such restriction. At its height of popularity, it is believed that 4,000 boys were castrated in one year. In the nineteenth century the practice became unpopular and eventually illegal (1861). In 1878, the Roman Catholic church prohibited the hiring of any new castrati.

impresario: opera producer

libretto: the text of an opera or other long vocal work

divas: famous opera singers who made their fortunes on stage; see prima donna

prima donna: famous opera singer who made her fortune on stage; divas

castrato: a male who had been castrated before puberty in order to retain a high voice and develop a powerful vocal range

DID YOU KNOW?

Scripture talks about the God-created body and how Christians should steward it as a gift. I Cor 6:19-20 states, "Your body is a temple of the Holy Spirit within you…you are not your own, for you were bought with a price. So glorify God in your body." This passage makes clear that the Spirit dwells within man and that man's body is thus a temple for that holy dwelling, just as God dwelt within the Holy of Holies of the temple. Furthermore, the reminder that "you are not your own," indicates that Christians bear a great responsibility to steward the body that ultimately belongs to God because He has purchased it at great price with His own blood.

> The practice of castration can be viewed as a voluntary mutilation of the human body. The few instances where the practice of self-mutilation is mentioned in the Bible are negative in connotation. They are either related to pagan practices (Lev 19:28, I Kgs 18:28) or to demon possession (Mk 5:5). Much more emphasis in Scripture concerns the positive qualities of the human body and its care. Christians must be content with their God-given bodies and take care of their health with sobriety and in sanctification. In this way they may glorify God in their physicality.

This led to a codification of opera during the Baroque era. Some characteristics became so popular and expected that a sub-genre emphasizing these features, **opera seria**, developed and spread throughout Europe. *Opera seria*, or "serious opera," focused on stories from either Greek mythology or Roman history. Monteverdi's first and last operas illustrate this well. *L'Orfeo* drew from the story of the Greek demi-god Orpheus (Ch. 2), and his journey to the underworld to bring his dead bride, Eurydice, back to the land of the living. Orpheus's musical powers as an integral part of the story made this tale a natural fit for opera as an entirely sung performance. *L'incoronazione di Poppea* related the story of Roman Caesar Nero's illicit relationship with Poppea to her cunning rise to power. Like Greek drama, these stories would have been well known to audiences prior to attending a performance. *Opera seria* focused on large and fantastical characters, such as kings and gods, which were distant and often unrelatable. They represented lofty themes, such as loyalty, ambition, or love.

The popularity of the singing, however, pushed the familiar stories into the background, dropping an emphasis on action and, instead, centering on the singer's solo performance. A scene typically began with a recitative followed by an aria, and then the exit of the singer to conclude the scene. Segments in this format would follow in rapid succession, with the audience craving the virtuosic singing, especially the expected improvisatory ornamentation. A typical aria was in a form known as **da capo**. *Capo* in Italian means "head;" thus it is a form that requires the singer to return to the "head" or top of the aria to sing the first half of it again. During the second time through, the diva would display her skill in ornamentation, giving the audience the equivalent of musical fireworks, and which would draw enthusiastic applause. Thus, this type of scene and song structure, while showcasing the singers' virtuosity, made the dramatic action static.

Handel's Operas

One of the most influential of all Baroque composers, Handel took the conventions of *opera seria* well into the eighteenth century. He played a prominent role

---

opera seria: "serious opera" focused on stories from either Greek mythology or Roman history

da capo: typical aria form; *capo* in Italian means "head;" thus, is a form that requires the singer to return to the "head" or top of the aria to sing the first half of it again

in bringing the Italian art form to the London stage. Born and raised in Germany, Handel was exposed to Italian opera as a youth by playing violin in an opera house orchestra. At nineteen, he wrote his first opera, in Italian, and it garnered great success. Desiring to hone his skills, he traveled to Italy to learn directly from the masters. He eventually found opportunities in London and gained the lifelong support of the British royalty. From 1711 to 1741, a span of thirty years, Handel wrote Italian operas for the British public. Some of them were masterpieces and others were failures. He worked diligently to make opera a success in a country that had been enamored with Shakespearean drama for more than a century. Since listening to a completely sung drama in a foreign language was not an easy sell, Handel was forced to turn to another direction, the English oratorio, where he found a much more enthusiastic public awaiting him.

Handel's best operas contained all the conventions of *opera seria*. Based on Roman history, *Giulio Cesare in Egitto* (1724), highlights Julius Caesar's escapades in Egypt as he pursued his enemy Pompeo and then became entangled in a love affair with Cleopatra. Da capo arias abounded, providing ample opportunities for the divas and castrati to provide spectacular displays of vocal expertise. Handel created more dramatic interest by employing a greater number of principal singers and increased interaction among characters, sometimes even interrupting an aria. In Cleopatra's aria, "V'adoro pupille," for example, Cesare is so captivated by her singing that he interjects an exclamation right before her repeat of the opening section, an act that breaks with convention, but heightens the drama.

Listen to Cleopatra's aria, "V'adoro pupille." Listen here for Cesare's insertion and Cleopatra's return to the A section.

Section	Character	Italian	English
A 0:01	Cleopatra	V'adoro pupille, Saete d'Amore, Le vostre faville Son grate nel sen;	I adore you, pupils, Cupid's darts. Your sparks Are welcome to the heart.
B 1:46	Cleopatra	Pietose vi brama Il mesto mio core, Ch'ogn'ora vi chiama L'amato suo ben. (Da capo)	Pitiable, for longs My gloomy heart, Which every hour calls you, Its beloved treasure.
0:01	Cesare (insertion)	Non ha in cielo in Tonante melodia, Che pareggi un si bel canto.	Jupiter in heaven has no melody That matches such beautiful song.
A 0:16	Cleopatra	V'adoro pupille. . . . (libretto by Nicola Haym)	I adore you, pupils. . . . (tr. J. Peter Burkholder)[23]

> **DID YOU KNOW?**
>
> Cleopatra refers to Cesare as "pupils." This is a poetic device called synecdoche whereby a part of something represents the whole. This literary technique is used in Scripture, where, for example, "soul" is used to represent the whole of a person (Ps 7:1-2), both body and soul. Cleopatra's mention of only the pupils (not even the entire eye!) represents the entirety of Julius Caesar. The focus on his pupils shows a special emphasis, however, on her power to captivate his gaze. She is making full eye contact with him and holding him in her command as she sings her seductive aria.

Opera in Other Languages

Handel did not attempt vocal works in English until he gained success with the English oratorio (see Music, this Ch.). The popularity of Shakespeare made any other English dramatic production a hard act to follow. Thus, it is rather difficult to find a strong example of English opera. However, a modest opera created for a girl's boarding school production has made its fame by being among the very few in the Baroque period. Henry Purcell (1659-1695), wrote this piece with only four main roles and a running time of about one hour. Yet, because of its rarity, *Dido and Aeneas* has become the most famous example of Baroque English opera. Like *opera seria*, its tale is of Roman writer Virgil's Queen Dido of Carthage and her lover, Aeneas (see Fig. 7.24.). When Aeneas abandons her for his greater call to establish the foundations of Rome, she takes her own life, singing one of the most beautiful laments in opera. This is not a da capo aria, but one where organization and structure are achieved with a repeated descending bass pattern known as a ground bass. It was a characteristic pattern for laments, and its presence reinforced the idea of intense grief.

Listen to Dido's When I am Laid in Earth and pay attention to the movement in the lowest notes.

Like the English, the French public (primarily the literary elite), loved spoken drama in their own language, particularly tragedy. For French opera to compete with this art form as well as with the popularity of ballet entertainment would take a genius who could combine the best of drama, dance, and music. The gifted Lully (see Music, this Ch.) was able to develop a style of opera that met all these demands. A central scene of most acts was a spectacular display of dance, drama, singing, and set, known as the divertissement (see Fig. 7.25). It was unique to French opera and became a cherished part of the form. Thus, French opera grew prolifically under Louis XIV. The powerful French monarch used this genre as political propaganda to intensify his prestige and influence. The subjects of most French operas contained clear allusions to the power of Louis,

Fig. 7.24. *Aeneas Departs from Carthage*, enamel painting of Aeneid (Bk IV), ca. 1530–1535, Master of the Aeneid, Metropolitan Museum of Art, NY.

also known as The Sun King, famous for his saying, "L'état, c'est moi," or "I am the State." While containing subjects from ancient mythology and history like Italian opera did, the French vocal style did not develop into the formulaic Italian recitative with da capo aria. Rather, in keeping with the taste for the French language, the singing blended elements of both recitative and aria into a more continuous delivery and was better able to imitate the natural inflection and cadence of the French language.

Fig. 7.25. Theatrical divertissement offered at a gala evening party (although this painting does not depict the theatrical stage, it does show the elements of the *divertissement* minus the dance), ca. eighteenth century, attributed to Gabriel de Saint-Aubin, Metropolitan Museum of Art, NY.

Study Questions

1. What are the characteristics of the counter-reformation?
2. Why is there an eventual shift in painting from religious imagery to an emphasis on portraiture, genre scenes, and still lifes?
3. In what ways did the Renaissance affect the Baroque Era?
4. What were the goals of the earliest composers of opera and how was opera different from any other musical styles that came before it?
5. What were common characteristics of Baroque music?
6. What is an oratorio and how did it compare to opera?

Notes

1. Kurt Vonnegut, Conversations with Kurt Vonnegut, 91.
2. David Hume, *Enquiry Concerning Human Understanding*, 165.
3. Ruskin, 92.
4. Legend has it that when a princess during the 17th or 18th centuries heard that peasants had no bread to eat, she uttered, "Let them eat cake." The phrase, which

is often used to show how elites are both out of touch with common life and are uncaring about those whom they consider beneath them, is often attributed to Antoinette. However, no record exists of her having said it.
5. Stolba, 3rd ed., 229.
6. Burkholder, 7th ed., 296.
7. Wold, 83.
8. Mortensen, 1-2.
9. Burkholder, 7th ed., 291.
10. Burkholder, 7th ed., 418.
11. Locke, 174.
12. Burkholder, 7th ed., 297.
13. Stolba, 3rd ed., 244.
14. Wold, 105.
15. Stolba, 3rd ed., 265.
16. Wold, 74.
17. Wold, 102.
18. Mark, 37-38.
19. Burkholder, 7th ed., 399.
20. Stolba, 280.
21. Stolba, 315.
22. Wold, 83.
23. Burkholder, 7th ed., 842.

8 Enlightenment
The Age of Reason

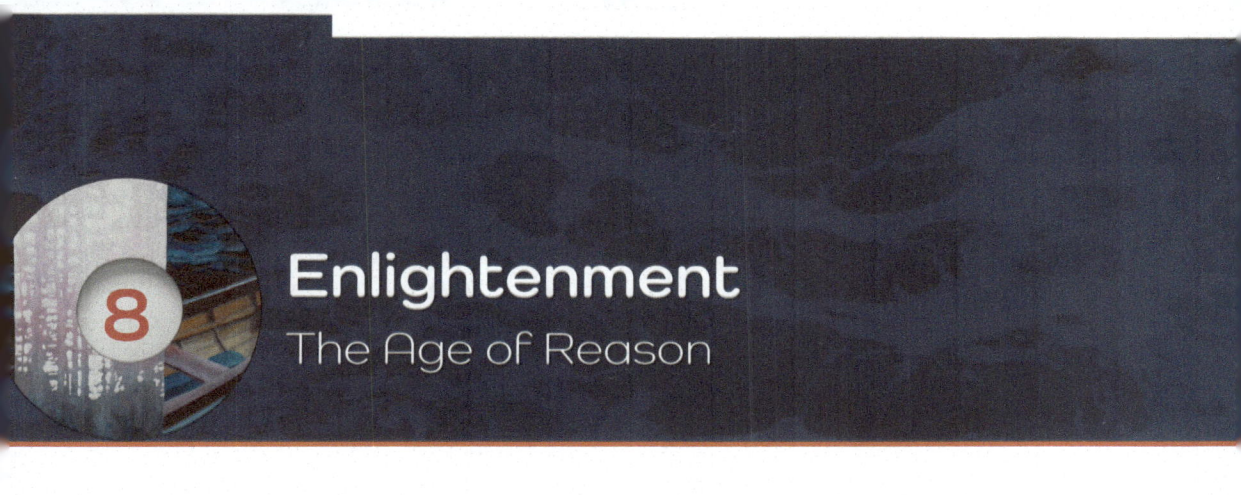

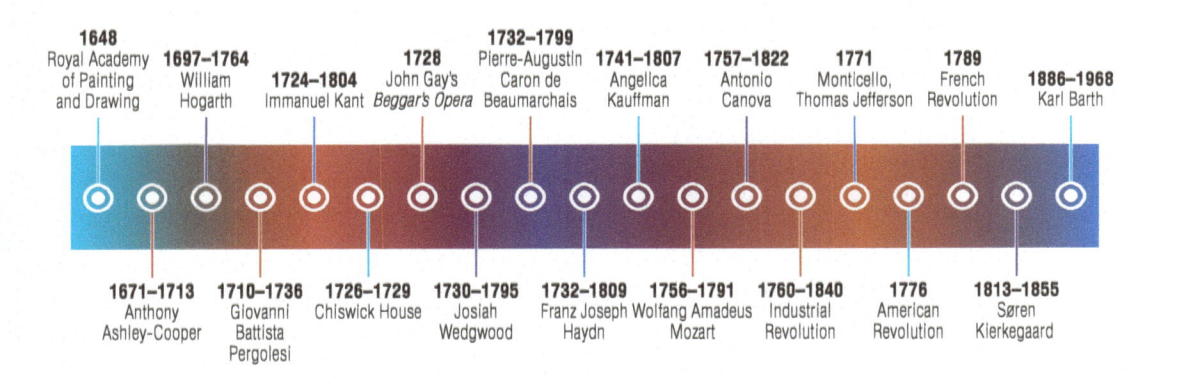

1648 Royal Academy of Painting and Drawing
1697–1764 William Hogarth
1724–1804 Immanuel Kant
1728 John Gay's *Beggar's Opera*
1732–1799 Pierre-Augustin Caron de Beaumarchais
1741–1807 Angelica Kauffman
1757–1822 Antonio Canova
1771 Monticello, Thomas Jefferson
1789 French Revolution
1886–1968 Karl Barth

1671–1713 Anthony Ashley-Cooper
1710–1736 Giovanni Battista Pergolesi
1726–1729 Chiswick House
1730–1795 Josiah Wedgwood
1732–1809 Franz Joseph Haydn
1756–1791 Wolfgang Amadeus Mozart
1760–1840 Industrial Revolution
1776 American Revolution
1813–1855 Søren Kierkegaard

Philosophy

It could be argued that what the Renaissance was to art, the Enlightenment was to philosophy. Against the backdrop of the growing successes of the sciences and with the newly developed skepticism of Christianity's ability to do what it claimed it could, Enlightenment era thinkers began to look to philosophy, with optimism, as that which could improve the human condition. Whereas scriptural depictions of God and His relationship to the world promised salvation, happiness, and a future, the rise of religious wars, the corruption of the Catholic church, and social problems had led to the search elsewhere for answers to the difficulties and ambiguities of human life.

By concentrating on the power of philosophy, the Enlightenment had a few overarching characteristics, despite the diversity of the key thinkers during the era. First, as was previously mentioned, was the hopefulness that humans could progress in its fight against injustice, suffering, and conflict by the power of its own thought. Second was the attempt to find solutions to problems without recourse to religious tradition, rituals, or scriptures. Thus, the Bible was

Fig. 8.1. Anthony Ashley-Cooper—3rd Earl of Shaftsbury, engraving from *Characteristicks of Men, Manners, Opinions, Times*, ca. 1702-1711, Simon Gribelin.

no longer a trusted source of truth, but was something that should only be used as a last resort. Third, was the belief that proper methodology could give one certainty at arriving at the truth. This view could already be seen in Descartes, the century prior, but found its zenith in the many Enlightenment philosophers who came to view humans as neutral observers who could come to objective truth by looking at the world and using their unhindered reason. Thus, the common strain in all of these characteristics was the autonomy of human thinking. It was this belief that would complete the process of art distancing itself from religion (especially Christianity) that had begun during the Renaissance.

Although the Enlightenment produced many significant philosophers, especially in Britain, France, and Germany, two thinkers deserve mention because of their influence on art and the field of aesthetics. The first is Anthony Ashley-Cooper (1671-1713; Fig. 8.1),[1] who is typically known by his title as the Third Earl of Shaftsbury. As a scholar, he was lesser known, but more influential than his popularity would suggest. As a nobleman, Shaftsbury was afforded a few luxuries that influenced his thinking. He had John Locke (1632-1704; Fig. 8.2), the famous British empiricist, as his tutor. Locke believed that humans were born as a *tabula rasa*, or blank slate, and all that one knew came from experiencing the world through one's senses.[2] Shaftsbury, though intrigued by his predecessor's emphasis on experience, believed that all people must have innate ideas, or it would be difficult to make sense of commonalities of various individual's perception of beauty. Furthermore, having access to travel and accounts of the New World, Shaftsbury was intrigued by the wildness of frontier life. Europe, in its history of glorifying the idea of "civilization," often saw cities as beautiful and the untamed wilderness as chaos to be subdued. Yet, Shaftsbury's investigation of the beauty of the uncontrolled lands of the Colonies would set off a trend that would culminate in Romanticism, which, as will be explained in the next chapter, stressed emotions, the individual, and the splendor of nature.

Fig. 8.2. John Locke, 1697, Godfrey Kneller, The Winter Palace, St. Petersburg.

Shaftsbury's influence on Kant (Fig. 8.3) was significant as the latter rose to prominence, becoming the most influential Enlightenment philosopher. Kant worked in various areas of philosophy, but three significant areas, mirroring three of his major works, were epistemology, or theory of knowledge, ethics, and aesthetics. For Kant, one could separate the world into things as they are in themselves, or the noumena, and how those things appear to people, or the phenomena. Kant believed that humans only dealt with appearances and could not actually know what things were like in themselves. The danger with this, was that in placing divinity, soul, and the afterlife in the noumena, the German philosopher believed one could not have knowledge of God. This challenge would eventually be taken up by Søren Kierkegaard (1813-1855), the father of existential philosophy, and Karl Barth (1886-1968), arguably the most important Protestant theologian of the twentieth century. Barth noticed, as had been historically recognized, that even if one could not pierce the mystery of God,

noumena: the realm of things in themselves

phenomena: the realm of things as they appear to humans

Fig. 8.3. Immanuel Kant, Prussian Philosopher, ca. 1790, unknown artist.

this did not mean that God could not come and manifest Himself to humans (John 1:1-18). Thus, his answer to Kant was to argue that the noumenal could appear to His people through revelation.

More *apropos* to this book was the manner in which Kant affected the trajectory of the arts. Recognizing, in line with influence from Shaftsbury, that beauty is perceived by most as having intrinsic value, Kant was reluctant to term anything as beautiful if one simply was attracted to it because it was useful or because they wanted to possess it. Thus, he differentiated what is "agreeable," which one desires because it gives them pleasure, and the beautiful.[3] That which is agreeable includes one's own interest because the goal is to possess that which gives them pleasure. Different things can be agreeable to different people because different things give different people pleasure. Thus, where one person takes pleasure in coffee and another abhors it, the agreeable is going to be subjective and individual. Beauty, however, requires one to be "disinterested," wanting only to continue the experience of the beautiful because it is beautiful. Moreover, it is universal, because when one claims that something possesses beauty, they are, in essence, prescribing that all people should react similarly.

Thus, Kant, along with Shaftsbury, sets the foundation for the idea of **rapture**, or intense pleasure or awe one experiences in the presence of something that possesses beauty, which became significant during Romanticism. This was also important because, eventually, Kant's idea of disinterest was used to argue that beauty must be for the sake of beauty and, therefore, art must be for the sake of art. As this occurred, some artists used this as an excuse to assert autonomy and treat art as an end in and of itself. Scripturally, all humans, as creatures, are to treat every aspect of their lives under the authority of the Creator.

ture: intense asure or awe experiences the presence something t possesses uty

In Their Own Words

"For as God is infinitely the greatest Being, so he is allowed to be infinitely the most beautiful and excellent: and all the beauty to be found throughout the whole creation, is but the reflection of the diffused beams of that Being who hath an infinite fulness of brightness and glory."[4]
—Jonathan Edwards

As was noted above, Kant followed Shaftsbury in thinking that beauty had commonality because something undergirded all beauty. However, they differed on the foundation. Shaftsbury held a view, which was echoed by Jonathan Edwards[5] (most likely because Edwards read books by Shaftsbury's tutor, Locke), that God was the ultimate beauty and all other beautiful things were mere reflections or representations of that beauty. Shaftsbury was **pantheistic**, seeing everything as being part of God and essentially equating nature with the divine. Edwards, however, developed a similar view, but did so with a scriptural view of the Trinitarian God who was known in Jesus Christ. Kant, however, saw the commonality and universality of beauty not in the object (i.e., God), but in the subject (i.e., the observer). He thought that all people had minds that were structured the same way so that they frequently took pleasure in the same types of things. Thus, even though people could vary in the pleasure they took from something like a specific food, all people would typically take pleasure when contemplation led their mind to be at "free play."[6] In other words, he could see commonality in what people called beautiful, because their minds would tend to take gratification in the use of their imagination. However, part of this could only occur when one's faculties were developed enough to be able to contemplate in such a way as to allow free play. Thus, like Shaftsbury before him, Kant believed one's aesthetic sense could be refined and developed.

pantheistic: the view that everything in the universe is God or part of God

One last offshoot that deserves mention based on Kant's view that the pleasure one gets when their imagination is running wild is what makes something beautiful, was that he preferred those experiences that he believed were more conducive to the working of said imagination. Thus, although he respected ideas like form and symmetry as found in classical art, he had a propensity for dwelling on the wildness of nature, once again echoing Shaftsbury, because he thought it was the best at evoking the pleasure of contemplation. In this way, Kant gave philosophical underpinnings for some of the movements that will be seen not only in the Enlightenment, but also in Romanticism.

Art

As the late Baroque style culminated in the lavish style of Rococo, art and architecture in the mid-1700s was flamboyant and decorative. Frivolity reigned, most dramatically illustrated in the Palace of Versailles and Louis XIV's court life. Rococo represented the attitude and power of the bourgeois class and poorly veiled the needs for social and economic change. Eventually, the Rococo style fell out of fashion in the early 1780s as **neoclassicism** emerged. This was in part because of the ideas of the Enlightenment that placed an emphasis on reason and social progress. Concurrently, archeological excavations of Pompeii (1738) and Herculaneum (1748) uncovered architecture and objects from antiquity. Once again, European culture revived the classical ideas of Greek and Rome. In the visual arts, neoclassicism turned to austere themes, compositions, and styles, the development of which was mostly centered in France and England.

neoclassism: revival of classical style in arts, architecture, music, referring to the movement of eighteenth century

Architecture and Sculpture

Architecture of the eighteenth century transitioned from an ornamental style to neoclassical ideas of proportion. The Chiswick House in London (Fig. 8.4) is an elegant example of neoclassical architecture, including its grounds and gardens. Designed by Richard Boyle (1694-1753), it rejected the showy Rococo approach for simpler, symmetrical designs based on the classical architecture of Italy. The Chiswick House includes the classical architectural elements of columns, a dome, pediments, and porches in the plan. Clean, simple lines contrast the theatrics of Baroque and Rococo.

Neoclassical ideas traveled to North America as well. In addition to being the third President of the United States, Thomas Jefferson (1743-1846) was also an amateur architect. In 1769, he designed his Charlottesville, Virginia home Monticello (Fig. 8.5) based on neoclassical design principles. Jefferson was one

Fig. 8.4. Chiswick House, 1726-1729, Richard Boyle, London.

of the earliest proponents of the style in the United States, believing that art had the power to bring social progress and catalyze the public to seek education.

Because of the lack of talented artists in the United States at the time, Thomas Jefferson commissioned Jean-Antoine Houdon (1741-1828) to sculpt a statue of war-hero George Washington (1732-1799) for the Virginia General Assembly. Houdon, a Frenchman, was trained at the Royal Academy of Painting and Sculpture and at twenty years of age, won the prestigious Prix de Rome. By the mid-1780s, as Jefferson was looking for a talented artist, Houdon was the most famous neoclassical sculptor at work in France. With two assistants and Benjamin Franklin (1706-1790), Houdon traveled to Virginia to take precise measurements of Washington's body and face. Washington rejected Houdon's first bust during his Virginia visit (Fig. 8.6). Washington thought it too idealized and preferred contemporary clothing to the historical garments of ancient Greece and Rome. The final dignified, realistic statue of the war-hero and future president sits at the Rotunda of the Virginia State Capitol (Fig. 8.7). It practically captures the likeness of the revered, but nondeified, Washington in military uniform and contrapposto stance.

Neoclassical artists often reached back to history and mythology in their subject matter to serve as allegory for contemporary themes. Such was the case for sculptor Antonio Canova (1757-1822). His sculpture, *Cupid and Psyche* (Fig. 8.8), was inspired by the legend written by Latin author Apuleius (ca.124-ca.170) in the *Metamorphosis*. The various trials Psyche underwent in order to be reunited with her lover Cupid symbolized the challenges and sufferings a human must

Fig. 8.5. Monticello, 1772, Thomas Jefferson, Virginia.

Fig. 8.6. *George Washington*, plaster, ca. 1786, Jean-Antoine Houdon, National Portrait Gallery, Washington, DC.

undergo to achieve happiness. Romans 5:4 describes suffering as well. Rather than producing happiness, the apostle Paul writes that suffering produces hope; hope in the redemption of the present and the promise of eternity. Canova's depiction of Cupid and Psyche, although considered neoclassical in style, has qualities of the later movement of Romanticism in his loose figurative proportions and tender emotional qualities.

The Academy

Eighteenth century painting was ruled by established art academies. In France, the Royal Academy of Painting and Sculpture, established in 1648, became the model for many such institutions across Europe and in the Americas. It maintained a monopoly over art production in France until 1793. The academy was born out of a nationalist desire to produce talented painters and a need to fulfill the commissions of the royals. Jean-Baptiste Martin (1659-1735)

Fig. 8.7. *George Washington*, 1788-92, Jean-Antoine Houdon, State Capitol, Richmond, Virginia.

painted the meeting of the gentlemen who established the academy (Fig. 8.9). The telling scene illustrates the intellectual nature of the institution as well as those who were its doorkeepers, mainly gentlemen of the upper class.

202 Chapter 8: Enlightenment

Fig. 8.8. *Cupid and Psyche*, plaster study, 1794, Antonio Canova, Metropolitan Museum of Art, NY.

Fig. 8.9. *A meeting of the Royal Academy of Painting and Sculpture*, ca. 1712-1721, Jean-Baptiste Martin, Louvre Museum, Paris, France.

Through the academy, a hierarchy of categories in painting were classified according to the prestige of subject matter and technical difficulty. In order of rank, greatest to least, they listed: history painting, portraiture, genre painting, landscapes, and still lifes. **History painting** covered subject matter drawn from history, mythology, literature, and Scripture. It was considered complex because it required mechanical proficiency as well as the intellectual prowess to represent grand ideas through imagery. Portraiture was considered a practice of copying rather than inventing. Genre painting depicted everyday life and landscapes illustrated rural or urban topography. Still lifes rounded out the list, theoretically requiring the least amount of skill and intellectual imagination in describing inanimate objects.

Within the hierarchies of categories, values were placed on specific skills. One such focus was **design composition**, meaning how one arranges figures, backgrounds, accessories, and areas of light and shade to achieve pleasing aesthetic effect. Also valued was the degree to which an artist was able to successfully show emotion in figures through facial expression, pose, and gesture. Additionally, perspectival effects and proportion were prized. There was not a great emphasis on color, as painted brushwork was embedded and supportive of the image, but not intended to distract. Finally, oil painting was positioned over watercolor painting. Interestingly, all of these hierarchies would be subverted in subsequent eras.

Angelica Kauffman (1741-1807) was a Swiss neoclassical painter and one of the only two female founding members of the Royal Academy in London. Most women were forced to train outside of such institutions. Impressively, Kauffman primarily worked as a history painter. As a woman, she was not allowed to attend life-drawing classes that used live, nude models. To compensate, she spent time in Rome and Florence studying literature, history, and language in order to make work that was "masculine enough" to function in the history painting genre. *The Sorrows of Telemachus* (Fig. 8.10) is a history painting drawn from the French novel *The Adventures of Telemachus*, which depicted the sadness of Odysseus's son when he was shipwrecked on sorceress Calypso's island. As one might observe in the painting, Kauffman's work was criticized for feminized male bodies, which may be a result of her lack of formal training in studying the nude figure.

Mary Moser (1744-1819), the second female founder of the Royal Academy of London, focused on the traditionally feminine skill of flower painting within the still life category of the academy, although she also painted portraits and history paintings. Her skill in floral artwork (Fig. 8.11) led to a position as drawing mistress to the Royal Princess Elizabeth and several royal commissions.

---

history painting: paintings whose subject matter drew from the history, mythology, literature, and Scripture, ranked highest according to prestige and skill in the academy

design composition: how formal elements in a visual work are arranged to achieve a specific purpose

Fig. 8.10. *The Sorrow of Telemachus*, 1783, Angelica Kauffman, Metropolitan Museum of Art, NY.

Courtesy MET Museum, Bequest of Collis P. Huntington, 1900

Craft and Industry

Ceramic potters began to employ plaster molds in the process of **slip casting**, in which a specially prepared slip was poured into a mold to produce thin-walled products. This process increased the production of identical pieces and allowed for the greater circulation of affordable cups, plates, and more complex serving objects like teapots and tureens. Rather than hand-painting surfaces, craftsman mechanically applied patterns, using transfer prints to stamp images on surfaces. The ceramic wares of the period were heavily influenced by the forms, surface decoration, and function of eastern imports brought to Europe through trade routes.

English potter Josiah Wedgwood (1730-1795) formalized and pioneered the development and production of thin **earthenware** (clay that is fired to relatively low firing temperatures), in cream-colored bodies that could compete with the quality of porcelain imported from the orient and continent of the Americas. One of his greatest commissions was from Catherine II of Russia, who ordered a dinner and dessert service set for fifty guests. Wedgewood delivered with the "Frog" service (Fig. 8.12), so titled for the emblem of the frog appearing on all 952 individual pieces representing the commissioning house. Each piece boasted detailed landscape and country houses from England as requested by the royal.

The popularity of neoclassicism in the era is seen in Wedgwood's partnership with Thomas Bentley (1720-1790) to produce vases and ornamental pieces. Together, they opened a factory in 1769 appropriately named Etruria,

slip casting: a ceramic production technique in which a specially prepared slip is poured into a mold in order to produce thin-walled object

earthenware: a type of clay that is fired to relatively low firing temperatures

Fig. 8.11. *Flowers*, still life, ca. 1780, Mary Moser, Brooklyn Museum, NY.

Courtesy Brooklyn Museum, Gift of Mr. and Mrs. Daniel L. Silberberg

a nod to the Greek vases recently discovered in Etruscan tombs. With crisp, uncluttered lines, shallow relief images depicted scenes of Greek myth and antiquity. They were often copies of Roman originals, such as the black Portland vase (Fig. 8.13). Wedgwood was notably an abolitionist, supporter of the American struggle for independence, and involved in the early stages of the French Revolution.

Artist as Satirist

Certain artists, such as English William Hogarth (1697-1764), used their paintings and prints as social commentary. Hogarth acted as social critic, **satirist** (one who censures human vices through means of parody or irony, sometimes with the intent to inspire social reform), and editorial cartoonist. He made the print *Gin Lane* (Fig. 8.14) in support of the Gin Act, which aimed to reduce

satirist: one who censures human vices through mea of parody or irony, sometimes with th intent to insp social reform

Chapter 8: Enlightenment

Courtesy Birmingham Museum of Art, Gift of Mr. and Mrs. Dwight M. Beeson (The Dwight and Lucille Beeson Wedgwood Collection), 1983.7

Fig. 8.12. A platter from the Green Frog Service, depicting Ditchley Park in Oxfordshire, 1774, Josiah Wedgwood, Birmingham Museum of Art.

Courtesy MET Museum, Gift of Henry G. Marquand, 1894

Fig. 8.13. Portland Vase, ca. 1840-60, Josiah Wedgwood and Sons, Metropolitan Museum of Art, NY.

Chapter 8: Enlightenment 207

Fig. 8.14. *Gin Lane*, 1751, William Hogarth, British Museum, London.

the consumption of the strong drink. In his print, those on "Gin Lane" are drunken and inebriated. Figures are skeletal in unhealth and in the background a coffin is carried to be buried. Hogarth's social commentary warned of the dangers of alcohol and the effects of poverty.

In Their Own Words

The accompanying poem at the bottom of Hogarth's print reads:

> Gin, cursed Fiend, with Fury fraught
> Makes human Race a Prey.
> It enters by a deadly Draught
> And steals our Life away

> **IN THEIR OWN WORDS**
>
> Virtue and Truth, driv'n to Despair
> Its rage compels to fly,
> But cherishes with hellish Care
> Theft, Murder, Perjury.
>
> Damned Cup!
> That on the Vitals preys
> That liquid Fire contains,
> Which Madness to the heart conveys,
> And rolls it thro' the Veins.[7]

Music

The Classical era in music was noted for its focus on apparent simplicity, transparency, and clarity of style. The later Baroque style was seen by mid-eighteenth century audiences as heavy, cluttered, and practiced only by those who were well-educated or representative of a privileged class. It was also seen as overly burdened with affectation and artificiality. The Classical style developed as a reaction against this and used the model provided by the lighter, more egalitarian dance forms to become an expression of all that the Baroque was not.

There are many cultural threads that came together to create this more balanced and seemingly streamlined style. These include the effect of the Enlightenment on artistic decisions, the rise of the middle class, and the influence of the many revolutions of the eighteenth century. The resultant style included simpler structures, less complex melodies and harmonies, and more straightforward forms that were coupled with a greater flexibility in rhythm and mood.

Cultural Influences on Classical Music

Enlightenment: reflected a growing dependence on reason rather than emotion; that rationality would bring about a just and equitable society in which ability was more important than birth

The **Enlightenment** reflected a growing dependence on reason rather than emotion; that rationality was believed to have the power to bring about a just and equitable society in which ability was more important than birth. Thus, in the fine arts, reason and logic influenced artistic decisions. Arts, including music, exemplified this and participation in the fine arts was seen as the result of fine, cultivated, civilized, and educated minds. This rational approach to music was reflected both in the structures of music and in the types of music that were produced.

Revolutions, whether political or cultural, radically changed the relationships between classes. The French Revolution (1789) and the preceding societal pressures led to the displacement of the aristocracy as chief patron of the arts, with the more common people taking over that role. The Industrial Revolution (1760-1840) changed the economic system resulting in shifts in financial influence, again leading to the increased power of the middle class over artistic decisions. Furthermore, change in industry also encouraged the development of musical instrument technology. For instance, machinery allowed for consistent metal tubing that enabled the development of valve technology in brass instruments. Furthermore, increased mechanization heightened the production and stability of pianos, enabling them to reach a broader market.

The middle class, although wishing to mimic the culture of the aristocracy, had less leisure time for sustained musical training and so required music that could appear to be cultured and charming yet not requiring a high technical skill. Composers responded to the changes in these cultural trends by balancing between the requirements of the remaining aristocratic patronage system while also providing music for an enlightened and increasingly wealthy middle class. This can be seen in the heightened significance of dance and dance-like features in composition and the rise of public concerts, where the audience bought tickets to attend, rather than watching as a guest of an aristocratic patron.

Stylistic Features of Classical Music

Dance and Classical Music

The dance forms of the Enlightenment were elementary in structure, often based on folk melodies and dances and emphasized the regularity of the dance with which it was associated. This regularity often consisted of even musical phrases or sentences that made dance movements easy to remember and reflected the concept of alternating movements that were balanced between the right foot and the left foot. The dance steps themselves became simpler at this time and musical contrast in melody and mood delineated the different sections of the dance.

The Rise of Public Concerts

While oratorio was one response to the closing of opera theatres during religious holidays and seasons, there was also the rise of *Concerts spirituels* (initially in Paris) that were concerts with an ostensibly sacred repertoire that included more than just modified opera. They not only included vocal music, but also pieces that were instrumental in nature. These concerts proved to be highly popular, particularly with a paying, middle-class audience, whose taste for music tended to be less involved and complex than that of the aristocracy. The symphony orchestra became the basis of the instruments used in this type of concert. Over time, these performances became increasingly secular in nature, could be performed at any time of the year, and spread throughout Europe.

> **DID YOU KNOW?**
>
> Dances were important as there was a new fashion at this time for young ladies to lead healthier, more active lifestyles, of which regular dancing was a part. Balls and informal dance gatherings were also important for social interaction and courtship rituals. This led to an increased market for music for those dances and musicians to play for them. Often, with informal social dance gatherings, the music was provided by members of the family. These important social occasions were often important settings for significant events in the novels of Jane Austen.

As part of the influence of the Enlightenment on musical compositions and the spread of public concerts throughout Europe, music and musical ensembles became more organized, so that music written for an ensemble in one geographic area could also be performed in another. This can be seen in the standardization of performance ensembles, such as the symphony orchestra, the string quartet, and in solo works, such as the sonata and the concerto.

The Symphony Orchestra

The symphony orchestra became the model of the large ensemble that was ubiquitous across Europe. A composer could write a work in Vienna that could be performed with little alteration in London or Paris. Its basic instrumentation consisted of roughly half string instruments (violins, violas, cellos, and basses) with the remaining complement of woodwind instruments (flutes, oboes, later clarinets and bassoons) and some brass (French horns, trumpets). Whereas the string instruments were much as they are today, the woodwind instruments had fewer keys and were therefore more difficult to play than their contemporary counterparts. The brass instruments were little more than different lengths of metal tubing, thus limiting the notes they could play. This meant that the woodwinds and brass were used more for moments of contrast rather than consistently throughout a piece. Although most orchestras consisted of professional or semi-professional players, there were also some that consisted of talented amateurs who enjoyed playing the music, but owing to various social constraints, chose not to be professional performers.

The Solo Concerto

The solo concerto consisted of a soloist performing to the accompaniment of a symphony orchestra. Advancing instrument technology increased the reliability and facility of an expanding number of instruments that enabled virtuoso performers to play more difficult pieces. The existence of the symphony orchestra allowed composers to create works that showcased an instrument (or a famous performer on that instrument) knowing that there would be a predictable ensemble to accompany the soloist. Most often, composers would write concertos either for themselves to play, as a commission from a famous virtuoso, or at the request of a friend.

The String Quartet

The string quartet was a versatile and small ensemble that consisted of two violins, a viola, and a cello. This company, more than any other, represented the egalitarianism of the Classical era; it combined the individual efforts of talented musicians of any class, who had to work together empathetically to produce an integrated work of art. In a string quartet, there is no absolute leader, but all members contribute to the way in which the music is performed (see Fig. 8.16). Strings quartets could, and often did, bring together diverse members, as aristocracy would play with professional musicians or members of the middle class on terms of musical equality. Such an ensemble also allowed proficient amateur players the opportunity to participate in music-making of high quality without having to gather together an entire orchestra.

The Solo Sonata

The solo sonata was performed either on the piano alone or by a solo instrument accompanied by the piano. This was the most personal music of the era as it was best suited for performance in the home (or smaller public venues) and required the fewest number of players. This was a genre ideally suited to the middle-class ideals of the cultivated amateur that played music for personal enjoyment and not for the entertainment of the aristocracy.

Songs

Songs were also popular. Some were based on opera arias, but many were based on folk music that had been arranged for performance with piano and one or two singers. These, like the string quartet, the sonata, and other similar groupings of instruments, allowed the middle class to participate in the luxuries of the aristocracy, providing a variety of level of repertoire, as well as the simplified harmonies and melodies that best supported the ideals and talents of the middle-class amateur.

Opera

Opera remained a popular form of entertainment, and the taste of the middle class also influenced the emotional immediacy of the plot (libretto) by supporting the drift from the high drama of Greek and Roman myths toward comedy and satire based on the everyday occurrences of contemporary life. In these plots, the aristocracy was increasingly portrayed as intolerant, cruel, unjust, abusive, and, at times, dim-witted.

Chapter 8: Enlightenment

Joseph Haydn: The Quintessential Classical Composer

One composer who worked as both a freelance musician and, at other times in his life, under the patronage system, was Franz Joseph Haydn (1732-1809). As a young man, he carved out a living by teaching private music lessons, playing wherever he could, including during church services or at private gatherings and dances, as a valet and accompanist for another composer, and even as a coffee shop performer and street **busker**. In his spare time, he learned his craft as a composer by studying any music on which he could lay his hands. He also gained work playing for the dances and other special occasions at the court of the Emperor of Austria-Hungary. Ultimately, Haydn gained full-time employment for the Esterhazy family in 1761, when he was twenty-nine years old. He never forgot his struggles as a freelance musician and remained a servant to the Esterhazy family until he went into semi-retirement with a pension in 1790, some twenty-nine years later (although he was recalled to a part-time position after 1794). The security of his position allowed him to experiment in composition, and he is credited with the consolidation of both the symphony and the string quartet, often referred to, even in his own time, as the "Father of the Symphony" and the "Father of the String Quartet." He was even affectionately known as "Papa Haydn" (see Fig. 8.15).

Fig. 8.15. Franz Joseph Haydn, Bust, Tiergarten Park, Berlin, Germany.

busker: a person who performs music or other entertainment in the street or another public place for monetary donations

Haydn's humility as a servant despite being recognized during his own lifetime as the best and most influential composer serves as a reminder that it is possible to strive for the highest quality of skill and recognition without seeking personal glory. Certainly, as a fallen human, there were times when he struggled against the constraints placed upon him, but he responded to those constraints with good humor and a playfulness that rose above the oppression he sometimes felt and the disappointments that he faced during his life. This was expressed in his music. While there were times when his works displayed tragedy and deep melancholy, he worked his way through to find a place of balance and optimism, often displayed in joyous melodies and musical jokes.

String quartets were very similar in structure to symphonies of the Classical era. They consisted of four movements that were contrasted through structure, key, mood, and speed. The structure of the first movement was often in **sonata form**. This structure consisted of two melodies or themes (labeled A and B) that were presented in the **exposition** (changing key for the second theme), a **development** section that explored the musical possibilities of some aspect of the exposition, and a **recapitulation** that returned the piece to a restatement of the two themes, both remaining in the same key. This form was rational, gave a sense of balance and completeness, and was, in many ways, the perfect expression of the Enlightenment in music.

Haydn composed his earliest string quartets in the early 1750s when he wrote chamber works for that patron with whom he was staying, using only instruments available to him at the time: two violins, a viola, and a cello. This grouping of instruments, because of its nature as a skeleton version of an orchestra, became the standard chamber ensemble of the Classical era, and is still in use today (see Fig. 8.16). By the end of his career, Haydn had completed sixty-eight quartets.

During his time in semi-retirement, Haydn continued to write string quartets, usually published in groups of six. His final set of quartets was published in 1799 and were dedicated to the Hungarian count, Josef George Erdödy. These quartets show the inventiveness that Haydn displayed throughout his life. The so-called "Quinten" Quartet is the second quartet in this set and is named the "Quinten" or the "Fifths" because of the way he uses the interval of a fifth throughout the first movement. This interval becomes, in essence, a two-note first melody (A) that he continues to use as an accompaniment figure even when he introduces the much more melodic second theme.

sonata form: musical form consisting of two melodies or themes (labeled A and B) that are presented the exposition (changing key for the second theme), a development section that explores musical possibilities of some aspect of the exposition, and a recapitulation which returns the piece to a restatement of the two themes but they both remain in the same key

exposition: the first section of sonata form; presents the principal themes and moves from the primary to the secondary key area

development: in sonata form the middle section explores the musical possibilities of some aspect of the exposition

recapitulation: in sonata form the return to restatement of the two principal themes in the primary

Fig. 8.16. Modern string quartet in a typical arrangement.

Here are some features and time markings to watch for in listening to this string quartet. Pay close attention to the communication that is going on between the four players. They all have to know when to come in at the right time so that no one plays out of place and all need to perform their part in a way that matches all the other musicians.

Listen for the elements below in Haydn's String Quartet Op. 76, No. 2, in D Minor ("Quinten").

Time	Description
0:01	They start playing. **Exposition**. The "fifths" theme (A) is there at the very beginning in the first violin and the other players play the notes of the chord at the same time to accompany the melody. This theme is highly dramatic and emotionally raw. It is in minor.
0:08	A is repeated higher, and the musicians play softer. The second violin, viola, and cello join the 1st violin in harmony, leading to a suddenly loud unison section. This finishes out the move to the new key in preparation for the second theme (B).
0:22	Theme B. Longer melody and less tragic. It is in major. The viola, 2nd violin, then the cello play theme A under the happier theme B. Tragedy is always nearby and often re-surfaces as it does at 1:02; Life is a balance between the joyous and the disastrous, and often joy is felt to its full extent only as it is a contrast to the devastating. The exposition closes with a cello solo that is a premonition of tragedy to follow.
1:39	**The exposition is repeated**. This is standard in Classical era sonata form. This enables the audience to understand the key changes that have occurred and the importance of the two melodies in preparation for the development, where the composer is going to play around with some of the musical potential of the melodies. He invites his audience to catch the melodic ideas and to see what he makes of them.
3:16	**Development.** Try to identify which melody he uses and how. (He even has a fa se return to the recapitulation; he can't resist a joke, even with his more serious works.)
4:29	**Recapitulation**.
4:36	Notice that the second statement of the theme A is now loud (whereas in the exposition it was soft). Haydn is never static. The character of the second theme is radically changed as it is no longer in the brighter major key but has been transformed by the tragedy of the minor key.
6:17	End of the first movement.

This movement ends tragically. Throughout the rest of the quartet, Haydn moves to a more settled conclusion. In many ways, this quartet shows a man at the end of a hardworking and productive life, still creative, yet all too aware of how the tragedies and disappointments of life can add a touch of melancholy to any sweetness; salvation comes at a price. Haydn does not often allow his music to be so reflective, and his music is more often characterized by lively humor.

Once in semi-retirement, Haydn continued to write for the Esterhazy family but was free to compose for commissions and for friends. One of these friends was a virtuoso on a recently invented instrument; the keyed trumpet, which allowed the trumpet to play using all the notes available to other instruments. Haydn wrote a solo concerto for orchestra and keyed trumpet that has often delighted audiences, as it combined all of Haydn's exuberance with his creativity as he tackled the challenge of writing for a newly devised instrument.

The concerto itself displays many of the features that define the Classical era. In keeping with the Classical concerto structure, his Trumpet Concerto consists of three movements: a fast movement that uses the requisite sonata form, a slower movement that is similar to an operatic aria, and then a faster tempo for the final movement. The orchestra consists of the standard orchestral grouping of the time with a string section that consists of 12 violins, 4 violas, 4 cellos, and 3 basses, and a wind section that consists of pairs of flutes, oboes, clarinets, bassoons, horns, and natural trumpets (trumpets without keys or valves, see Fig. 8.17), with the addition of timpani. The form of the final movement is referred to as rondo-allegro, which, like the sonata form of the string quartet, uses two contrasting melodic ideas, although the two melodies alternate several times in the exposition section before the key change and the development. While maintaining the external structure of the Classical concerto,

Fig. 8.17. Natural trumpet, brass, late seventeenth century, Johann Wilhelm Haas, Metropolitan Museum of Art, NY.

Courtesy MET Museum, The Crosby Brown Collection of Musical Instruments, 1889

Haydn inserts his jocular and undying optimism in his work while, at the same time, writing to emphasize the unique qualities of the keyed trumpet.

Listen to "The Treasure of the Trumpet Repertoire."

As you listen to this work the first time, concentrate on the way Haydn writes for the trumpet. The first melody (A) consists of two phrases that are balanced, and relatively straightforward. Then Haydn incorporates his own humor. There are small parts of the melody that are repeated, which leads the audience to wonder just where the melody is going to go or if it is going to be endlessly repetitive. While the two phrases are balanced, they are not the standard eight measures, but are an unusual twelve measures long. The rhythm of this melody is bright, predictable, bouncy, and joyous. The second melody (B) is where Haydn really shows off the increased notes now available to the new instrument. The keyed trumpet can now play all the notes in the octave, just as the violin can, and Haydn demonstrates this in a lyrical melody that is also rhythmically more variable than that of the first melody (A). This second melody is more fragmented than the first, but still maintains the balance and small-scale repetitions that he used in the first. The work unfolds with many features that showcase the flexibility available to the new instrument.

Listen to Haydn Trumpet Concerto, Third Movement played on a keyed trumpet with fortepiano accompaniment.

Listen to this work and pay attention to the interplay between the violins and the solo trumpet played on a modern instrument with orchestral accompaniment.

Wolfgang Amadeus Mozart: Child of the Classical Era

Wolfgang Amadeus Mozart (1756-1791) was a composer who grew up as many of the changes of Neoclassicism were occurring. A precocious musical child, he and his sister Maria (nicknamed "Nannerl") spent most of their childhood travelling to, and performing in, the main courts and concert houses of Europe (see Fig. 8.18). Mozart's father, a composer himself, encouraged the musical skills of his son through extensive training in composition, which he received from masters in the various cities which they toured. Thus, Mozart was able to assimilate the regional styles of Europe and combine them to produce a cosmopolitan mix that exemplified the Classical style.

Mozart wrote in all the genres that were popular at that time, but he was most known in his own time as a composer of opera. Those operas that he wrote during the last few years of his life are still popular today. These include *Don Giovanni* (1787), *The Magic Flute* (1791), and *The Marriage of Figaro* (1786). Mozart's operas were able to capture and amplify, through music, the inner emotional states of his characters. For instance, Mozart captured the discontent of Leporello, the servant of Don Giovanni, in the way he pattered through his introductory aria with quick rhythm and limited pitch selection, or the self-satisfied obsequiousness of Don Basilio, a servant to the Count in *The Marriage of Figaro*, whose music slid and slithered as he described how he needed to pretend to be a fool so that he could survive in life.

Examine an aria from *Le nozze di Figaro (The Marriage of Figaro)*. First, watch this video clip to provide an introduction to the opera: Introduction to The Marriage of Figaro.

Not only did Mozart capture and honestly present the concerns of the servants in his works, but he also sympathetically portrayed other human emotions that are universal to the human condition. Such can be seen in the quiet agony of the Countess in *The Marriage of Figaro* as she recalled the loss of the love of her husband, the indignity, shame, and humiliation of having to conspire with her servants to try to bring him back to her, and the hope that she felt that it might, at last, work. While much of this could be presented in a prose monologue, it is through its amalgamation with music that the audience gains a deeper empathy with the character.

Fig. 8.18. Leopold Mozart with daughter Maria Anna (Nannerl) and young Wolfgang, print, etching and engraving, 1764, Jean-Baptiste Joseph Delafosse, Metropolitan Museum of Art, NY

Watch: Mozart: Marriage of Figaro "Dove sono."

The excerpt is from the Countess's aria, "Dove sono," where she explores the depths of her emotions as she exposes her lost love and her belief that her own love will win back the love of her husband. Mozart is able to touch the heart of his audience and enable them to feel empathy for her condition as one who has been betrayed by the one for whom she had the most affection. She seeks to redeem his love through the strength of her own, as well as through her forgiveness, even though he has done nothing to deserve her constancy.

Chapter 8: Enlightenment

Time	Description
0:00	The aria opens with the Countess asking, where is the love that they once shared? Here, the aria is slow and she sings with a very limited range, as if she had a great weight hanging on her that drags her emotions down. As she asks her question, the pitch rises slightly, as pitch does when a question is asked, and as her despair builds, but this slowly sinks away. The orchestra plays a very simple accompaniment, rather like a guitar, alternating a bass note and then a plucked chord, which is sometimes punctuated by the oboe, her melodic companion.
0:26	The oboe hauntingly echoes her melody before drooping downwards to emphasize her loneliness.
	This opening idea is repeated with new words that reinforce the idea of her lost love, yet, the orchestral accompaniment is slightly fuller, a subtle composition feature that helps to gently push the drama along, even though the melody and sentiment are relatively static.
1:00	The oboe takes the lead and the Countess falters as she reveals her despair at how all has failed.
1:11	She dips momentarily into self-pitying minor. (Mozart only uses a **minor key** a couple of times in this opera, so his choice here is very important as to how he presents this moment in the development of this character.) The minor section does not last long as she remembers the happiness she once had.
1:28	The music moves at a slightly faster pace.
1:30	The melody has a few modest upward leaps of joy, saddened by experience.
2:04	As memories are themselves a repeat of what has happened before, so Mozart repeats the opening.
2:57	He does not stay wallowing in the past for long. The Countess recalls that her love is faithful and that it may bring about a return of the Count's affections. The melody becomes faster, the range wider and rises in anticipation of success, whereas before, it fell from disappointment. As this end section (or coda) progresses, the accompaniment and the singer combine to bustle their way to the end of the aria as they build in the excitement of the commencement of the plan.

nor key: a sical key or ality in the nor mode; a od of melan-ly or pathos

Listen to this excerpt again, and this time focus on those features that are part of the Classical style. The main melody is simple and singable with a balancing of a musical question and answer that echoes her verbal question and answer (Question: "Where are those lovely moments…?" Answer: "of gentleness and pleasure gone"). The range of this melody is not too wide. The form of the aria is also straightforward, with the first section ("Where are those moments") contrasting the second section ("If everything has turned to tears and sorrow"). Mozart then returns her to the first section of the music. This form can be written simply as ABA. Mozart moves the drama along by adding what is called a **coda** (or a tail) where she moves forward with her plan. So the form can be fully written out then as ABA Coda. The orchestra that accompanies her is mostly strings, with the addition of the poignant oboe to punctuate and highlight her loneliness.

coda: tail or additional section of music to extend the length of a piece

Ultimately, the Countess's tears of rejection turn to grateful, yet sorrowing grace and forgiveness as the Count confesses his failings in his responsibilities to protect those over whom he has authority, his failings as a human, and his failings as a husband.

Theatre

Satire and Comedy

Europe in the eighteenth century was a tumultuous and dangerous time. As political unrest developed in many countries, social class structures, which had been largely unchallenged since the breakdown of the feudal system, had experienced clear and present threats to their very existence. The aristocratic classes lost their positions in several swift moves of revolution, ironically led by the American Revolution (1776) and quickly followed by its French counterpart (1789). Constitutional governments replaced centuries-old monarchies with promises of liberty, equality, brotherhood, and, perhaps most universally, a voice to be heard and a vote that would count. As seen throughout this book, the arts were quick to reflect on changes in society and even to predict coming trends. Theatre, in particular, was a fairly accurate barometer of the times with its ability to mix satire and comedy in a way that displayed the people's sentiments to all classes, especially putting them in the unavoidable view of the aristocratic audiences.

Pierre-Augustin Caron de Beaumarchais (1732-1799) was one of the most successful French playwrights in portraying the class struggles of his times (see Fig. 8.19). He was the son of a master watchmaker and grew up in Paris. With such a background, he had the opportunity to learn both scientific technology and the arts. He read widely in French, English, Latin, and Greek. Although he was not born an aristocrat, he married an aristocratic widow, thus vaulting himself to the privileged class. His wife died not long after their marriage and he lost both his new status and her fortune. He managed to maneuver his way among the French royalty, even teaching the harp for a time to Louis XV's daughters. Perhaps because of his first-hand experience in both worlds of French society,

Beaumarchais could portray, with acute sensitivity and realism, the characters found in his plays. His famous trilogy, a set of three plays known as the "Figaro" plays, explored issues of master-servant relationships that came under question in the revolutionary era. The themes of these plays could hit so close to home that at times Louis XVI, Napoleon, and even the restored Bourbon monarchy in France banned its performances. Eventually the bans were lifted and the plays enjoyed enormous success. On at least one occasion, Queen Marie Antoinette herself played a leading role in a performance at Versailles.

The most famous plays of the trilogy are *The Barber of Seville* and *The Marriage of Figaro*. In the first play, Figaro is the barber of Seville, Spain. As the town barber, he knows everyone in the community and their business. When approached by the Spanish noble, Count Almaviva, to assist him in winning the heart of Rosine, a young noblewoman under the guardianship of the much older Dr. Bartholo, Figaro complies. The task is not easy, for Dr. Bartholo keeps a careful watch over Rosine to the point of locking her in her room. Figaro arranges for the Count to serenade her under her window and Rosine's heart is easily won. The great escape from Dr. Bartholo becomes a major part of the action and, of course, Figaro and the Count outwit the old doctor. *The Marriage of Figaro* is a true sequel to *The Barber*. The opening of *The Marriage* finds Figaro, now a valet to the Count, on the eve of his wedding to Suzanne, the Countess Rosine's personal attendant. Although in *The Barber* Figaro and the Count worked together for a common goal, in *The Marriage* Figaro is at odds with the Count because the Count has his eyes on his own bride-to-be. Through a number of comedic twists and subplots, the Count is outwitted, his sin is uncovered, and he responds by repenting to the Countess for his wayward thoughts. As with the prequel, the sequel also ends well. Both plays, however, convey the clear and singular message that the lower class, represented by Figaro, is smarter and more capable than the higher class, represented by Count Almaviva.

Fig. 8.19. Pierre-Augustin Caron de Beaumarchais, bronze statue, 1895, Louis Clausade (1865-1899), Rue St.-Antoine and Rue des Tournelles, Paris.

Fig. 8.20 gives a good example of this proposed intellectual superiority. In a scene from Act I, the Count seeks a moment with Suzanne alone by asking Bazile (dark-clothed figure with wide-brimmed hat) to leave, but matters become complicated when he discovers young Chérubin hiding in a chair. Suzanne raises her arms in astonishment, afraid of the Count's assured rage. As the Count attempts to accuse the youth of the same sinful actions that he himself intends to carry out with Suzanne, quick-witted rebuttals and the arrival of the Countess and Figaro foil the Count's intention to divert blame to Chérubin. It takes the rest of the play before the Count is forced to admit that the "speck" in Chérubin's eye is nothing compared to the "log" in his own eye (Matt 7:3).

Although these plays were popular in their day, they are most well known and most often performed today in their adaptations as operas. *The Barber of Seville* is arguably one of the most popular operas in all of the repertoire. It was composed by Gioachino Rossini in the early nineteenth century (see Theatre, Ch. 9). *The Marriage of Figaro* by Mozart (see Music, this Ch.) is a close rival, never failing to delight contemporary audiences. Its message of social inequality in outdated systems of privilege still rings true today.

Beyond Serious Opera

Several musical genres emerged that specifically focused on satire and comedy as an alternative to the heaviness and elitist focus of serious drama and opera prevalent in many major cities throughout Europe. The **ballad opera** was a play with singing, popular in eighteenth century England. It offered a biting satire both of British politics under Sir Robert Walpole's leadership and of the high-class *opera seria* tradition made popular by Handel (see Ch. 7). Ballad operas presented an upside-down world in which low class became high, serious art became ridiculed, simple tunes replaced the reigning recitative and da capo arias, and evil morals were touted as good.

ballad opera: play with singing, popular in eighteenth-century England

The most successful ballad opera was John Gay's *Beggar's Opera* (see Fig. 8.21). The title itself juxtaposes a class of society that would never have the money to attend opera with an elitist genre that catered only to the highest classes of society. The plot replaces the highly revered royalty and gods with leading characters who are criminals and prostitutes. The leading man, Macheath, operated a gang of thieves for a living. Mr. Peacham was a thief-catcher and supposedly opposed to crime. When his daughter Polly announced that she had married Macheath, Peacham decided to kill Macheath—not for honor, but only because Polly would not be free to help the Peachams in their own work. A series of such twists and turns makes the play both funny and critical of society at the same time. Corruption at every level and in every corner of this play left no sector of British society unscathed.

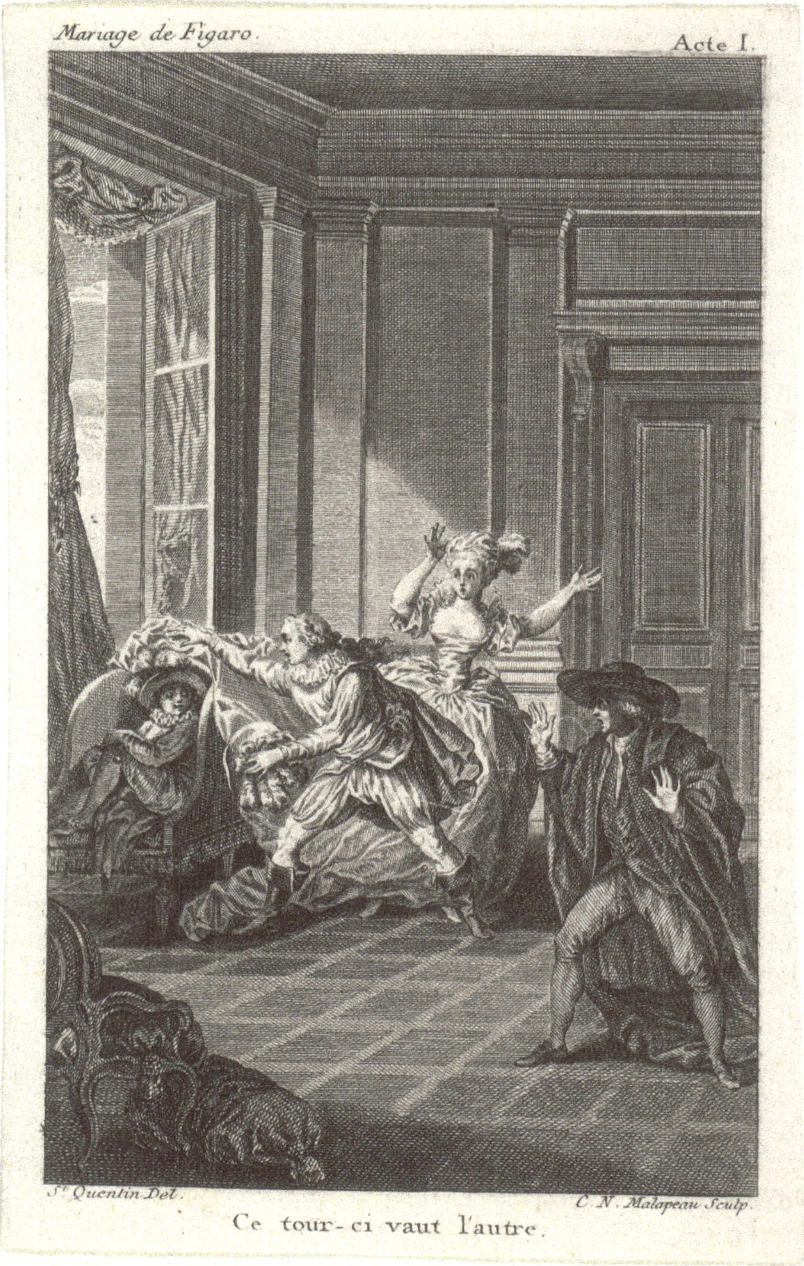

Courtesy MET Museum, Bequest of Phyllis Massar, 2011

Fig. 8.20. The Count discovers Chérubin hiding in a chair, from *Five Illustrations after Jacques Philippe Joseph de Saint Quentin for The Marriage of Figaro,* the caption states, "This turn is worth the other," print, etching with engraving, ca. 1784, Claude Nicolas Malapeau, Metropolitan Museum of Art, NY.

Fig. 8.21. The Beggar's Opera, print, etching and engraving, 1728, formerly attributed to William Hogarth, Metropolitan Museum of Art, NY.

In the opening to Act II, listen to the satire in replacing the lofty recitative and aria of *opera seria* with coarse dialogue and a simple tune. The link will take you to all of Act II; just listen from the beginning to 1:47.

Watch Mrs. Trapes (a woman of ill repute) sing, "In the Days of My Youth" to Mr. Peacham and Mr. Lockit (a jail keeper).

Watch Macheath sing, "Since Laws Were Made" from his jail cell.

Although John Gay's *Beggar's Opera* made the genre a popular one, it remains the only play of its type to continue to be performed today. Although banned during Victorian and Edwardian times because of its purported impropriety, it has been revived numerous times since then. It is the basis for the equally famous *Threepenny Opera* by Bertolt Brecht and Kurt Weill first performed exactly 200 years after *The Beggar's Opera*.

In Italy, the empty stage between acts of *opera seria* became a principal location for experiments in lighter forms of opera that did not conform to the established rules. With the popularity of satirizing society with comedy and song, one such composer worked in this direction, essentially creating a "serious" alternative

opera buffa: comic opera

to *opera seria*: *opera buffa*, or comic opera. With characters looking no different from the audience, situations common in contemporary society and politics, and volatile emotions that could change at a moment's notice, Giovanni Battista Pergolesi (1710-1736) found the secret to success. His most famous work, *La serva padrona* (*The Maid as Mistress*) portrays the conniving Serpina, maid to well-to-do bachelor Uberto, as she tricks him into marrying her.

Listen to Uberto's changing emotions as he is considering the prospect.

Translation:

> I am all mixed up / I have a certain something in my heart. / Truly I cannot tell / whether it's love or pity. / I hear a voice that tells me: / Uberto, think of yourself.
>
> I am between yes and no, / between wanting and not wanting, / and I get more confused all the time, / unhappy fellow. / What will ever become of me?[8]

Singspiel: literally sing-play; a German form of musical theatre with both singing and spoken dialogue

Alternative opera also found an audience in German-speaking lands. Its focus was not necessarily a critique of society, although it did connect with contemporary philosophy. Whereas Italian *opera seria* remained popular among Germans, the lighter genre of *Singspiel* (lit., sing-play) began to draw large audiences to its public venues. Akin to modern-day musical theatre, *Singspiel* included some spoken parts along with singing. The vocals could be either virtuosic or less demanding, depending on the character. One of the most famous examples in this genre is Mozart's *The Magic Flute* (see Fig. 8.22). Although on the surface

DID YOU KNOW?

Free Masonry is a secret fraternal organization dating back to the fourteenth century. They require members to believe in a supreme being and they espouse some of the same virtues that Christians do. The question arises, were they really Christians? The Word of God, which is living and active, and discerning the thoughts and intentions of the heart makes the decision (Heb 4:12). Scripture states that the name of Jesus Christ, the Lord and Savior, must be uplifted and recognized as the name of God. "No man can say 'Jesus is Lord' except in the Holy Spirit" (I Cor 12:3); "By this you know the Spirit of God: every spirit that confesses that Jesus Christ is come in the flesh is from God, and every spirit that does not confess Jesus is not from God" (I John 4:2-3). Are Free Masons Christians? As an organization they are not, since it is not enough to believe in a supreme being, but one must believe in the supreme being who came incarnate as the Savior of the world. In other words, one must believe and confess the lordship of Jesus and believe in His resurrection (Rom 10:9).

Fig. 8.22. Set Design for Hall of Stars, Queen of the Night Palace, Act 1, vi. The Magic Flute, print, aquatint printed in color and hand-colored, after Karl Friedrich Schinkel, 1847-49, Karl Friedrich Thiele, Metropolitan Museum of Art, NY.

it portrays a fantasy world with evil pitted against good, a damsel in distress, and even a dragon, underlying themes of knowledge, justice, wisdom, and truth present themselves throughout. *The Magic Flute* explores the tenets of Free Masonry, of which Mozart was a member. Many Enlightenment writers were also Masons, and thus the message of this opera resonated with several contemporary thinkers.

Listen to the Queen of the Night (with an extremely high vocal range) sing her aria, as she convinces her daughter Pamina that Sarastro (with an extremely low vocal range) is the enemy. In the end, the truth triumphs and justice wins.[9]

Study Questions

1. What were some of the specific formal principles of antiquity returned in neoclassicism in architecture, sculpture, and painting?
2. How are social and economic progress and concerns illustrated in the artwork of the eighteenth century?
3. In what ways was visual art used as social commentary?
4. How did the Enlightenment influence musical styles and forms in the eighteenth century?
5. How did dance influence musical composition in the eighteenth century?

6. How is the oboe used in the aria "Dove Sono"?
7. Why is the string quartet a complete musical expression of the Enlightenment?

Notes

1. See Anthony Ashley-Cooper, Characteristicks of Men, Manners, Opinions, Times.
2. John Locke, *An Essay Concerning Human Understanding*, 1-39.
3. Immanuel Kant, *Critique of Judgment*, 5: 209-210.
4. Jonathan Edwards, *The Nature of True Virtue*, 8: 550.
5. Jonathan Edwards, *The Nature of True Virtue*, 8: 550-562.
6. Immanuel Kant, *Critique of Judgment*, 5:209-244.
7. https://en.wikipedia.org/wiki/William_Hogarth#/media/File:GinLane.jpg
8. Burkholder, 7th ed., 14.
9. Classic Fm Digital Radio https://www.classicfm.com/composers/mozart/guides/queen-of-the-night-translated/.

Romanticism
Nineteenth Century Part I

1746–1828 Francisco Goya

1765–1833 Joseph Nicéphore Niépce, inventor of heliographs, early forerunners of photographs

1770–1827 Ludwig van Beethoven

1774–1840 Caspar David Friedrich

1789–1851 James Fenimore Cooper

1797–1828 Franz Schubert

1801–1848 Thomas Cole

1810–1856 Robert Schumann and Clara Schumann (1819–1896)

1818–1883 Karl Marx

1748–1825 Jacques-Louis David

1768–1834 Friedrich Schleiermacher

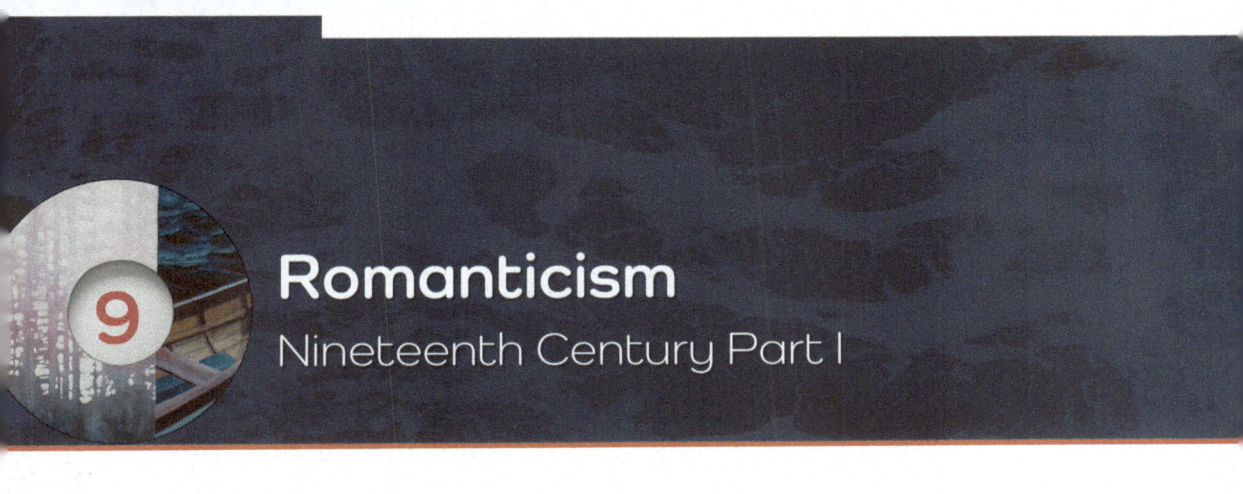

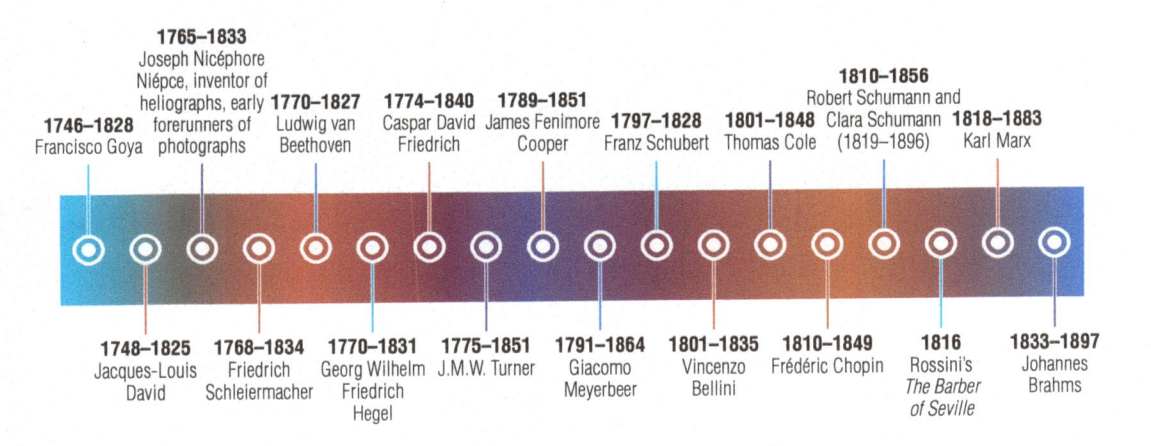

1770–1831 Georg Wilhelm Friedrich Hegel

1775–1851 J.M.W. Turner

1791–1864 Giacomo Meyerbeer

1801–1835 Vincenzo Bellini

1810–1849 Frédéric Chopin

1816 Rossini's *The Barber of Seville*

1833–1897 Johannes Brahms

Philosophy

As was mentioned previously, the dawn of the nineteenth century was fraught with turmoil. Coming on the heels of the American and French Revolutions, the West experienced severe shifts in civil power. Furthermore, the Age of Imperialism had dawned at the end of the eighteenth century, changing global perceptions. Tales of the East, the Sahara, and the New World were fertile grounds from which the tree of Romanticism could sprout. Nature became a common fixture of artistic content and those that dwelled in newly discovered areas became a subject of literature, as can be seen in the *Leatherstocking Tales* of James Fenimore Cooper (1789-1851). These were a series of stories about Natty Bumppo, a child of white parents who was raised by Native Americans. Such stories had depictions of the dangers and vast beauty of the forested areas of eastern North America, as depicted in Thomas Cole's (1801-1848) painting of a scene from *The Last of the Mohicans* (Fig. 9.1), the second volume of Cooper's series. The author's portrayal was stylized and idealized, often perpetuating myths about the inhabitants of the Americas that supported European settlement. The reactions to such descriptions were varied, with some responding by idealizing the wilderness and its inhabitants, whereas others viewed the

Fig. 9.1. Cora Kneeling at the Feet of Tamenund, 1827, Thomas Cole, Wadsworth Atheneum Museum of Art, Hartford, CT.

frontier as something to be subdued for civilization. Both views had damaging moral effects, with the former infantilizing indigenous peoples and the latter treating them as commodities to be used. Where the biblical perspective is to see all people as bearing the image of God (Gen 1:26-27), loved by their Creator (John 3:16), and those whom God desires to save (1 Tim 2:3-4), many in Western nations, often using the guise of Christianity, saw the natives as opposition at best and animals at worst.

> **DID YOU KNOW?**
>
> The *Leatherstocking Tales* have been adapted into multiple television series, including a children's show. Moreover, the most popular of the volumes, the aforementioned *The Last of the Mohicans* has been made into multiple movies, including a 1992 adaptation that starred three-time Academy Award winner Daniel Day-Lewis. The movie, itself, won the Oscar for best sound.

The philosophical world, too, was reeling from the immense movements of the Enlightenment. As the eighteenth century drew to a close, philosophy had cemented its drift away from viewing knowledge as faith seeking understanding, as was the view previous to the Renaissance, to seeing knowledge as human reasoning finding truth apart from any external influences, including

Fig. 9.2. Karl Marx, 1875, John Jabez Edwin Mayal, International Institute of Social History, Amsterdam.

Christianity. When that was combined with growing skepticism arising from Hume and with Kant's attempt to centralize beauty and knowledge solely on the perceiver, it is not surprising that the nineteenth century closed with four of the most influential atheistic scholars that the world has seen. In the field of history, government, and economics, it was Karl Marx (1818-1883; Fig. 9.2) whose development of communism saw religion as the "opium of the people."[1] He thought that Christianity kept people in something akin to a drug-induced haze, unable to think clearly enough to take action against their oppressors. Interpreting the world in light of power dynamics led to the rise of critical theories of the twenty-first century.

Fig. 9.3. Georg Wilhelm Friedrich Hegel, 1970, East Germany Postage Stamp.

The three other significant atheist academics were Sigmund Freud (1856-1939), who developed a view of caring for the mind apart from Scripture; Friedrich Nietzsche (1844-1900), who developed a philosophical perspective that critiqued Western religion and declared "God is dead;"[2] and Bertrand Russell (1872-1970), who was one of the most significant bridges between nineteenth- and twentieth-century philosophy in the West. Yet, even with the rise of opponents to religion, there remained many influential philosophers who viewed Christianity in a positive light, not the least of which was Georg Wilhelm Friedrich Hegel (1770-1831), whose work precipitated the works of Marx and Nietzsche. So influential was Hegel that he even appeared on German postage stamps (Fig. 9.3).

Hegel viewed world history as the outflow of Absolute Spirit,[3] a phrase he used to give a somewhat philosophical view of what God was like. Absolute Spirit could not be conscious of itself apart from the world, and thus, the development of the world was the process by which the Spirit was recognizing itself through the consciousness of humanity. As difficult as that may sound, it is much more complicated than most could imagine and has led to many disputes in philosophy as to what Hegel meant. Yet, one thing that is known for certain is that he believed that the history of the world developed necessarily and rightly toward a goal. This development he believed occurred dialectically, whereby some sort of movement, or *thesis*, is met with resistance, or *antithesis*, and those movements combine to produce a third element that has some characteristics in common with each, or a *synthesis*. This synthesis would then become a thesis for a new dialectic and the process would continue. He used this type of thinking to interpret the succession of world powers and empires.[4] This mentality led to two extremely influential beliefs. First, was the belief that any moment in history is a necessary part of its overall development, a view which many used to legitimize any activity undertaken by an empire. This perspective became a significant factor in the rise of nationalism in the second half of the nineteenth century. Second, as Hegel arrived at a picture of the ultimate end of the development of history, his depiction looked very similar to the Germanic Empire. Thus, the sense of triumphalism that was fervently held in Germany at the beginning of the twentieth century was in many ways shaped by Hegelian philosophy. Thus, the World Wars, though perhaps not directly caused by philosophy, were definitely influenced by it.

Hegel also addressed art, often understanding it in distinction from philosophy and religion. He believed that all three of the fields were coming at the same truth, but with different methodologies. Philosophy understood truth through concepts, which were universal ideas in the mind. Religion understood truth by representation of Absolute Spirit through given images and metaphors. However, art understood truth by representation through created images. Since Hegel saw freedom as central to the life of Absolute Spirit, then the artist was producing something that represented the ultimate freedom of spirit in using her own freedom. As Houlgate writes,

> The principal aim of art is not, therefore, to imitate nature, to decorate our surroundings, to prompt us to engage in moral or political action, or to shock us out of our complacency. It is to allow us to contemplate and enjoy created images of our own spiritual freedom—images that are beautiful precisely *because* they give expression to our freedom.[5]

Although Hegel believed that true human freedom had constraints, his perspective was used to continue the trend of art's autonomy from religion.

Kierkegaard (see Fig. 9.4) was another philosopher who had a positive view of Christianity; one so positive, in fact, that he should also be categorized as a theologian. The Danish scholar was concerned about the products of the Enlightenment, especially the work of Kant and Hegel. He felt that human life was too complicated to be described by merely having a simple, rationalistic methodology. In a parallel to twentieth-century naturalism, which denied the spiritual and understood all things in terms of what was natural (i.e., physical), many had come to see humanity as the product of external forces. Yet, Kierkegaard believed that if individuals really had freedom, then they were much more

naturalism: an idealized representation of the visual world

existentialism: belief that one's existence is what he imagines it to be, thus leaving man to be responsible for his actions and consequences. Believing there is no higher power, existentialists challenge man to derive his own truth rather than one handed down to him by authorities or deities

postmodernism: the view that reacted to the Enlightenment by being radically skeptical of all values and any attempt to understand truth

theological liberalism: view that denies the inspiration of Scripture and thereby rejects historically significant doctrines of the Christian faith

than the sum total of influences from history, nature, and society. This appears to be a biblically supportable view. Humans are more than their lineage (Gal 3:7-9), and Christians are more than their past (2 Cor 5:17). However, Kierkegaard's view would eventually give rise to **existentialism**, which was a philosophical movement that focused on humanity's freedom and the difficulty of analyzing human life, including its development and suffering, in natural terms.

Kierkegaard's existentialism was developed, though in a manner that would likely have been opposed by the Danish writer, into a view that was radically skeptical at all values and at any attempt to understand truth. This development, which is termed **postmodernism**, ends up being one of the most defining movements in twentieth-century philosophy, popular culture, and, indeed, art. The unfortunate byproduct of this type of postmodernism was the relativism of morality and truth and the focus on experience. Because values were not real or, at the very least, unknowable, one should simply produce art that evoked the types of experiences that people desire. This caused a greater focus on popular culture in the twentieth century and a lesser focus on art. For example, music became a means of diversion and not a way to stir one toward contemplation. Ironically, Kierkegaard already critiqued this type of view. In his work *Either/Or*, he developed a view of the world where people are aesthetic, moral, or religious. For him, the aesthetic individual, who focused on experience and freedom from boredom, is engaged in the lowest form of life. Greater was the life of conviction, or the moral life devoted to principle. The greatest, in Kierkegaard's view, was the religious life where individuals were devoted to something beyond themselves.

Theology in the nineteenth century was not spared from the disorder coming out of the eighteenth century. One of the most important developments was the rise of **theological liberalism**, a view that denied the inspiration of Scripture and thereby rejected historically significant doctrines like the truth of the

Fig. 9.4. Søren Kierkegaard, 1918, Louis Hasselriis, Royal Library Garden, Copenhagen.

Bible, the substitutionary atonement of Jesus Christ, and the hope in a bodily resurrection. Friedrich Schleiermacher (1768-1834), who is often considered the father of theological liberalism, attacked the inerrancy of Scripture. He placed the centrality of Christianity not in thought or action, but in feeling, or the direct intuition of God. This would eventually feed into many subjectivist theories, or theories that deny objective truth and make truth the function of individual experience. Though Schleiermacher believed that art should be subservient to religion, he himself provided arguments that undercut the value of religion in general and Christianity in particular.

Art

For artists, the early nineteenth century was a time of continued change, pushback, and rebellion against the established styles and themes of their predecessors. Particularly in Europe, turmoil brought on by the ruling upper class went hand-in-hand with the advent of the Industrial Revolution. The working class labored under appalling conditions with no hope for improvement. The frivolous paintings of Rococo became entirely out of touch with the common person. Artists found continued camaraderie with the idealism and virtue found in classical Roman and Grecian artwork of the past. Others found that the way forward wasn't by revisiting the past, but forging a new path forward embracing emotion, and reveling in nature; what became known as **Romanticism**.

Romanticism: the movement in visual art to move toward emotion and revel in nature

Neoclassical

Although neoclassical work emerged in the eighteenth century, it also continued into the early nineteenth century. The neoclassical style was known for its depiction of idealized figures and scenes. The subjects of these paintings were people without flaws—well-shaped bodies in their prime. The artists wanted to portray these characters as virtuous and heroic, standing up for what was right. Some of their artwork even fueled the fire of revolution.

Where Christian virtue rests in the finished work of Jesus, neoclassical works called upon the stern Roman virtue of old to denounce injustice and raise up a new order. Such neoclassical sentiments are clearly portrayed in how Jacques-Louis David (1748-1825) painted *The Death of Marat* (Fig. 9.5) at the turn of the century. Jean-Paul Marat (1743-1793), a former doctor and scientist-turned journalist, advocated for basic human rights during the political unrest of the **French Revolution**. He was considered radical in his beliefs and was assassinated in his tub for the stance he took in politics.

French Revolution: revolutionary upheaval of t French aristo racy in 1789

In this painting, Marat is depicted as a strong and yet humble martyr with a heavenly light shining down on his lifeless body. Despite having a chronic skin condition for which he was taking a medicinal bath, he is portrayed as healthy

Fig. 9.5. *The Death of Marat.* Oil on canvas, 1793 (165 × 128 cm). Royal Museums of Fine Arts of Belgium, Belgium.

and without blemish. His pierced skin echoes that of Christ's pierced side. Christians can identify with this imagery of a virtuous self-sacrifice that stands in the gap for the common person. The shallow stage-like space and dramatic posture of characters in neoclassical artworks lend themselves to being read as having a theatrical presence. In some cases, this allowed artists to venerate their heroes beyond their natural presence, lifting them up to a saint-like status, believing that their motives were equally pure.

Jacques-Louis David is the most notable neoclassical painter as his paintings embody so much of the emotions and spirit of his time. He was substantially involved in politics, which is reflected in the content of his artwork. While living in France, he allied himself with various political groups that had succeeded in rising to power, and when Napoleon Bonaparte (1769-1821) rose to prominence, it was no different. Napoleon desired to legitimize his reign by utilizing the power and acclaim of neoclassical art that David graciously provided. This began the **Empire Style**, which was a particular brand of neoclassical art relating to the first Empire of France from 1804 to 1814.

Empire Style: a certain brand of neoclassical art related to the First Empire of France from 1804 to 1814

One of David's most notable commissions came from Napoleon Bonaparte himself after he traversed the Alps to reinforce French troops and regain land that had been taken by the Austrians. After the successful campaign, Napoleon established diplomatic relations with Charles IV (1748-1819) of Spain. The relations included an exchange of gifts during which David was commissioned to make a painting of Napoleon crossing the Alps. The French leader requested three more versions to be used as propaganda. David ended up making five versions in total.

When Napoleon was asked to pose for the painting, he refused stating that the painting's resemblance to him was not as important as capturing his character and genius—a truly neoclassical sentiment. The paintings liberally embellished the scene featuring a majestic and fearless Napoleon on a stormy precipice. Despite the depiction being entirely fictitious, it was effective in capturing the imagination and awe of his followers (Fig. 9.6).

In Their Own Words

Of portraiture, Napoleon stated:

"It is not the exactness of the features, a wart on the nose which gives the resemblance. It is the character that dictates what must be painted."[6]

Completed for a royal commission in 1786, David's *Oath of the Horatii* (Fig. 9.7) typifies neoclassic painting as an allegory of subject matter paired with classic formal qualities to speak to the contemporary moment. The composition, taking its linear style from that of classical relief sculpture and ancient friezes, shows the ancient Roman story of the Horatii family swearing to fight their three cousins, the Curiatii of Alba Longa, to settle a dispute between the two cities. Their stances are tense, especially in relation to the languid figures of the women grieving in the background. To the public eye, *Oath of the Horatii* signaled David's promotion of revolution in the time of unrest leading up to the French Revolution. It served as an exhortation for resolution of character and willingness to sacrifice individual liberties for the greater good.

Fig. 9.6. *Napoleon Crossing the Alps*, oil on canvas, 1800, Jacques-Louis David, Château de Malmaison, Paris, France.

Neoclassical works gave fuel to the revolutionary fire. However, like most fires, they eventually ran their course and were consumed. By the year 1824, Jacques-Louis David could be found attempting to stem the tide of carnage left behind by civil unrest and war. Perhaps this was most literally depicted in the last painting he ever produced, titled *Mars Being Disarmed by Venus*, completed in 1824 (Fig. 9.8). In this painting, David chose to portray the literal disarming of Mars, the God of war. He had lived through a period of great unrest, seeing the rise and fall of numerous political parties and powerful figures. It seems that he was convinced that the way forward was a less bloody one, where people willingly replaced weapons and armor with vulnerability. This exchange was necessary to make room, in David's view, for love.

Fig. 9.7. *Oath of the Horatii*, 1785, Jacques-Louis David, replica at Toledo Museum of Art, Ohio.

Romanticism

In the same way that the Rococo of the eighteenth century was far removed from the plight of the average person, so the taste of revolution and war had turned bitter in the mouth of those who had so craved it before. Some artists began to describe these fresh atrocities without virtuous idealized heroes. Art in this period began to depict the grim realities of tragedy. At this point, there was a fraying of styles where artists split off to describe things from their own viewpoint. This was the beginning of a new age known as Romanticism. The Romantics didn't have a particular style of painting as much as a desire to show life as they experienced it. For some artists like Francisco Goya (1746-1828), this meant describing the horrors of war where reality looked significantly more like mass execution of the helpless than the virtuous heroes and martyrs of neoclassicism.

Goya's *The Third of May 1808* (Fig. 9.9) made a clear break with tradition in his handling of paint as well as the subject matter. There is no glory or heroism in this execution scene; there is only injustice and actual violence. The desperate laborer has his arms thrown up in helpless disbelief, his white shirt a final outcry against the darkness threatening to swallow him up in crimson.

Fig. 9.8. *Mars Being Disarmed by Venus*, oil on canvas, 1824, Jacques-Louis David, Royal Museums of Fine Arts of Belgium, Belgium.

Where Goya chose to portray a grittiness of life, other artists felt a beckoning back to nature. With industrialization changing the way people had been living for centuries past, large amounts of rural populations were driven into overcrowded cities to look for work. Once there, they found unregulated, demanding, and thankless jobs.[7]

Where Rococo provided escape through titillating moments of upper-class fantasies, the Romantic depictions of landscape offered escape through a refreshing encounter with nature. Artists began infusing their work with a sense of the **sublime**—an almost mystical encounter with nature where the viewer is simultaneously awe-struck and humbled. This feeling of the sublime was typically encountered alone, an experience that could bring an individual to the brink of destruction, only to be undone by the sheer beauty of their encounter

Chapter 9: Romanticism 239

Fig. 9.9. *The Third of May 1808*, oil on canvas, 1814, Francisco Goya, Museo Nacional del Prado, Madrid, Spain.

with nature. The artists of such landscape paintings most typically represented a scene that confronted the smallness of mankind in a vast and majestic world. These artists had discovered that the world was a harsh and unforgiving place, full of beauty as well as danger. People were no longer the main subjects of the artwork. Nature had taken primacy.

In the example *Snow Storm: Hannibal Crossing the Alps* (Fig. 9.10), we see J. M. W. Turner's (1775-1851) choice to depict Hannibal's (247 BC-ca. 181 BC) incursion into Italy. Where Jacques-Louis David depicted a heroic Napoleon crossing the Alps, Turner chose a two millennia older event to paint. The contrast is made even more stark when one notices that the vast number of Hannibal's army, which included war elephants, is hardly distinguishable. The few people that are discernible are cowering against the rocks, hiding from the untamable power of the oncoming snowstorm. The entire army is almost an afterthought. Turner depicted what was one of humanity's greatest warfare achievements as nothing compared to the raw power of nature.

All of the years of strife and recent revolutions had come at a sobering price. The Enlightenment of the eighteenth century did not fix society's problems. There was still so much that could not be controlled or explained. Enlightenment rationalism had given way to Kierkegaard's existentialism. Nature always seemed to have the final word. Despite all the advancements of industrialization and scientific discovery, mankind was merely a temporary passenger in this world,

Fig. 9.10. *Snow Storm: Hannibal and His Army Crossing the Alps*, oil on canvas, 1810-1812, J. M. W. Turner, Tate Britain, London, England.

Fig. 9.11. *Monastery Ruin Eldena*, oil on canvas, 1824, Caspar David Friedrich, Old National Gallery, Berlin, Germany.

unable to even make a scratch on the earth's surface. Caspar David Friedrich (1774-1840) often capitalized on these notions employing ruins of civilizations gone by, such as in the painting *Monastery Ruin Eldena* (Fig. 9.11).

Friedrich had the uncanny ability to capture the beauty and power of nature and contrast it with the fragility of mankind. In his painting *The Sea of Ice* (Fig. 9.12),

Fig. 9.12. *The Sea of Ice*, oil on canvas, 1823-1824, Caspar David Friedrich, Hamburger Kunsthalle, Hamburg, Germany.

there is a majestic landscape full of jagged ice formations. They are a fascinating subject upon which to gaze, but the scene is quite uninviting—a frozen desolate tundra, hostile to practically all forms of life. However, upon closer inspection, there is the hull of shipwreck—the only reference to mankind is a mere footnote tucked into the cracks of nature.

There is a lot about the sublime that works hand-in-hand with Christianity. Some have argued that Friedrich's goal in painting was to cause contemplation of the metaphysical. Much of these landscapes inspire a sense of awe and humility at God's creation, which can impart a healthy sense of reverence. However, one should also hold in mind that God is not as distant and unforgiving as these landscapes depicted. As Paul stated to the Greeks at the Areopagus, "Yet he is actually not far from each one of us, for 'In him we live and move and have our being'" (Acts 17:27b-28).

A wonderful moment of the sublime in the Bible appears to be the event when Moses spoke with God in Exodus 33:18-23, asking God to reveal His glory. God directed Moses to turn away, then allowed Moses to see the glory of his passing back. In this moment, Moses had one of the truest experiences of the feeling of the sublime. He witnessed as much of the glory and beauty of God as he could without dying.

Not only Moses, but everyone will experience this moment of true sublimity when they pass from this life and come face-to-face with God. The author of Corinthians writes, "For now we see in a mirror dimly, but then face to face. Now I know in part; then I shall know fully, even as I have been fully known" (1 Cor 13:12). Not only will they see the face and full glory of God, but some will find that by the power of the Holy Spirit at work in them, they were being made into the very image of God. The author of Corinthians later continues, "We all, with unveiled face, beholding the glory of the Lord, are being transformed into the same image from one degree of glory to another" (2 Cor 3:18). Even unbelievers will eventually recognize that Jesus Christ is Lord (Phil 2:10-11).

> ### DID YOU KNOW?
>
> In 1825, French inventor Joseph Nicéphore Niépce made the first permanent photograph, prepared through a process of fixing an image on a treated plate through exposure to light. The invention of photography and its subsequent development in the nineteenth and twentieth century drastically changed the function and purpose of fine art. With the ability to capture a perfectly illusionistic image, photography served as a tool for portraiture, landscape, and the documentation of world events.

Music

Ludwig van Beethoven (1770-1827)

Beethoven's (see Fig. 9.13) career as a composer began the romantic period while at the same time bringing a close to the Classical period. Early in Beethoven's career, he was known as a "second Mozart." By 1812 when he was forty-one, Beethoven's career finally exceeded the careers of Mozart and Haydn and in the process had revolutionized the musical language. Beethoven's success came about through his sheer determination to continue creating music despite struggling with deafness. His music depicts his struggles, triumphs, individualism, and self-expression.

Beethoven wrote a variety of music, including symphonies, sonatas, chamber music, concertos, operas, and vocal music. Beethoven is especially credited for creating the genre known as **song cycle,** which is a group of songs that are played one after the other. The songs in the cycle typically tell a story. Even though Beethoven is credited with its creation, the vocal works of Schubert, Brahms, and Schumann overshadowed his own well-composed pieces. Beethoven began a tradition that would put other composers in the limelight, instead of himself.

One of Beethoven's most well-known works is Symphony No. 5 in C minor. In this symphony, Beethoven highlights his struggle to overcome his physical

song cycle: group of songs designated by a composer to be performed at the same time as a set

Chapter 9: Romanticism   243

Fig. 9.13. Ludwig van Beethoven.

limitations by starting the piece in C minor and then shows his triumphant success by highlighting the key of C major. As a whole, the piece inspired subsequent composers by its optimism and relationship to Enlightenment ideals. The piece seems to take the listener from a place of darkness to a place of light.

Listen to Beethoven's Fifth Symphony. Although it takes a while to listen to all four movements, it is well worth the time to benefit from the overall effect. The opening 4 notes (da-da-da-DUM, sometimes called "Fate knocking on the door") recurs in many different guises throughout all 4 movements. Listen for those similarities. Note also the contrast of the somber and heavy opening of Movement 1, with the triumphant opening of Movement 4. Beethoven was deliberate in placing every note in this grand, heroic work.

Franz Schubert (1797-1828)

Schubert (see Fig. 9.14) was known during his life for his *Lieder* (pl. of *Lied*), chamber music, and piano works. As a composer, his financial support came from publishers instead of the patronage system upon which Beethoven and other composers depended. Schubert followed in Beethoven's footsteps as he took the song cycles that his predecessor founded and advanced them even further in the Romantic era. Schubert's songs are perfect examples of Romantic *Lied*. Overall, Schubert composed over six hundred *Lieder*. Schubert's songs were frequently paired with poems, as he became known for composing captivating melodies.

One of Franz Schubert's best known song cycles is *Winterreise*. It was not well received during his lifetime and was actually only performed once for friends. The song cycle features a jilted lover who is fixated on death as he goes on a long journey in the bleak winter. Schubert often struggled with depression and as he finished writing *Winterreise*, he had descended into despair once again. In order to express the bleakness and despair in his music, Schubert often featured the

Lieder: German art songs for solo voice and piano accompaniment

chamber music: instrumental music for a few performers, meant to be performed in a hall room, or chamber

Fig. 9.14. Franz Schubert.

singer unsupported by the accompaniment, emphasizing the performer's vulnerability. Schubert also used fewer notes in both the accompaniment and the melody, a type of composing that gave the music a riveting intensity. The last song in *Winterreise* exhibits these characteristics. The lonely traveler meets "Der Leiermann," which means "The Hurdy-Gurdy Man" (see Fig. 9.15.). Examine the lyrics in translation and then listen to the music. Think about what Schubert is portraying in this song.[8]

Listen for the ways Schubert uses the piano to paint the bleak picture: Winterreise, "Der Leiermann."

Fig. 9.15. *Je joueur de vielle* (The Hurdy-Gurdy Player), from *Les gueux suite appelée aussi les mendiants, les baroni, ou les barons*, print, etching, ca. 1623, Jacques Callot. Metropolitan Museum of Art, NY. Note: the hurdy-gurdy is a portable stringed instrument with keyboard that requires the turning of a circular bow to produce sound; hence the traveler's question at the end of "Der Leiermann."

Robert Schumann (1810-1856) and Clara Schumann (1819-1896)

Robert and Clara Schumann (see Fig. 9.16) were one of the most famous artist couples in history, working as composers and pianists during the Romantic era. Robert was much older than Clara; he met her when she was young and waited for her to come of age before marrying her. Clara's father did not approve but they proceeded to get married and had several children. Robert was a prolific musician and composer who injured his right hand and subsequently had to stop performing. After the injury, Schumann focused on his composing, while suffering heavily from depression and other mental illnesses. He died in 1856 at a mental asylum near Bonn. After Robert's death, Clara stopped composing and instead edited and promoted her late husband's compositions.

Robert Schumann produced compositions for piano, chamber music, vocal music, as well as others. As he composed, Clara was often the pianist who performed his music. Both encouraged each other as they composed, often exchanging secret messages through the music they were creating.

Fig. 9.16. Portrait of composer Robert Schumann and his wife, musician, Clara Schumann.

Robert idolized his wife and wrote many love songs to her as a result, some of which added to the Romantic *Lieder* of this time period.

Clara Schumann was a child prodigy who was trained to become a concert pianist. By the age of twenty, she was known throughout Europe for her skill. Even though women were not often respected as composers in this time period, Robert encouraged her to compose. Clara's best known work is her *Trio for Piano, Violin, and Cello*, Op. 17. She was not confident when composing and often second guessed herself. Her colleagues who performed her compositions disagreed with her insecurities and expressed their surprise that a woman could compose so well.

> **IN THEIR OWN WORDS**
>
> Robert Schumann was impressed with his wife's talent at composing and had this to say about her: "Clara has written a number of small pieces that show a musical and tender invention that she has never attained before. But to have children and a husband who is always living in the realms of imagination do not go together with composing. She cannot work at it regularly and I am often disturbed to think how many profound ideas are lost because she cannot work them out. But Clara herself knows her main occupation is as a mother and I believe she is happy in the circumstances and would not want them changed."[9]

As with Symphony No. 5, it is well worth the time to listen to all the movements in a continuous sitting. Recall the discussion of sonata form from Ch. 8 and try to hear the structural markers of theme and key in the first movement. Pay attention to how the themes pass among the three instruments, as if in a conversation. Every instrument is equally important in chamber music. Listen also to the beauty of the different timbres of the instruments woven together.

Clara Schumann: Trio for Piano, Violin, and Cello, Op. 17 (Tracks 17-20).

Johannes Brahms (1833-1897)

Except for opera, Johannes Brahms (see Fig. 9.17) led every field in composition during his time. Brahms composed music that was meant for all people. He had a special skill in being able to preserve the treasured style of music from the past two centuries and combining it with lyricism, expressivity, and excellent craftsmanship. Brahms revered the past composers, believing that no other modern composers could compare to their greatness. In addition, Brahms was known for composing music that was accessible to the amateur musician as well as to the professional.

IN THEIR OWN WORDS

What Brahms thought of the past composers: "How must those Gods Bach, Mozart, Beethoven have felt, whose daily bread was to write things like the St. Matthew Passion, Don Giovanni, Fidelio, [the] Ninth Symphony!"[10]

Brahms lived with the Schumanns and studied under Robert. He created a love triangle between himself and the Schumanns by falling in love with Clara. As far as it is known, however, Clara and Brahms never had any more than a platonic relationship, even after Robert died.

chamber music: music for three or more musicians of varying instruments

Brahms's chamber music, or music for three or more musicians of varying instruments, is considered some of his most prolific compositions, being considered a successor of Beethoven in that genre. He thought that as a composer, one should be able to compose well in the chamber music genre as

Fig. 9.17. Photo of Johannes Brahms.

preparation to compose symphonies. His gifts as a composer shone in this genre, as his music was appealing to musicians for its "ruthless clarity, economy, invention, emotional intensity without sentimentality, and unerring sense of proportion."[11]

Frédéric Chopin (1810-1849)

Frédéric Chopin (see Fig. 9.18) was originally from Poland and was traveling with the intention of going to Italy and Germany when he heard of Poland's revolt against Russia. Instead, Chopin changed his itinerary and made his way to Paris. He was never again able to return to his homeland, but much of the music he created is reminiscent of his life in Poland. Chopin is best known for his piano music, redefining how it was written. Chopin had a skill in composing idiomatic music that was easy for amateurs to enjoy but was challenging for professionals to perform. His pieces are characterized by his innate ability to write singing melodies for the piano.

ballade: a one movement work for solo piano, usually in a lyrical style

Chopin and Clara Schumann were among the first composers to use the name **ballade** for instrumental music. Chopin combined harmony, form, and transcendental melodies to create ballades that were full of charm and fire. In Ballade No. 1 in G minor, Op. 23, Chopin explores the potential of the new and improved piano that was developed by the French company, Érard, in the first half of the nineteenth century. Its steel frame, the arrangement of the strings crossing over one another, the addition of a foot pedal, and the innovation of a double-action mechanism for the hammers, allowed for an instrument of unparalleled versatility, range, and volume. This instrument and its virtuosic performers captured audiences' attention in such a way that entire solo recitals could be performed on piano in large halls. This had never been done before. Chopin and other pianists, such as his contemporary Franz Liszt (1811-1886), became the first solo super-stars, with

Fig. 9.18. Frédéric François Chopin, portrait of the Polish composer and pianist, ca. 1849, Louis-Auguste Bisson.

audiences swooning over them and fighting for seats at their concerts. Ballade No. 1 presented an aural display of fireworks, something that earlier versions of keyboard instruments could never dream of doing.

Listen for the idiomatic writing for the modern piano—its versatile capabilities to be very smooth, slow, soft, and connected as well as very loud and clearly articulated with rapid-fire delivery. Listen also for the memorable, singable melodies that Chopin was so adept at writing, between which he showed off the new piano's features. Be prepared also for another of Chopin's tricks—he leads the hearer to think the piece is coming to an end several times, only to take off again on yet another display of piano virtuosity: Ballade No. 1 in G minor, Op. 23.

Time	Description
0:05	Slow, smooth, connected, lazy, and quiet introduction
0:38	Theme 1: Pensive and halting, in short segments that question and answer each other
1:06	Theme 1
2:57	Theme 2: Soaring and lyrically gorgeous
4:04	Theme 1
4:35	Theme 2
5:58	Theme 2
7:01	Theme 1
7:41	Fast, loud, and fiery conclusion, in contrast to the slow beginning

Theatre

The success and versatility of opera in the eighteenth century, in large part because of the ingenious works by Mozart, laid a strong foundation for the continued popularity of serious opera, comic opera, and variations of sung plays, or **musical theatre**, such as *Singspiel*. By the early nineteenth century, the French Revolution had dealt a fatal blow to the old aristocracy of Europe and a new social order, with its accompanying tastes and goals, took its place as the dominant, decisive culture.

The eighteenth-century experiments in theatre that showcased contemporary social commentary, both with and without music, proved to resonate with the changing times. This direction would continue in the nineteenth century, especially in opera. It became so popular in the first half of the nineteenth century that its effectiveness as an art form that accurately captured the pulse of society, became a major factor in its continued triumph. In fact, this period in history is commonly referred to as the "Golden Age of Opera," owing to the success of the genre. Furthermore, many of the works produced between 1800 and 1850 are now part of modern opera companies' standard offerings.

In addition to musical theatre's ability to reflect society, several other factors contributed to the success of opera in particular. One of these was the development of *bel canto* singing, especially in Italian opera. Simply defined, bel canto means "beautiful singing," and its continued progress from the earliest experiments in monody led to its blossoming in this era. Turning away from the static formula of the da capo aria, with its required return to the capo (beginning), early nineteenth-century composers developed the aria with more dramatic action in mind. While a character might still begin a scene with recitative and the first part of an aria, she would move on to a second half of her aria that was new material. Whereas the first section might present a character's dilemma or conflict, often in a slow, contemplative mood, the second section was frequently faster and more resolute, showing that the character has chosen a path of action and intends to take it. The two sections become so distinct that they each have their own names. The slower opening section is the cantabile and the second feistier one is the cabaletta.

bel canto: Italian style of vocal delivery marked by beautiful singing

An excellent example occurs in Rossini's *The Barber of Seville* (1816). In this aria, Rosina (Beaumarchais's "Rosine," see Ch. 8 Theatre) has just fallen in love with Count Almaviva (known to Rosina as Lindoro) after he serenades her outside her window (see Fig. 9.19). Under the close scrutiny and "house arrest" by her guardian, however, it would take a certain amount of scheming to break free from his control. Yet, Rosina was determined.

cabaletta: second part of a nineteenth-century Italian aria

Listen to Rosina's aria, comparing the level of energy at the beginning to that at the end. The orchestra does a fine job of matching Rosina's hesitant opening sentiments with her fiery resolve at the end. The music at the end intensifies her warning to Dr. Bartolo ("Bartholo") that although she is usually docile and loving, she can be a viper when necessary to get her way.

Translation:

Cantabile: A voice a short while ago / here in my heart resounded. / My heart is already wounded, / and Lindoro is the culprit. / Yes, Lindoro will be mine. / I swore that I would win.

The guardian I shall refuse. / I shall sharpen my wits. / In the end he will be appeased, / and I shall be happy. / Yes, Lindoro will be mine. / I swore that I would win.

Chapter 9: Romanticism

Fig. 9.19. *The Barber of Seville*, Count Almaviva (Lindoro) serenades Rosina, assisted by Figaro, 2011, Dnepropetrovsk State Opera and Ballet Theatre, Dnepropetrovsk, Ukraine.

Cabaletta: I am docile, I am respectful, / I am obedient, sweetly loving; / I let myself be governed, be led.

But if they touch my weaker side, / I will be a viper, and a hundred tricks / I'll play before I give in![12]

(librettist Cesare Sterbini)

Listen for the change in tone that reflects Rosina's determination in "Una voce poco fa."

A second factor of success came with a heightened view of opera *as* drama. As seen with changes to the organization of arias, audiences desired to see more action, even in moments of reflection. As the focus of opera turned to plot, psychological characterization, staging, conflict, and **denouement**, composers sought ways to reinforce this new emphasis in music. They used it most effectively in three areas: enhancing character, propelling action, and creating atmosphere.

Rossini has already shown how music can enhance character with Rosina's aria. A contemporary of his, Giacomo Meyerbeer (1791-1864) effectively used music in his medium of French Grand Opera to generate and accelerate action. Meyerbeer's opera, *Les Huguenots* (1832-1836), clearly shows this. It is a historical opera portraying the St. Bartholomew's Day Massacre of Aug. 24, 1572,

nouement: final part of lay or opera en everyng is unraved or resolved when Roman Catholics in Paris massacred more than 3,000 French Protestants (known as Huguenots). Over the following several days, it is estimated that 20,000 Huguenots were killed in the massacre. The tension of that event resonated with political unrest in nineteenth-century France during the aftermath of the Revolution and Napoleon's failed imperial reign. The Huguenots' fight for freedom of religion mirrored the causes championed by the French Revolutionaries. Needless to say, this subject provided much opportunity for action-packed drama, in spite of the somber reminder of the outcome of the real event (see Fig. 9.20).

Les Huguenots, as an opera, is a dramatization, but it does portray the attempts by Queen Marguerite de Valois (1553-1615) to create peace between the Catholics and the Protestants. Her idea was a marriage between two prominent members of each group. Raoul, the Protestant, agreed to marry Valentine, the Catholic, sight unseen. In the listening excerpt, the bride-to-be is presented to her groom in a solemn ceremony that brought many leaders from both sides together. Unbeknownst to either side, however, Raoul recognized Valentine as his former lover who had supposedly jilted him. As he cries out, "Treason! Treachery," the entire company breaks out in pandemonium. Marguerite's plan is thwarted and the Catholics and Protestants resume their animosity. Only the voice of Marcel, Raoul's servant and staunch Protestant who saw through the futility of this attempt, can calm the storm briefly. Listen to how Meyerbeer uses music to accelerate the action to a rousing end, and likewise uses Marcel's interruption with strains of Luther's chorale, *Ein feste Burg* (A Mighty Fortress).

Fig. 9.20. St. Bartholomew's Day Massacre, Aug. 24, 1572.

Time	Chorale
2:27	Marcel, *Ein feste Burg*
2:36	Marcel, *Ein feste Burg*
4:03	Marcel, *Ein feste Burg*
4:08	Marcel, *Ein feste Burg*

(Note: The translation is not included here due to the many, many voices singing in the riot. Marcel is also singing different words—in French—to *Ein feste Burg*, but the tune is what sends the clear message to return to God and to sensibility.)

DID YOU KNOW?

Theatrical performances were conducted with house lights on. By the early nineteenth century, oil lamps, gas lighting, and limelight were in use. Because of this, most attendees had their personal copies of libretti in hand and were able to follow along with complicated plots and many voices singing simultaneously.

The phrase "in the limelight" comes from the use of stage lighting produced by heating calcium oxide, otherwise known as lime. It produces a white light that was flattering to actors, but it was unable to produce a sharp focus. The less flattering bluish light created by the safer and more efficient electricity later in the century created a nostalgia for "limelight."

Finally, music can create an atmosphere akin to staging and lighting. Vincenzo Bellini (1801-1835) effectively set the stage for *Norma* (1831) in her titular role as the High Priestess of the Druids in Roman occupied Gaul (see Fig. 9.21). As she and her maidens collect mistletoe to appease the moon goddess at such a time of threat and anxiety among her people, her own sense of calm and reassurance for her people is reflected in the music. The rolling arpeggios in the violins and the slow unfolding of the solo flute reinforced a sense of calmness. The 12/8 meter creates a sense of floating as 12 beats languidly fill out 1 measure. It is a meter frequently used for slow, tranquil music, and is very effective here in the moonlight. The audience is almost put to sleep by this introduction, and nearly unaware of Norma's quiet entrance at 1:52.

Chapter 9: Romanticism

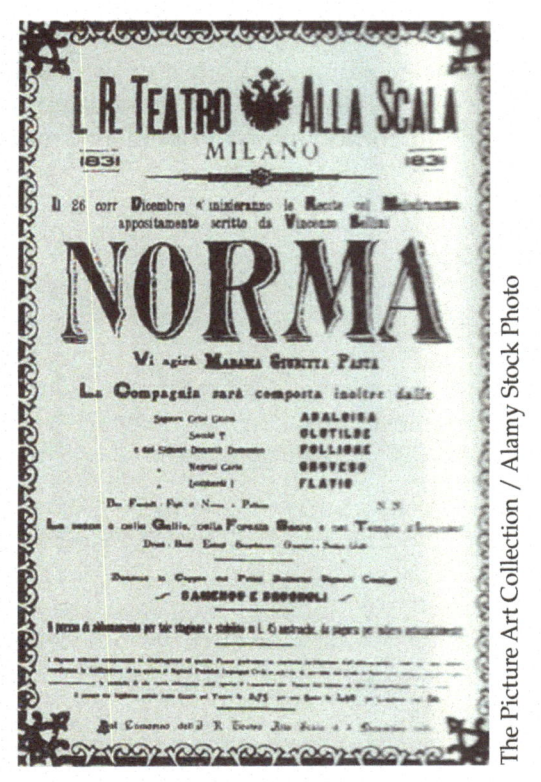

Fig. 9.21. Advertisement for *Norma*, 1831, La Scala, Milan.

Time	Description
0:00	Instrumental introduction in 12/8 with slow, rolling accompaniment
1:52	Norma begins singing, "Casta diva..."

Translation:

> Chaste goddess, who plates with silver / these sacred ancient plants, / towards us turn your lovely face, / without clouds and without veils.
>
> Temper, O goddess, these ardent hearts, / temper also their bold zeal. / Spread over the earth that peace / that you make reign in heaven.[13]

Listen to this excerpt.

In summary, opera developed a number of effective dramatic techniques while maintaining a high level of artistry in singing. During the nineteenth century, dramatic opera offered contemporary social commentary to audiences through satire, history, and comedy. Composers effectively combined music with the drama to reinforce characterization, action, and atmosphere. As such, opera became a powerful voice of the times and at times became a catalyst for change, as will be seen in the potent combination of opera and nationalism in Ch. 10.

> **IN THEIR OWN WORDS**
>
> Joseph Kerman, an important musicologist of the late twentieth century, expounded on the critical roles of music in drama in his seminal work, *Opera as Drama*. His words below might seem a little academic and hard to grasp; however, in a listener's experience, music conveys these ideas in a much more natural, simple, and effective way than words can do.
>
> "One agency of music in opera is to round out information about a character's thought and action with insight into his or her inner life of feeling. A second agency has to do with action. Music, like action, exists in time and articulates time. So music is especially well adapted to mirror, underpin, shape, or qualify individual actions. . . .A third contribution of music, though more ineffable, is also very important. . . .Music of a particular sort established a particular world or a particular field in which certain types of thought, feeling, and action are possible (or at least plausible). This is what we mean, ultimately, when we say that music imbues atmosphere."[14]

Study Questions

1. How did romanticism influence musical style? Give some specific examples.
2. How did opera become a very popular art form in the nineteenth century?
3. What historical events influenced Romanticism in art?
4. Which aspects of classical style most affected Neoclassicism?

Notes

1. Karl Marx, *Critique of Hegel's Philosophy of Right*, 131.
2. Friedrich Nietzsche, *Thus Spoke Zarathustra*, 212-213.
3. The phrase that Hegel uses may also be translated as Absolute Reason, as the German term *Geist* can mean spirit or reason. However, in keeping with the connections he makes between history, religion, and Christianity's past, it will be translated "Spirit" here. See Georg Friedrich Wilhelm Hegel, *Phenomenology of the Spirit*.
4. Georg Friedrich Wilhelm Hegel, *Lectures on the Philosophy of World History*.

5. Stephen Houlgate, "Hegel's Aesthetics".
6. Thibaudeau, quoted in Zarzeczny, 121.
7. https://www.history.com/topics/industrial-revolution/industrial-revolution
8. Oxford Lieder https://www.oxfordlieder.co.uk/song/2046
9. Reich, 228.
10. Musgrave, 92.
11. Botstein, 87-89.
12. Burkholder, 7th ed., 631.
13. Burkholder, 7th ed., 644.
14. Kerman, 215.

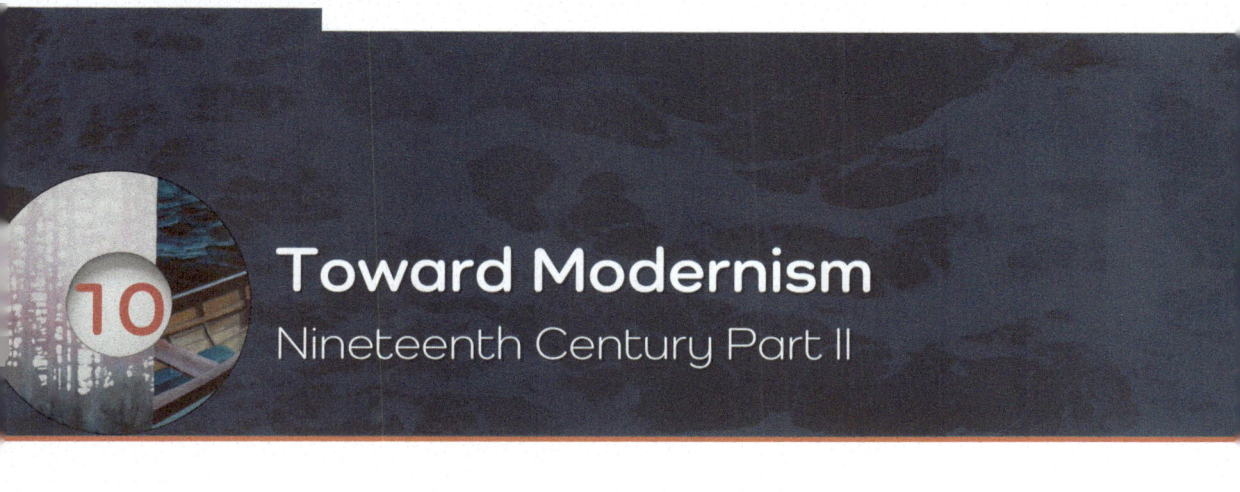

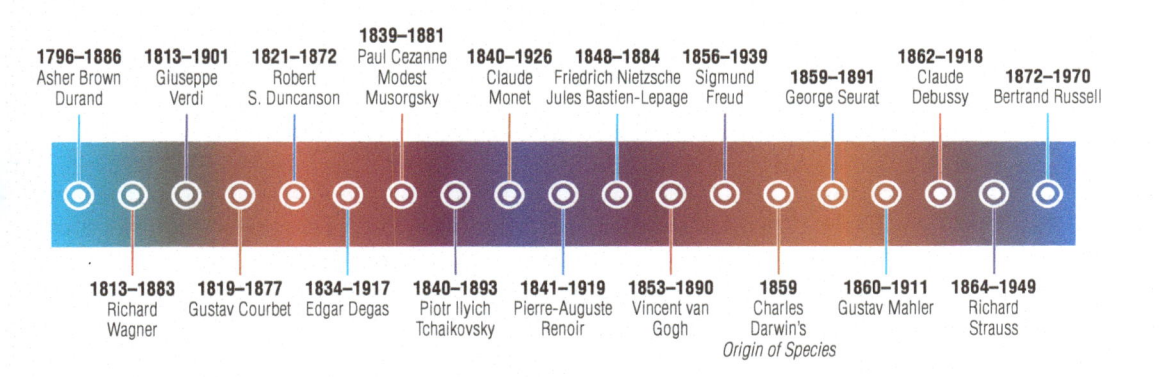

10 Toward Modernism
Nineteenth Century Part II

1796–1886 Asher Brown Durand
1813–1883 Richard Wagner
1813–1901 Giuseppe Verdi
1819–1877 Gustav Courbet
1821–1872 Robert S. Duncanson
1834–1917 Edgar Degas
1839–1881 Modest Musorgsky
1840–1893 Piotr Ilyich Tchaikovsky
1840–1926 Claude Monet
1841–1919 Pierre-Auguste Renoir
1848–1884 Friedrich Jules Bastien-Lepage
1853–1890 Vincent van Gogh
1856–1939 Nietzsche Sigmund Freud
1859 Charles Darwin's *Origin of Species*
1859–1891 George Seurat
1860–1911 Gustav Mahler
1862–1918 Claude Debussy
1864–1949 Richard Strauss
1872–1970 Bertrand Russell

Paul Cezanne (listed 1839–1881 area near Musorgsky dates shown as Paul Cezanne)

Art

Although most of the previous chapter focused on the early nineteenth century art in Europe, there was a peculiar brand of art happening in America that spanned the period from early to late nineteenth century. The untamed natural beauty of the American landscape had become a driving passion for many painters during this time. Another distinct movement that developed out of the mid-1900s in Europe was that of realism. The focus of these paintings was no longer legends of the past or portraits of those rich enough to buy them. The motivation behind realist paintings was to depict life as it truly was, often from the vantage point of the common person. Out of realism came impressionism. The realists went out and gathered data to bring back to their studio in order to complete a painting, whereas impressionists sought to complete their works on site. This led to more inventive techniques and stylized works. These stylized works reached their zenith through the postimpressionist artists that followed.

American Landscape Painting

Where European Romanticism was largely invested in the sublime depicted in the fiery seascapes of J. M. W. Turner, and the frightful and looming landscapes of Casper David Friedrich, American artists were mesmerized by the sheer beauty of the world. They sought to capture the magnitude of deep space and the warmth of the earthy vegetation surrounding them. A number of these landscape painters were established in New York, where they found ample inspiration in the Catskills and Adirondack mountains upstate. They eventually gained the title of Hudson River School, an appellation that was not meant as a compliment. Numerous paintings were from upstate New York, but this sentiment carried across the vast interior of the budding nation. Much of the preliminary work for these paintings was done from direct and meticulous observation. However, the works were typically finished in the studio where the landscape became idealized and edited as they saw fit.

Robert S. Duncanson (1821-1872) was heralded the "best landscape painter in the West" by *Daily Cincinnati Gazette* on May 30, 1861.[1] His artistic career took off after having made a name for himself while living in Cincinnati. Between his accolades in Ohio and international travel, he acquired renown in Canada, Great Britain, Sweden, Scotland, and Ireland.

> **IN THEIR OWN WORDS**
>
> Duncanson is believed to have started as a house painter before deciding to pursue a career in fine art. In the book *A History of African-American Artists: from 1792 to the Present*, Romaire Bearden states the following about the time in which Duncanson lived:
>
> "Most of Cincinnati's artists began as sign or house painters. But many became awed by the magnificence of the untamed wilderness at their doorstep and turned to landscape painting with a spiritual feeling. They saw the wilderness as God's work, allied with freedom and nature, but threatened by the destructive wastefulness of civilization."[2]

In his painting *Landscape with Rainbow* (Fig. 10.1), Duncanson portrays a marvelous display of luminescence in his treatment of the rainbow, coupled with the waning light of the setting sun as it cascades over the Arcadian landscape. Despite a significant downpour having just subsided, evidenced by the numerous trickles of water bubbling down the adjacent hills, the landscape is serene and quiet. This sensation is enhanced by the shimmering rainbow pointing the way home for a young couple. They seem to be taking their

Fig. 10.1. *Landscape with Rainbow*, oil on canvas, 1859, Robert S. Duncanson, Smithsonian American Art Museum, Washington, DC.

time, enjoying the moment as they casually stroll the last bit of road barefooted. Duncanson had captured some of the natural charm of rural life in America. The only visible threats are the deepening shadows of evening. However, even with tensions rising in America around the debate over slavery, Duncanson finished this peaceful painting close to a year from the onset of the American Civil War. Duncanson, himself a free African American, was preeminent in his artistic ability and unique in forging a prominent career in the arts.

Asher Brown Durand (1796-1886) was a leader and pillar for this emerging group of landscape painters in New York. Durand helped in the founding of the New York Drawing Association and was elected to various artistic clubs. He went on to write monthly for a publication where he gave his opinion on landscape painting with practical application points as well as answers to the reader's questions. Durand's writings, collectively referred to as *Letters on Landscape Painting*, were published over the course of nine entries. He was also the president of the National Academy of Design for over a decade.[3]

In his work *In the Catskills* (Fig. 10.2), Durand's thoughts are put into action. The landscape is lush and warm. There is a friendly exchange of travelers on a dirt road. The path is inviting, and it trails off into the distant green fields at the foot of a majestic mountain. The scene is peaceful and the weather is fair. Nature is still the main focus, but unlike the prior emphasis of artists on the sublime, here it is welcoming. The plants and vegetation are not wholly untouched by

© San Diego Museum of Art / Museum purchase with funds provided by the Gerald and Inez Grant Parker Foundation / Bridgeman Images

Fig. 10.2. *Landscape Composition: In the Catskills*, oil on canvas, 1848, Asher Brown Durand, San Diego Museum of Art, San Diego.

decay and death as seen in the broken tree stumps and withered branches in the foreground. There is a genuine attempt to depict nature as it is and not overly manipulated or stylized. In his *Letters on Landscape Painting*, Durand emphasized the need to go outside and draw directly from nature, reproducing it with exactness.

> **IN THEIR OWN WORDS**
>
> Asher Brown Durand in the 1855 issue of *The Crayon*: "Take pencil and paper, not the palette and brushes, and draw with scrupulous fidelity the outline or contour of such objects as you shall select..."[4]

Realism

In a similar way that Durand insisted on drawing nature with faithful precision in the United States, parallel beliefs can be found driving the concepts of realism in Europe. Where American landscape painters sought naturalism in the untamed remote places, some European artists applied these methods to the everyday lives of common people. In some circles, there was a general sense of displeasure toward the idealized paintings of neoclassical art as well as the dramatic and emotional paintings of the Romanticists. These artworks were

Fig. 10.3. *The Stonebreakers*, oil on canvas, 1849, Gustave Courbet, Gemäldegalerie Alte Meister, Dresden, Germany.

often highly edited, dramatized, and typically fictitious. Realism was not tied to a specific group of artists as much as to an attitude toward what should and should not be depicted.

Gustave Courbet (1819-1877) was most notable for setting this standard. He regularly pushed against the status quo with his brash attitude and stunning paintings.

In his massive work *The Stonebreakers* (Fig. 10.3), Courbet dedicates the entire canvas to the grueling work of poor laborers. There is no glory in their work, only the impersonal description of their plight. Torn clothes, heavy stones, and a steady hammering, describe their lot in life. There is no joy in their work or pleasure in their rigid monotony. The hammer seems barely large enough to do the job—the old laborer seems almost frozen in place without any real sense of strength or leverage. These are not heroes showing the dignity of hard work, these are faceless peasants barely holding on. By painting these commoners on such a large scale, Courbet was pushing the boundaries of what is worth portraying in paintings, blurring the lines between art and everyday experiences.

Jules Bastien-Lepage (1848-1884) found substantial success as a realist painter during his all too brief career. One of the works that established his notoriety was *Hay Making* (Fig. 10.4). The clarity with which Bastien-Lepage was able to paint is truly remarkable. He was able to achieve a level of naturalism that was almost unparalleled in his time. From muddy boots to a polished metal canteen, he skillfully depicted various materials with mastery. The empty

Fig. 10.4. *Hay Making*, oil on canvas, 1877, Jules Bastien-Lepage, Musée d'Orsay, Paris.

stare of the woman complements her tired arms hanging limply by her side. The scene is not describing anything of significance. It is merely a break in an otherwise average day, a moment so uninteresting that the man is literally taking a nap.

Another of Bastien-Lepage's paintings depicting common life can be seen in *The Little Chimney Sweep* (Fig. 10.5). The scene has a strong composition while still maintaining a candid sensibility. The figures in his paintings have very natural poses, almost as if the viewer happened to catch the subjects unaware. Despite *The Little Chimney Sweep* being technically unfinished in places, the parts that are finished have every bit of detail. Lepage not only depicted the soot on the boy's hands, but even the flour on the bottom crust of the bread he is holding. It is in paintings like these where the artist captures a mundane moment with such grace and virtuosity, that the beauty of God's creation can be seen in a fresh way. It can be a delicate reminder that not every moment in life needs to be grandiose, adventurous, or entertaining to be worthwhile—beauty and value can be found throughout all of life.

Fig. 10.5. *The Little Chimney Sweep*, oil on canvas, 1883, Jules Bastien-Lepage, private collection.

A number of those who lived through the recent upheaval, revolutions, and war became disillusioned with the static faith of religious activity. God must have seemed far off to those seeking refuge from a turbulent world. The notion of **materialism**, which dictated that all there is to life is what can be seen and touched, came to influence many. This philosophy coincided with the publication of Charles Darwin's *Origin of Species* in 1859 and his subsequent advocacy of evolution. Some artists began to scrutinize reality not as a way to find hidden meaning and value but simply to document and reinforce its empty physicality.

Impressionism

Impressionism was born from the desire to paint life at the moment that it was happening. To do this, several changes needed to happen. Up until this point, artists or assistants were making their oil paint by hand and storing them in pig's bladders or glass syringes. The industrial revolution allowed for the mass production of paint, the manufacturing of capped tin paint tubes, and the introduction of a number of new colors. With the advent of the collapsible and portable easel and readily available, stable pigments, artists were able to become significantly more mobile, further encouraging them to take their craft outdoors, a practice known as **plein-air** painting.

materialism: philosophy th all there is to life is what ca be touched ar seen

impressionis the style of painting that uses general, ten loose mar to make the "impression" of details rath than naturalis ones

plein-air: pai ing from life outdoors in a natural settin often comple in one sitting

Chapter 10: Toward Modernism

alla prima: meaning "to the first," the process of completing a whole painting in one session

To be able to work outside with natural daylight, an artist needed to work quickly. The term *alla prima* meaning "to the first" describes the process of creating the whole painting in just one session. This was distinct from more traditional painting methods that would use multiple layers and slowly build up to the finished image.

Claude Monet (1840-1926) was trained as a realist painter, but he gravitated toward the quick sketchy style that allowed him to paint quickly on location. He was one of the founders of Impressionism, the title of his painting (Fig. 10.6) being the inspiration for the label given to this movement.

Impression, Sunrise, aptly named, does not have the clarity and exactness of realism. There is no longer distinction between known objects, as much as an effort to simplify everything into broad shapes and colors. There is no time to develop the various riggings or number of sails on distant ships. There is not even enough time to clearly denote the number of passengers in their dinghies. However, the fact that this is a harbor in the misty morning sunrise is unmistakable. Monet used short and energetic strokes of paint to describe the big picture. Everything is nearly lost in a blue haze, except for the main subject of the painting, which is the burning light of the morning sun.

Another of Monet's paintings, *The Sheltered Path* (Fig. 10.7), shows a frenzy of blurred vegetation. The dappled brushstrokes mimic the leafy vegetation as it

Fig. 10.6. *Impression, Sunrise,* oil on canvas, 1872, Claude Monet, Musée Marmottan Monet, Paris.

Chapter 10: Toward Modernism 267

Fig. 10.7. *The Sheltered Path*, oil on canvas, 1873, Claude Monet, Philadelphia Museum of Art.

catches the sunlight. Even a botanist would be hard-pressed to identify any of the plants included in this landscape painting. However, Monet's goal was not to document with scientific exactness. His goal was to describe the *impression* of what he saw.

> ### IN THEIR OWN WORDS
>
> "When you go out to paint, try to forget what objects you have before you, a tree, a house, a field, or whatever. Merely think, here is a little square of blue, here an oblong of pink, here a streak of yellow."[5]
> —Claude Monet

Impressionists were more concerned with depicting the atmosphere and natural daylight—even capturing the difference between the light in the morning and afternoon as seen in Figs. 10.8 and 10.9. These paintings are from a series Monet painted of the same cathedral at different times of the day. Sometimes a plein-air painting would need multiple sessions to complete simply due to the size of the canvas and the changing direction of the sun. In order to circumvent this problem, artists would come back to the same spot during the same time of day until the painting was finished.

268 Chapter 10: Toward Modernism

Fig. 10.8. *Rouen Cathedral, West Facade, Sunlight*, oil on canvas, 1892-1894, Claude Monet, Musée d'Orsay, Paris.

Another leader of the impressionist movement was Pierre-Auguste Renoir (1841-1919). In his painting *Luncheon of the Boating Party* (Fig. 10.10), he has captured a whimsical scene of a crowded café in the summertime. Through his paintings, Renoir celebrated beauty; in particular the female form. His works were most often vibrant and colorful portraits depicting the easygoing middle-class life. With the exciting development of new synthetic colors for paints and pastels, the impressionists used them liberally, often leaving colors and brushstrokes unmixed on the canvas to heighten the contrast.

Edgar Degas (1834-1917) also significantly contributed to the impressionist movement. Best known for his depictions of ballerina dancers, Degas worked in a number of different mediums, including printmaking, painting, pastels, and sculpture. His piece *Swaying Dancer* (Fig. 10.11) is typical of his pastel work. Focusing more on the gesture of the ballerina and the simplified shapes and marks of color that compose the image, Degas was able to represent the fast-paced, ethereal, and fleeting qualities of dance. There is no rigid structure of perspectival lines to give a true sense of space. Degas is relying on his impression of the

Chapter 10: Toward Modernism 269

Fig. 10.9. *Rouen Cathedral, Facade (Morning effect)*, oil on canvas, 1892–1894, Claude Monet, Museum Folkwang, Essen, Germany.

Fig. 10.10. *Luncheon of the Boating Party*, oil on canvas, 1880–1881, Pierre-Auguste Renoir, The Phillips Collection, Washington, DC.

Fig. 10.11. *Swaying Dancer (Dancer in Green)*, pastel and gouache on paper, 1877-1879, Edgar Degas, Thyssen-Bornemisza Museum, Madrid.

moment to communicate the dynamic movement of the dancer. The various intricacies and decorative elements of the costumes are translated into mere specks and scrawls of color.

Impressionists sought to convey the big picture without getting lost in the meticulous details. In essence, they were not painting objects, people, and landscapes, as much as they were painting light itself. Similarly, it can be tempting to overemphasize the details of daily life and lose track of the true Light of the World. Impressionism can also serve as reminder that the substance of life isn't simply a series of details and checklists, but the bigger picture of the gospel lived out.

Postimpressionism

Postimpressionism is one of the last signposts before the jump to modernism. Up until this point, art had been a fairly consistent stream of styles and ideas—each new generation gradually changing the previous patterns and visions by degrees. However, in comparison to modernism, none of these movements had amounted to a truly unique and innovative form of art. Postimpressionism was the first step in an entirely new direction. Postimpressionist artists took notes from the formal qualities of impressionism and then split off into a variety of directions. Artists had grown weary of the subjects of their forebearers.

Georges Seurat (1859-1891) moved the impressionist style into an almost scientific use of color application by applying dots of pure color to the canvas in order to create his images. From a distance, the viewer would experience a harmonious landscape with various figures, but as one drew near to the surface of the painting, the illusion would disintegrate into a spattering of contrasting colors. Seurat believed these dotted color combinations could actually be imbued with varying emotions of happiness, sadness, and calm.

Sunday Afternoon on the Island of La Grande Jatte (Fig. 10.12) is Seurat's most significant work. His painting uses his meticulous technique of **pointillism** combined with his theories of harmony, balance, and the emotional potential of color. The stiff figures have been carefully placed in favor of composition over naturalism. They give off a sense of discomfort, each person in contemplative silence. It is unclear whether the severity of the people was a critique of Parisian society or a nod to classical Greek friezes. Either way, each figure was given what seems to be the personality of a tree, rigid, unmoving, and hiding in shadows.

pointillism: the laborious use of individual dotted marks form the whole of an image

With the close-up in Fig. 10.13 of a leaping dog and pet monkey on a leash, the individual color dots of his telltale technique start to become more distinguishable.

One of the most celebrated artists in the Western canon, Vincent van Gogh (1853-1890), was virtually unknown during his time. His life was a series of struggles and difficulties up until his death. His emotional turmoil alternately led from tremendous zeal to bitter sadness and depression. During his fifteen-month stay in Arles, France, he completed 200 paintings, over 100 drawings and watercolors, and roughly 200 letters.[6]

Van Gogh had encountered the works of Georges Seurat while living and working in Paris. He was influenced by Seurat's use of color and pointillism, experimenting and mimicking the technique until he landed on his own peculiar style. In *The Night Café* (Fig. 10.14), one can see thicker and longer brushstrokes

Courtesy of The Art Institute of Chicago, Helen Birch Bartlett Memorial Collection

Fig. 10.12. *Sunday Afternoon on the Island of La Grande Jatte*, oil on Canvas, 1884, Georges Seurat, Art Institute of Chicago.

Fig. 10.13. *Sunday Afternoon on the Island of La Grande Jatte*, close-up, oil on Canvas, 1884, Georges Seurat, Art Institute of Chicago.

Fig. 10.14. *The Night Café*, oil on canvas, 1889, Vincent van Gogh, Yale University Art Gallery, New Haven, CT.

that have been left patchy and unblended. This painting is one of Van Gogh's explicit attempts at using color in a symbolic way. In a letter to his brother, Vincent relays his attempt at using complementary colors of red and green to express "the terrible passions of humanity," instilling a moralizing quality to the painting of this venue, which he likens to a "devil's furnace of pale sulphur."[7]

Chapter 10: Toward Modernism   273

Fig. 10.15. *Wheat Field with Cypresses*, oil on canvas, 1889, Vincent van Gogh, Metropolitan Museum of Art, NY.

Wheat Field with Cypresses (Fig. 10.15) is indicative of Van Gogh's stylistic undulating treatment of his subjects. The rippling movement of everything gives a psychological intensity to an otherwise typical landscape painting. The eye of the viewer has nowhere to rest in the swirling strokes of paint, giving the sensation that the painting is always in motion. Van Gogh used loads of thick paint with each brushstroke to build up a rich texture, also known as **impasto** painting.

Paul Cézanne (1839-1906) must also be included among the most influential postimpressionists. His vision for art was to move beyond representing things from a rigid single point of view. He sought to represent life from multiple perspectives—similar to the way one's eyes naturally rove around moving from place to place to take in their surroundings. In doing so, his paintings have a very odd and detached presence to them. In *The Artist's Father Reading His Newspaper* (Fig. 10.16), this disconnect is happening with the shallowness of the chair where his father seems to be unnaturally perched.

In *Still Life with Dresser* (Fig. 10.17), everything seems to be occupying the same space, causing some significant discrepancies in the painting. The front edge of the table is misaligned and hidden under the fabric. The pottery is simultaneously depicted from lower and higher perspectives, which is off-putting. Also, the tabletop is considerably shallow in depth compared to all the items on its surface. Cézanne is suspending the natural and intuitive understanding of

impasto: the very thick application of paint to a surface

Courtesy of National Gallery of Art, Collection of Mr. and Mrs. Paul Mellon

Fig. 10.16. *The Artist's Father Reading His Newspaper*, oil on canvas, 1866, Paul Cézanne, National Gallery of Art, Washington, DC.

space, forcing the viewer to accept his unrealistically crowded tabletop. Many of his paintings have a compressed sense of space as if he is cramming a still life or portrait into half of the depth that the subject was actually taking up.

Cézanne's work had a polarizing effect on people. Younger artists greatly admired his paintings, while many others held them in disdain. After attending a group show with Cézanne's work in it, right-wing journalist Henri Rochefort described the artists as having "diseased minds, traitors to their country, lovers of physical and moral filth." Rochefort's review sparked outrage in Cézanne's hometown where Cézanne received abusive messages advising him to leave "the city that he was dishonouring."[8]

The modern art movement of the twentieth century, following post-impressionism, pushed Cézanne's ideas even further, catapulting the artworld into uncharted waters. This further opened the door to creativity and controversy. The renowned Pablo Picasso (1881-1973) even declared, "Cézanne's influence gradually flooded everything" regarding him as a "mother hovering over (all)."[9]

DID YOU KNOW?

Paintings have been loaned to presidents of the United States during their administration. Typically, the artwork served as the backdrop for the Senate Inaugural Luncheon and a symbol of the incoming administration's agenda before heading to the Oval Office for display. First Lady Jill Biden helped choose Robert Duncanson's painting *Landscape with Rainbow* (Fig. 10.1) for the occasion of President Joe Biden's inauguration.

Fig. 10.17. *Still Life with Dresser*, oil on canvas, 1883-1887, Paul Cézanne, Neue Pinakothek, Munich.

Music

Nationalism

Following the revolutions of 1848 and 1849, Germany entered a period of restructuring. Tradition was highly valued as a way to celebrate the past while also reasserting dominance in the present. As musical scholarship developed, German composers such as Bach, Handel, and Mozart grew to fame far beyond their influence during their lifetimes. The undeniable presence of German masters in Western music's development was the catalyst for nationalism and bolstered the agenda of the New German regime. With the conventions of the past as their foundation, and the growing Romantic movement highlighting current musicianship and innovation, state-led unification embraced what they considered to be the authenticity and purity of the German sound and encouraged its continuation.

While Germany sought to achieve a unified state through authoritarian rule, the **Risorgimento** was already in motion in Italy, following the defeat of Napoleon in 1815. The movement inspired zealous patriotism in pursuit of unity and reestablished national identity. Although their breadth of musical tradition did not match Germany's, Italian music still served as a means through which a collective national voice was revered.

Risorgimento nineteenth-century political movement that fought for the unification of Italy

In response to German dominance, Russia and many Eastern European countries sought to celebrate the unique traditional elements of their individual countries as they endeavored to forge their own musical identities and assert their presence in the artistic world of the late nineteenth century. Folk melodies, rhythms, and harmonies were incorporated into traditionally structured works, as composers emphasized the authentic and worthy heritage of their respective countries.

Germany

A discussion of German nationalism in music would be incomplete without mentioning opera composer Richard Wagner, who is discussed in greater detail in the theatre section of this chapter. His support of the quest for German unification established him as a staunch nationalist, and he used symbolism throughout the music and librettos of his operas to demonstrate his leanings; the presence of strong male characters was often set in contrast to weaker, less masculine roles, highlighting both his anti-Semitic and sexist views. Wagner's influence extended beyond the art world, however, as he penned many essays on a range of topics from composition to politics, where he argued for the superiority of German music, from both artistic and philosophical perspectives.

Italy

In Italy, composer Giuseppe Verdi (1813-1901), also discussed in more detail in the theatre section of this chapter, was widely hailed as a champion of Italian nationalism, eventually serving as an elected member of the first Italian Parliament. Historians differ regarding the degree to which Verdi actively contributed to the nationalist cause. However, it is established that his works were subject to Austrian censorship. He often resorted to changing words in his librettos, both preemptively and by specific direction. One such instance was in the chorus "Immenso Jehova" from his opera *Nabucco*. The original line, "Often you gave your people tears, but you broke their chains if they believed in you" was rewritten without the reference to breaking of chains. The imagery of escaping from bondage was often associated with the Risorgimento, and as the movement continued, Verdi's operas were celebrated as a driving musical force in the crusade. His name ultimately became synonymous with the cry for unification. "Viva Verdi!" (**Vittorio Emanuele Re d'Italia**, which meant "Long live Victor Emmanuel, king of Italy") was proclaimed throughout Italy—spoken, written, and even graffitied—to demonstrate patriotic allegiance (see Fig. 10.18). Although he was not the original inspiration for the phrase, the association endured.

Fig. 10.18. Italian nationalists inscribing "Viva Verdi" on the city walls.

Russia

While music in Germany and Italy served to promote the sanctity and solidarity of a national identity through reliance on tradition, Russian music began to depart from tradition, forging a character of its own. Leading the way in this divergence was a group of laymen-by-day, composers-by-night, now known as The Mighty Five or The Mighty Handful. These five men united around the goal of establishing a distinctly Russian sound and presence, without entirely dismissing the Western European tradition in the process. They closely studied the work of the greatest German composers, whose influence can be discerned in the harmonic structure of many late nineteenth-century Russian works.

Modest Musorgsky (1839-1881; see Fig. 10.19) is one of the most widely recognized of The Five and his music embodies their quest. The distinctive presence of Russian folk tradition in his melodies, coupled with Western compositional structure, clearly presents the marriage of the two schools within the newly established Russian style. His *Pictures at an Exhibition*, originally written for solo piano in 1874 and later orchestrated by composer Maurice Ravel, demonstrates these qualities in abundance. This suite of ten movements was inspired by a collection of paintings created by artist Viktor Hartmann. Each movement within the suite represents one of Hartmann's works and

Fig. 10.19. Portrait of Modest Musorgsky, 1881, Ilya Repin, Tretyakov Gallery, Moscow.

the subsequent scenes Musorgsky envisioned occurring within the art. The pieces are joined by a recurring promenade, representing the composer's walk through the exhibit.

The inspiration for the final scene in the suite, Hartmann's *The Great Gate of Kiev,* mirrors the dichotomy of ideals in Musorgsky's music—the columns and arches represent the presence of classic architectural technique while decorative Russian elements adorn the face of the gate (see Fig. 10.20). The grandeur and ceremony of this movement resemble a sacred hymn or anthem, while the presence of bells both in the painting and in the composition is a direct homage to the religious influence in the Russian tradition.

Chapter 10: Toward Modernism

Fig. 10.20. *The Great Gate of Kiev*, 1869, Victor Hartmann, Pushkin House, St. Petersburg.

Listen to the treatment of the themes in The Great Gate of Kiev, from Musorgsky's *Pictures at an Exhibition.*

Time	Description
0:00	The main theme (representing the gate) is declared by the force of the full brass section.
0:25	Woodwinds enter under the brass, but the sound of the brass carries over them until you can hear the change of the color of the sound at 0:33.
0:46	The string section finally enters, and the full force of the orchestra loudly plays this iteration of the theme.
1:06	The full orchestra drops out and a new theme (the Russian hymn "As you are baptized in Christ") is played by only 4 performers: 2 clarinets and 2 bassoons.

(*Continued*)

Time	Description
1:37	The lowest voices in the orchestra take over the melody of the main theme, with the high strings and woodwinds playing descending and ascending scales above.
1:53	The roles are reversed, the higher voices (led by the trumpets and violins) take over the main theme, and the scales are played by the lower strings and woodwinds.
2:13	The hymn returns, beginning with the same instrumentation as the first time, but eventually adds flutes and the bass clarinet to the mix.
2:46	Transitional material that creates a sense of heaviness, almost as if building the massive gate.
3:14	The trumpets lead the way in the playing of a theme that is presented throughout the entirety of this work, known as the "Promenade" theme. This theme is played (in various forms) between each of the pictures represented in the whole work. As this is the end, Musorgsky is giving one last statement of the theme, this time in a proud and stately manner.
3:45	The main theme is stated again, this time in the musical score, the note values are twice as long as they have been to this point. This is referred to as augmentation.
4:56	Final augmented version of the main theme, punctuated by bells, drums, and cymbals.

Late Romantic Composers

Gustav Mahler

Bohemian-born composer and conductor Gustav Mahler (1860-1911) was another presence whose works shaped the music of the era (see Fig. 10.21). While his Jewish heritage placed him at odds with German nationalist ideals, he was influenced by Wagner's desire to build upon the principles of past Romantic composers as they sought to establish a new approach to sound and symbolism. His works were a strong contribution to the continuation of German dominance within the musical world. Mahler's early symphonic works are marked by their massive instrumentation and unique combinations of instrument voicings. His music often contained Austrian folk elements in an attempt to evoke rural scenes familiar to his listeners; the low art of folk music met the high art of the symphony. *Symphony No. 2 in C minor, "Resurrection,"* is an example of a **program symphony**, a musical work with an extramusical association. Its subtitle, *Resurrection*, offers clues to the purpose of this symphony. Throughout his life, Mahler

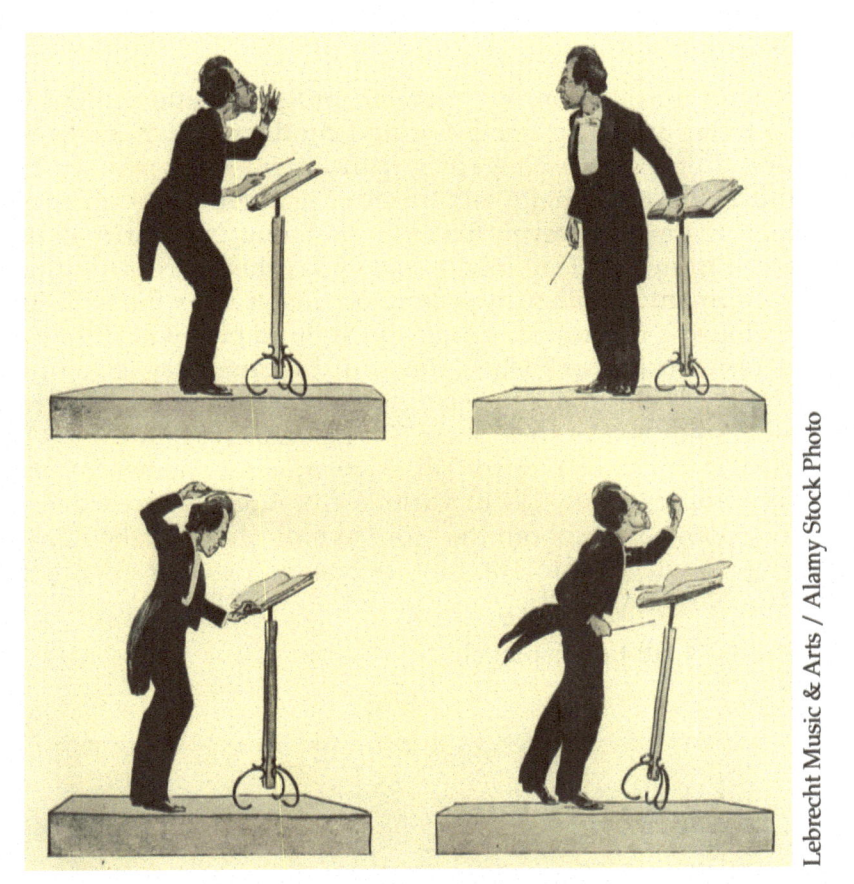

Fig. 10.21. Caricatures of Gustav Mahler, who was known for his expressive conducting style.

maintained a certain fascination with death and life beyond the grave. Inspired by the passing of a close friend, this piece is his musical journey through the reckonings of loss and grief, and his reflections on the meaning of life. From the somber, funeral-like opening movement to the apocalyptic Final Judgment in the finale, the hauntingly beautiful string melodies and magnificent brass presence usher the listener through every imaginable emotion as Mahler masterfully probes the mysteries of finite existence. While his religious conviction and affiliation changed throughout his lifetime, his familiarity with Christian tenets is evident in this work as he presents his understanding of events following death. The *Resurrection* is a powerful display of the role music can play both in personal introspection and in the exploration of the most meaningful questions.

Listen to the opening final movement of Mahler's Symphony No. 2 in C minor.

Richard Strauss

tone poems: ne-[vement] symphonic work [that] depicts a [spe]cific program, theme, or [stor]y

Where Mahler's music often incorporated programmatic content to present its meaning to his audience, composer and conductor Richard Strauss (1864-1949) created a new genre altogether with his **tone poems** (see Fig. 10.22). Strauss's music did not contain any traces of nationalism or alliance with the New German regime; however, his overwhelming popularity earned attention and honor from state leadership, as they saw his success inviting national acclaim for Germany. While he was certainly inspired by the work of Wagner, Strauss developed a musical language and style all his own. His compositions challenged previously established limits of instrumental technique, requiring a new level of skill from musicians, which in turn introduced revolutionary orchestral sounds. His tone poem *Till Eulenspiegel* follows the humorous adventures of a trickster named Till. Two musical themes recur throughout the piece, representing Till in various situations. Strauss even included specific story points throughout the score to indicate what the musical effects are depicting. In reference to Till, Strauss noted, "das war ein arger Kobold" (he was a troublesome devil!).

Listen to Strauss's *Till Eulenspiegel*.

Fig. 10.22. Photograph of composer Richard Strauss.

Time	Description
0:01	Once upon a time….
0:23	The French horn enters and plays a repeated motive that fits the syllables of "Till Eulenspiegel," and again at 0:34 and by the oboes at 0:41, you will continue to hear it traded around the orchestra.
1:08	Clarinet enters with the second main motive. Strauss notes here, "he was a troublesome devil!" The motive gets developed and passed around the orchestra.
3:05	Cymbal crash. Strauss notes, "Hop! On horseback straight through the market women" and at the silence at 3:27, Till has escaped.
3:56	Disguised as a priest, he delivers a blasphemous sermon
5:17	He meets some girls and falls for one of them. Rejected by her, he "vows revenge on all mankind."
6:54	He challenges some old school-masters, making fun of them for their beliefs, this section ends with a "big grimace" at 8:20.
9:44	We hear the Till Eulenspiegel theme from the solo French horn again as he plans another adventure.
12:13	The snare drum enters, Till is arrested, he continues to make fun of those around him as he is accused, but they hang him (shrieking clarinet playing the motive at 13:01) for his blasphemous acts.
14:18	Music similar to the introduction, this time seemingly stating the moral "it is best to be good and behave," but the Till Eulenspiegel theme makes its way through one last time.

Piotr Illyich Tchaikovsky

While Musorgsky and the rest of The Five established a revolutionary legacy in the development of Russian music, their nationalistic emphasis held them back from the global acclaim enjoyed by their contemporary, Piotr Ilyich Tchaikovsky (1840-1893). Tchaikovsky (see Fig. 10.23) is universally acknowledged as one of the greatest composers of the nineteenth century. His music deftly balances Western European romanticism and Russian nationalism. It features the structure, harmony, and emotion found in German music, while also celebrating Russian culture both in melodic and rhythmic elements and through the stories he featured in his dramatic works. Tchaikovsky was a passionate, mercurial man who internalized both the ecstasy and pain he experienced. Though his professional life and work were highly successful, a lack of stability marked both his personal affairs and mental well-being. He battled depression, struggled with

Fig. 10.23. Photograph of Piotr Ilyich Tchaikovsky.

his homosexuality, and experienced financial distress throughout his career. His final piece, *Symphony No. 6 in B minor, "Pathetique,"* is the culmination of his life's work.

> ### IN THEIR OWN WORDS
>
> Tchaikovsky ultimately dedicated his Sixth Symphony to his nephew Vladimir "Bob" Davydov. In a letter to Davydov, dated August 1893, Tchaikovsky wrote of this symphony:
>
> "I'm very pleased with its content, but dissatisfied, or rather not completely satisfied, with the instrumentation. For some reason it's not coming out as I intended … But I absolutely consider it to be the best, and in particular, the most sincere of all my creations. I love it as I have never loved any of my other musical offspring."[10]

While there is disagreement among music historians regarding the extent to which this symphony is autobiographical, his regard for the work, as revealed in his letter to his nephew, lends credence to the idea of a deeply personal connection. The somber mood of the piece displays Tchaikovsky's mastery of colorful orchestration and his ability to communicate deep-seated emotion, while the drama of the rich string melodies and heaviness of the minor key in which the symphony is set add to the darkness the music evokes. While a typical symphony of the time would end with a majestic or celebratory finale, the *Pathetique* quietly fades away into silence, which proved to be hauntingly prescient, as Tchaikovsky died only nine days after the premiere of the work in October 1893.

Listen to the first movement of Tchaikovsky's Symphony No. 6 in B minor.

Impressionism

In a marked step away from the realism and emotion of romantic art, the impressionist movement introduced new ideals of restraint and understatement. Just as impressionist paintings presented images with soft, muted colors and a marked absence of sharp lines and details, so impressionist music emerged with an emphasis on subdued aesthetic and mood.

The work of French composer Claude Debussy revolutionized the realm of music (see Fig. 10.24). Though his compositions are considered a part of the impressionist movement, he renounced the idea that his work was influenced by the paintings of artists such as Monet and Renoir. Inspired in part by the progressive thinking of The Mighty Five, Debussy engaged in innovative departures from established conventions and the excessive emotion and drama in the music of his Romantic predecessors.

> **IN THEIR OWN WORDS**
>
> When describing his music in a conversation with Ernest Guiraud, Debussy said:
>
> "There is no theory. You merely have to listen. Pleasure is the law."[11]

He created a musical language of his own, with influences ranging from medieval parallel organum (see Ch. 5) to Javanese gamelan music. The new level of symbolism he introduced, and his pioneering of unique instrumental **timbres** and original harmonic colors were subversive contributions to the development of the late nineteenth century music. In contrast to the "always more" mentality of Romanticism, Debussy's music contended for the value of restraint. His *Prélude à "L'après-midi d'un faune"* (Prelude to "The Afternoon of

timbre: the distinguishing qualities properties of sound

Fig. 10.24. Photograph of Claude Debussy.

a Faun"), based upon a poem by symbolist Stéphane Mallarmé, utilizes all of Debussy's newly established musical vocabulary as he paints with sound, bringing the scenes from the poem to life. The opening lines feature a solo flute, representing the faun sleepily playing his pipes in the woods as he drifts seamlessly into peaceful dreams. The muted swells of the strings and horns usher the listener into the faun's dream world, and the harp adds to the sense of magic and fantasy as his visions unfold.

Listen to Debussy's Prélude à "L'après-midi d'un faune."

The bold, yet understated revolution of Debussy represents some of the first steps toward musical modernism—a development that gained momentum at the dawn of the twentieth century.

Theatre

From German Romanticism to Nationalism

The Romantic era (see Ch. 9) was largely the first time that literature became an important factor in shaping music, but it was also the first time that German ideas became an important force in shaping European thought. Ever since the 30 Years' War (1618-1648), the German language and German people seemed to be inferior to the cultures of Italy and France. The rise of the latter nation under Louis XIV made French culture and language a status symbol. Napoleon later exerted influence in Germanic areas as he conquered the lands for his short-lived French Empire. As Germans recovered from foreign domination, ideas of nationalism began to grow. The core identities of a people bound by language, a common culture, shared history, and a defined sovereign territory gave impetus to writings in the German language. Not since Luther translated the Bible into German in the sixteenth century was prominence given to such linguistic growth.

One of the main writers in the nineteenth century generation of thought was Johann Wolfgang von Goethe, whose literature and poetry were heavily influenced by Romanticism. Since this movement largely began with literary figures, it was very much intertwined with German nationalism. From this close relationship, the idea of opera as a marriage of the literary world and the nation served as a vehicle to elevate the importance of these two arenas in building the ideas of German identity. No one saw the potential of this medium more than Richard Wagner did. His 13 operas in German all reflected ideals of Romanticism on the surface and of nationalism on a much deeper level that managed to resonate with many German speakers of the late nineteenth century. This resonance would last well into the twentieth century and erupt with great vehemence and destruction with the rise of Hitler in 1933.

In Their Own Words

Richard Taruskin, musicologist and author of the six-volume seminal work, *The Oxford History of Western Music*, reflected on Wagner's Christian beliefs in light of his contemporaries Charles Darwin and Karl Marx, who challenged Christianity in their own ways:

"Wagner was in an important sense a religious thinker in his own right… But his religion was not Christianity … [I]t was German myth and legend that formed the basis of Wagner's mature work. The ecstatic and redemptive religion his works proclaimed was in effect a new paganism born of ethnic rather than political nation-worship, and anyone who knows the history of the twentieth century knows that ethnic nationalism has been an even more volatile force in that history than Darwinism or Marxism have been."[12]

Richard Wagner and Music Drama

For Richard Wagner (see Fig. 10.25), music, art, and drama had to work effectively together to create what he termed *Gesamtkunstwerk*, or total artwork. With such alignment, his music drama pointedly sent messages of nationalism through characterization, libretto, plot, setting, action, and melody. In fact, Wagner weaves motives into his music that tells the story in a more effective way than language could do alone. These music motives are call *Leitmotives*. They are short statements, usually just a few notes, that are easily remembered. They stand for a person, a thing, a feeling, or an idea, and when they are heard, the audience recognizes the presence of what is represented by the music. The Leitmotives give the music equal responsibility in conveying the message of the opera and not merely in serving as an accompaniment.

Gesamtkunstwerk: German for total artwo[rk]

Leitmotives: short musical motives that represent a person, idea, thing, or even and that occu[rs] whenever som[ething] thing related [to] that is on stag[e]

Chapter 10: Toward Modernism

RICHARD WAGNER.
WAGNER

Courtesy MET Museum, The Crosby Brown Collection of Musical Instruments, 1901

Fig. 10.25. Portrait of Richard Wagner, print, lithograph after a photograph, after 1861. Pierre Petit, Metropolitan Museum of Art, NY.

Two of the main messages that Wagner continuously sought to portray in his music dramas were the strong male character of the German ideal male and the weak, inferior characteristics of non-Germans. In the world of the nineteenth century Germany, there was no doubt that he meant the Jews (see Music, this Ch.). Anti-Semitism waxed and waned throughout Europe's history following the diaspora of Jews beginning in AD 70 with the destruction of Jerusalem and the temple by Titus. While some European Christians refused to participate in anti-Semitic movements, many did ostracize the Jews and were even guilty of persecuting them.

> **DID YOU KNOW?**
>
> Nationalism sounds like a noble and worthy cause, but Christians should think twice about the implications of nationalist movements. Although there may be promises of identity, inclusion, and safety, there is an equally insidious side of nationalism that leaves no place for persons who failed to share the dominant characteristics of a particular nation. As Christians, there is no place for prejudice and hate crimes against other human beings. The Bible does not support a justification for any such actions or attitudes.
>
> What does the Scripture say? For the many people who were not born Jews, God considered them "separated," "alienated," and "strangers," "having no hope and without God in the world." With Christ's death on the cross, however, those same people were "brought near by the blood of Christ." One of Christ's many great accomplishments on Calvary was to create one new body. Whether Gentile or Jew, all could be included in this unified institution by believing in Jesus Christ as the Son of God and Savior. "For He Himself is our peace, who has made us both one and has broken down in his flesh the dividing wall of hostility…that He might create in Himself one new man in place of the two, so making peace" (Eph 2:12-15).

Wagner's crowning work, *The Ring of the Nibelungs* (*Der Ring des Nibelungen*), a cycle of four operas that has a total running time of about fifteen hours and is often performed as a week-long extravaganza, contains strains of both sides of nationalism—the insider and the outsider. This story is the long saga of a search for possession of a magic gold ring, similar to *The Lord of the Rings* film series by Peter Jackson, based on the novels by J. R. R. Tolkien. In the titular role of Wagner's work are the Nibelungen, a subhuman race of creatures who steal the gold from aquatic maidens in the Rhine River (the river dividing Germany from France) and forge some of it into a ring. Whoever possesses the ring gains power over the world and all its forces, but it brings sure devastation to whoever wields it. The ring is stolen from the Nibelungen and passes into several hands throughout the four operas, eventually bringing final destruction to the hero and heroine of the entire cycle, the demigods, Siegfried and Brünnhilde, in a fantastic, fiery finale to the work.

Siegfried does not appear until the third opera, which is eponymously so titled. By this time, however, the audience knows how the gold was stolen, what has happened to some of the rings' possessors, the identity and fate of Siegfried's parents, and how Brünnhilde ended up on a rock for eighteen years surrounded by an eternal fire. Wagner needed two full-length operas to provide the backstory alone! *Siegfried* opens with young Siegfried at eighteen

Chapter 10: Toward Modernism

Fig. 10.26. *The Young Siegfried*, drawing, pen and brush and gray ink, 1839, Julius Hübner, Metropolitan Museum of Art, NY.

years old, having been raised as an orphan by a Nibelung. He questions his heritage, noting his own physical superiority over his adopted community. Disgusted and dissatisfied, he takes his sword, Nothung, and leaves daringly to find his own answers in the world (see Fig. 10.26). His fearlessness is a principal characteristic of the perfect German that Wagner portrays in the work. Naturally, he is the only one who can brave the flames to set Brünnhilde free. As a reward for this, he wins her love and they marry. Until the end of the entire cycle, Brünnhilde remains faithful in her love and devotion to Siegfried, a prized characteristic of the ideal German woman.

Listen to Siegfried calling for his sword Nothung as he is forging it, incorporating part of the "sword" *leitmotif*, a very wide descending interval, into his music. This leitmotif is present throughout the Ring cycle, whenever the sword is present.

The non-German in *The Ring* is no doubt portrayed partly by the Nibelungen. Throughout the Ring cycle, they have no admirable qualities. Wagner paints them as a race of dwarves who mainly live and work underground. Their greed initiates the entire cycle and the theme only continues to develop throughout. In the listening example above, you can see Siegfried's guardian, Mime, lurking and watching as Siegfried forges his sword. It takes only a little imagination to realize that he is ready to steal Nothung at the first opportunity. Siegfried's realization that he is very different from his guardian and his new hatred for him is but a mirror of the situation in nationalist Germany.

Chapter 10: Toward Modernism

In Their Own Words

Richard Wagner makes his anti-Semitic beliefs more than clear in his essay, "Das Judentum in der Musik."

"The Jew speaks the language of the nation in whose midst he dwells from generation to generation, but he speaks it always as an alien… if the aforesaid qualities of his dialect make the Jew almost incapable of giving artistic enunciation to his feelings and beholdings through talk, for such an enunciation through song his aptitude must needs be infinitely smaller. Song is just Talk aroused to highest passion: Music is the speech of Passion. All that worked repellently upon us in his outward appearance and his speech, makes us take to our heels at last in his Song, providing we are not held prisoners by the very ridicule of this phenomenon. Very naturally, in Song—the vividest and most indisputable expression of the personal emotional-being—the peculiarity of the Jewish nature attains for us its climax of distastefulness; and on any natural hypothesis, we might hold the Jew adapted for every sphere of art, excepting that whose basis lies in Song."[13]

Giuseppe Verdi and Opera à la Risorgimento

The Italian Giuseppe Verdi (see Fig. 10.27), a contemporary of Richard Wagner, displays many parallels to the German composer. He was also born in 1813, became a prolific opera composer, and followed a similar path toward national unification. Although some claim there was a fierce rivalry between the two, such tension cannot entirely be determined because neither would admit his jealousy of the other. Although both used their operas as a voice for nationalism, they used that medium in different ways.

Whereas Wagner drew keen character sketches of both the desirable and undesirable

Fig. 10.27. Giuseppe Verdi, engraving, in Harper's Monthly Magazine, 1876.

© Stocksnapper/Shutterstock.com

traits of the German people, Verdi relied more on the use of choruses to rally a collective sense of patriotism and unity. From the same opera that produced "Immenso Jehova" (see Music, this Ch.), Verdi wrote another chorus for the enslaved Hebrew slaves. Nabucco is the Old Testament Nebuchadnezzar, and while the opera contains fictionalized matter, it still gives the true account of the Israelites in captivity in Babylon. "Va, pensiero" is sung as a contrast to the sorrowful captivity the Hebrew slaves were experiencing. The music takes them out of their bondage and carries them to the promised land, if only in their momentary thoughts. The text in translation nostalgically describes the sights, sounds, and smells of the former days of freedom.[14]

Listen to this chorus.

The words of this chorus reflect the longing for Jerusalem, mirroring the sentiment of the psalmist in Ps 137. According to this psalm, the enslaved Hebrews were so homesick for their own country that they could no longer sing the songs of Zion. In Verdi's adaptation, he encourages the rekindling of their music to inspire them to endure their captivity. Longing for one's homeland bore poignant resonance within the hearts of Italian nationalists. At various moments in history, their beloved Italy had been occupied by France, Austria, and Spain (see Fig. 10.28). Now they longed for an independent Italy, completely united, and ruled by Italians. Not surprisingly, "Va, pensiero" became a popular song during the Risorgimento and for a time, was even the unofficial national anthem.

Did you know?

Nationalist movements show man's longing to be identified with something larger than himself. As the theory of race and the science of genetics were growing in importance in the nineteenth century, the idea of being part of a collective group in which one belongs by virtue of a common blood was very appealing to many people. This was especially so among Europeans that had lost trust in Christianity due to several centuries of religious wars. Man's search for identity in nationalism, however, was misplaced. Man's real identity can only be found in Christ. Until man finds Christ as his Lord and Savior, man will continue searching for who he is. Furthermore, unity can only be found in Him. Ephesians states that man in his sin was apart from Christ, a stranger to the covenant of the promise and without God in the world. As Paul writes, "There is one body and one Spirit—just as you were called to the one hope that belongs to your call—one Lord, one faith, one baptism, one God and Father of all, who is over all and through all and in all" (Eph 4:4-6).

Chapter 10: Toward Modernism   293

Fig. 10.28. *Barricade in Milan, Porta Tosa*, revolt against the Austrians, 1848. Risorgimento Museum, Milan, Italy.

Study Questions

1. What were the main differences between Realism and Impressionism? What were the main driving ideologies of each?
2. What role did nationalistic music play in Germany? In Italy? How did nationalism appear in Russian music?
3. What were some of the main characteristics of Tchaikovsky's music?
4. In what ways was Debussy's music a departure from the Romantic style?

Notes

1. Brummel, 2020.
2. Bearden, 20.
3. Avery, 2009.
4. Durand, 34-35.
5. Van Dycke, https://www.denverartmuseum.org/en/blog/20-quotes-claude-monet
6. Sayre, 468.
7. Van Gogh, 1888.
8. Spurling, 250.

9. National Gallery of Art, "Paul Cézanne."
10. Tchaikovsky, 549-550.
11. Lockspeiser, 207.
12. Taruskin, 480.
13. Wagner, 15-16.
14. Lyrics Translate. https://lyricstranslate.com/en/Chorus-Hebrew-Slaves-Chorus-Hebrew-Slaves.html

11

Modernism
Twentieth Century Part I

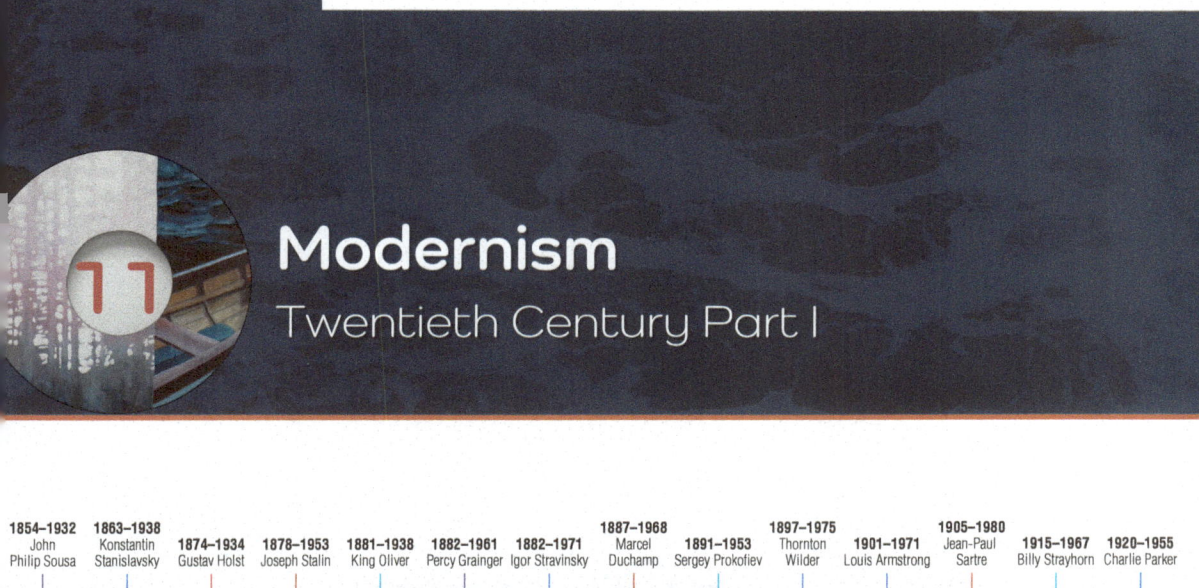

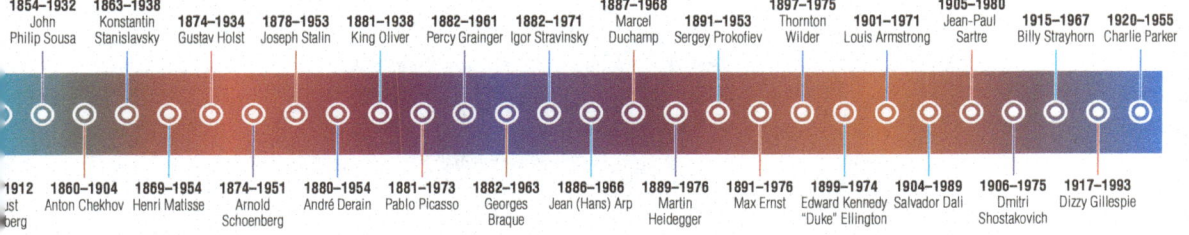

| 1854–1932 | 1863–1938 | 1874–1934 | 1878–1953 | 1881–1938 | 1882–1961 | 1882–1971 | 1887–1968 | 1891–1953 | 1897–1975 | 1901–1971 | 1905–1980 | 1915–1967 | 1920–1955 |
| John Philip Sousa | Konstantin Stanislavsky | Gustav Holst | Joseph Stalin | King Oliver | Percy Grainger | Igor Stravinsky | Marcel Duchamp | Sergey Prokofiev | Thornton Wilder | Louis Armstrong | Jean-Paul Sartre | Billy Strayhorn | Charlie Parker |

| 1912 | 1860–1904 | 1869–1954 | 1874–1951 | 1880–1954 | 1881–1973 | 1882–1963 | 1886–1966 | 1889–1976 | 1891–1976 | 1899–1974 | 1904–1989 | 1906–1975 | 1917–1993 |
| ust berg | Anton Chekhov | Henri Matisse | Arnold Schoenberg | André Derain | Pablo Picasso | Georges Braque | Jean (Hans) Arp | Martin Heidegger | Max Ernst | Edward Kennedy "Duke" Ellington | Salvador Dali | Dmitri Shostakovich | Dizzy Gillespie |

Philosophy

In the early part of the twentieth century, many nations faced a crisis of identity. Economic disasters, World Wars, and an accelerating rate of intellectual disputes caused different countries to reconsider their place in the world and, indeed, their place in history. This can be seen, for example, in the radical turns in German literature and theology[1] following the recognition that Germany had been unequivocally in the wrong in its conquest of neighboring peoples, genocide of the Jews (Fig. 11.1), and hypernationalism. No longer sustainable was the Hegelian view of the Germanic empire as the pinnacle of civilization. Similarly, the artist and the artworld went through a crisis of conscience. Technology, like photography, made art seem obsolete, tragedies made art seem trivial, and intellectual attacks on communication and interpretation made art seem meaningless. As the artist attempted to justify her own significance, she became more entangled with the philosophical movements of the day. The artworld, as one can see throughout the preceding chapters of this volume, has often followed the philosophical musings of earlier periods in their self-understanding. In the search for purpose, the artworld continued this trend at an even quicker rate within the twentieth century.

Chapter 11: Modernism

Fig. 11.1. Auschwitz, Sergej Borzov, Poland.

Arguably, the most significant philosopher of the twentieth century was Martin Heidegger (1889-1976), a German scholar whose influence extended beyond philosophy to theology, historical studies, technology, linguistics, education, politics and, indeed, art. Heidegger's effect on the academic world has often been overshadowed by his well-known, though ambiguous, relationship with the Nazi party, an involvement for which he never clearly apologized. Yet, ethical quandaries aside,[2] his effect on the intellectual landscape of the West was monumental. In terms of art, as was mentioned in Ch. 1, Heidegger recognized the significance of the disruptive nature of art in forcing one to reckon with the world or things in the world that one would normally ignore. This type of disruption, unfortunately, has been seen by some to be the only characteristic of art and thus some contemporary artists simply create in order to shock.

However, apart from this, Heidegger was also significant in his development of a theory of language that saw words as a way that one constructed their relationship with the world. For example, when one sees a mustang, depending on if he calls it "pet," "friend," or "transportation," he will treat the horse differently. Thus, the words are used to define one's interconnection with things. While such a view has far-reaching consequences in literary theory and interpretation, it affected artists, who saw the similarity in the symbolic nature of words and the symbolic nature of art. In light of this, they began to view art as constructive of the way people interact with the world. Such a view is significant but can be taken to excess. Various scholars believed that individuals construct everything through their own thoughts and actions, including truth. In this way, truth became subjective and unstable according to the whims of humankind. Yet, it is impossible to be a faithful believer without being an objectivist, since Christ is truth (John 14:5), whether individuals recognize Him or not.

> ### Did you know?
>
> Martin Heidegger spent two weeks in the Jesuit order, an educational division of Catholicism, before turning to philosophy. He did, however, have a continual relationship with theology and theologians during his lifetime, including a friendship with the famous biblical scholar Rudolf Bultmann (1884-1976).

Existentialism, though finding its origins in the nineteenth century, continued to be prominent in the West, especially in France, through the latter half of the twentieth century. One thinker who helped to reinvigorate existentialist thought was Jean-Paul Sartre (1905-1980). Incredibly famous due both to his academic work and his social activism, Sartre carried on themes of previous existential thinkers, especially in his pessimistic worldview. Though he encouraged a type of **nihilism**, or view that life was without intrinsic meaning or value, ironically, Sartre believed that humans had to either act like there were values or had to create, in their own humanity, their own values.[3] Thus, even though he could not consistently account for what in life was worthwhile, he believed that individuals should act in accordance with the ideals they created. Furthermore, though from a very different perspective, Sartre agreed with Christians that the artist had "social responsibility."[4] This perspective facilitated the rise of activist art, as can be seen in the work of the anonymous street artist Banksy (Fig. 11.2).

nihilism: the view that life was without intrinsic meaning or value

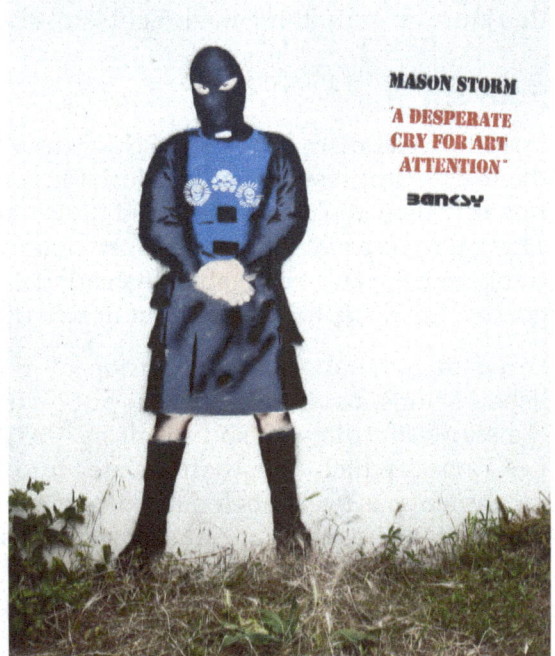

Fig. 11.2. Photo of Banksy art, 2011, Weston-super-Mare, UK.

One last philosophical influence of note in the twentieth century was the rise of postmodernism, a philosophical perspective that reacted against the optimism and objectivity of the Enlightenment, frequently with skepticism and subjectivism. The loss of truth, meaning, and values, which was precipitated by the separation of philosophy and art from religion, found its most extreme expression in the postmodern philosophical perspective. The outcomes of this view often included moral relativism, or the view that morality depended on people's perspectives, and the relativism of truth. Art, with this backdrop, had to reckon with a valueless and meaningless world. The reaction, as will be seen later in this chapter, was a drastic rebellion against the historical and the traditional.

Art

Whether or not the art of the twentieth century is found to be appealing or repulsive, it is undoubtedly the period of the most upheaval. Up until this point, there was a broadly accepted understanding by society of what was considered to be art. This began to be challenged with each succeeding movement that followed. During the early twentieth century, the limits and boundaries of art were tested repeatedly, revealing that art was an extremely flexible term that has grown to encompass just about everything. The early twentieth century began this journey with fauvism and cubism, ending up with surrealism and Dada.

Fauvism

Postimpressionism opened the door for a whole host of creative possibilities. If the artists' impression could allow for color to be used symbolically and emotionally, then the forms depicted could also be interpreted and manipulated. The value of artists was no longer determined by their ability to paint something realistic and believable. Instead, it came from their ingenuity and creative genius. Early on, this played out in two different ways, fauvism and cubism.

Fauvism came about from a group of artists who were rejected by the established salons, having decided to put on an exhibition themselves. After seeing the show, a critic was so put off by their art that he referred to the group as Les Fauves which directly translates into Wild Beasts. The name stuck and the movement has been labeled fauvism ever since Henri Matisse (1869-1954) made a name for himself as a leader among these artists. The group was only loosely connected and the movement dissolved within a few years. Matisse, however, went on to become a pillar of the artworld.

Fauvist artwork was so distinct from the works of previous, mainstream painting that it was considered primitive and savage in comparison. Where past artwork saw subtle shifts in subject matter or minor stylistic changes, fauvist artists threw out nearly everything and reimagined the world in haphazard application of chaotic flat colors. Craftsmanship became entirely subjective, value structure was incidental, and correct proportions were unnecessary. A painting was complete whenever the artist decided so. Fauvist artists were inspired by postimpressionists' creative uses of color, but beyond that there was a complete break with tradition.

One of the works Matisse submitted to the first collective exhibition, that marked the beginning of fauvism, was *The Open Window* (Fig. 11.3). The painting is of the view from the artist's apartment. The image is made up of blotchy colors placed in no particular order. There is no consideration given to clarifying wobbly edges or blending colors to create soft gradients. In effect, the painting is completely devoid of traditional craftsmanship. The visual thrust of the work relies entirely on the prismatic color combinations.

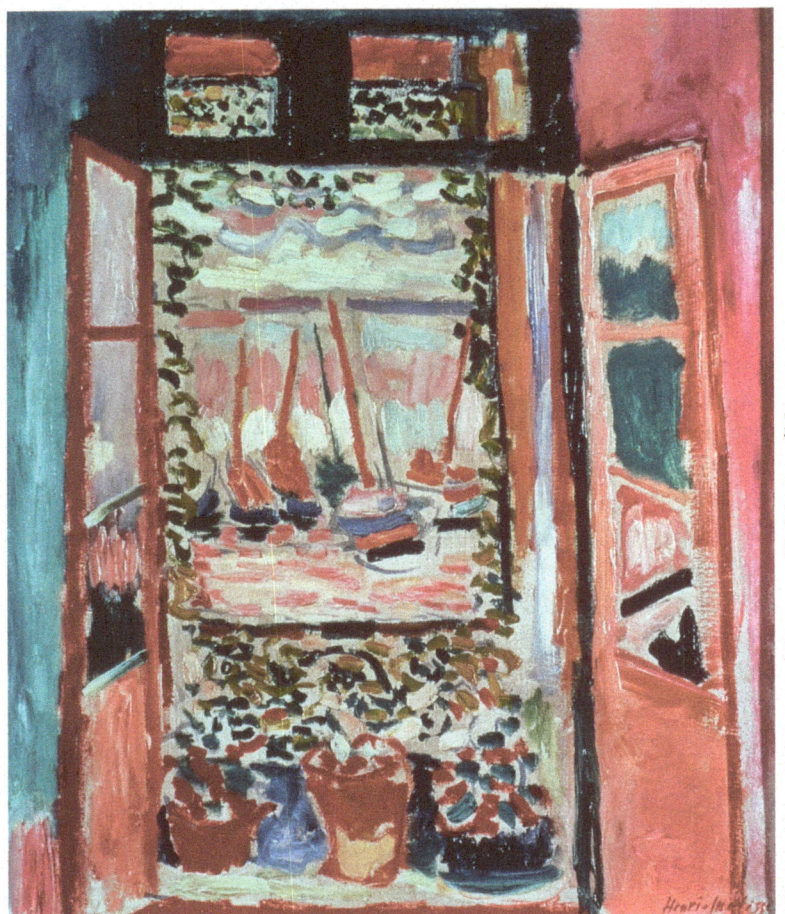

Fig. 11.3. *The Open Window*, oil on canvas, 1905, Henri Matisse, National Gallery of Art, Washington, DC.

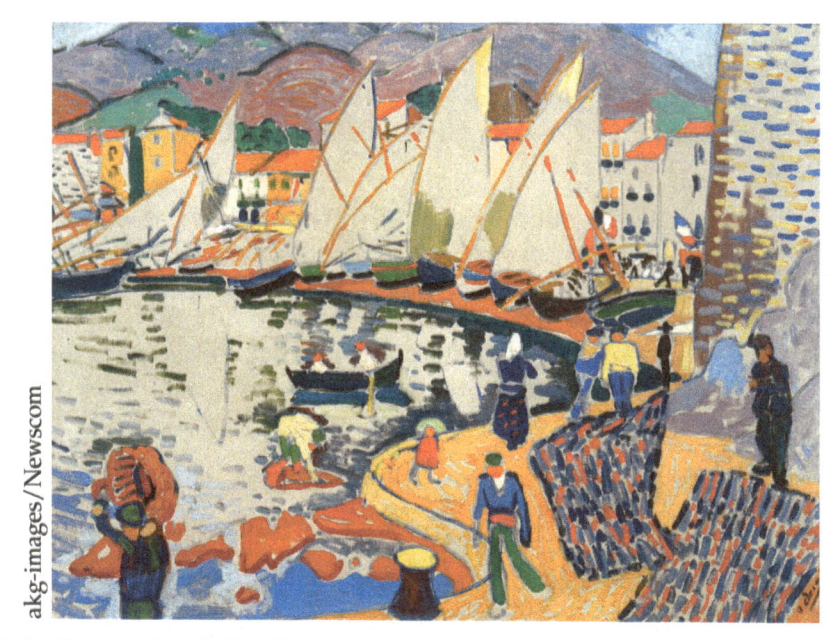

Fig. 11.4. *Drying the Sails*, oil on canvas, 1905, André Derain, Pushkin Museum, Moscow.

Another fauvist and friend of Matisse, André Derain (1880-1954), reflected on the emergence of photography as one of the catalysts that pushed their paintings in the seemingly opposite direction of representation. If photography was taking the place of realist paintings, it would naturally cause painters to consider their role in society. What could paint offer that photography could not? Derain embraced the brushy streaks of paint and expressive color to give life to the harbor scene in Fig. 11.4. The liberal and emphatic pigment choices elevate a sense of lighthearted playfulness. His choices echo the kaleidoscope of colors and light that people would experience if they had the opportunity to walk the curvy path between the sails on a sunny afternoon.

> ### IN THEIR OWN WORDS
>
> André Derain describing the movement of fauvism:
>
> "Fauvism was our ordeal by fire…. It was the era of photography. This may have influenced us and played a part in our reaction against anything resembling a snapshot of life. No matter how far we moved away from things, it was never far enough. Colors became charges of dynamite."[5]

Cubism

Cubism was another movement that was born from postimpressionism. Where fauvists touted color as supreme, cubists continued in the direction opened up by Cézanne. Cézanne looked to break down the world into basic shapes and different perspectives. Artists were not bound to one particular point of view, as was the case with young Pablo Picasso (1881-1973) who showed up in Paris at the age of 19. There he fell under the influence of Van Gogh, Paul Gauguin (1848-1903), and Cézanne.

Cézanne's influence was particularly strong and foundational to the friendship between Picasso and Georges Braque (1882-1963). The two bonded over his work, constantly checking in on each other to see what the other had painted that day. Through this process, they experimented and pushed the boundaries of depicting form, developing the movement of cubism.

In contrast to fauvism, cubism gravitated toward a muted color palette, often various tints and shades of brown. Braque's painting *Fruit Dish* (Fig. 11.5) is an example of early cubism. His work grew to be more complex with a greater number of divisions and complications. In this painting, the representation of

Fig. 11.5. *Fruit Dish*, oil on canvas, 1908-1909, Georges Braque, Moderna Museet, Stockholm, Sweden.

Fig. 11.6. *Woman Writing*, oil on canvas, 1934, Pablo Picasso, Museum of Modern Art, NY.

fruit is still distinctive in places. Braque's creative use of value allowed the various forms to stand out, but without a uniform light source. This allows for contradictions within the forms creating a disorientating camouflage effect. It simultaneously gives the illusion of multiple perspectives as well as creating a pictorial puzzle of which the viewer is trying to make sense.

In Picasso's work *Woman Writing* (Fig. 11.6), the painting is broken down into the basic shapes present in the subject. No longer is there a singular face; instead, Picasso presents a jumble of overlapping pieces. The subjects are fractured along these various contours, each one being treated separately and distinct from the neighboring shapes. Each outline is a new opportunity to make a different value structure, color, and intensity. The effect is similar to looking into a broken mirror where each piece is misaligned and therefore reflecting back a multiplicity of slightly different perspectives. When this effect is applied to a person, and to a face in particular, it can project a psychological quality.

Picasso and Braque's experiments in art led them to become the first artists to really popularize and legitimize **collage** as well as **mixed-media** as fine art. In Picasso's collage (Fig. 11.7) the piece of yellowed newspaper is a prominent part of the design. Both he and Braque incorporated other nontraditional elements such as oilpaper, rope, spackle, sand, enamel, and cardboard.

From the viewpoint of the cubist, to draw or paint exactly what one saw only showed the surface of those things. This can be a limiting factor if the majority of what a person actually experiences in life is what is interior—thoughts, emotions, conscience, and spirit. Using exaggerated or symbolic employment of color and form allowed artists the freedom to express those internal realities in a way that, in their view, realism could not achieve.

Chapter 11: Modernism   303

Fig. 11.7. *Pipe, Glass, Bottle of Rum*, cut-and-pasted colored paper, printed paper, and painted paper, pencil, and gouache, 1914, Pablo Picasso, Museum of Modern Art, NY.

> ### In their own words
>
> Stéphane Mallarmé (1842-1898), a poet and critic who was inspirational to cubism, futurism, Dadaism, and surrealism has said:
>
> "To *name* an object is to suppress three-fourths of the enjoyment of the poem which is made up of gradual discovery: to *suggest* it, that is the dream...."
>
> Although he was speaking about poetry, Mallarmé's words applied to visual art as well. As Christians are aware, there is value in learning to appreciate and express the invisible aspects of the world. The manner in which physical objects could symbolize spiritual realities, as seen in the Lord's Supper, shows that there is more to life than meets the eye.[6]

Dada

The origin of the name "Dada" isn't entirely certain, but the movement itself was clearly linked to World War I. Many who took up the banner of **Dadaism** did so out of a rejection of the ideology, values, and logic that had led to the war. The

Dadaism: an a tistic moveme based in absu ism and satire

Chapter 11: Modernism

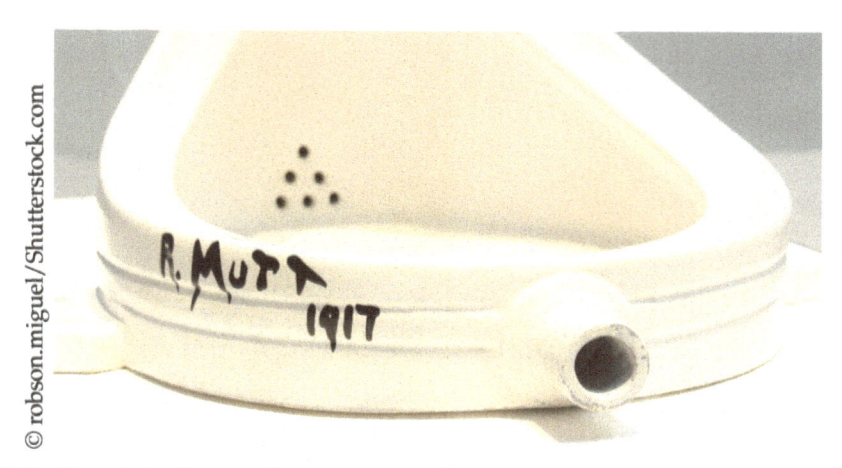

Fig. 11.8. *Fountain*, found object, original lost or destroyed, replica, 1964, Marcel Duchamp.

goal of the movement was largely to cause controversy and upset tradition. In essence, the movement was artistic sabotage of nationalism, manifesting itself in numerous capitals across the world and in a variety of expressions. The appearances showed up as complete irreverence and nonsense, a determined antilogic.

If the goal of Dadaist art was to infuriate and disrupt, then Marcel Duchamp (1887-1968) was probably the most successful. The artworld had already been provoked and enraged by modern artists practicing fauvism, cubism, and various levels of abstraction and expression. However, these would seem tame and sensible compared to the disrespect and irreverence flaunted by Duchamp. He submitted a piece titled *Fountain* (Fig. 11.8), a prefabricated porcelain urinal, to the Society of Independent Artists under the pseudonym R. Mutt. Not surprisingly the urinal wasn't displayed during the show. However, pushing the envelope even further, Duchamp had his piece photographed and defended in an article published by a magazine run by his friends. They argued that the merit of the piece is based on the artist's choice to present the work as art, not the artist's labor. His propositions and controversy completely blurred the lines between what art can and cannot be, changing the future of the field.

readymades: a term for prefabricated or found objects displayed as art

Not all Dada-related art took the form of Duchamp's readymades, a term for prefabricated or found objects displayed as art. There were numerous other ways artists engaged with Dada's anti-art movement. One of these artists was Jean (Hans) Arp (1886-1966). Many of these artists, including Arp, emphasized the role of chance in the making of their artwork. In *Untitled* (Fig. 11.9), Arp claimed to have dropped torn pieces of paper onto the substrate at random and glued them down where they fell. Judging by the evenly spaced and aligned rectangles, it is highly doubtful that the composition was left entirely up to chance.

However, the claimed role of chance, its implications, and its impact on other artists was immense.

Arp continued to invoke chaos in his work by creating simple shapes with which to play his game of chance. Despite his feigned attempts to rely on arbitrariness to dictate his compositions, he could never truly let go of the control as seen in *Constellation according to the Laws of Chance* (Fig. 11.10). Arp embraced these ambiguous organic forms that allowed him to work with balance and harmony at a very basic level without the necessary baggage of recognizable objects. He was still very much concerned with balance and harmony, eventually moving on from Dada to surrealism.

Surrealism

The main interest of surrealism was to harness the subconscious, as well as chance, as the basis for the artwork's content.

Fig. 11.9. *Untitled (Collage with Squares Arranged according to the Law of Chance)*, torn-and-pasted paper and colored paper on colored paper, 1916-1917, Jean (Hans) Arp, Museum of Modern Art, NY.

Fig. 11.10. *Constellation according to the Laws of Chance*, painted wood, c. 1930, Jean (Hans) Arp, Tate Museum, London.

Surrealist artists had idiosyncrasies that made their work unique. However, the movement as a whole is one of the easiest to distinguish in relation to other art movements. Some descriptors of surrealist works would be absurd, comical, flexible, and dreamlike, all completed with precision and craftsmanship reminiscent of realism. A large influence on this group was Sigmund Freud's *The Interpretation of Dreams*, which drew connections of bizarre dreams with very real implications of an individual's waking reality.

Salvador Dali (1904-1989) was the most notorious of the surrealists. At times, he gained more attention because of his ostentatious persona than his art—which is saying something. Known for his iconic upturned mustache and outrageous publicity stunts, he was one of the most famous artists of his time. His paintings, like *The Persistence of Memory* (Fig. 11.11), are equally unbelievable and palpable. The precision and accuracy in the craftsmanship of his paintings demand realism, while the ephemeral and absurd subject matter precludes any truth to his images.

Dali often used certain objects as symbols which would resurface in other paintings he produced. In *The Metamorphosis of Narcissus* (Fig. 11.12), we see an egg prominently displayed in the top middle of the painting. Dali's personal symbology of the egg represents hope and love. The thumb-like rock directly beneath the egg has ants crawling all over it, the ants typically representing decay and death.

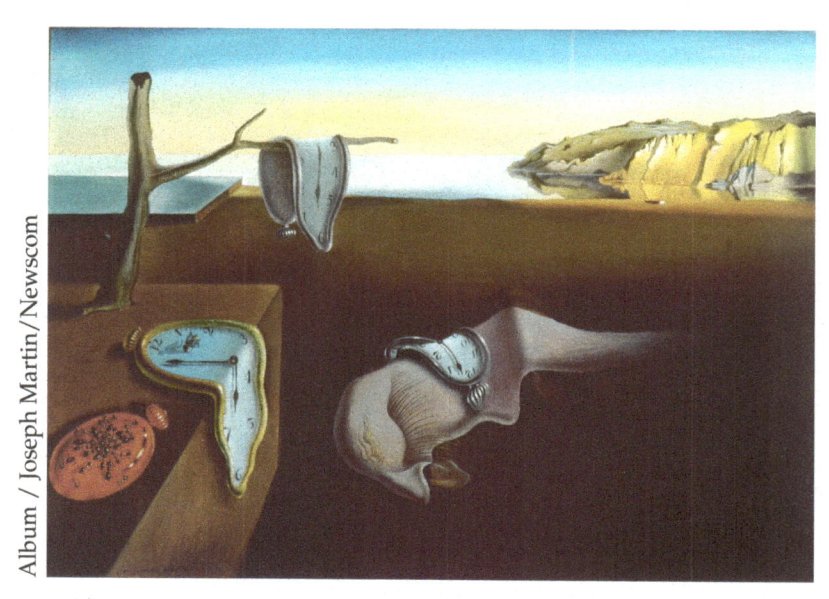

Fig. 11.11. *The Persistence of Memory*, oil on canvas, 1931, Salvador Dali, Museum of Modern Art, NY.

Chapter 11: Modernism 307

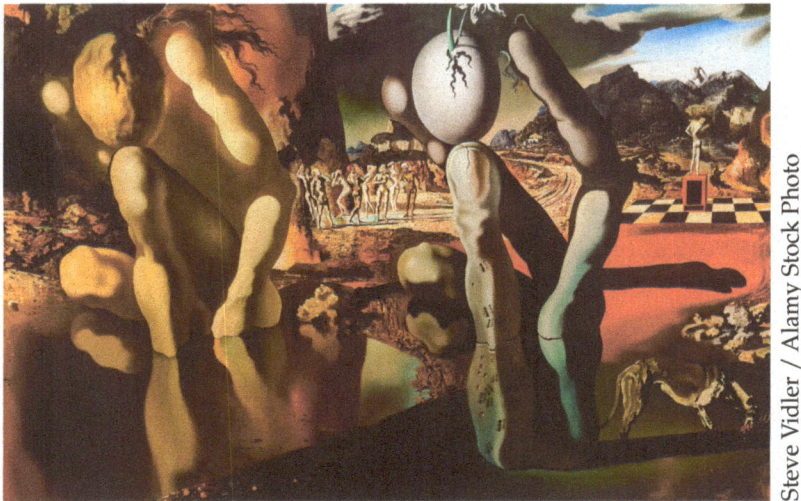

Fig. 11.12. *The Metamorphosis of Narcissus*, oil on canvas, 1937, Salvador Dali, Private collection.

Another surrealist painter worth noting would be Max Ernst (1891-1976). *Europe After the Rain, II* (Fig. 11.13), portrays an unworldly postapocalyptic scene indicative of postwar Europe. The complex maze of what looks like coral and organic matter originates in a technique he invented called **grattage**. Grattage involved the scraping of paint off a canvas that has been laid over a textured surface. The effect would create complex and unexpected details on the painting. The experimentation and ingenuity of this technique allowed surrealists to create new inspiration and solutions without having to consciously direct the work.

grattage: the painting technique of scraping paint off a already textur or painted surface

The early twentieth century was a time of tremendous change and upheaval. People experienced some of the most tragic and horrific calamities the world

Fig. 11.13. *Europe After the Rain, II*, oil on canvas, 1940-1942, Max Ernst, Wadsworth Atheneum, Hartford, CT.

has ever seen. It changed the very fabric of society. It is no small wonder that the art world was similarly traumatized and transformed. These disruptions had shaken the art world, upsetting much of the comfortable traditions of the past. It was also an opportunity to hit the reset button, prompting some of the most foundational questions: What makes something a work of art? What makes quality art? These questions opened up the doors to chaos as well as creativity. For Christians, creativity is an opportunity to reflect the gifts of God to humanity, and these questions can help to stimulate and inspire new ways of doing just that.

Music

Classical Music

The first half of the twentieth century was marked by writers of music who broke with tradition. This movement, called **modernism**, was led by composers who sought to create their own musical language. Some would develop new rhythmic practices, while others would focus on new tonal techniques in their works. Many composers were innovative in their approach but were still grounded in the past traditions of the classical repertoire, while others were influenced by these changes, but were compelled to avoid the trends. Government dictates determined the degree to which their native composers engaged in these new conventions.

Stravinsky Connects to Previous Traditions

Igor Stravinsky (1882-1971; see Fig. 11.14) was one of the most recognizable and influential composers of the twentieth century. He was a leader of **musical neoclassicism**, which rejected the heightened emotionalism of the Romantic movement and sought to revive styles common to the seventeenth- and eighteenth-century music.

Stravinsky's early works were influenced heavily by his Russian homeland. His first ballet, *The Firebird* (1910), is one of his best-known compositions. The ballet depicts a Russian legend, in which the hero, Ivan Tsarevitch, captures the titular character. In exchange for its release, the firebird gives Ivan a feather that helps him defeat an evil ruler, free beautiful maidens, and ultimately marry the most beautiful among them. In his score, Stravinsky continues to expand tonal language, just as Wagner, Debussy, and others had done. In developing his style, Stravinsky also stretched his rhythmic vocabulary in revolutionary ways. He regularly grouped beats in an unconventional manner and used **syncopations** and accents that would become his trademark. His music, despite being recognized today as masterful, was not immediately celebrated and would first challenge the musical preconceptions held by many. In fact, Anna Pavlova, a

Fig. 11.14. Stravinsky in 1934.

principal dancer for the Ballet Russes, refused to dance in the premiere of *The Firebird* after hearing the score and declaring it "horrible music."[7]

Another of Stravinsky's most famous, yet controversial, works was *The Rite of Spring* (1913). This ballet tells of a pagan sacrificial ritual in which a young girl dances herself to death in order for Spring to return—an idea Stravinsky claims appeared in a vision.[8] During the premiere of *The Rite of Spring*, a riot purportedly broke out due to its incongruence with previous musical tradition. Stravinsky's score used primitive beats, dispensing of the rhythmic conventions typically found in Western music. His use of various techniques to mask the meter, along with the dissonances in his harmonies left many critics and theatregoers shocked at what they had experienced.

Listen to the primitive nature of the opening of Stravinsky's The Rite of Spring.

Around 1920, Stravinsky entered his neoclassical phase while creating orchestrations from the music of eighteenth-century composer Pergolesi. Familiarity with works of the past led him to focus on forms and techniques of bygone eras while applying his new tonal language and style. During this time, seventeenth-century Baroque and eighteenth-century. Classical tradition became his primary influences. *The Symphony of Psalms* (1930) highlights his neoclassical style. Within the symphony, the listener will hear perpetual motion in the accompaniment, a fugue (second movement), and sequences typical of Baroque music.

Another neoclassical element of *The Symphony of the Psalms* is Stravinsky's elimination of the violin, viola, and clarinets from the orchestration. Without these instruments, the emotional sound palette of Romantic tradition was nearly impossible to achieve, creating the objectivity for which he strove. Stravinsky's unique style and popularization of the neoclassical idiom influenced many other composers and established him as the leading composer in the resurgence of this style. His ability to maintain a personal flair while connecting with forms of the past achieved a synthesis previously unmatched.

> **IN THEIR OWN WORDS**
>
> Igor Stravinsky commented on the problem of an overemphasis on orchestration:
>
> "Orchestration has become a source of enjoyment independent of the music, and the time has come to put things in their proper places. We have had enough of this orchestral dappling and these thick sonorities; one is tired of being saturated with timbres, and wants no more of all this overfeeding, which deforms the entity of the instrumental element by swelling it out of proportion and giving it an existence of its own."[9]

Schoenberg Reorganizes Music

Arnold Schoenberg (1874-1951; see Fig. 11.15) was a Viennese composer. As a young musician, he performed and wrote chamber music, an experience that would influence his compositions for the rest of his career. Through this, he learned to highlight each instrumental voice using counterpoint.[10] A largely self-taught composer, he quit school to focus on composing, but, surprisingly, only studied with a composition teacher for a few months.[11] His early works were influenced by Wagner and generally fit within the prevailing musical styles of the time. *Pelleas und Melisande*, Op. 5 (1902) is an example of Schoenberg's early style. In keeping with tradition, he focuses on counterpoint throughout his piece,[12] emphasizing the relationship between orchestral parts through such counterpoint despite employing nonconventional harmonies. In *Pelleas und Melisande*, he built chords on fourths and used the whole-tone scale, similar to Debussy. This was just the beginning

Fig. 11.15. Arnold Schoenberg.

of Schoenberg's radical tonal evolution. He continued to explore ways to remove Western music's prevailing harmonic language and produce *atonal* music.

A piece that highlights Schoenberg's atonal work is *Pierrot lunaire*. This piece has no established tonality and prominently features dissonance while also maintaining an advanced contrapuntal style. One striking aspect of this piece is the use of *Sprechstimme*, a method of performing where the vocalist sings the initial notated pitch but then falls or rises away from the pitch immediately. One music critic, upon hearing the premiere of *Pierrot lunaire*, remarked, "If this is music, then I pray my Creator not to let me hear it again!"[13] Indeed, as he ventured further into his own style, his pieces were met with hostility, which led him to create the Society for Private Performances. There, his pieces, along with others, could be performed away from the ever-listening ears of music critics.[14] Regardless of the reception of his music (his music was received much more favorably toward the end of his life), it is evident that the ideas he introduced had a profound impact on the Western music tradition.

After experimenting with atonality and realizing its limitations, Schoenberg sought yet another new system to organize his musical material without giving the impression of tonality. This search led to the *twelve-tone row*, the arrangement of the twelve chromatic tones in a specific order. This order dictated the sequence, or row, of notes in a piece of music. Each of the notes in the row had to be used once before anything could be repeated. The row could also be manipulated to create retrograde (backward), inverted (upside down), and inverted retrograde (backward and upside down) variations. Doing this would prevent the listener from hearing any one pitch as "home" and, as a result, the music would lose all tonality. The first of Schoenberg's twelve-tone works, *Five Piano Pieces*, Op. 23 was finished in 1923.

Schoenberg has an interesting place in music history because his music tends to be appreciated at a theoretical level instead of aurally. While his contributions to music are impactful—his twelve-tone method was adopted by many composers, including Stravinsky—his music hasn't received the programming of other musical revolutionaries. The twelve-tone method changed the way many composers approached music composition, but it took some time for the taste of his music to be acquired.

atonal: music that does not have a perceptible tonal center

Sprechstimme: vocal method which the singer sings an approximate pitch followed by a quick ascent or descent from the original pitch

twelve-tone row: Schoenberg's method of musical organization; the row was a preset sequence of the 12 chromatic pitches; tended to avoid tonality, but also to give unity to the final composition

In Their Own Words

Arnold Schoenberg defends the intellectual artistry of the twelve-tone method.

"While a 'tonal' composer still has to lead his parts into consonances or catalogued dissonances, a composer with twelve independent tones apparently

> possesses the kind of freedom which many would characterize by saying: 'everything is allowed.' 'Everything' has always been allowed to two kinds of artists: to masters on the one hand, and ignoramuses on the other."[15]

Stalin Hampers Musical Progress

While individual aesthetics and the opinions of both audiences and composers can have a large impact on musical styles, one must not forget the impact a government can have on the arts. Dmitri Shostakovich (1906-1975; see Fig. 11.16) and Sergei Prokofiev (1891-1953; see Fig. 11.17) were both Russian-born composers who reached international acclaim during their musical careers. Their paths to becoming synonymous with Russian music were quite different, but both ultimately spent the majority of their careers composing as representatives of the regime of Joseph Stalin (1878-1953).

Shostakovich began his musical career as a pianist but turned to composing in order to provide for his family. In Soviet Russia, the only source of commissions was the state, which viewed music as a powerful tool for propaganda. Shostakovich had to align himself politically with the Stalin-led government in order to receive commissions, an arrangement that could lead alternatively to a lucrative career or ruin, imprisonment, and even death. Shostakovich, himself, would find this out many times throughout his career.

Shostakovich's Symphony No. 1, Op. 10 was written in 1925 while the composer was just nineteen. The symphony catapulted Shostakovich to fame: its success was immediate and the symphony started to be performed internationally by 1927. However, things would change in 1934, when Shostakovich's opera, *Lady Macbeth of Mtsensk*, debuted.

Initially, *Lady Macbeth of Mtsensk* was well received, both in Russia and internationally. However, in 1936, Stalin attended a performance of *Lady Macbeth* and the following day brought Soviet-led condemnation of both the

Fig. 11.16. Shostakovich composing in 1950.

Fig. 11.17. Sergei Prokofiev.

opera and the composer. An article titled "Muddle instead of Music" was found in *Pravda*, the Russian government's primary newspaper, and it unequivocally denounced Shostakovich's work. One reason for this condemnation was the inclusion of sexually explicit content in the opera. Stalin would not tolerate sexually explicit material and under his leadership, naked bodies had disappeared in films and art. The newspaper article decried its inclusion in the opera, but the criticism was not limited only to the content of the work.[16] The anonymous author (whom Shostakovich believed to be Stalin himself[17]) condemned the "confused stream of sound" and the "nervous, convulsive and spasmodic music" found in the opera.[18] In short, Shostakovich had shown himself to be out of step with the prevailing artistic vision of the Soviet government, both stylistically and morally. This reaction to *Lady Macbeth*, along with a scathing review of another Shostakovich work (*The Limpid Stream*) left Shostakovich depressed, with little work and in the bad graces of a totalitarian government despite the critical acclaim his music had garnered internationally. He canceled the premiere of his Fourth Symphony and focused on writing film music to make ends meet.

IN THEIR OWN WORDS

In the scathing words of the unknown author of "Muddle instead of Music," published in *Pravda* following the doomed performance of *Lady Macbeth of Mtsensk*:

> "The composer apparently never considered the problem of what the Soviet audience looks for and expects in music. As though deliberately, he scribbles down his music, confusing all the sounds in such a way that his music would reach only the effete "formalists" who had lost all their wholesome taste. He ignored the demand of Soviet culture that all coarseness and savagery be abolished from every corner of Soviet life."[19]

Meanwhile, in 1936, another Russian composer would make his return. Sergei Prokofiev, a composer born in Russia, had established himself as a powerful composer in the neoclassical tradition, as evidenced by his Symphony No. 1 (1917). Symphony No. 1 (also known as the *Classical Symphony*) is a piece that is influenced by the symphonic tradition of Haydn and Mozart. While the form is similar to the classical tradition, the harmonies are modern and typical of a work produced by Prokofiev. Shortly after writing this symphony, Prokofiev left Russia for about 18 years.

Listen to the first movement of Prokofiev's Symphony No. 1.

The Soviet government followed Prokofiev's musical success closely and tried to convince Prokofiev to return to Russia by offering him commissions, housing, and performances that would guarantee him a lucrative career. In 1935, he had accepted and carried out numerous government-sponsored commissions that led to a profitable year. Knowing that failing to return risked the loss of guaranteed commissions, he decided to return home. The precipitous fall of Shostakovich helped to reinforce that this was the right choice: the events of 1936 seemed to point to Prokofiev immediately assuming the title of Russia's most prominent composer.[20]

IN THEIR OWN WORDS

Prokofiev spoke about his reasons for returning to Russia:

"[I] had not grasped the significance of what was happening in the U.S.S.R. I did not realize that the events there demanded the collaboration of all citizens—not only men of politics, but men of art as well."[21]

The year 1937 marked Shostakovich's restoration to Stalin's good graces when Shostakovich's Fifth Symphony premiered to great acclaim, a symphony that was largely seen as Shostakovich's answer to being censured. In fact, Shostakovich himself had called it an answer to criticism. What exactly that answer was, however, is still debated. On the one hand, the Symphony was a continuation of the great symphonic tradition of composers like Beethoven and Mahler. Its tonality was simple and it was easily accessible by musical experts and laymen alike. The fact that it had become a symbol of Shostakovich's "rehabilitation" indicates that the government approved of this piece, and Shostakovich was restored as a prominent composer of Russian music. However, there were many who still heard dissent within the notes of his masterpiece. The finale is interpreted as falsely enthusiastic and, even though it is in a major key, critics still heard a vengeful and threatening tone within the music. Regardless, the Fifth Symphony was an immediate success and allowed Shostakovich to further his career.

As their careers continued, both Prokofiev and Shostakovich found themselves balancing the propagandizing intent of Stalin with their creative freedom. They needed to find a compromise that allowed musical progress while also pleasing Stalin's musical taste. This resulted in a careful balancing act that generally worked out well for both sides. However, both found themselves as objects of Stalin's wrath in 1948, despite the fact that they had achieved status as two of the Soviet Union's preeminent composers and were highly decorated, including having received the People's Artist award in 1947. A public resolution issued by the Central Committee of the Communist Party denounced the leading Russian composers as being out of touch with the people. Shostakovich and Prokofiev, among others, were being accused of embracing Western atonality and dissonance while forsaking clear tonal language. Once again, Stalin, with the help of his totalitarian government, reminded the prominent composers who ultimately controlled the direction of Russian music. Prokofiev's career never regained the popularity he enjoyed previous to 1948 and he died in 1953, on the same day Stalin passed away. He would be remembered for elevating Russian music through pieces such as *Romeo and Juliet, Peter and the Wolf,* and *Cinderella*.

Following the death of Prokofiev and Stalin, Shostakovich's Symphony No. 10 premiered. This symphony portrays the relationship between an artist and a tyrant, and it is through this lens that Shostakovich's body of work is considered.[22] Shostakovich, for the most part, outwardly complied with Stalin's artistic mandates, but he was also able to show his dissatisfaction, if not outright opposition, toward the Soviet government through his music, despite its heavy moderation. As for Stalin, the case can be made that he, in a perverse way, "inspired" a neoclassical giant (Prokofiev) and extended the symphonic tradition of Beethoven and Mahler (Shostakovich) through his manipulation of the state composers.

> **DID YOU KNOW?**
>
> Shostakovich and Prokofiev both spent significant periods of their lives composing as representatives of a murderous regime led by Joseph Stalin. This naturally broaches the question of moral responsibility for artists. Knowing the depravity of the Stalin-led government, should Prokofiev and Shostakovich have refused to be involved in its propaganda (a decision that very well could have resulted in their deaths)? Or did Shostakovich do the right thing in using his position and art to show the evil of Stalin? How does this line up with Paul's admonition to submit to and pray for government authorities (Rom 13, 1 Tim 2)? Though one's answers to these, even among Christians who believe in the truth of Scripture, may vary, what is not debatable is the unavoidability of such questions.

American Voices

George Gershwin (1898-1937) began his career as a songwriter, with little formal training in his craft. Often working with his brother, Ira (1896-1983), he wrote a number of Broadway musicals early in his career. Not content in only writing musicals and popular tunes, Gershwin expanded into other avenues of music. He composed what is probably his most well-known work, *Rhapsody in Blue*, for one of the most influential and popular jazz bands of the 1920s, the Paul Whiteman Orchestra. Gershwin's composition was full of influences not just from jazz but also blues. He also wrote an opera that was premiered in 1935, entitled *Porgy and Bess*. Gershwin even added in a stipulation for the performance rights: *Porgy and Bess* could only be performed by black artists. Early reviews of the opera were mixed, and while some songs such as "Summertime," "It Ain't Necessarily So," and "I Loves You Porgy" remained popular, the opera fell out of popularity for a time. However, it was revived in the 1950s, and it is one of the few works that has enjoyed stagings in both opera halls and on Broadway, most recently in 2020. Gershwin's ability to combine jazz and concert music was a natural extension of the music styles that he heard and in which he had worked.

Listen to one of Gershwin's most recognizable songs from *Porgy and Bess*, the haunting "Summertime."

Aaron Copland (1900-1990) was also known for the creation of a very American voice in the world of classical music. His early works embraced the use of material from jazz, blues, and ragtime, though over the course of time his music crafted the sound that would for many be synonymous with Americana. There is an openness and clarity in Copland's music, which, at times, makes it sound much simpler to the listener than it actually is to perform. Many of Copland's most iconic music was written first for ballet, including *Billy the Kid* and *Appalachian Spring*. He also wrote a number of cinematic scores, including such notable early films as *Of Mice and Men* (1939) and *Our Town* (1940). His well-known work, *Fanfare for the Common Man* was written for a series presented by the Cincinnati Symphony Orchestra in 1943. More than simply a composer, Copland wrote about music and was a mentor to many musicians, including composer and conductor Leonard Bernstein (1918-1990).

Music for ballets, musicals, and other staged works, are often arranged for a smaller ensemble, frequently between 10-15 musicians. Like many composers before him, Copland arranged the music from his ballets into suites to be played by full orchestra. *Appalachian Spring* contains one of Copland's most popular settings. In the ballet, this music accompanies the daily activities of a newly married couple who find their home in rural Pennsylvania in the early 1800s, accompanied by the use of the familiar Shaker melody, *Simple Gifts*.

Listen for the variations of the tune "Simple Gifts" in this movement of Copland's *Appalachian Spring*.

Time	Description
0:02	The clarinet plays the initial statement of the melody, "Simple Gifts."
0:34	The oboe and bassoon take over the melody at a slightly faster pace.
0:59	Over an almost music box-like accompaniment, the violas enter with the melody, followed later by the violins playing the melody above them, almost as if in a round. The cellos and double basses enter (1:15) with a figure that vaguely outlines the opening notes of the melody. This is the first time that the entire orchestra is playing.
1:45	Following a short transition, the trumpets and trombones take the lead with the melody at twice the speed that it was just played at, in an almost fanfare-ish manner.
2:10	The tempo slows slightly, and the mood changes as the woodwinds and low strings take over the melody and create an almost idyllic sounding setting.
2:30	The entire orchestra enters, as the last variation of "Simple Gifts" begins with a majestic and grand setting, led by the flute, trumpet, and violins playing the melody. Unlike the earlier setting with the full orchestra (1:15), this time the ensemble is used for the full amount of power and sound it can generate.

Jazz

Jazz music is often described as America's artistic contribution to the world. A combination of written and improvised music, jazz grew from a melting pot of cultures found in the American south.

The beginnings of jazz are rather nebulous. It evolved from the influences of folk and popular music, ragtime, and brass bands in the cultural melting pot of New Orleans. In the early 1900s, New Orleans was home to American, French, Spanish, African, and Caribbean cultures, and was the most significant port city in the Gulf of Mexico. It was the combination of cultures and music in this one unique location, one of the most cosmopolitan in the world at the time, which created the cultural foundation for what would become jazz.

Fig. 11.18. Louis Armstrong.

Louis Armstrong (1901-1971; see Fig. 11.18) is often considered the first great improviser in jazz. He grew out of the New Orleans tradition and played in King Oliver's (1881-1938) band. Armstrong began working at the age of seven. At the age of thirteen, he was arrested for firing blanks into the air and was sent to the New Orleans Colored Waif's Home for Boys. He played in the home's band, ultimately progressing to being the leader of the band while playing trumpet. Once out, he apprenticed with King Oliver, trading work for lessons.

Armstrong's importance to jazz grew with his exceptional ability to improvise solos. Early New Orleans Jazz, or Dixieland music, centered on collective improvisation. The trumpet would improvise along the melody of the tune being played, the clarinet would improvise lines above the melody, the trombone would play below, while the rhythm section would provide the chords and beat underneath. Armstrong's strength as a soloist surpassed his contemporaries and defined the role of the improvised solo in jazz. Armstrong, through his performances, also codified what would later become central components of jazz, including the use of blues, improvisation, and the rhythmic energy of the music that would become known as swing.

While Armstrong was known widely for his trumpet playing, he increasingly asked bandleaders he worked with for the opportunity to sing. His idiosyncratic style of vocalization consistently led bandleaders to refuse him the opportunity to do so in performance. Eventually, Armstrong struck out with his own group and began to sing in performances and recordings. It is somewhat ironic to consider now that Armstrong's singing style is one of the most easily identified voices in the history of American popular music when he was so often denied the opportunity to sing. An important aspect of Armstrong's vocalization was his development of the technique of what became known as **scat** singing. Scat is the vocalization of syllables in a manner that is similar to what an instrumentalist would play, comparable to a musical onomatopoeia. Wind players use their tongue to articulate different sounds with their instrument, and Louis used this technique as another way to improvise, with the same type of sounds and ideas, but with his voice, rather than his trumpet.

Scat: the vocalization of syllables in a manner that is similar what an instrumentalist would play; a musical onomatopoeia

Listen for the components of New Orleans Jazz in Louis Armstrong's performance of the tune, "Hotter Than That."

Time	Description
0:00	The full band begins in classic New Orleans Style. Trumpet playing melody, clarinet improvising a line above, trombone playing glissandos between notes, and the rhythm section keeping the beat.
0:09	Armstrong plays an improvised solo, based on the chords to a popular tune of the time, *Tiger Rag*.
0:25	The rhythm section stops playing, allowing Armstrong to solo unaccompanied. This is called a break and happens throughout the piece. The soloist often will use this as an opportunity to build excitement into the solo.
0:43	The clarinetist (Johnny Dodds) begins his solo.
1:03	Dodds ends the break on a blue note (slightly off pitch—typically flat—from what it would normally sound).
1:19	Armstrong begins a scat solo.
1:55	At the break, Armstrong begins a call and response with the guitarist in the group, Lonnie Johnson. (Louis sings an idea, which Johnson plays with in reply)
2:14	The pianist, Lil Hardin, and trombonist, Kid Ory, pull the tune back into tempo after the call and response section.
2:34	Armstrong takes over on the break after the trombone solo.
2:36	The group performs collective improvisation.
2:46	The band stops and plays only the first beat of four successive measures, in a technique referred to as "stop time," as Armstrong continues to solo.

Chapter 11: Modernism

Fig. 11.19. Duke Ellington.

mute: a device that changes the timbre or reduces the volume of a musical instrument. For brass instruments, it is a stopper that fits into the bell

growling: a harsh tone made by a wind instrument by humming or singing into the instrument while playing. Also, a vocal technique of making guttural sounds while singing

While Armstrong's small groups were important to the early development of the style of jazz, these small groups eventually became larger ensembles. One trumpet or saxophone grew to sections of three to five, assembled to create more sound, and fill larger rooms. In Harlem in the late 1920s, places like the Cotton Club, a mixed-race social establishment, sought the best musicians in the city to play the extravagant floor shows. It was the young, up and coming pianist and bandleader Edward Kennedy "Duke" Ellington (1899-1974; see Fig. 11.19) that would use the opportunity to launch his career as head of the Cotton Club's house band. In the 1920s, radio was supreme, and performances as the house band for significant locations meant that not only was a band's music heard by the people in attendance, but its performances could be broadcast through the nationwide affiliates of corporations like the National Broadcasting Company (NBC). These opened up opportunities for audiences to become familiar with the bands and allowed them the opportunity to generate fans across the country, which further led to tours and record sales.

Ellington, while serving as the pianist for his band, became known as the most accomplished composer of jazz music. Duke preferred hiring musicians who had a distinctive voice or sound to their instrument. Musicians in Duke's band incorporated the use of mutes, growling, and other techniques to create distinctive sounds with their instruments. Each had his own individual style of playing. Whereas most composers wrote parts for particular instruments, Duke wrote for the individuals in his band. Rather than considering the sound of a trumpet, he would write specifically for trumpeter Bubber Miley or Cootie Williams, using their particular sound as an orchestral technique. Over the decades of performances of the Duke Ellington Orchestra, they would always sound their best in the periods where his band's personnel was stable, allowing Duke the opportunity to explore the richness of his individual players, and inspiring the creativity of his compositions. Ellington is credited with writing over 1,000 different works, with many of his tunes being considered among the canon of great works that every working jazz musician should know. Eventually, Duke Ellington hired his "writing and arranging companion" Billy Strayhorn

(1915-1967), and together they collaborated on a variety of short and long-form compositions, including suites and sacred concerts.

Listen to "Black and Tan Fantasy."

Ellington's Orchestra was one of many that rose to prominence during the swing era. Other artists such as William "Count" Basie (1904-1984), Benny Goodman (1909-1986), Artie Shaw (1910-2004), and Glenn Miller (1904-1944) rose to prominence during the 1930s and 1940s. Swing was the popular music of the era, playing in halls across the country for the Lindy Hoppers who would dance the night away. Glenn Miller's recording of "Chattanooga Choo Choo" was the first recording to receive a gold record, selling 1.2 million copies after its release in 1941. Swing turned the early folk style music of jazz into the pop music of the era. The solos were less important and the arrangements were meant to keep the dancers happy and moving.

During the 1940s, a group of black jazz musicians began to experiment in after-hours engagements, called jam sessions, with increasingly complex chord progressions and faster tempos. Complex melodic lines with syncopated accents led to the creation of bebop. Alto saxophonist Charlie Parker (1920-1955; see Fig. 11.20) and trumpeter Dizzy Gillespie (1917-1993) became the primary figures associated with this new style of jazz. Less concerned about the arrangements, and sometimes even disregarding the melody that the chord changes were built upon, bebop focused on the skill of improvisation. It would become the *lingua franca*, or common language, of jazz for future generations. Much as the music of Bach would lay a template for what would follow in Western European music, bebop laid the foundation for future jazz. Its musicians viewed their music more as art rather than entertainment. Many swing-era fans found the music undanceable and incomprehensible, and Armstrong observed there was "No melody to remember, and no beat to dance to."[23]

Lindy Hopper: dancers who danced the Lindy Ho a dance developed in th late 1920s in Harlem's Sav Ballroom, wh became synor mous with th big bands of swing era

Fig. 11.20. Charlie Parker.

Charlie Parker is often remembered as the brightest shining star of the bebop era, in many ways setting the standard for the style. He grew up in Kansas City, one of the early incubators of jazz. Parker was exposed to many great musicians and began practicing hours a day after being embarrassed in a jam session. He idolized the lyricism of Lester Young, one of the early great tenor saxophonists, and learned his solos. It was often said that Parker played like Young, but twice as fast. He set the benchmark not only for saxophonists, but for all jazz musicians with the breakneck speed of his lines and dynamic phrasing. However great his genius, he became addicted to heroin, and repeatedly fell victim to its terrible effects. Parker died at the age of just thirty-five. When the coroner examined his body, he thought he was examining the body of a fifty-year-old man. More tragically, the influence of his music was equaled by the influence of the lifestyle that he lived. Many jazz musicians, attributing Parker's musical genius to his heroin habit, followed suit and fell into drug use, looking for the key to his success. For many years, heroin (and other drugs) took hold of many in the jazz community, as they looked to reach Parker's heights.

Listen to Charlie Parker's solo on the bebop classic, Donna Lee.

The early explosion of jazz music saw it progress from folk music to pop music, to art music, in just two short decades. And all three versions of early jazz (New Orleans, swing, and bebop) continue to be important forms of the music.

The twentieth century saw the rise of compositions written for bands. By definition, an orchestra is a large instrumental ensemble featuring a large string section, complemented by a smaller component of wind instruments and percussion. A band, by contrast, is composed almost entirely of wind and percussion instruments.

Ensembles composed primarily of wind instruments have been used throughout the history of music; many times they were assembled to play for outdoor events. Composers such as Mozart, Beethoven, Dvořák, and Strauss composed a variety of smaller wind ensembles. Larger assemblies of wind instruments formed into bands, most famously by the likes of John Philip Sousa (1854-1932), who helped standardize compositional forms and programming for these ensembles. Most often, programs consisted of transcriptions of famous orchestral or operatic works and marches.

As bands continued to develop in the twentieth century, bandleaders sought compositions to be written specifically for band, other than just marches and novelty works. Composers such as Gustav Holst (1874-1934) began to write for the medium. Holst's *First Suite in E-flat* (1909) and *Second Suite in F* (1911) were early works written for a band that utilized its unique features while developing the style of orchestrational techniques that would become common for the ensemble. Percy Grainger (1882-1961) wrote his masterpiece for band, *Lincolnshire Posy*, in 1937. It is a setting of six folk songs that he recorded in the English countryside during the early part of the century, and each movement reflects the specific style of the folk singer recorded. More importantly to the development of the band, Grainger experimented with combinations of instruments, creating unique and interesting timbres, turning the band into a much more interesting ensemble than the full-on sound common to the typically played marches.

Listen to the setting of the tune "Horkstow Grange," the second movement of Grainger's *Lincolnshire Posy*.

Time	Description
0:00	The French horns lead the first statement of the melody. The melody is notated in such a way that it lingers longer on some notes than others and does not stay in strict time, varying between 4, 5, and 6 beats per measure.
0:45	The second variation of the tune begins, this time led by the upper woodwinds, this time spending considerable time on the note that begins at 1:01.
1:34	With the snare drum rolling softly underneath, the solo trumpet begins to play the melody in a manner much faster than heard to this point, but it is still somewhat irregular and free in its statement.
2:22	The final variation of the melody begins with a crescendo bringing the band to full volume.
2:31	The low brass (trombone, euphonium, and tuba) mark their moving notes underneath the melody, pushing the music forward even though the melody is sustaining above them.
2:45	The final moments of the piece begin with the loudest the band gets, and as it slows down, the music gets quieter and ends at a whisper.

Theatre

Theatre during the modern era was constantly evolving, seeking to facilitate a path by which an audience could better connect to and evaluate the culture around it. The theatre's modern transformation can be traced through its break from traditional practices in the Western world between 1875 and 1945. Two notable types of theatre emerged during the modern period. The first was **theatrical realism** and the second was its polar opposite, often classified as **anti-realism**. Both styles are still commonly practiced in the theatre

theatrical realism: a style of theatrical production th[at] imitates real l[ife] through its ac[t]ing, costumes, and sets

anti-realism: any style of theatrical produc[-]tion that does [] not imitate re[al] life

of today and their creative scope has given directors countless possibilities for casting the artistic vision for a production.

Realism

Key proponents of the modern theatre movement included playwrights and performers with new methodologies. Their drive toward realism emerged from a desire to represent life more authentically on stage, creating a type of theatre that would more closely resemble everyday living. Scenic designs would also incorporate such a style, often going as far as to build houses with multiple stories and cultivate yards sodded with real grass (see Fig. 11.21).

Three playwrights were hugely influential within the modern realism movement. Norwegian writer Henrick Ibsen (1828-1906) was considered the father of modern realism. Ibsen was controversial for writing plays that showcased more truthful characters than those typically hidden behind their societal facades. Some of his best-known titles include *A Doll's House* (1879), *Ghosts* (1881), and *Hedda Gabler* (1890)—all of which are commonly produced today.

Swedish playwright August Strindberg (1849-1912) dove deeper into the realm of realism by crafting plays that reflected an honest, inner turmoil within his characters, who often seemed to be at war with themselves and each other. Strindberg's most notable plays indicative of this battle were *The Father* (1887) and *Miss Julie* (1888). Strindberg's stylistic depth became known as naturalism.

Russian playwright Anton Chekhov (1860-1904) was the third major contributor to modern realism with *The Seagull* (1896), *Uncle Vanya* (1899), *The Three Sisters*

Fig. 11.21. Cedarville University's production of Arthur Miller's *All My Sons*, photo, 2020, scenic design by Jonathan Sabo, directed by Stacey Stratton.

(1900), and *The Cherry Orchard* (1904). Chekhov cleverly utilized both tragic and comedic components in his writings to create an entirely new genre of dramatic literature called **tragicomedy**, which became widely used in the modern and postmodern eras.

In addition to a new style of plays that mimicked real life, modern realism required a new style of acting. Konstantin Stanislavsky (1863-1938) was a famous actor/director who founded the Moscow Art Theatre in Russia. He was notable for his development of an internal (mentally driven) acting technique that was vastly different from the traditional external (physically driven) approach to the art. His method was based on *affective memory*, a term Stanislavsky coined to describe an actor's ability to recall past experiences to invoke the same emotions onstage. The ability to relive past experiences during a performance provided a deeper way for actors to connect to their characters. As a result, audiences felt a stronger connection to the story based on the actors' authenticity. Stanislavsky used his method to create a systematic process by which actors could recreate the same emotionally compelling performance night after night for an extended run. His technique also became foundational for the development of additional acting methods, some of which have evolved into programs for training the most prestigious actors of today.

The acting found in modern realism is commonly referred to as a **representational style of acting** in which the actor *represents* his character as a real person living out a real situation. This new style of realistic acting changed the way audiences interacted with a play. A boundary was established between the actors and the audience through an imaginary **fourth wall**. This theatrical convention contends that although the audience can see through the invisible "wall" to witness the action onstage, the actors act as if they cannot. Audiences felt they had privileged access to the events unfolding before them, which in turn prompted a stronger emotional connection to the characters and their stories. Fig. 11.22 from a contemporary production illustrates representational acting as an embittered son threatens his father. It is evident that the realism of the actors and setting can have a profound emotional impact on the audience.

This approach was much different from the traditional **presentational style of acting** in previous centuries where actors acknowledged their audience, even speaking directly to them at times. The traditional acting style utilized archetypal characters and static settings to tell the playwright's story, but the more modern methods invited audiences to lay aside reason, willingly suspend their disbelief, and experience the play as if the action and characters were uniquely authentic. From its naturalistic dialogue to the ways characters were dressed and behaved in very realistic settings, the dramatic style of realism approached everything differently, a shift that was not embraced by all proponents of the theatre.

tragicomedy: a hybrid genre of dramatic literature containing elements of comedy and tragedy

representational style of acting: an internal (mental) approach to acting rooted realism which utilizes the fourth wall

fourth wall: mutually agreed upon convention based on an imaginary invisible wall separating the audience from the stage through which the audience can see but actors act as if they cannot

presentational acting: an external (physical) approach to acting that acknowledges an audience present

Fig. 11.22. Cedarville University's production of Arthur Miller's *All My Sons*, photo, 2020, directed by Stacey Stratton, performed by Hunter Johnson and Blake Hansher.

> ### IN THEIR OWN WORDS
>
> Stacey Stratton, Director and Assistant Professor of Theatre at Cedarville University, evaluates the idea of "honest realism" as she integrates biblical theology into her instruction.
>
> "Isn't it interesting to think that theatrical realism sought to be more 'honest,' and yet there is nothing inherently honest about the convention of a theatrical production? Just think about it … an audience willingly goes along with what it knows is not true—momentarily exchanging truth for a lie—and then reacts to the story as if it were occurring in real time with real characters in a real setting, with a genuine emotional response! This speaks volumes about the influence the arts have on the culture. In a world where sinful man attempts to redefine truth as something with which the majority agrees, or what man simply wants to be true, believers must continually seek to glorify God through their art. Christians understand that ultimate truth can only be defined by God, and that man will never have the authority to alter truth."

Anti-Realism

At the same time theatrical realism was growing in popularity, some were fighting against it. By nature, this new style eliminated many widely used theatrical devices such as music and dance, symbolism and poetry. Many felt modern realism restricted its audience to a simplistic experience based on the manipulation of emotion. The anti-realism movement sought a different experience for both its performers and its audience, one that promoted artistic creativity and challenged audiences to think for themselves. Even some of the major playwrights known for moving realism forward, such as Ibsen and Strindberg, eventually moved toward anti-realism later in their careers.

Anti-realism took on various forms of experimentation, sometimes referred to as **avant-garde** theatre. Avant-garde is a very broad category of experimental theatre that developed out of a rebellion to the traditional style, encompassing all theatre that was produced in a nonrealistic manner—embracing the idea that theatre should, in fact, be theatrical. Incidentally, one form of this style was actually called **theatricalism.** It highlighted the setting and space, calling attention to the mechanics of the theatre's operation during performances to remind the audience that they were indeed watching *a performance*. Fig. 11.23 is a current example of theatricalism with two sisters interacting from different "locations"—a Harvard observatory office and a living room in Wisconsin—using minimalistic set furnishings to suggest the multiple locales.

Perhaps one of the best modern examples of the anti-realism style is demonstrated by Thornton Wilder's (1897-1975) famously minimalistic play, *Our Town*. Wilder was already an award-winning writer by the time he crafted the play, which eventually earned him his second Pulitzer Prize in literature. Written in

avant-garde: a term used to describe new-found, often experimental artistic ideas

theatricalism: a category of avant-garde theatre employing an exaggerated performance style as to highlight the artifice of a production

Fig. 11.23. Cedarville University's production of Lauren Gunderson's *Silent Sky*, photo, 2021, directed by Stacey Stratton, scenic design by Jonathan Sabo, performed by Ava Ramsey and Haven Sidell.

1938, Wilder issued clear directions in his script detailing how simplistically the play should be staged.

> *No curtain. No scenery. The audience, arriving, sees an empty stage in half-light. Presently the STAGE MANAGER, hat on and pipe in mouth, enters and begins placing a table and three chairs downstage right. He also places a low bench at the corner of what will be the Webb house.*[24]

props: an object held or carried by an actor character, separate from costumes or scenery

pantomime: a detailed style of movement in which an actor pretends to be something that is not there, such as the simple movement of tossing a ball without using an actual ball

Fig. 11.24 additionally shows how no **props** were to be used in *Our Town* as actors were instead required to **pantomime** all stage business. The walls of the stage remained bare, exposing ladders and other backstage mechanics which reminded its audience that the action was indeed occurring inside a theatre. Wilder also utilized an unconventional role in *Our Town* with the character simply called "Stage Manager" who guides the audience through the play with his storytelling. The Stage Manager, as his name suggests, is considered just another member of the crew staging the play and narrates from scene to scene, often performing as different characters.

Through the convention of theatricalism, the minimalistic nature of *Our Town* still has an enormous impact on the contemporary theatre scene. The play's endearing story of the brevity of life and the importance of cherishing each moment continues to resonate with audiences. *Our Town* remains one of the most widely produced titles in high schools, colleges, and community theatres today.

Fig. 11.24. Thornton Wilder performs the role of Stage Manager in his play, *Our Town*. This character breaks the fourth wall to guide the audience through the play's action.

It has even seen several Broadway revivals—including one scheduled in 2021 to celebrate the reopening of Broadway after New York's theatre district shut down during the COVID pandemic. This is further proof that the art of storytelling is timeless and that the theatre will always be a means by which a culture may be transformed, for better or for worse. In light of this, Christians should be poised and ready to use their gifts in the art setting to reach the world for Christ.

Study Questions

1. What were the two main movements that transformed theatre in the modern era?
2. What are the major differences between presentational and representational acting?
3. What is neoclassicism, and how did Stravinsky exemplify this movement?
4. What was Schoenberg's greatest contribution to Western music? What was he trying to accomplish?
5. How did writing music for the Stalin regime both help and hinder the careers of Prokofiev and Shostakovich?
6. Why was the city of New Orleans important to the evolution of jazz?
7. How was Duke Ellington's style of writing music for his band different from the approach of others?
8. How did the jazz establishment react to the new style of bebop?
9. What is the difference between an orchestra and a band?
10. What kind of elements did Gershwin and Copland incorporate into their music to make it American?

Notes

1. Ingolf Dalferth, "God and the Mystery of Words".
2. The willingness to learn from Heidegger's work should not be interpreted as approval, tacit or otherwise, of his association with Nazism. As mentioned frequently in this volume, God declares his desire for the salvation of all peoples (1 Tim 2:4) and will eventually compose Christ's church of individuals from every nation (Rev 7:9-12). With such a perspective, there is no biblical justification for hatred of another "race."
3. See Jean-Paul Sartre, *What is Literature?* and *Existentialism and Humanism.*
4. Thomas Flynn, *Jean-Paul Sartre.*
5. Duthuit, 29.
6. YourDictionary.com, "Stéphane Mallarmé."
7. Ewen, 403.
8. Ewen, 405.

9. Stravinsky, 119.
10. Leibowitz, 36.
11. Leibowitz, 36.
12. Leibowitz, 41. Counterpoint is a driving force throughout Schoenberg's body of work.
13. Ewen, 351.
14. Ewen, 350.
15. Schoenberg, 96.
16. Volkov, 95.
17. Volkov, 105.
18. Seroff, 204-207.
19. Seroff, 204-207.
20. Morrison, 41.
21. Ewen, 282.
22. Volkov, 257.
23. Fordham, *The Guardian*, 2009.
24. Wilder, 5.

Postmodernism
Twentieth Century Part II

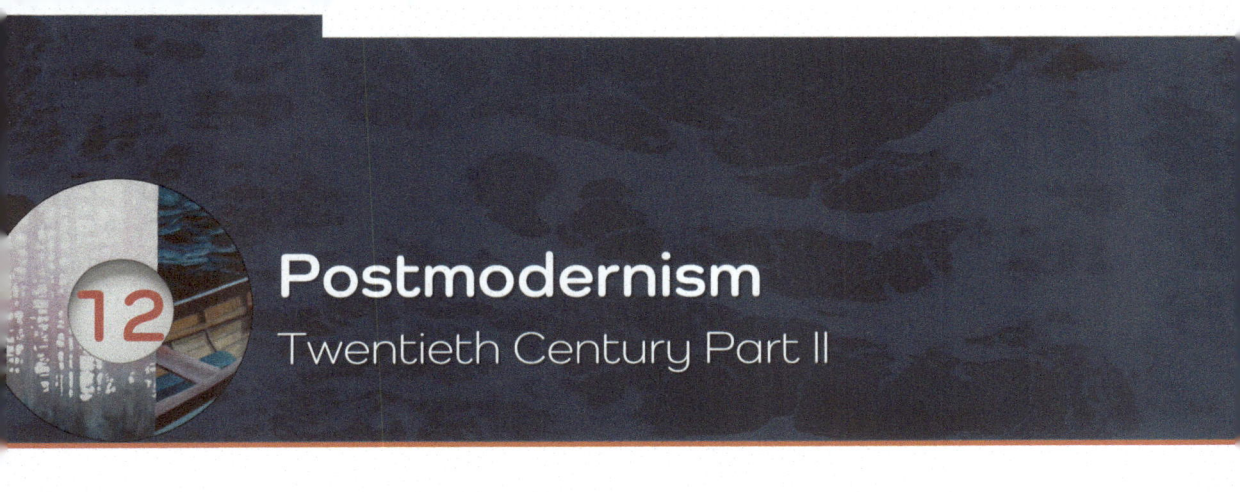

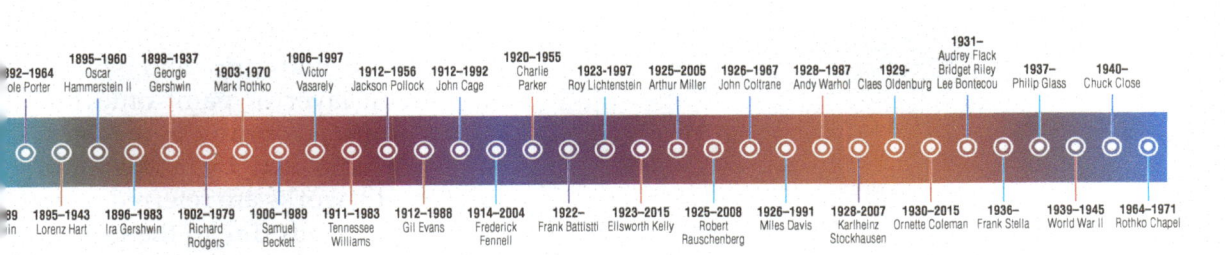

Art

One of the challenges presented in the continued study of Western art during the late twentieth century and beyond is that there has been a great splintering of art movements with an untold number of hybrid and unique adaptations that make it difficult to neatly categorize. Even individual artists have changed their own artistic style multiple times throughout their life. To add to the challenge, the increasingly interconnected world caused a significant cross-pollination of influences.

As mentioned in Ch. 11, the value of artists was no longer determined by their ability to paint something realistic and believable. The value of artists in the late twentieth century has been placed on their creativity and concepts. Naturally, this means that there has been less and less of a motivation to identify with a particular group or movement. That said, the rest of this chapter will seek to untangle and clarify some of the main contributors to the Western canon of art.

Abstract Expressionism

Abstract expressionism is a fairly ambiguous term that is broad out of necessity. The artists and works outlined in this section have significantly different stylistic elements in their work. It is also the first significant and uniquely American form of visual art. Some of the common elements of the artists represented here

abstract expressionism: movement in that focused subjective em tional expression and artis spontaneity

Chapter 12: Postmodernism

Fig. 12.1. Photograph of Jackson Pollock creating a painting using his drip technique. ca. 1950.

are the following: There is a hand-touched expressive quality to their art—these are not machine made, as manifest in the organic quality to the work. The scale of their work is typically quite large. Also, the work is completely abstract, or nonrepresentational.

Jackson Pollock (1912-1956) is best known for his **action paintings**, where he would drip and splash layer upon layer of paint onto the canvas until practically every inch has been activated by a dynamic splotch. His works are referred to as all-over paintings due to the lack of any singular focal point.

In Fig. 12.1 Pollock can be seen working on one of his paintings with the canvas lying flat on the ground. He is known for using commercial enamels and house paints that have a more fluid consistency. This allows him to create the string-like rhythmic textures on the canvases.

In Fig.12.2, a woman can be seen walking in front of Pollock's painting. She provides a good example of the scale of these monumental works. Pollock saw his paintings as records of his motions and intuitions. They are stamps of his rhythmic dance—an attempt to channel nature itself. Pollock sought to balance his control with the chance qualities produced by the materiality of the paint. The scale and amount of effort it took to create one of these mazes of layered paint is substantial. Toward the end of his career, he moved on from this technique to pursue a new direction in his artwork. This was short-lived, however, as he had a long history of alcoholism and consequently died in a single-car accident while driving under the influence.

Mark Rothko (1903-1970) is best known for his large **color field paintings**. Color field paintings focus on large swaths of color to create their minimalist compositions (see Fig. 12.3). Rothko discovered a formula that worked for him, referred to as multiforms by critics. The term refers to the broad bands of color that stack onto each other. Although the work is minimalist and deals with only a few formal qualities of color and rectangles on a vertical canvas, Rothko saw his work as conveying spiritual content. One of Rothko's influences was

Fig. 12.2. Photograph of a woman in front of *Blue Poles*, enamel and aluminum paint with glass on canvas, 1952, Jackson Pollock, original in National Gallery of Australia, Canberra, Australia.

Friedrich Nietzsche's book *The Birth of Tragedy* (see Ch. 2, 9). Originally, it led him to explore these tragic concepts through surrealism but finding his products ultimately unsuccessful for his intended purpose, he moved on to complete abstraction.

The culmination of his work is neatly tied up in what is known as Rothko Chapel (see Fig. 12.4). He worked on the paintings for more than three years starting in 1964. Rothko was also instrumental in the design and layout of the chapel building, working with multiple architects to bring about his vision for the experience. His desire for the visitor was to create a sense of being enveloped in the paintings. The paintings themselves are made of various shades of deep purples and black—a melancholy atmosphere to promote personal meditation. Rothko sought to replace faith-based religion with his spiritually stirring works of art. He borrowed some of the designs of traditional Christianity but then stripped them of their content. The attempt at creating transcendental art that could replace spiritual experiences within religion ultimately failed in saving its own creator as Rothko died by suicide a year before the opening of the chapel. However, Rothko's efforts highlight a universally experienced desire for an immaterial fulfillment.

Early on, Robert Rauschenberg (1925-2008) was strongly influenced by Dadaism. His lack of technical skill at the outset of his career did not hold him back as he pursued art with great zeal. Taking Duchamp's idea of readymades,

334 Chapter 12: Postmodernism

Fig. 12.3. *Grey, Orange on Maroon, No. 8*, oil on canvas, 1960, Mark Rothko, Museum Boijmans Van Beuningen, Rotterdam.

Fig. 12.4. Photograph of man inside of Rothko Chapel, installation of 14 murals, oil on canvas, 1971, Mark Rothko, original in Houston.

Rauschenberg became known for his **assemblages**, also referred to as combines, which were found objects that he manipulated and compiled into sculptures.

Fig. 12.5 is an example of Rauschenberg's combines, a work possessing a list of various found materials that is extensive. He has created a curiosity, a history without a narrative. The jumble of flat collaged elements on the ground plane are contrasted with the clearly recognizable forms on top. His work is some of the first to blur the lines between painting and sculpture.

Fig. 12.6 is an excellent example of how Rauschenberg combined abstract expressionistic painting with sculpture. Despite the majority of the surfaces being flat, Rauschenberg chose to offset the surfaces so that they physically overlapped each other. This is partly due to the nature of its creation to be a collaborative experience that dancers could interact with. As with sculpture in general, the three-dimensionality creates the need to physically walk around the freestanding object in order to see all of its parts. The rich painterly surface and collaged material makes this piece vibrant and expressionistic.

> **assemblage:** also called combines, usually sculptures made up of found objects

Fig. 12.5. 'Monogram,' combine: oil, paper, fabric, printed reproductions, metal, wood, rubber shoe-heel, and tennis ball on two conjoined canvases with oil on taxidermied Angora goat with brass plaque and rubber tire on wood platform mounted on four casters, 1955-1959, Robert Rauschenberg, Moderna Museet, Stockholm.

Fig. 12.6. Minutiae, combine: oil, paper, fabric, newspaper, wood, metal, and plastic with mirror on braided wire on wood structure, 1954, Robert Rauschenberg, private collection.

Lee Bontecou (1931-) is an artist that does not fit neatly into a particular art movement and yet her work was greatly influential to numerous artists. Her 1961 work *Untitled* (Fig. 12.7) evokes a sensation of a mystery looming. The main focus of the piece is actually the absence of everything, including light, causing an eerie and unsettling effect. Using steel, rawhide, and canvas, she creates abstract forms with ominous voids punctured through a skin that is reminiscent of a cyborg. The fractured surface with a limited and muted, color pallet recalls the works of Cubism, but with a modern and more sinister flare. Created at a turbulent time in history, which experienced the beginnings of the Vietnam war, the invasion of Cuba, and the construction of the Berlin wall, her work expressed the collective anxiety of society at the time.

Photorealism

Artists have used the projection of images as early the fifteenth century in the making of their artwork. They did this using what was called the camera obscura, which translates to dark chamber. Aptly named, this technique would use a dark room with a small hole in it to project an upside-down image of the

Chapter 12: Postmodernism   337

Fig. 12.7. *Untitled*, welded steel, canvas, fabric, rawhide, copper wire, and soot, 1961, Lee Bontecou, Museum of Modern Art, NY.

scene outside of the room. This image could be traced onto canvases and used to make art. Photography was the ability to fix that projected image with light sensitive materials. The earliest of these were called daguerreotypes after their inventor in 1839. These fixed images on polished metal plates held perfect still images of their subjects. It was no longer necessary for clients to sit for hours for a portrait painting. Daguerreotypes, however, were still only black and white, which is why artists quickly took to hand painting in order to colorize them. At times, complete portrait paintings were made from daguerreotypes.

daguerreotype: an early kind of black-and-white photograph

IN THEIR OWN WORDS

The Cleveland Morning Leader, January 7, 1861, reports on the skill of painting portraits from daguerreotypes.

"Miss Ransom possesses very fine talents as an artist, as several of her later specimens will testify. Her portrait of Senator Wade is worthy of much praise, though it is not better than several others which she has executed here. Her work has given very general satisfaction. She particularly excels in executing portraits from Daguerreotypes."[1]

The photographic process continued to improve, even incorporating color as early as 1890. However, reliable and commercially available color photography

Fig. 12.8. *John*, acrylic on canvas, 1971-1972, Chuck Close, The Broad, Los Angeles.

photoreal-
...: an artistic
... based in
...roducing
...errealistic
...ictions akin
... photograph

didn't reach the public until 1907 in the form of glass autochrome plates. These were replaced with film-based versions beginning in 1930. By 1960, **photorealism** became a movement in America. Artists often used film slides to project their images onto canvases, which they would trace and paint, creating images that had the integrity and detail similar to photographs.

One of the most well-known photorealists to come out of the movement was Chuck Close (1940-). His paintings are portraits done from an uncomfortably close point of view, as seen in Fig. 12.8. This nearness to the subject and the cropping of everything except for the face, invites the viewer to study the details presented over and above having the portrait function as a means for representing the sitter.

Not only did photography provide the ability to document with an exactness previously unheard of, but it also changed the general attitudes and understanding of composition. Due to the nature of photography, subjects would often get cropped in interesting and inadvertent ways, encouraging artists to incorporate these phenomena in their work.

An early adopter of photorealism, Audrey Flack (1931-) would use airbrushes to create her larger-than-life paintings. Airbrushes allowed her to eliminate the personal touch and physicality of the paint, aiding the illusionistic quality of the image. At times she toyed with the concepts of *trompe l'oeil*, a seventeenth-century French term meaning "to fool the eye," as seen in her painting *Queen* (Fig. 12.9).

Fig. 12.9. *Queen*, acrylic on canvas, 1976, Audrey Flack, Metropolitan Museum of Art.

This is most evident in the way she used the illusion of a frame to simultaneously hide, and break out of it, as a barrier. Flack's choice of subject matter has strong ties to the history of still life painting, which was firmly established by the sixteenth century. However, her contemporary adaptations have a lighthearted and colorful sensibility that is more reflective of pop art.

Pop Art

Pop art gets its name from the word popular. The artists in this movement believed that art could be about anything and not just weighty and serious subjects. They found inspiration in all areas of popular culture. From soup cans to comic books and celebrities, there was no distinction in high and low forms of culture.

> ### In Their Own Words
>
> Andy Warhol, in his *The Philosophy of Andy Warhol*, comments on the deeper meaning of drinking Coke.
>
> "A Coke is a Coke and no amount of money can get you a better Coke than the one the bum on the corner is drinking. All the Cokes are the same and all the Cokes are good. Liz Taylor knows it, the President knows it, the bum knows it, and you know it."[2]

Chief among these artists was Andy Warhol (1928-1987). After about a decade mostly dominated by abstract expressionism, it seems as though society was hungry for something more recognizable and relatable. Warhol's first big splash into the world of fine art was with his screen prints of Campbell's soup cans. He made thirty-two different prints (Fig. 12.10) reflecting the different flavors offered at the time of their making. The screen prints are graphic and simplistic in nature, the only difference between them being the flavor displayed on the cans.

Fig. 12.11 shows another silkscreen print by Warhol. He chose to depict Marilyn Monroe, a very famous actress, singer, and film star of the time that died by suicide. Warhol did numerous prints of Monroe in a variety of color combinations. His experimental printmaking created images that would at times cause the various layers of color to be offset. The large format, iconic portrait, and vibrant colors became an instant success.

Like Warhol, Roy Lichtenstein (1923-1997) also sought to incorporate clearly recognizable imagery that society would be able to relate to. His mature works in pop art largely incorporate various comic magazine motifs.

In *Yellow and Green Brushstrokes* (Fig. 12.12), Lichtenstein isolates a couple of brushstrokes as depicted in the comic book style. The sheer scale at which these are depicted separates it from its native low-class medium, and makes the viewer consider it in a new way. In choosing very expressive brushstrokes

Fig. 12.10. Close-up of Andy Warhol's iconic silkscreen prints of *Campbell's Soup Cans*, 1962, Andy Warhol, Museum of Modern Art, NY.

Chapter 12: Postmodernism 341

Fig. 12.11. *Green Marilyn*. Silkscreen on canvas, 1962, Andy Warhol, National Gallery of Art, Washington, D.C.

Fig. 12.12. *Yellow and Green Brushstrokes*, oil and magna on canvas, 1966, Roy Lichtenstein, Museum für Moderne Kunst, Frankfurt.

at this point in time, he is cleverly taunting the abstract expressionist works that had previously held the artworld's attention. His painting had all of the expressive form of his predecessors, but the way in which he depicted it is calculated and ironic. The photograph of Roy Lichtenstein in his Long Island studio (Fig. 12.13) shows the large scale of some of his works. In the picture he is leaning onto a sizeable comic-style cup sculpture.

Claes Oldenburg (1929-) is a sculptor that found his place in the art world through the use of scale. His monumental sculptures bring a level of playful wonder and comedy to otherwise trivial objects. His work typically interacts with its environment, which is often outdoors in public places. Oldenburg's pieces fit with pop art by nature of the subject matter he chooses to depict, which are everyday objects to which society can easily relate.

Fig. 12.14 shows 1 of 4 massive shuttlecocks on a museum's lawn, strewn about as if they were left by a couple of giants practicing badminton. The scale of these objects also takes them out of the normal context in which one would recognize them and puts them in a new light. With this fresh perspective, the observer

Victor Watts / Alamy Stock Photo

Fig. 12.13. A photograph of Roy Lichtenstein in front of his work, Roy Lichtenstein.

Chapter 12: Postmodernism   343

Fig. 12.14. A photograph of 2 of 4 *Shuttlecocks*, aluminum and fiber-reinforced plastic, painted with polyurethane enamel, 1994, Claes Oldenburg, Donald J. Hall Sculpture Park, Kansas City, MO.

hard-edge painting: a style of painting based in geometric swathes of co with abrupt transitions

minimalism: movement in based around grandiose and simplistic figures; a movement in music that uses a sm amount of mu sical material to create long works

op art: an artitic movement based in optic illusions to ch lenge the eye

is asked to reconsider the virtue of the object's form, which would otherwise go unnoticed.

Sometimes, a change in perspective can help one to reconsider what is truly valuable in life. How often do the dropped metaphorical ice cream cones ruin one's attitude to the point of missing God's will for them? The temptation is to see setbacks on the scale of Oldenburg's ice cream (Fig. 12.15) when the reality is not as dire.

Hard-Edge Painting, Minimalism, and Op Art

Other variations of art during this period come in the forms of **hard-edge painting**, **minimalism**, and **op art**. There is common ground between these movements. The works they represent are neither expressionistic nor representational. They work in the purity of design and color to achieve

Fig. 12.15. *Dropped Cone*, stainless steel, reinforced plastic, balsa wood, and painted with polyester gelcoat, 2001, Claes Oldenburg, Neumarkt Galerie, Cologne, Germany.

Fig. 12.16. *Hagamatana II*, polymer and fluorescent polymer paint on canvas, 1967, Stella, Berardo Collection Museum, Lisbon.

their goals. Where hard-edge painting and minimalism sought balance and harmony of shapes, op art sought challenging and unnerving retinal phenomena.

Frank Stella (1936-) is probably the most renowned artist of this movement (Fig. 12.16). His lively color combinations and clever use of interactive shapes make his work interesting and playful. His paintings have a highly organized and exacting quality that allows the shapes and colors to exist without any distracting, painterly brushstrokes. This type of machined precision allows the viewer to see the mind of the artist and not their hand.

Ellsworth Kelly (1923-2015) works with even fewer elements and complications (Fig. 12.17). His art is heavily invested in the purity of form and color. Where Stella plays with complex patterns, Kelly takes his stand in minimalism.

> **IN THEIR OWN WORDS**
>
> Ellsworth Kelly writes about his painting,
>
> "The form of my painting is the content. My work is made of single or multiple panels: rectangle, curved or square. I am less interested in marks on the panels than the 'presence' of the panels themselves."[3]

Victor Vasarely (1906-1997) was the leader of the op art movement. Op art got its name from the word optical (Fig. 12.18). Artists working in this field concerned

Chapter 12: Postmodernism 345

Fig. 12.17. *Red Panel, Dark Green Panel, and Dark Blue Panel*, oil on canvas, 1986, Ellsworth Kelly, The Modern, Fort Worth, TX.

Fig. 12.18. *Gestalt-Hideg*, acrylic on canvas, 1977, Victor Vasarely, private collection.

themselves with the various optical phenomena created by the interplay of contrasting values and colors that are difficult for the brain to process. His work was critical to ushering in the movement that had a profound influence on the world at large. His work often presents two-dimensional dichotomies of form and space, causing the still images to vibrate as the mind works to process the contradictions. In his work *Gestalt-Hideg* (Fig 12.18), Vasarely presents a pair of gridded interlocking "U" forms that seem to both stand out and recede.

The career of Bridget Riley (1931-) kickstarted in the 1960s with her exploration of various optical effects in black and white. Gaining broad acclaim for her optical artwork she began to add color to broaden her style. Her work defied the static boundaries of the two-dimensional picture plane, giving the illusion of movement through waves of varying form and gradients of black and white as seen in Fig. 12.19.

As portrayed in this chapter, art underwent a complete metamorphosis, becoming hardly recognizable in comparison to its past. The focus of the art world shifted from Europe to New York City where new types of artwork were praised

Fig. 12.19. *Hesitate*, emulsion on board, 1964, Bridget Riley, The Tate Modern, London.

for their originality. Art critics also played a role in portraying American abstract expressionism as the new avant-garde, drawing artists from all over the world. Supportive collectors with deep pockets helped bolster the new movements, creating an ideal atmosphere for artists who were eager to make their mark on the art world.

It is worth noting that the newly formed capital of the art world was devoid of significant Christian representation and influence. It does not take much effort to peel back the façade to see the spiritual darkness that came to be during this period. Beyond the famed canvases and celebrated sculptures were broken people looking for worldly success but missing eternal life.

Music

The second half of the twentieth century saw continued experimentation and innovation in the classical music tradition. Some composers continued and expanded the practice of previous composers like Arnold Schoenberg, while others created music antithetical to his theories, or any other musical theories for that matter. In this time frame, three main composition philosophies came to the forefront of classical music: serialism, avant-garde, and minimalism.

serial music: music in which the pitch, duration, timbre, and/or dynamics are all determined through rows or other systems to create composition

Stockhausen Controls Music

Karlheinz Stockhausen (1928-2007; see Fig. 12.20) was a German-born composer known for his **serial music**. The development of this style began with

Fig. 12.20. Karlheinz Stockhausen in 1960.

Schoenberg's twelve-tone row (see Ch. 11) but expanded to include all aspects of composition. In addition to pitch, Stockhausen and other composers added rows for duration, dynamics, and timbre. Musical notes, at their most basic identity, are vibrations, so Stockhausen endeavored to begin his creative process at this fundamental level.[4] Before this period, the Western use of acoustic instruments was simply accepted and, as a result, composers did not begin their work at the genesis of sound. While Stockhausen's aesthetic was driven by his quest for new sounds, his religious ideologies heavily influenced his musical philosophy. Though raised Roman Catholic, his theology ultimately embraced tenets from various religions.

Kreuzspiel (Cross-play, 1951) was the first piece that Stockhausen considered an original composition. In *Kreuzspiel*, Stockhausen creates his tones in a row so that different notes do not compete against each other. For instance, you may hear a sustained low note sounding against a short high note, but both notes are clearly distinguishable. As the piece progresses, the tone rows are permuted in a way that gradually changes the original high notes into low notes, and the original low notes into high notes. This creates a musical crossing of tones, which gives the piece its name. This piece exemplifies the point music that Stockhausen wrote early in his career, in which each note was treated and appeared as an individual. These tones do not contribute to a human expression, but are thought to be of a higher order, and therefore pure. It was only through the ordering of sounds and rejection of human expression that music could be pure and therefore represent God's perfect ordering of the cosmos.[5] Unfortunately, this method was limited in its creativity and Stockhausen said, "the drawback to point music is that if one wants the music to be different all the time, it becomes very monotonous."[6]

point music: music in which each note can be heard as an individual entity

Listen to Kreuzspiel.

After composing point music, Stockhausen introduced groups to his compositions in *Kontra-Punkte* (Counter-Points, 1953).[7] The use of the term counterpoint is not the traditional musical use, but instead is the literal sounding of one note against another. In this piece, he begins the practice of grouping notes by common characteristics. The piece begins in the pointed style of his early works, but then groups of notes are introduced. The piece ends with each instrument fading out until only the piano is left, reflecting Stockhausen's view that "in time every different thing becomes One," a view found in Eastern religions such as Buddhism.[8] The One gives order to the world and anything different ceases to exist. By fading out each instrument, Stockhausen depicted this worldview through his music.

Stockhausen also pioneered the use of electronic music in high art. Stockhausen's shift in this direction was due to the fact that the timbre of a given instrument is set; that is, a trumpet will always sound like a trumpet. However, when composing with electronics, the composer could manipulate sound to achieve the timbres he had assigned. Stockhausen, in ordering the aspects that made up sound, now controlled every aspect of his music.

Stockhausen's strict adherence to serialism and the concept of setting up a system in which the music grows ultimately led to his inability to create the living pieces for which he strove. Controlling every aspect of music ultimately did not achieve Stockhausen's intended result. While his pieces had the unity he sought, he ultimately had to give up some control of the composition in order to give the piece life. One of the solutions to this problem was the use of **indeterminacy**. By allowing his pieces to have an element of chance to them, Stockhausen created music that allowed every performance to be unique. *Klavierstücke XI* (1956) is an example of the incorporation of indeterminacy. In it, he has short segments of music arranged on a sheet. The performer plays the segments as he sees them: Stockhausen prescribes no set order. The piece continues until one pattern has been played three times, so the length varies between performances as well. Indeterminacy allows it to be "living" in that no two performances will ever be the same.

Stockhausen's ideas of organizing his compositions challenged assumptions and created new ways of thinking about compositions. His focus on the creation of sound led to many new ways of composing music through his serial and electronic compositions. Through his music, he also sought to reveal his concept of God. His career served to inspire and inform the careers of many other musicians.

indeterminacy: an approach to composing in which the composer leaves part of the performance to chance

IN THEIR OWN WORDS

Karlheinz Stockhausen on religion:

"The next step is the untangling of the particular religions. A new orientation has to occur, which embraces all of humanity and in which no one feels excluded and fought against by others simply because he or she thinks differently or has a different sense of life. A new religiosity has to be established. I believe that, for example, the pure, abstract arts acquire a new purpose in this development—to connect man with the mysterious vibration structures of the entire cosmos. Therefore it can be said that if one sees, grasps, and understands the deeper meaning of a musical work of art, one will eventually become a humble admirer of God. One will become aware of the intelligence of the universe that pulsates through everything. And one will also realize that the composer is a servant, an assistant to the universal God who creates such a wonderful work of art."[9]

John Cage Gives Up Control

If Stockhausen was the picture of complete control in music, John Cage (1912-1992; see Fig. 12.21) should be seen as the musical opposite. While the serialism of Stockhausen prescribed every element of music, John Cage's music gave up control of the sounds in favor of chance music. Cage's music is heavily influenced by his adherence to Zen Buddhism and his belief that life on earth is random.

The early music of John Cage was experimental and marked by his invention of the **prepared piano,** a piano in which various objects were placed in the piano strings to create new timbres. The effect would be that the piano would take on the characteristics of a variety of percussion instruments. *Sonatas and Interludes* (1946-1948) is a series of sixteen movements that explore the timbres Cage achieved with his new instrument. John Cage's early works were influenced by his studies with Arnold Schoenberg, but he would eventually venture into even more experimental and **aleatoric** methods of composition.

Listen to Cage's Sonata No. 2 for prepared piano.

Cage's biggest contribution to the tradition of Western music came through his chance processes. One way that he composed was through the use of tossing coins according to the tradition of the *I-Ching*, a Chinese book of prophecy. Like a serial composer, Cage would create charts for all of the possible sounds, then use the method of the *I-Ching* to determine the order for his composition. When he would write an indeterminate work, he would not specify exactly what

prepared piano: piano in which objects such as bolts and felt are placed in the strings in order to create nontraditional sounds

aleatoric: depending on chance

Fig. 12.21. John Cage in 1958.

should happen, but instead would set up a framework within which the music will take place. The most famous example of this is 4'33" (pronounced four minutes thirty-three seconds, 1952).

4'33" is a silent piece of music: The performer sits silently at a piano for three silent movements that total four minutes and thirty-three seconds. Influenced by modern art (particularly Robert Rauschenberg's *The White Paintings*), Cage wrote a piece of music that highlighted the world in which it took place. As audience members listen to 4'33", it is inevitable that they will not hear silence. Instead, they will hear environmental sounds that will make up the composition of the piece. With Zen as an influence, Cage created a structure in which listeners would have to sit and listen to sounds all around them. This is similar to the Zen discipline of *zazen*, a meditation in which the practitioner attempts to silence their ego in order to achieve clear perception of the surrounding world.[10] Cage attempted to write his music in the same way, which is a large part of the emergence of chance composition processes. The *I-Ching* allowed Cage to quell his ego in order to produce music free of his personality. Zen includes the belief that the world is an illusion. There is no good or bad, no happiness or sadness, except that which happens in a person's thoughts. If humans are one with nature, there is no difference between humanity and nature. When that thinking is then applied to music, it is natural that silence and sound are considered the same: there is no difference, intellectually, between organized sound and its absence. Additionally, the presence of a note from an instrument and the squeak of a concert hall chair are equally valid musical sounds. With these concepts in mind, it becomes easier to understand 4'33". Cage was not creating a musical prank. Instead, he was acting out his worldview through the medium of music. Just as in *zazen*, Cage emptied his musical structure to highlight the sounds around the listener.

zazen: a meditation in which practitioners attempt to silence their ego in order to achieve clear perception of the world around them

In Their Own Words

In her book *Saving Leonardo,* apologist Nancy Pearcey discusses the work of John Cage and the implications of a Buddhist worldview. She writes,

"The problem with this approach ... is that it 'represents a virtual denial of any transcendence over nature.' In fact, it expresses the Eastern idea that human transcendence over nature is an illusion ... Thus the goal of meditation is to dissolve all sense of being a separate self by merging with the cosmic One, the undifferentiated All. A poem by Li Po, an eighth-century Chinese poet ends with these words:

> We sit together, the mountain and I
> until only the mountain remains.

> This poem is frequently quoted in books on meditation. *Such peace! Such oneness with nature!* But what is the poet really saying? That a person's goal should be to dissolve into the rock of the mountainside. It's a radically dehumanizing message. The poem implies that the human being has less value and dignity than a rock.
>
> As created beings, of course, we do sense at times our unity with the rest of creation, and these can be powerful and moving experiences. The brilliance of snow-capped mountains, or the calm of a sunny summer day can lift us beyond the superficial demands of daily life. This might be called a biblical form of nature mysticism. Yet as personal beings, we are also infinite to a deeper mysticism—to share in the life and love between the three persons of the divine Trinity, in whose image we were made. In communion with the personal yet infinite God, we actually get in touch with our own personality at deeper levels than we ever thought possible."[11]

Indeterminacy and chance remained a constant throughout the work of John Cage. His philosophy and compositions have inspired many composers, including Stockhausen, and installed him as the de facto face of avant-garde music. Simultaneously, his pieces caused great amounts of controversy and debate about what really constitutes music. Regardless of classification, Cage deserves to be listed as one of the most influential twentieth-century composers due to the acceptance of his ideas into the mainstream of Western fine arts.

Philip Glass

Philip Glass (1937-) is the most well-known and commercially successful of those composing music in the style known as minimalism. In many ways, minimalism is a reaction to the overly complex music of the first half of the twentieth century. It is often composed using simplified rhythmic, melodic and harmonic ideas, is often very consonant, and does not typically engage in a great deal of harmonic dissonance. Rhythmically, the music can be incredibly complex for the performers to realize, but that is not always apparent to those listening to it. Glass began his career writing film music, but as his mature style began to take shape, he formed his own ensemble, bearing his name, to perform and record his music in the 1960s and 1970s. Unlike many composers, who would release performance rights for their music to any orchestra or ensemble who might want to perform their music, Glass maintained the rights to be performed only by his ensemble, ensuring that both his music was performed correctly and to his standard, and that his ensemble would be paid through the performances of his work all around the world. Performances were held in a variety of venues, such as art galleries and museums, not just the concert hall. Glass collaborated with artists in the visual arts, dance, theatre, and film in the loft scene of New York City during this era.

Glass's collaborations led to some of his most creative and well-known works. He composed the opera *Einstein on the Beach* in collaboration with Robert Wilson, whose theatre work combined multiple forms of media. Unlike traditional opera, the work does not present a plot in a normal timeline, but draws upon a libretto formed of poetry, solfege, and numbers used to learn the music, and monologues. The music, choreography, and libretto are presented in similar manner, repeated melodic ideas that might undergo slight changes to the rhythm, or movements by the cast that are repeated in a pattern, but then slightly changed, or stopped. The phrases spoken or sung may be repeated suddenly, one line, and then commencing on, only to return to a certain phrase again, or even a single word. Two people might be reciting the same lines of poetry but will be speaking at different points at the same time in the poem, or one will repeat a word or phrase that the other does not. The music requires intense listening to capture the slight changes or pick up the two or more distinct voices speaking at the same time. The opera lasts approximately five hours, but the audience is encouraged to come and go as they please during the performance. While it may seem nonsensical at times, the work should be experienced as a whole to be fully appreciated.

Watch this excerpt from Einstein on the Beach. Note how the choreography and monologue is similar to the music through the repetition in part or whole, or through the slight changes made in the patterns.

Always a collaborator, Glass has continued to work with others on a variety of projects, producing an incredible amount of music including many operas, symphonies, concertos, chamber works, and additional independent film and documentary scores, as well as Hollywood studio film scores. Just as entrepreneurial as he was in the 1960s, Glass continues to work with his self-named ensemble, and created recording labels to catalog his music, maintaining his control over his music in a way that few composers have been able, or even interested, in doing. Yet these decisions have led to not only professional acknowledgement as one of the great composers of the second half of the twentieth century, but also as one of the most commercially successful composers, reaping the full financial rewards of his artistic endeavors.

Jazz

During the second half of the twentieth century, jazz music continued to develop and branch out into numerous different styles. While many jazz musicians were important to the continued development of the art form, many of the

Fig. 12.22. Miles Davis.

important changes in jazz can be traced through the careers of two musicians, Miles Davis (1926-1991; see Fig. 12.22) and John Coltrane (1926-1967).

Miles Davis grew up in East Saint Louis, Missouri, and was accepted into the famed Juilliard School in New York City to study trumpet. Aware that opportunities for black musicians in orchestras were virtually unattainable, Miles dropped out, and began working the New York City jazz scene. He apprenticed by playing with Charlie Parker and eventually struck out on his own as a leader. Davis is credited with innovating the direction of jazz in six different ways. His album *Birth of the Cool* slowed down the feverish tempos of bebop and used unique instrumentations to create new textures over which to improvise. His record *Walkin'* established the style of hard bop. Hard bop incorporated funky grooves and maintained the tempos similar to cool jazz. Davis's collaborations with the arranger Gil Evans (1912-1988), with whom he had worked on *Birth of the Cool*, created large-scale jazz compositions that resembled the classical concerto more than a typical jazz small group or even big band setting, of which the album *Sketches of Spain* is a classic example. In 1959, Davis recorded what is regarded as the best-selling jazz album of all time, *Kind of Blue*. Continuing his direction away from the frenzied tempos and complex chord changes of bebop, Miles and his bandmates soloed over single chords for long periods. This style focused on melodic improvisation and the exploration of the scales that worked over each individual chord and became known as modal jazz. In the period beginning in 1963, Davis's quintet incorporated some of the elements with avant-garde jazz, within the context of much of the music familiar from his hard bop period. Finally, in 1969, Davis began to incorporate elements of rock and roll into jazz, creating a hybrid often referred to as fusion. Davis's continued development was a credit to his desire to not be satisfied with success or accolades. Moreover, he benefited from his openness to surround himself constantly with younger musicians with different influences and ideas than his own.

Listen for the different soloists and their approaches in "So What" from Davis's album *Kind of Blue*.

Time	Description
0:01	Bill Evans, the pianist, plays an introduction with Paul Chambers on bass.
0:34	Chambers transitions into the melody of the tune accompanied by the drummer Jimmy Cobb. Evans interjects a two chord hit that essentially sounds the syllables, "So What."
0:51	The horns (Miles Davis—trumpet; Cannonball Adderley—alto saxophone; and John Coltrane—tenor saxophone) play the *So What* hit.
1:04	Since the tune started (0:34), the band has played over one chord (d minor), the chord finally changes here, up a half-step to e-flat minor.
1:18	The chord changes back to d minor. The form of this tune translates to 16 measures of d minor, 8 measures of e-flat minor, and then back to d minor for the last 8 measures. The musicians will repeat this same type of format for their solos. Listen for that change during the solos.
1:31	Davis begins his solo, the first phrase of which ends with two eighth notes (doo-dot) at 1:36—this will become a motif that can be heard throughout this solo.
3:26	Coltrane begins his solo. Whereas Miles's solo was laid back, and had space to breathe, Coltrane plays with a sense of direction and plays flurries of notes at times.
5:17	Adderley begins his solo. Similar to Coltrane, Adderley plays a lot of notes, but in the slower moments, he maintains a stronger sense of swing and blues to his solo.
7:06	The horns play the "So What" motif, and Evans solos underneath on piano with a more chordal approach.
8:17	After a transition from Evans solo, Chambers begins playing the melody to the end of the tune.

Fig. 12.23. John Coltrane.

Davis's role as a mentor to younger up and coming musicians is one of the most important aspects of his career. While he may not have viewed himself as a mentor, many of the greats would work with him, and many current musicians including Herbie Hancock (1940-), Ron Carter (1937-), Kenny Garrett (1960-), and Dave Holland (1946-) all played with Miles Davis at various points of his career. His influence is still felt in the jazz world today by those who played with him over his lengthy career.

John Coltrane (see Fig. 12.23), similarly, was an artist who was constantly exploring and searching for new sounds and ideas. A tenor saxophonist, Coltrane's first major job was playing in the Miles Davis quintet. Though they were born the same year, Davis was a seasoned veteran when they began playing together, due to his early apprenticeship with Charlie Parker. Coltrane was noted early on for his long, searching solos, and was accused of practicing on the band stand. Coltrane was an obsessive student of his instrument, and many stories exist of him practicing up to twelve hours a day, and even falling asleep with his instrument at his side in bed. Due to the prodigious technique that he developed, he was able to play extremely fast and his aggressive runs of scales and arpeggios became known as "sheets of sound." While playing with Davis, Coltrane started recording albums as a leader of his own group, most notably the album *Giant Steps*, which, like *Kind of Blue*, debuted in 1959. While *Kind of Blue* looked for ways to slow down the harmonic rhythm of jazz (slowing down the speed that the chords changed), *Giant Steps* took the challenge of bebop a step farther. The title track was based on a chord progression that Coltrane developed as a practice tool, which moved in a much more unfamiliar pattern than standard chord progressions of the bebop era did.

Coltrane would continue searching, and in 1964 released his album, *A Love Supreme*. The album is a document of Coltrane's musical and spiritual search. Both Coltrane's father and grandfather were preachers; however, Coltrane's father and mother both passed away when he was just twelve years old. Coltrane was a spiritual seeker, which can be clearly seen in the final movement of *A Love*

Supreme, entitled *Psalm*. Coltrane plays a prayer that can be found in the liner notes of the album. It is filled with many lines with which a Christian would have no problem, many of which have their source in the Bible: "Glory to God" (Luke 2:14), "acceptable in Thy sight" (Ps 19:14), and "He will wipe away every tear" (Rev 21:4). Digging deeper, however, one starts to perceive ideas contradictory to the historical Christian view, such as referring in a vague way to all paths leading to God. While Coltrane was raised in a Christian home, he took a more general view of religion, and one can see influences from Eastern religions in some of his lines. In his poem, he appears to be earnestly seeking God. However, Coltrane approaches it from the viewpoint of inclusivism or universalism and not, as Jesus said in John 14:6, that "I am the way, and the truth, and the life. No one comes to the Father except through me."

Listen to "Psalm" from Coltrane's album *A Love Supreme*.

In 1959, another genre-defining album was recorded by the alto saxophonist, Ornette Coleman (1930-2015). The album shook the jazz world as it sounded very little like the jazz that anyone was familiar with. It sounded chaotic and experimental, musicians would play in the extremes of their range, or even scream through their instrument. Gone were many of the elements that had defined jazz: chord changes, blues, and consistent rhythmic swing feel. Performers even sometimes played on toy instruments, like a plastic saxophone. These performers were serious about their craft, but the jazz community did not take them seriously until Coltrane, the constant searcher, started to incorporate elements of this avant-garde style. His constant probing led him to now be totally free, and eventually his titanic presence brought others into this style of music and legitimized it within the jazz community.

The influence that Davis and Coltrane exerted over jazz over the 1950s and 1960s shaped what would become of jazz through the end of the century. Jazz artists continued to look for ways to remain relevant, and fusions of jazz with R&B, hip-hop, funk, and even pop followed. In the 1990s, jazz musicians began to look back at the styles of bebop and hard bop and reinvigorated the traditional jazz style that had mostly been fused with other genres of music. While this was viewed by some within the community as looking backward, when the style had always looked forward, it allowed jazz to approach the music anew from within its own established language, rather than working to join with whatever new genre had popped up. Thus, they breathed new life into the art form.

Bands

The 1950s were an important time to the development of the modern band. While band leaders sought out composers to write for their ensembles in the first half of the century, many famous composers were reluctant to write for the medium. Composers, used to writing for orchestras, were accustomed to a standard of performance that was not often heard by bands. Many composers associated the term "band" with a poorly run high school ensemble, or an out-of-tune group of community performers. While many fine college bands existed at this time, they were large ensembles, featuring 80 to 100 musicians, with multiple musicians playing each part, which did not necessarily feature the flexibility or fleetness of which a modern orchestra was capable. Frustrated with the lack of quality repertoire available for bands, Frederick Fennell (1914-2004) director at the Eastman School of Music in Rochester, NY, changed the format of his ensemble in 1952 to a single player per part. He exposed his ensemble to a variety of music, using only the musicians needed for each piece. A concert may feature an octet by Mozart, followed by a larger piece by Stravinsky, but the defining nature was the high-quality literature and exacting performances. Immediately Fennell raised the standard of the band and changed its name to the Eastman Wind Ensemble.

Fennell, and adherents like Frank Battisti (1922-) who would go on to lead the wind ensemble at the New England Conservatory, sought to raise the level of compositions available to the modern wind ensemble and commissioned numerous composers to write for their groups. The make-up of the ensemble allowed for flexible instrumentation, and the composers were encouraged to write what they wanted, as long as it was mainly for winds and percussion. (Many wind ensembles have a double bass as the lone string instrument in the ensemble.) The quality of literature improved, and Pulitzer Prize-winning composers such as Aaron Copland, William Schuman (1910-1992), Gunther Schuller (1925-2015), Joseph Schwantner (1943-), John Harbison (1938-), and Michael Colgrass (1932-2019) all wrote major works for the wind ensemble. While the stigma of the "band sound" remained, the work of conductors like Fennell and Battisti helped pave the way for interesting and challenging music to be written for the medium. Conservatory and university programs promised the ability to rehearse the music in a way that modern orchestras would not. Some composers, like Vincent Persichetti (1915-1987), Alfred Reed (1921-2005), and later David Maslanka (1943-2017) and Frank Ticheli (1958-), began composing a significant number of works for bands and wind ensembles, leading to the development of an impressive repertoire.

Listen for the elements in the triumphant finale of David Maslanka's Symphony No. 4.

Time	Description
0:01	The flutes and harp perform a setting of a chorale written by J.S. Bach ("Christ, Who Makes Us Holy")
0:13	Clarinets playing only the mouthpiece section of their instrument. (Maslanka refers to this in the score as "the babies"—for Maslanka—part of this work is about rebirth, and this is a reference to that.) Eventually, the clarinets join with the flutes and add their voice to the chorale.

Time	Description
1:22	A solo euphonium joins in, adding a mellow brass voice to the group.
2:22	A theme from earlier in the symphony returns here, but brighter and more powerful.
3:23	Flutes, oboes, and clarinets begin a rapid passage of notes above the melody.
3:42	Now saxophones, bassoons, and mallet percussion (marimba, vibraphone, and xylophone) play the furious passages of notes over the melody.
4:14	A theme that has been called the "shout for the joy of life" (due to a note from the composer) serves as a transition to the next section.
4:19	The hymn tune Old 100th (also known as the Doxology) is introduced by the trombones, while swirling passages of notes fly above and the bass line is pounded below.
5:07	The music quiets but maintains an intensity and direction as the ensemble moves together. Maslanka quotes material from his 3rd symphony in this section.
5:53	Maslanka was inspired by the landscapes of western Montana and central Idaho, near his home, and the end of this work pays tribute to that magnificent creation. This theme continues to rise majestically, as do the mountains, ending on a powerful major chord.

Theatre

Each successive theatrical style found in previous eras sought to become the newly defined approach to drama and any attempt to modify those styles were viewed negatively. This fundamentalist attitude is what sets the postmodern era apart from its predecessors. **Theatrical postmodernism** intentionally pursued ways to combine newer methods with the old to tell stories in inventive ways. While modern realists refused to revert to techniques of earlier methods, postmodernists abandoned those convictions to embrace, and even showcase, ways of blending multiple cultures and performance styles.[12]

Changes in political, economic, social, and religious climates had a major influence on theatrical movements over the centuries. As the mid-twentieth century progressed, artists were reeling from recent political unrest and relied on their creativity to move the world forward. Playwrights suddenly had a desire to inform and challenge their audiences, rather than to simply entertain them. The result was a new approach that faced off with traditionalism by rebelling against it, celebrating it, disregarding it, and everything in between.

theatrical postmodernism: a style of theatre that arose after the modern era which utilizes a mixture of traditional methods with more experimental ones

Toward the Absurd

An immense amount of theatrical experimentation occurred in the years following World War II (1939-1945) and a new writing style emerged wherein playwrights asserted that life was meaningless. This mentality arose from the existentialist philosophy that there was no God, that all of life was pointless, and that man was alone in an irrational universe with no choice but to accept it. This new approach sought to enlighten its audience of this "truth" by presenting life as illogical and wildly unreasonable—the very definition of *absurd*. And, thus, a new theatrical approach was born that combined the existentialist philosophy with the avant-garde dramatic form to become the theatre of the absurd.

A classic example of absurdist theatre is found in Samuel Beckett's (1906-1989) famous play written in 1953, *Waiting for Godot* (pronounced in the United States as "guh-DOW," in the UK as "GAW-dow," and by Beckett's family as "GUD-OW"). The play is based around a cyclical plot structure[13] where the main characters, two vagabonds named Vladimir and Estragon (see Fig. 12.24), spend the entire play ... waiting. For whom or what, the audience is uncertain, and the two accomplish nothing during the first act, which ends when a messenger arrives to tell them that Godot will not come that day. The second act is basically more of the same and ends with a messenger bearing the same word that Godot will not come. Hearing this news, Vladimir and Estragon resolve to go and return the next day to wait, but they never leave, and the curtain falls.

theatre of the absurd: a theatrical approach born out of existentialism, expressing life as illogical and unreasonable through experimental performance styles

Fig. 12.24. The characters of Vladimir and Estragon in a 2015 production of *Waiting for Godot* at the Barbican Theatre in Sydney.

Although *Waiting for Godot* contains several religious references, Beckett never claimed to be a believer and his works contain no reverence toward God. Many speculate the character of "Godot" actually represents "God" although Beckett would never comment on it. It is likely that as an existentialist, his religious references were an attempt to mock man's dependence upon God. It is interesting to note that, much to Beckett's chagrin, *Waiting for Godot* might actually be seen as an archetype of the Ecclesiastical point: if man believes in a god who does not see him, care for him, or come for him, then his life truly is meaningless. For the believer, Beckett's depiction of "Godot" serves to further illustrate man's hopelessness without the one true God.

Toward Selective Realism

Another notable theatrical style emerged from multiple hybrid techniques. As playwrights Tennessee Williams (1911-1983) and Arthur Miller (1925-2005) veered away from the strict style of realism, a **selective realism** emerged. Plays written in this style dictated the use of some realistic components in the action, dialogue, or scenery, while omitting others. Nonrealistic conventions such as flashbacks, dreams, memories, and imagery were merged with a representational acting style (see Fig. 12.25).

Tennessee Williams wrote some of the most prolific plays of the twentieth century. Two of his many writings included *A Streetcar Named Desire* (1947) and *Cat on a Hot Tin Roof* (1955), for which he won Pulitzer Prizes. The disturbing plot lines and controversial characters likely paralleled Williams's own troubled life

selective realism: a style that only highlights certain thematic elements of a production (scenery, action, language) using realism, but omits others

Fig. 12.25. From the 2016 Broadway revival of *The Glass Menagerie* by Tennessee Williams.

Fig. 12.26. A scene from The Royal Shakespeare Company's 2006 production of *The Crucible* by Arthur Miller.

and spirit. He was notorious for including very detailed stage directions in his scripts that established what conventional and unconventional techniques the story would employ.

Like Williams, Arthur Miller also wrote many American classics including his famous *Death of a Salesman* (1949) where he combined simplistic sets and flashbacks with realistic characters and action. He also wrote other hits including *All My Sons* (1946), *The Crucible* (1953), and *A View from the Bridge* (1955). Miller's writings were influenced greatly by the social and political climates of the time as demonstrated by the flawed worlds of his characters and the idealistic qualities that symbolized their downfall (see Fig. 12.26.).

Toward the Musical

Picture a typical musical—a lavish backdrop, a man who finally wins the girl and the two immediately burst into a harmonious song and elaborate dance—this is a theatrical style all its own. Precursors of the modern musical can be traced back to vaudeville and operetta as lighthearted musicals with catchy tunes that grew in popularity during the period following World War I with contributions from **composers** and **lyricists** like George and Ira Gershwin, Jerome Kern (1885-1945), Richard Rodgers (1902-1979), Lorenz Hart (1895-1943), Oscar Hammerstein II (1895-1960), Irving Berlin (1888-1989), and Cole Porter (1892-1964). Kern and Hammerstein partnered in 1927 to write *Show Boat*. Dealing with more serious themes than its musical predecessors, *Show Boat* was a groundbreaking musical with songs that were integrated into its plot.

Two of the most important contributors to the musical theatre genre were Rodgers and Hammerstein, who paired up for the first time in 1943 to write *Oklahoma!* which signaled another new era in musical theatre. It showcased character-driven lyrics and tunes that naturally emerged from the dialogue. *Oklahoma!* also became the first musical to produce an original cast recording and is credited with being the first American **book musical**—a dramatic style of contemporary musical theatre where both the "book" (or *script*, which is also called the *libretto*) serve equally to tell the story. The **book-writer** (or librettist) became a fundamental part of the musical writing team and, as in the case of Hammerstein, would often also serve as the lyricist. Rodgers and Hammerstein continued to work together to create *Carousel* (1945), *South Pacific* (1949), *The King and I* (1951), *The Sound of Music* (1959), and others including the musical that premiered on TV in 1957 starring Julie Andrews, *Cinderella*.

Over the following years, many other musical genres emerged including the antiestablishment **rock musicals** *Hair* (1967) and *Rent* (1996) as well as **concept musicals** like *A Little Night Music* (1973) and *Into the Woods* (1988). The design styles and performance techniques of postmodern musicals were as varied as the ideas for their storylines. Productions emerged based on religion (*Jesus Christ, Superstar*, 1971), novels (*Les Misérables*, 1986, and *The Phantom of the Opera*, 1987), poetry (*Cats*, 1982), wives of dictators (*Evita*, 1979), and even stories of struggling artists (*A Chorus Line*, 1975). The popularity of musical theatre drew the Walt Disney Corporation onto the scene to produce the box-office hits *Beauty and the Beast* (1994) and *The Lion King* (1997). The popularity of the American musical grew substantially during the postmodern era and it continues to soar even higher today.

Toward Another Broadway

The epicenter of theatre in America has always been New York City, and the term "Broadway" had become synonymous with theatre by the modern era, but what does the term **Broadway theatre** really mean? This complicated question has multiple answers as the expression can refer to a "street, a district, a form of theatre, a union classification, or a state of mind."[14] In the context of this chapter, the term will refer to a theatre's house size (Broadway venues typically have an audience seating capacity of 500 or more) *and* its physical proximity to **New York's theatre district**.

As professional theatres popped up across the country as "testing grounds" for potential Broadway hits, postmodern theatre artists had to work harder for a debut. Mounting a production on Broadway in New York had become substantially more expensive after 1950. Increased competition from the entertainment industry through film and TV, as well as the expensive price tag for theatre labor union memberships, greatly impacted artists' ability to earn a living.

---

book musical: a contemporary style of musical where the music and lyrics are fully integrated into the story and emerge as a natural continuation of a character's dialogue (the book/script, is also called the libretto)

book-writer/librettist: the one who writes the spoken dialog in a musical which weaves the story together (the book/script, is also called the libretto)

rock musical: style of musical theatre using a rock genre of music and whose themes are often in opposition to someone in authority (government, landlord, etc.) and/or a idea (war, disease, etc.)

concept musical: a style of musical theatre where the words and music convey story based on a theme or message, instead of a character driven plot

Postmodern artists needed alternative ways to produce shows amid increasing financial burdens. A logical solution was found in the creation of a new Broadway experience[15]—one that was less costly and offered more artistic freedom—and **Off-Broadway theatre** was born. Off-Broadway theatres had smaller house sizes than traditional Broadway (100-500 seats) and offered cheaper ticket prices. The shows were also smaller in scale with fewer cast members, less lavish scenery and costumes, and less popular titles. The goal was to make theatre available to more people, artists and audiences alike.

It did not take long for yet another branch of the Off-Broadway movement to emerge around 1960. With an influx in many avant-garde and experimental theatres springing up around New York, the **Off-Off Broadway theatre** emerged. The term was coined at the time[16] by *The Village Voice* as artists in New York found nontraditional performance spaces in churches, basements, coffee shops, restaurants, and abandoned schools. The increasingly experimental nature of Off-Off Broadway appealed to a smaller faction of people whose minds were open enough to appreciate its edgier art-form. The Off-Off Broadway performance spaces were more intimate, seating fewer than 100, and soon became known as a place where new artists could experiment with controversial subject matter and methods.

Broadway theatre: popular productions staged in a theatre within the New York Theatre District and which seats over 500 (the audience house)

New York Theatre District: area around Times Square in Manhattan where most Broadway theatres are located (runs roughly between West 41st and West 54th Streets, and Sixth to Eighth Avenues)

Off Broadway theatre: less-popular productions staged in a theatre located relatively close proximity to the New York Theatre District and which seats between 100 and 499 in (audience house)

Off-Off Broadway theatre: experimental productions staged in non-traditional theatre spaces outside the New York Theatre District and which seat fewer than 100 (its audience house)

Did you know?

Out of the roughly forty "Broadway theatres" in New York today, only five have physical addresses on Broadway Street? These include The Broadway Theatre, Circle in the Square, The Marquis, The Palace, and the Winter Garden. All Broadway theatres are nestled within a larger area, called New York's Theatre District, which includes the area in mid-town Manhattan around Times Square that runs roughly between West 41st and West 54th Streets (south to north), and Sixth to Eighth Avenues (east to west). There are likely upward of a hundred additional theatres classified as Off or Off-Off Broadway theatres in New York City, but only Broadway productions are eligible for the Tony Awards.

In their own words

The history and progression of the theatre is indeed multifaceted. By its very nature, theatre's evolution represents man's grand story. Bruce King, theatre scholar and editor of *Contemporary American Theatre* writes a succinct summation that could be poignantly applied to man's rebellion against his creator:

> "In the evolution of art, every period of intense innovation is a response to—a revolt against—established tradition. And this response is always followed by a period of consolidation, in which a sort of cultural triage takes place: classical culture is re-evaluated in the light of recent developments, and the value of recent experiments are weighed against the truth and usefulness of art that has remained vital across centuries and continents. The collage that results is the basis of a new tradition, against which future innovators will inevitably rebel. The cycle is as simple (and violent) as nature itself."[17]

Theatre would continue to evolve, as the next chapter demonstrates. It will be part of Western culture as long as there are passionate artists with stories to share. Although the theatre can be a place where controversy abounds, it can also be a place where God's truth and beauty are extolled.

Study Questions

1. What ideas guided the movement of abstract expressionism?
2. Why did photorealism become an artistic movement in such close proximity with abstract art?
3. What was the pervasive philosophy behind the theatre of the absurd?
4. What was different about the "book musical" as compared to its predecessors?
5. What are the differences between Broadway, Off-Broadway, and Off-Off Broadway theatre?
6. What aspects of music did Karlheinz Stockhausen, and other serial composer, seek to control through serialism?
7. Explain how the music of John Cage differed from the music of Stockhausen.
8. In what way does modal jazz differ from bebop?
9. How did Frederick Fennell change the concept of the symphonic band?
10. What is minimalism in music?

Notes

1. *Cleveland Morning Leader*, January 7, 1861.
2. Warhol, 100-101.
3. Stiles, 92.
4. Ulrich, 8.

5. Ulrich, 12.
6. Stockhausen, 39.
7. Stockhausen, 39-40.
8. Ulrich, 19. From a letter to Goeyvaerts.
9. Peters, 110.
10. Gann, 138.
11. Pearcey, 203-204.
12. Balthrop, 65.
13. Fraser, 193.
14. Hischak, 193.
15. Robinson, 2019.
16. Wright, 2004.
17. King, 294.

13 Globalization
Twenty-First Century

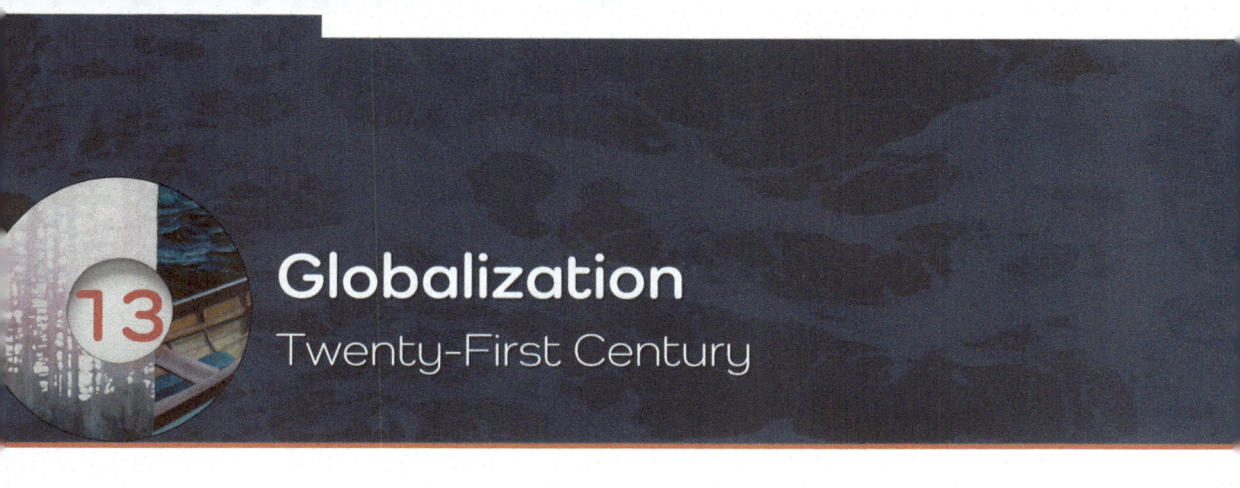

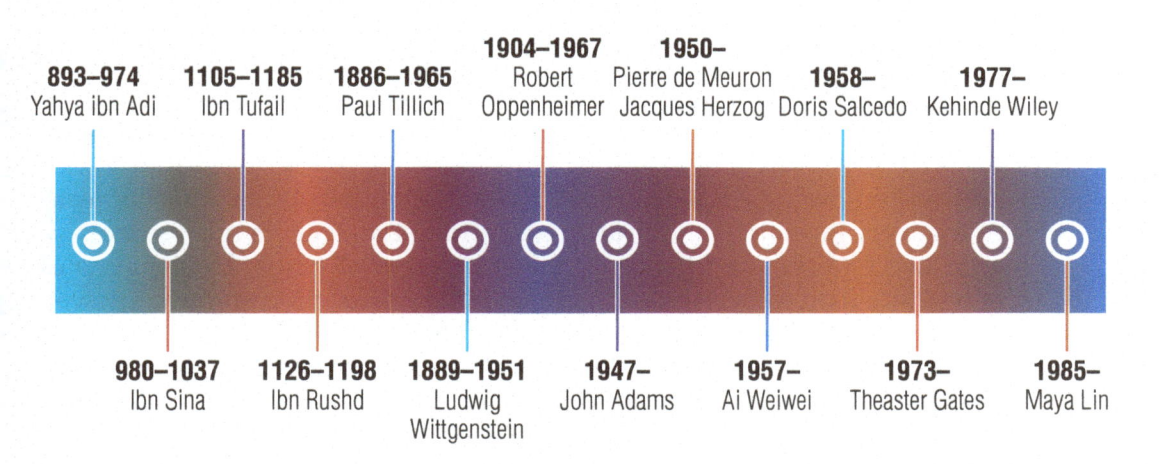

893–974 Yahya ibn Adi
1105–1185 Ibn Tufail
1886–1965 Paul Tillich
1904–1967 Robert Oppenheimer
1950– Pierre de Meuron Jacques Herzog
1958– Doris Salcedo
1977– Kehinde Wiley

980–1037 Ibn Sina
1126–1198 Ibn Rushd
1889–1951 Ludwig Wittgenstein
1947– John Adams
1957– Ai Weiwei
1973– Theaster Gates
1985– Maya Lin

Philosophy

The meeting of cultures has had a long and turbulent history. At times, such meeting involves the eventual decline of one culture due to attacks by another. At other times, such interchange has been fruitful, allowing for great progress in human thought. Frequently, however, **globalization**, or the process by which different geographical areas and cultures are becoming more interconnected, has been a combination of both. One can see this if one were to look at the history of Aristotelian philosophy. Aristotle, after the death of Plato, had fallen out of favor in Athens and eventually left to become the tutor of Alexander the Great. Alexander's conquest and development of the Greek Empire led not only a swath of destruction in the Mediterranean world but also allowed for the movement of Aristotle's ideas and works across the Middle East. It was there that his work was kept alive and given its most fruitful interpretation and use. This can be seen in Arabic philosophers such as Ibn Sina (Latinized, Avicenna; 980-1037), Ibn Tufail (Latinized, Avetophail; 1105-1185), and Ibn Rushd (Latinized, Averroes; 1126-1198). As the West and Middle East continued to

globalization the process by which different geographical areas and cultures are becoming more interconnected

globalize, Aristotle's work was reintroduced to Europe. This occurred as early as the Islamic incursions into Spain but was continued as international trade increased and with European conquests during the Crusades. The interconnection of peoples can be fruitful, but it has come at some deep historical costs.

> **DID YOU KNOW?**
>
> Though Islamic philosophers were among the most significant in the continuance of the influence of Greek philosophy, Arabic Christians had an important role as well. For example, Yahya ibn Adi (893-974) was a Syrian believer who was integral in translating Greek works into Arabic, works that became foundational for scholars that succeeded him.

The twenty-first century dawned with constant reminders of the effect of technology on every facet of life. Warnings concerning the dangers of a technological world that had occurred the century before, especially from Heidegger and Sartre, had fallen on unhearing ears. Exponential growth in computing power, the ubiquity of cellular devices, and the ascendency of social media made the interchange of information and disinformation quick and effortless. The process of globalization that had begun millennia earlier on a regional scale was now a governing cultural force. As different societies were now confronted with ideas and practices that they had not experienced, the way to navigate the tension came to the forefront of the philosophical mind. For art, it meant that classical ideas, though in some areas respected, were not allowed dominance. Contemporary artists, consequently, are much more likely to be influenced by content and techniques from non-Western sources and from Western sources that had been frequently ignored (i.e., South American and African).

Philosophically, one of the principal characteristics of twenty-first-century thought is the reaction to the perceived failures of postmodernism. Postmodern writers did both academia and Christianity a great service in convincing the world that individuals were not as objective as Enlightenment thinkers attempted to portray them. The interpretation of historical events, the living out of ethical principles, and the development of civil authority, as examples, do not arise from detached individuals who come into the world as "blank slates," to use the aforementioned terminology of Locke (see Ch. 8). Individuals are invested in situations, hold values that affect their understanding, and cannot help but enter into analyzing complicated issues with cultural baggage. Similar is the scriptural idea, frequently developed by Calvin, that humans are not neutral. All individuals are creatures who are affected by their upbringing, their social situation, and indeed, their own sin, in the way they approach the world.

Yet, with this important contribution by postmodernism came the deleterious effects of the attack on all values and truth.

The naming of this reaction to postmodernism has yet to reach consensus. Some people call the contemporary situation post-postmodern, while others speak of metamodernism (which will be used here, for the sake of ease). Since postmodernism had created such a chaotic situation societally and philosophically, responses to it have likewise been unsystematic and diverse. A few significant themes, all of which have had effects on art, can be discerned. First, the rise of social activism, in art and otherwise, is recognized more frequently as being impossible in the vacuum of values that postmodernism helped to create. Thus, the attempts to discover value have returned, though, admittedly, these attempts are typically secular. Second, there has been a pragmatic but conflicting relationship to truth. It is not unusual in the contemporary setting for an individual to treat certain truths as given when it suits an activist mindset, while acting as if truth is subjective when justifying activities and ideas that others may critique. In other words, individuals speak of the "the truth" when it helps to make an argument and speak of "my truth" when defending against criticism. Third, with the attempts to find values, some of which are arbitrary, there has been a type of return to dogmatism that had characterized various previous eras. Certain ideas, including general inclusivity and acceptance, have nearly unquestioned authority, even if the genesis of those ideas have long been forgotten.

Whereas the philosophical world may be post-postmodern, the theological world may be understood as post-liberal. Similar to metamodernism's reaction to postmodernism, post-liberal theologians of the latter half of the twentieth century became disillusioned with liberal theology (see theological liberalism in Ch. 9) and its promises. By questioning the truth of Scripture, liberal scholars began to downplay the significance of the Bible to theological studies. Thus, the textual foundation for knowledge of Christ was attacked and Christianity began to lose its uniqueness. For liberal theology, one's view of God was defined more by philosophy than by God's revelation through the speech of Scripture. One example of this would be the work of Paul Tillich (1886-1965), perhaps the most influential liberal theologian of the twentieth century, who wrote the entirety of the three volume *Systematic Theology* with very few direct quotations of Scripture.[1] Barth's withering attacks on theological liberalism, coupled with the rise of theologians, such as Hans Frei[2] and Georg Lindbeck,[3] who used the philosophy of Ludwig Wittgenstein (1889-1951) to argue for the intrinsic significance of the biblical text to the culture of the Christian community, led to a resurgence in **exegetical studies**, or studies concerning the interpretation of Scripture. Unfortunately, the return to the importance of the Bible in theology has had little effect in the artworld, since the secularization of art that began during the Enlightenment and that had continued through the twentieth century, prevented there

exegetical studies: the field that examines the interpretatio Scripture

from being, with a few notable exceptions, a noticeable influence of Christianity on the artistic endeavor.

Art

Within the age of globalization, individuals across societies and cultures easily connect through convenient travel and by means of the internet. Social media outlets like Twitter, Instagram, YouTube, TikTok, and Facebook are the great equalizers, giving people greater access to and easier exchange of information. In today's times, even social justice movements are built through these platforms. Information about visual art, art history, and individual artists is readily available to see, watch, and be the object of interaction.

Contemporary art is defined as art being made in the current moment of time; it is the art of *right now*. There is no one "ism" or a set of principles to confine or categorize it by, at least not yet being merely two decades into the twenty-first century. In contemporary art, the globally influenced world gives voice to the constantly shifting cultural landscape of identities, values, and beliefs held by present society. These extend to conversations, ideas, and concepts around science, sustainability, social activism, cultural identity, marginalized histories, and issues of gender and sexuality.

One explicit trend that impacts all of the themes cited is the dissolution of the medium-specific artist. There are few boundaries for artists working today, and artists are adept at moving across them fluidly without having to be solely defined as a "painter" or "sculptor." There is no academy or hierarchy of technical skills required to be an artist. Artists are often **interdisciplinary**, working not only across different materials and methods, like installation, painting, sculpture, performance, and video, but even across other areas of study. An artist might collaborate with a poet, a history scholar, a dancer, or a scientist. For all these reasons, one can easily walk into a museum today and be befuddled by what is on display. It might not look like "art" as had been conventionally conceived. Taking into consideration the greater influences surrounding art-making in the twenty-first century, common arcs can be found that can give context to viewing and interacting with contemporary art.

Bio-architecture

With an increased emphasis on the concerns of global warming and ecological dangers, architecture in the twenty-first century has placed high worth on sustainable designs that have low impact on the environment. **Bio-architecture** is defined by two parts: the design and construction of buildings in an eco-friendly manner and looking to nature for inspiration in solving design problems.

Interestingly, it points back to the intelligent design of God's creation, the efficiency of which man cannot match.

Swiss architects Pierre de Meuron (1950-) and Jacques Herzog (1950-) won the competition for the design of the Beijing National Stadium (see Fig. 13.1) for the 2008 summer Olympics in Beijing, China. Built in consultation with activist artist Ai Weiwei (1957-) and nicknamed "The Nest," the structure boasts a retractable roof and multi-functional design meant to accommodate a host of activities. The design mimics the structure of a bird's nest in the exterior with criss-crossing supports and an interior that opens up with a hollow in the center.

Environment and Ecology

Maya Lin (1985-) is an American-born artist who, as a college student, came to fame by winning the design competition for the Vietnam Memorial. Since that seminal project, her work has focused on environmental issues and environmental activism through earthworks, sculptures, and **installations** (a work of art made for a specific site that immerses the viewer in a three-dimensional space). In her projects, Lin attempts to make viewers aware of the impact humans have

installation: a work of art made for a specific site, that immerses the viewer in a three-dimensional space

Fig. 13.1. Beijing National Stadium, "The Nest," 2008, Herzog, de Meuron, Ai Weiwei, Beijing, China.

Fig. 13.2. *Wave Field*, 1995, Maya Lin, Storm King Art Center, Hudson Valley, New York.

on the environment. Her work *Wave Field* (Fig. 13.2) is an earthwork that is built into the landscape of the Hudson Valley. The earthwork is made up of seven long wave forms that run the length of nearly 400 feet and range in height from 10- to 15-feet high, referencing the visual rhythms of waves in the ocean. The location of the installation was once a gravel pit; thus, the project is a reclamation project. Lin worked with architects and conservationists to use the existing gravel and topsoil at the site while introducing new grasses and a natural drainage system.

Social Activism

As contemporary art has given voice to individuals all over the world, many artists use this voice as political criticism of corrupt governments, global trade, the effects of war, and issues of immigration. They do this in direct and indirect ways. Some are politically charged and urgent, while some are quiet and contemplative. Though most of these artists do not operate out of a Christian worldview, their work uplifts the values of Isaiah 1:17 to "learn to do good; seek justice, correct oppression; bring justice to the fatherless, plead the widow's cause."

Political Controversies

The aforementioned Ai Weiwei is a Chinese artist who grew up in north-west China under harsh conditions due to his father's exile. As an artist, he makes use of Chinese art forms like sculpture, ceramics, and installation to critique

Fig. 13.3. *Circle of Animals/Zodiac Heads*, Prague installation, 2016.

government corruption, cover ups, and human rights issues. Due to the politically controversial nature of his work criticizing the Chinese government, he has been detained multiple times.

In his 2010 work *Circle of Animals/Zodiac Heads* (Fig. 13.3), Ai made a set of twelve bronze animal heads based on the figures looted from the Summer Palace in Beijing by the British and French soldiers in 1860. The original heads are now scattered around the world, though the Chinese government is attempting to recollect them as an act of Chinese patriotism. In recreating them and installing the heads at various sites around the world, Ai points out the irony and false narrative of nationalism by the Chinese government, particularly in the era following pro-democracy protests and subsequent government crackdown in China. The bronze and gold variations of the heads have been displayed at nearly forty sites around the world, ironically displaying items looted by colonial Western countries in the west.

Immigration and Displacement

Doris Salcedo (1958-) is a Colombian-born artist who makes sculptures and installations that address the devastation of wars in her home country and the plight of refugees in Europe in the age of globalization. As an artist from a developing country, her perspective is from the experience of the victimized rather than the triumphant, which stands in contrast to the works of Western art produced by dominant culture.

In 2007, Salcedo installed *Shibboleth* (see Fig. 13.4) at Turbine Hall, the main entrance space at the Tate Modern in London, England (the same location of the choral performance *Spem in alium* referenced in Ch. 6). The installation is a large, man-made 548-foot fissure that cracks throughout the length of the concrete floor. The title "Shibboleth" refers to a word, language, or customs that identifies a person with a particular group of people (this word actually originates in Judges 12, in which the pronunciation of word "shibboleth" is used to distinguish the Ephraimites from the Gileadites). The negative space wrought by the fissure in the floor is meant to represent the experience of outsiders in segregation and racial hatred, which is often the plight of a third-world person immigrating to Europe. After the duration of the installation, the crack was filled in with concrete, which is still visible in the floor as a permanent scar.

Fig. 13.4. *Shibboleth*, 2007, Doris Salcedo, Tate Modern, London.

Marginalized Histories in the US

In the twenty-first century, all areas of the humanities, institutions, museums, galleries, and individuals have been challenged to increase representation and recognition of contributions of people of color. Though oppression occurs across continents and ethnic groups, in the US the drive towards racial reconciliation has become increasingly prominent. Particularly in light of the protests surrounding George Floyd's death in Minneapolis, Minnesota in May 2020, there has been a movement towards the representation of historically marginalized black artists and artists of color. Often, these artists use the visual language of the dominant narrative to critique it. Among such artists is African-American Kehinde Wiley (1977-), whose work infuses western art historical references with the contemporary perspective of the black experience.

Wiley is best known for his portrait paintings of black people in the highly naturalistic style of master painters, but adding ornate, colorful backgrounds that give individual autonomy and personality to his subjects. In 2018, Wiley painted

Fig. 13.5. *Rumors of War*, Kehinde Wiley, 2019, Virginia Museum of Fine Arts, Richmond, Virginia.

President Obama for the National Portrait Gallery. In *Rumors of War* (Fig. 13.5), Wiley created a thirty-foot tall statue of a young, contemporary-clothed black man in high tops and dreadlocks atop a horse. The meaning of appropriating the figurative style of monuments that memorialize the triumphant southern Confederate generals seen prolifically in the city of Richmond, Virginia, is pointed. The work is permanently installed at the Virginia Museum of Fine Arts in Richmond.

Art as Social Practice

Social practice in contemporary art focuses on engagement through human interaction and social discourse. It focuses on artist engagement, where the final product is not necessarily a work of "art;" rather, the work of art is created through interaction and experience.

Theaster Gates (1973-) is an African-American artist living and working in Chicago, Illinois. The overarching aim of his artistic work is to build disenfranchised communities in the city of Chicago through ongoing community revitalization projects. One such project is the Stony Island Arts Bank (see Fig. 13.6), once a community savings and loan bank. Through Gates's ongoing project, it now provides the South Side of Chicago with a place for artists to gather and houses important historical collections of African-American culture. Its collections include music records among its cultural artifacts. It is an active site that hosts weekly arts programming that support local artists and artists of color.

social practic art focused on engagement through hum interaction ar social discour

Fig. 13.6. Stony Island Arts Bank, 2015, Theaster Gates, Chicago.

Gender and Sexuality

In our contemporary society, views on gender and sexuality have moved away from the definition for those identities that Scripture teaches as God designed. The arts and humanities are often the first place those shifting conversations around said identities represented by LGBTQ+ communities occur. These include lesbian, gay, bi-sexual, transgender, queer, intersex, and asexual identifiers. In potentially interacting and viewing artwork that redefines God's terms of biological and sexual identity, it is important to go back to the source.

As believers, Christians have historically believed that God determines biological and sexual identity in his wonderfully and intentional design for humans as male and female. Together, the genders of male and female reflect God's nature (Gen 1:26-27). Some individuals have specific struggles regarding their sexual identity or determining their sex either genetically or physically because of the fall. All are called to live in a fruitful obedience to Christ finding their identity in Him through the gospel. In all matters believers are called to see and honor the *Imago Dei*, image of God, in others by treating others with dignity and respect. Though Christians may not agree ideologically with shifting gender and sexuality identifiers, they are still called to the first and second greatest commandments, to "love the Lord your God with all your heart and with all your soul and with all your mind" and to "love your neighbor as yourself." (Matt 22:37-39).

In Their Own Words

Cedarville Studio Art faculty member Cat Mailloux speaks to how she sees her identity as an artist grounded in her Christian faith.

"My artistic work spans across different mediums but is driven by methods that are closely tied to touch and tactility: drawing, sewing, mending, and stenciling. I find that a strong connection to material processes paired with a contemplative attitude in making allows me to reflect on my physical and spiritual nature. I am drawn to the stories of the Bible that center the corporeal nature of Christ as fully human while fully divine, one who broke bread with his friends, changed the physicality of matter through miracles, and healed bodies through touch. I am reminded by Romans 8:23-24 that I, along with all creation, wait in the tension of the physical while yearning for the New Creation. I hold both death and resurrection in me (2 Cor 4.10) and am called in obedience to new *creation*. In my life as an artist, this movement towards new creation manifests itself literally, in acts of creation.

"My visual work uses an intense, laborious touch to draw out patterns and atmospheres of traditional spaces of Christian worship. These drawings, collages, and fabric studies are based on the interior architecture of my church in Circleville, OH. They abstract from the lines and shapes of stained-glass windows and wood detailing of the church interior, contemplating the comfort and mystery of the space of the church sanctuary. I often use layers of drawing and text to reveal and obscure the surface. In the drawing *All Shall Be Well* (Fig. 13.7), I do this using the repetition of the words of medieval anchoress Julian of Norwich who famously wrote 'All shall be well and all shall be well and all manner of things shall be well.'

"Each iteration of my work brings a new combination of media gives a different perspective of materiality and touch. Some are sturdy, like *Blue Void* (Fig. 13.8) which is a sewn panel made of velvet stretched over a wooden frame. Some are ephemeral, like *Paper Window* (Fig. 13.9), a small sculpture made with thread and paper.

"In the Old Testament, the craftsmen Bezalel and Oholiab of Exodus were tasked by God with the creative work of making the Ark of the Covenant. In Exodus 35:31 Bezalel is described as being filled with the Holy Spirit. This is the first example in the Bible of a human being filled with the Holy Spirit. In the same way, I believe the Spirit of God fills me in order to create, so that in my art and in my life, I reflect resurrection in Christ (2 Cor 4:11)."[4]

Chapter 13: Globalization

Art © Cat Mailloux. Photo by Elisa Smith.

Fig. 13.7. *All Shall Be Well,* 2020, Cat Mailloux.

Art © Cat Mailloux. Photo by Elisa Smith.

Fig. 13.8. *Blue Void,* 2021, Cat Mailloux.

Fig. 13.9. *Paper Window*, 2020, Cat Mailloux.

Art © Cat Mailloux. Photo by Elisa Smith.

Music

After a century filled with modernism, experimental music, the avant-garde, and the "who cares if you listen" attitude of many classically trained composers, the twenty-first century witnessed a search for meaning and relevance in the arts. As with other eras, the pendulum swing was predictable and inevitable. In contrast to the objective abstraction of artistic experiments at the most extreme end, twenty-first-century artists sought to connect with audiences and to respond artistically to real events in life.

Global Relevance

Y2K is history for the present readers of this book. For the authors, however, it was a "clear and present danger" in which everything in human life that was controlled by computers might dissolve into thin air. The danger was that at the turn of the millennium, computers would revert to 1900 instead of 2000. Many people watched their screens with emotions that ranged from extreme anxiety to mild nonchalance. When midnight struck, however, nothing happened. The digital world moved on in sync with the "real" world and humanity entered the new millennium—not just a new century—together. Still, it was a big moment, even if uneventful. No one had ever predicted such a moment or such a concern.

Some things in 2000, however, were planned, and had been in the making for quite a while. The year 2000 marked the 250th anniversary of the death of J. S. Bach. What better way for a heralding in of the new millennium than to honor the biggest name in classical music? For this event, the International Bach Society commissioned a project called *Passion 2000*, inviting major composers from all over the world to write a passion for the occasion (see Ch. 7).

Knowing that Bach had written passions based on all four Gospels, although only two have survived, the Society wanted a passion for each of the four. From China, Buddhist Tan Dun (1957-) composed *Water Passion after St. Matthew*. From Argentina, Jewish-Russian Osvaldo Golijov (1960-) wrote *La pasión según San Marcos* (St. Mark). German Lutheran composer Wolfgang Rihm (1952-) wrote *Deus passus* (after St. Luke), and Russian Orthodox female composer Sofia Gubaidulina (1931-) wrote *Johannes Passion* (St. John). The representation of major world religions and languages, along with major geographic regions of the world illustrated an important trend of the twenty-first century: the breakdown of distinctions between the reigning elite Western classical music and all other world music traditions. The composers included styles inspired by their own cultural backgrounds in addition to their academic training.

Dun's *Water Passion* draws on the sounds of nature that might have been heard on Calvary. He divides the orchestra and choir among seventeen glass bowls of water arranged symbolically in a cross. The water bowls have microphones close by, and the **percussionists** have explicit instructions for "performing" the water.

View a special performance of the Water Passion at the Temple of Dendur in the Metropolitan Museum of Art. As a Christian, think about the message of this sacred musical account of the days leading up to the crucifixion of the Lord Jesus, composed and conducted by a Buddhist in a reconstructed ancient Egyptian temple in a secular museum of international renown. Does this compromise the name and work of Christ or does it strengthen the fact that He is far above all rule and authority and power and lordship (Eph 1:21)?

Listen again to the first few minutes of the "Baptism" from *Water Passion*, listening for the eerie howling of the wind, the drips of water, and the remote screeching of wild animals in the distance.

*[Sidebar: **percussionists**: performers on percussion instruments, who produce sound by striking, shaking, scraping, or otherwise manipulating the instrument]*

Time	Description
0:32	Echo
0:43	Howls
0:58	Water ripples
1:08	Distant beating
1:40	Cat cries
1:50	Metal against metal

As with Y2K, no one could predict the following two major global-impacting events of the twenty-first century: 9/11 and COVID-19. In spite of the most advanced technology to date, no one was prepared for these moments and no one had an immediate solution. They took humanity off guard. These events may not as yet have enough historical distance to make a fair assessment of their impact. However, humanity's responses to these moments arose almost immediately from artists, composers, writers, and performers who continued and will continue to create, comment, communicate, and respond in ways that humans have been doing since the dawn of history.

One of the first artistic arenas that responded to 9/11 was popular music. Toby Keith's (1961-) "Courtesy of the Red, White, and Blue (The Angry American)" inspired a new wave of American patriotism. Bruce Springsteen (1949-) took a slightly different spin with his song, "The Rising." He wrote the song as a tribute to the heroism of a New York City firefighter climbing one of the World Trade Center towers to rescue people trapped inside. The lyrics juxtapose the agony of a crumbling world with the reach of a saving hand. Although portraying humanity's need at an extreme moment of crisis, this song has a richer meaning for Christians—one of the hope of eternal salvation found in the risen Christ.[5]

Although written in a popular style and not considered elite in the Western tradition, popular music was quick to respond and its message was widely and quickly disseminated throughout the world (see Fig. 13.10).

The popular genre has something that Western classical music works very hard to achieve: a large fan base that relates well to it. Perhaps because of issues like this in the elitist world of music, this century has witnessed an increasing breakdown of these distinctions, in the same way as *Passion 2000* exhibits the dissolution of the wall between Western and other global traditions. Notice the breakdown of walls in the Kennedy Center Honors 2009 performance by rock star Sting (1951-) in his "classical" performance of "The Rising" for honoree Bruce Springsteen.

Fig. 13.10. Bruce Springsteen in concert, with musician Steven van Zandt of the E Street Band, 2002. During this 3-hour concert, Springsteen and the band performed "The Rising."

As symphony halls, museums, and theatres shut down one after another in the wake of the pandemic of 2020, many artists found themselves without commissions, without performance outlets, and in some cases, without any means of income. Under such challenging restraints, one such composer decided to rise above the difficulties and write a work in honor of the essential, but unsung heroes of the pandemic: the first responders, the health-care professionals, and the door-to-door delivery workers. Composer Austin Jaquith (1980-) offered *Heldenleben 2020*, an orchestral work depicting themes of the evil Coronavirus warring against the good of humanity seen through the victorious themes. Jaquith was inspired by a nineteenth-century tone poem (see Ch. 10) by German composer Richard Strauss, *Ein Heldenleben*. Whereas *Ein Heldenleben* means "A Hero's Life" and is speculated that it was an autobiographical reference, *Heldenleben 2020* refers to a collective group of heroes, many unsung. Jaquith offered this work free of charge to a major performing arts organization, in honor of those who sacrificed their lives to save others.

IN THEIR OWN WORDS

The following is part of Austin Jaquith's program notes for a virtual performance of *Heldenleben 2020* performed by a select group of socially distanced performers of the Dayton Philharmonic Orchestra on Nov. 13, 2020.

Chapter 13: Globalization   383

> "[The first responders] returned each night to their homes in obscurity. While they will never be known by name, we will remember what they did for us, and be forever in debt to their service. *Heldenleben 2020*, though only a token, is an encomium to each and every one of these individuals."[6]

Theatre

Opera

A few years after the devastating loss of 9/11 as the fear of holocaust and terror gripped the world, John Adams (1947-) produced his opera, *Doctor Atomic*. Adams, a post-minimalist, postmodernist composer is known for his operas that address serious, contemporary international political and social issues, such as *Nixon in China* and *The Death of Klinghoffer*. For *Doctor Atomic*, he collaborated with edgy, controversial librettist Peter Sellars (1957-) to produce a new angle on the unlikely subject of the Manhattan Project, the top-secret World War II operation to create the first atomic bomb. The work navigates through the agonizing decision that Robert Oppenheimer (1904-1967), the director responsible for the operation, had to make, unable to predict whether or not he was creating something capable of annihilating the entire human race. The opera ends with the countdown to 0 right before the first test at Trinity, New Mexico, is carried out.

DID YOU KNOW?

Trinity, New Mexico was named for John Donne's "Three Person'd God." The poem in the opera was chosen because it was a text that Oppenheimer knew well. Trinitite is the name of a brand new green glassy substance found at the test site after the detonation.

One of the most famous moments in the opera is Oppenheimer's famous aria, quoting John Donne's poem, "Batter My Heart, Three Person'd God," in which he grapples with issues of life and death, surrender and salvation, and enslavement and freedom. Oppenheimer's outward fears of the bomb's potential power, mirror his own inner war against sin and self.

View the entire aria.

Then, go back and listen once again to the audio only, paying attention to the interplay of text and music.

Chapter 13: Globalization

Fig. 13.11. Atomic bomb looming above J. Robert Oppenheimer, *Doctor Atomic* dress rehearsal, 2005, John Adams and Peter Sellars, San Francisco War Memorial Opera House, San Francisco.

In the video, which includes the theatrical context of the aria, the atomic bomb looms in the background above Oppenheimer (see Fig. 13.11). The set design implies that Oppenheimer's prayer to the "Three-Person'd God" is perhaps the bomb. Will the bomb have the power to destroy or preserve humanity? In addition to Donne's Christian prayer, other parts of the libretto are based on a Hindu text describing a god who is the destroyer of all mankind. This pagan god is the opposite of the Christian God as the giver of life portrayed in the Bible. The Bible describes death affecting humanity due to the fall caused by sin. Yet, the good news of salvation is that life triumphs over death and in eternity death will be no more. For now, Christians can enjoy the death-overcoming (1 Cor 15:54-57) life by receiving Jesus Christ as their personal Savior. "Because of one man's trespass, death reigned through that one man, much more will those who receive the abundance of grace and the free gift of righteousness reign in life through the one man Jesus Christ" (Rom 5:17).

Listen for:

Time	Description
0:00	Strings quietly entering on sustained pitch, growing in number and volume
0:10	Winds, brass, and timpani each repeat short motives in minimalist fashion
0:54	Strings ostinato
1:09	"Batter My Heart" aria begins, A section, orchestra moves to background, intensity drops way down

Time	Description
1:25	Music intensifies on "Knock," longer and calmer on "Breathe"
1:47	Repeat of "Batter My Heart" A section
2:14	Acceleration on "Break, blow, burn." Rising pitch and reflective slowing on "make me new," as though reaching up in hope.
4:25	"I like an usurped town" B section increases orchestral sounds
5:27	"Am betrothed unto your enemy" musical intensity matches the frustration of the singer's spiritual dilemma
6:45	Aria is over, orchestra continues minimalist motives moving in and out of sync, ending with a climactic timpani burst like a bomb. Is it speaking what Oppenheimer fears to utter?

Musical Theatre

Coming full circle from the Ancient Greeks to the twenty-first century, Orpheus still finds himself on stage as a star. There are few other figures in history than can make that boast! The 2019 Tony-award winning musical, *Hadestown*, puts a complex spin on the age-old tale of man's fragility and his limited attempts to solve his own problems (see Ch. 2). This telling, however, adds other voices to the conversation. By humanizing the gods Hades and Persephone with the sub-plot of their own centuries-old love story, these gods of the realm of the dead evoke the audience's empathy and understanding. The audience learns that those who come to work in Hadestown seek comfort and stability, but in reality become enslaved and blinded. Orpheus is able to intervene and soften Hades's heart with a song about the freeing power of love.

Composer and librettist Anaïs Mitchell (1981-) and director Rachel Chavkin (1980-) use the medium of a folk opera employing folk, jazz, and rock musical styles, along with dance, gesture, and design in combination with storytelling. It includes a nearly omnipresent narrator in the character of the god Hermes to remove the fourth wall (see Ch. 11) of the stage, drawing the audience right into the lives of the characters. Hermes takes the role of the Greek chorus in commenting on the action and the dilemmas of the characters. The prominence of storytelling draws on an age-old tradition of seeking understanding and meaning through stories. From Homer to *Hadestown*, humans will continue to understand themselves and the world around them through narratives. This emphasis makes *Hadestown* stand apart from the typical Broadway musical.

Beyond this, Mitchell and Chavkin apply metamodernist thought, which adds a contemporary lens that blurs—even to the point of erasing—the lines of good and evil, light and darkness, and high and low, and gives equal voice to the "Other," the marginalized. *Hadestown* presents Eurydice's death not as the traditional snakebite, but as the compelling personal call of Hades, who serenades her to the so-called better realm of death below. In Hades's song, "Hey, Little Songbird," listen to the contrast between the opening classical string ensemble with Hades's bass voice, speak-singing with a growl in his lowest range. The idea may recall Hildegard von Bingen's setting in *Ordo virtutum* of the Devil's words in speech only, for he is denied the ability to sing (see Ch. 4). The accompaniment turns into a slow blues-type background as he gradually convinces Eurydice to join him in the world below.

Although interesting and captivatingly entertaining, *Hadestown* sends a subtle, disarming message that the realm of death, darkness, and sin is not something to fear, but is an attractive option for living out an alternative worldview. It challenges the Truth of the Bible with Hades's and Hermes's "my truth." While this volume encourages an appreciation and even enjoyment of the fine arts, there is a concurrent hope to equip Christians to guard their hearts from subtle ideas that would corrupt good morals. Ephesians and Colossians remind believers to "walk as children of light" and "to share in the inheritance of the saints in light," having been delivered "from the domain of darkness" (Eph 4:8; Col 1:12-13).

Theatre: Resonant across Centuries

The author of Ecclesiastes writes, "What has been is what will be, and what has been done is what will be done, and there is nothing new under the sun" (Ecc 1:9). The public program Theatre of War illustrates this quite clearly. Theatre of War was established by Bryan Doerries and Phyllis Kaufmann as a public health project that partners with health organizations, veteran services, homeless shelters, prisons, and activist groups. The project seeks to generate discussion, confrontation, and shared empathy around social issues through the medium of theatre. The project is a series of live readings of historic plays and writings, ranging from classical Greek tragedies to The Book of Job, to the speeches and sermons of Dr. Martin Luther King Jr. and Frederick Douglass. The tailored program of reading events, read by professional actors and community stakeholders, are followed by live town-hall style discussions in which audience members or guest panelists share their reflections. The program reflects the sentience of the plays to our contemporary time.

Each performance-discussion is headlined by a contemporary social issue that is connected to a theme highlighted in the play. Social issues include domestic violence, caregiving and death, the climate crisis, posttraumatic stress disorder, addiction, natural disasters, and racialized police violence. The selected plays underscore the complexities of humanity, retold in a contemporary context. As the founder, Doerries often says during the events, "Remember, you are not alone in this room—and you are not alone across time."[7]

In the project *Storytelling after the Storm*, from 2012, a small group of actors participated in the dramatized reading of the Book of Job at a church in Joplin, MO, on the one-year anniversary of a tornado that tore through the city, killing 161 people and destroying homes, schools and businesses. The reading and discussion that followed bore witness to suffering, survivors' guilt, grief, and caring for one's neighbor in the wake of the tragedy.

See an excerpt from the performance and discussion in Joplin, MO: *Storytelling after the Storm: Book of Job in Joplin, MO. 2012*

Thinking all the way back to Ch. 2 of this textbook, recall the Greek tragedy *Oedipus Rex* by Sophocles. Sophocles's play centers around flawed leadership, metaphorical blindness, and a pestilence that plagues the city of Thebes. Re-contextualized through a contemporary lens, the Theatre of War uses the program *The Oedipus Project* as a space for discussion and communal empathy during the time of COVID, performed via Zoom. The production realizes the trauma of a global pandemic, through the story of Oedipus, allowing health workers and individuals to respond to what their experience has meant to them. The project underscores the relevance of the Greek tragedy across time and culture.

Watch a trailer from *The Oedipus Project* on the platform of Zoom.

Conclusion

Looking Back, Looking Forward

History needs time to assess these events and its artifacts. However, looking back after twenty-one years of the twenty-first century, the fine arts can provide clues. How is art of the new century the same as in the early Greek era? All can agree that art is still a creative expression, is metaphorical, and is rhetorical. It remains a creative expression both in terms of the individuality and personality and voice of the artist, while at the same time it is a collective expression of the civilization that produced it. Does the artist understand and know how a receiver will respond? Perhaps not, or perhaps he can make educated guesses based on collective experience. Can he predict how receivers will understand his art in the distant future? Probably not. Will he care? Perhaps or perhaps not.

However, the artist is keenly aware that art is metaphorical too. She knows that it stands for something, whether that be as a synecdoche, a simile, an allegory, or a metaphor. She expects that the receiver will get the message based on collective understanding. By the twenty-first century, the scope of that collective understanding grew far beyond the sovereign borders of a nation or an ethnic region; the collective region is now the entire world. In a world united by the speed of technology and by events that commonly affect all, art can convey meaning in complete disregard of physical borders. In fact, in the twenty-first century, what borders still exist? Definitely political and economic borders remain, and they are fiercely protected. One good example is the European Union and the recent Brexit phenomenon. But how about the borders of artistic expression? Arts have an uncanny ability to defy political, cultural, and economic restrictions. The visual arts can be understood by humans all over the world. Music can likewise convey universal desires and longings common to mankind. Theatre, while bound by its specific language, can still communicate through movement, gestures, and interactions on stage.

Finally, art is as rhetorical in the twenty-first century as it was in Ancient Greece. It frequently communicates. It may be the message of redemption in the musical works of *Passion* 2000 or it may be a collective praise of the everyday heroes of COVID-19 in *Heldenleben 2020*. No matter what new scenario befalls man, the arts are resilient, adaptable, and capable of responding. Humanity will continue to respond in art, and while there may be times where "art for art's sake" may not make much sense, art will adapt itself to some other "sake" or "cause," becoming in one situation a rallying cry for change and in another, a poignant message from the depths of the human soul.

Does art imitate life, as described in this chapter, or does life imitate art? The answer is not a simple one, but it matters profoundly to the Christian. Oscar Wilde argued that "life imitates art more than art imitates life,"[8] and there are many examples to support that idea. The trend toward normalizing and neutralizing sin has been continuing and even accelerating in contemporary society. Much of that was found decades earlier in art as the "harbinger" of immoral things to come. Particular situations played out on a theatrical stage, for example, which "pushed the envelope" a decade ago have served to transform an audience's initial shock into modern-day normalcy. The discomfort felt at one time while watching certain situations portrayed has fallen victim to a seemingly innocuous worldview shift that begins with an introduction to a different lifestyle (or view of sin), then moves on to the acceptance of it, then to an embracing of it, and finally an imitation of it.

That is why an understanding of the arts in light of Scripture is so important. If the arts move away from representing beauty as defined by God, they will continue to drift toward an open celebration of man's rebellion against God. Unfortunately, culture is always under the influence of the arts, as was the case even back in Exodus. The best way for Christians to impact the world of art is to guard their hearts in the stewardship of a discerning appreciation of the arts, rather than of a dismissingly passive nonchalance toward potential glorifications of sin. "You are the salt of the earth, but if salt has lost its taste, how shall its saltiness be restored?" (Matt 5:13).

Study Questions

1. What are some ways that you see life defining art and art defining life in the twenty-first century?
2. How did musicians respond in music to major global events of the twenty-first century?
3. How have theatre and musical theatre sought to maintain a relevance in contemporary society?

Notes

1. Paul Tillich, *Systematic Theology*.
2. Hans Frei, *The Eclipse of Biblical Narrative*.
3. George Lindbeck, *The Nature of Doctrine: Religion and Theology in a Postliberal Age*.
4. Norwich, 60.
5. Springsteen, "The Rising." https://brucespringsteen.net/albums/2002.
6. Jaquith, 2020.
7. Doerries, 2021.
8. Wilde, 10.

Authors' Picks

Symphony No. 4 in e minor, Brahms (Sandra Yang)

When I heard this for the first time, I was in my car and had to pull over and stop. I was just beginning to appreciate classical music, and this work completely grabbed my attention, especially the first movement. The rest is history! Listen here.

Stabat mater, Pergolesi (Sandra Yang)

This is a hauntingly beautiful work for soprano, alto, and small string ensemble. The words are from a 13th-century hymn about the suffering that the mother of Jesus experienced as she watched her son being crucified. The intertwining of the voices throughout the piece is compelling. Listen here.

Staged Gate, Mary Miss (Cat Mailloux)

In my first sculpture class, I read the seminal 1979 essay "Sculpture in the Expanded Field" by Rosalind Krauss, which describes the conceptual spaces between architecture, landscape, and sculpture. Shortly after reading the piece, I was able to see a work by Mary Miss, an artist cited heavily in the essay. The work "Staged Gate" is a permanent installation at Hills and Dales Park, which is part of the Five Rivers Metropark in the Dayton, OH, area. I wandered through the woods until I found the wooden installation, part architecture, part landscape, like a cathedral in the forest. For me, viewing the work in person reinforced the power of sculpture to serve as a physical and sensory experience. You can see images of the work at http://marymiss.com/projects/staged-gates/, or go see the work for yourself at Hills and Dales Park. You can read "Sculpture in the Expanded Field" here.

"A Letter to Young Artists," Makoto Fujimura (Cat Mailloux)

This is a letter of encouragement to young artists who are also believers, written by Makoto Fujimura, a contemporary painter in traditional Japanese painting techniques. Read the letter here.

Ginevra de' Benci, Leonardo da Vinci (Sandra Yang)

When I look at this portrait, one of only three great portraits that Leonardo da Vinci painted, I can't stop wondering what she is feeling. Is she sad about a life she is being forced to live against her will? Is she simply annoyed that the painter is taking so long? I can study this painting for hours, literally, every time I come across it. I still cannot unlock her inner soul, but I know that Christ is the answer to her sorrow and dissatisfaction. I found Christ as my Lord and Savior when I was about Ginevra's age, and I have been burdened to bring the Joy of the gospel to this age group ever since.

The End for Which God Created the World, Jonathan Edwards (Joshua Kira)

This is the book that caused me to revaluate my purpose in the world. It is insightful, if difficult, work on God's glory as the central feature of our lives. It not only made me rethink my vocation, but how the revelation of God's greatness should affect my understanding of art, culture, and society.

"Impressions," from the album *Infinity*, McCoy Tyner (Chet Jenkins)

This track features the saxophonist Michael Brecker, who is the most influential saxophonist post-Coltrane, and (as a saxophonist myself) my favorite saxophonist to listen to. The chord progressions are very simple (the same as "So What" which is discussed in Ch. 12). Brecker plays with incredible intensity and ferocity, and I always find this awe-inspiring. I can listen to any of Brecker's many albums, but I always come back to this.

Places we can no longer go, John Mackey (Chet Jenkins)

I had the privilege of attending the world premiere of this piece. The composer wrote it in memory of his mother, who suffered from rapid-onset dementia. Often uncommunicative, she would respond to some of her favorite music (she had played flute). Faced with the challenge of trying to write this piece to describe her plight, Mackey wrote it in reverse, starting the piece in a confused, broken manner, and ending in the past, before dementia had begun to set in. As both of my grandmothers suffered from forms of dementia, the piece resonated very personally with me. In performance, the piece is startling, as the vocal soloist begins singing in the middle of the auditorium, and in the premiere, she was two rows directly behind me. I was startled when she unexpectedly began singing so close to me. The composer has a full program note, and there is a video of one of the early performances of this work (with the same vocalist) on his website.

Lincolnshire Posy, Percy Grainger (Chet Jenkins)

One of the most famous works for band, this is absolutely my personal favorite. A setting of 6 folk songs (one of which is discussed in Ch. 11), it is full of beauty, drama, and power. One of the things that I think make it great—because it is based on folk songs—is that the music has an incredibly singable quality to it. I have often said that, Lord willing, on my retirement concert, this will be the last piece I conduct. It's a favorite, and even though I've conducted it a number of times, I learn something new from it every time I program it.

Timelines

Chapter 2

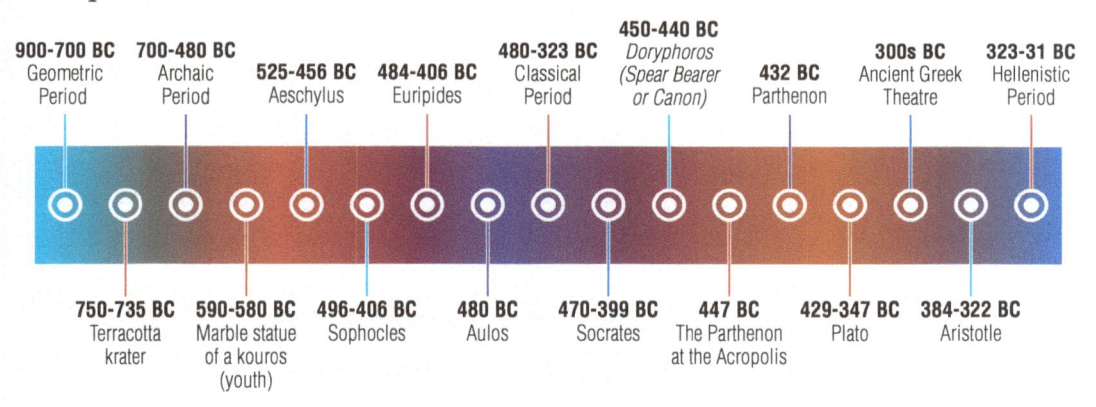

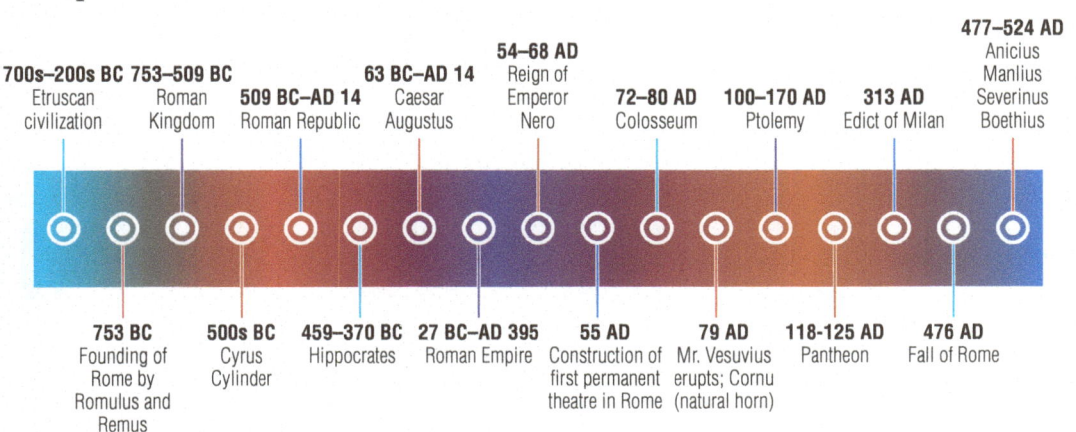

900-700 BC Geometric Period
700-480 BC Archaic Period
525-456 BC Aeschylus
484-406 BC Euripides
480-323 BC Classical Period
450-440 BC *Doryphoros (Spear Bearer or Canon)*
432 BC Parthenon
300s BC Ancient Greek Theatre
323-31 BC Hellenistic Period

750-735 BC Terracotta krater
590-580 BC Marble statue of a kouros (youth)
496-406 BC Sophocles
480 BC Aulos
470-399 BC Socrates
447 BC The Parthenon at the Acropolis
429-347 BC Plato
384-322 BC Aristotle

Chapter 3

700s–200s BC Etruscan civilization
753–509 BC Roman Kingdom
509 BC–AD 14 Roman Republic
63 BC–AD 14 Caesar Augustus
54–68 AD Reign of Emperor Nero
72–80 AD Colosseum
100–170 AD Ptolemy
313 AD Edict of Milan
477–524 AD Anicius Manlius Severinus Boethius

753 BC Founding of Rome by Romulus and Remus
500s BC Cyrus Cylinder
459–370 BC Hippocrates
27 BC–AD 395 Roman Empire
55 AD Construction of first permanent theatre in Rome
79 AD Mr. Vesuvius erupts; Cornu (natural horn)
118–125 AD Pantheon
476 AD Fall of Rome

Timelines

Chapter 4

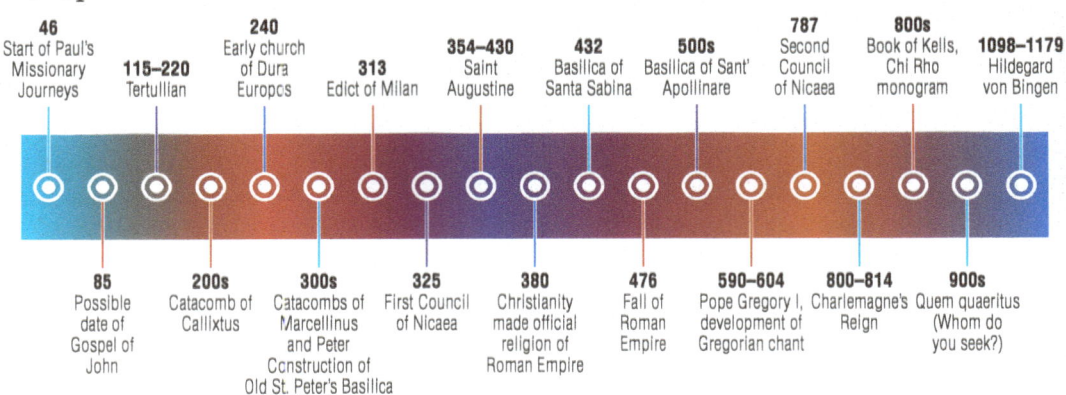

- **46** Start of Paul's Missionary Journeys
- **85** Possible date of Gospel of John
- **115–220** Tertullian
- **200s** Catacomb of Callixtus
- **240** Early church of Dura Europos
- **300s** Catacombs of Marcellinus and Peter Construction of Old St. Peter's Basilica
- **313** Edict of Milan
- **325** First Council of Nicaea
- **354–430** Saint Augustine
- **380** Christianity made official religion of Roman Empire
- **432** Basilica of Santa Sabina
- **476** Fall of Roman Empire
- **500s** Basilica of Sant' Apollinare
- **590–604** Pope Gregory I, development of Gregorian chant
- **787** Second Council of Nicaea
- **800–814** Charlemagne's Reign
- **800s** Book of Kells, Chi Rho monogram
- **900s** Quem quaeritus (Whom do you seek?)
- **1098–1179** Hildegard von Bingen

Chapter 5

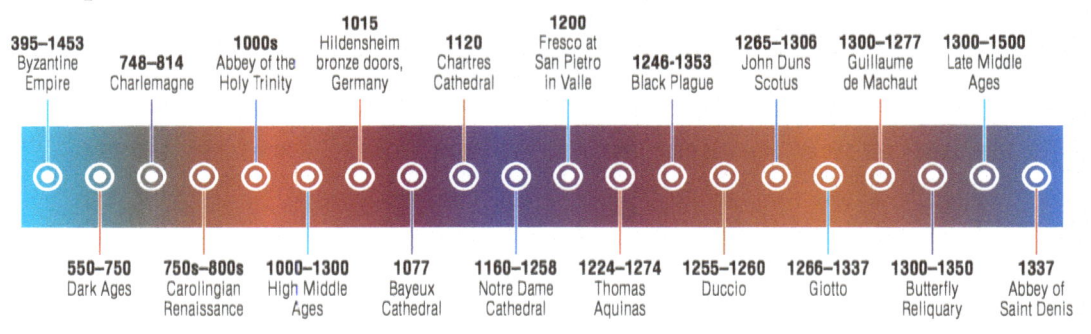

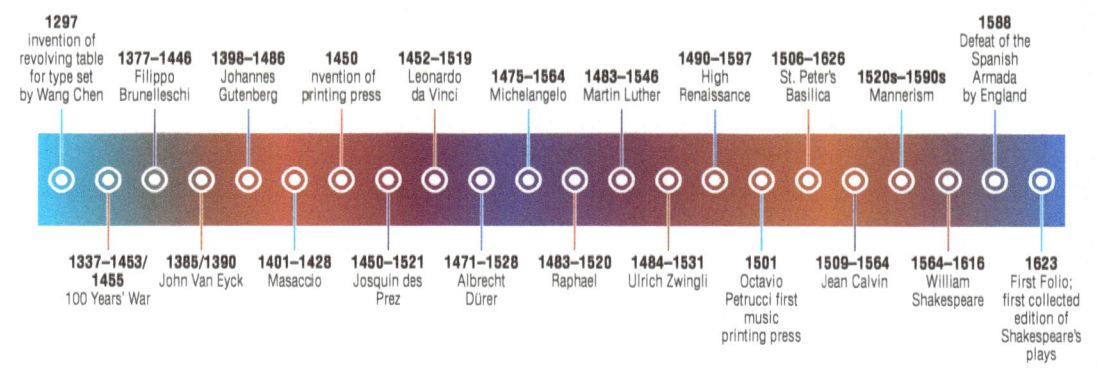

- **395–1453** Byzantine Empire
- **550–750** Dark Ages
- **748–814** Charlemagne
- **750s–800s** Carolingian Renaissance
- **1000s** Abbey of the Holy Trinity
- **1000–1300** High Middle Ages
- **1015** Hildensheim bronze doors, Germany
- **1077** Bayeux Cathedral
- **1120** Chartres Cathedral
- **1160–1258** Notre Dame Cathedral
- **1200** Fresco at San Pietro in Valle
- **1224–1274** Thomas Aquinas
- **1246-1353** Black Plague
- **1255–1260** Duccio
- **1265–1306** John Duns Scotus
- **1266–1337** Giotto
- **1300–1277** Guillaume de Machaut
- **1300–1350** Butterfly Reliquary
- **1300–1500** Late Middle Ages
- **1337** Abbey of Saint Denis

Chapter 6

- **1297** invention of revolving table for type set by Wang Chen
- **1337–1453/1455** 100 Years' War
- **1377–1446** Filippo Brunelleschi
- **1385/1390** John Van Eyck
- **1398–1486** Johannes Gutenberg
- **1401–1428** Masaccio
- **1450** nvention of printing press
- **1450–1521** Josquin des Prez
- **1452–1519** Leonardo da Vinci
- **1471–1528** Albrecht Dürer
- **1475–1564** Michelangelo
- **1483–1520** Raphael
- **1483–1546** Martin Luther
- **1484–1531** Ulrich Zwingli
- **1490–1597** High Renaissance
- **1501** Octavio Petrucci first music printing press
- **1506–1626** St. Peter's Basilica
- **1509–1564** Jean Calvin
- **1520s–1590s** Mannerism
- **1564–1616** William Shakespeare
- **1588** Defeat of the Spanish Armada by England
- **1623** First Folio; first collected edition of Shakespeare's plays

Timelines

Chapter 7

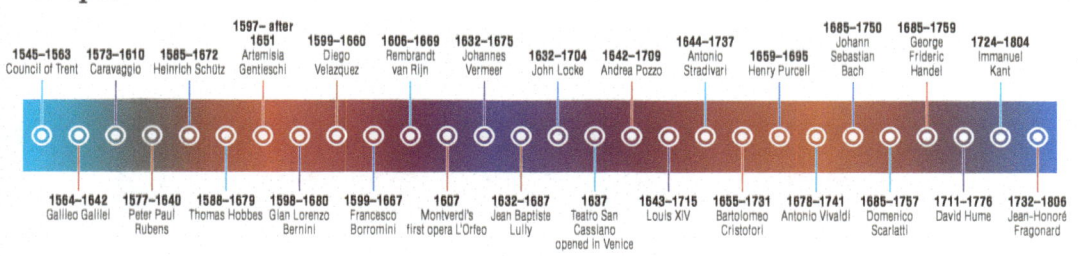

Above timeline:
- 1545–1563 Council of Trent
- 1573–1610 Caravaggio
- 1585–1672 Heinrich Schütz
- 1597–after 1651 Artemisia Gentileschi
- 1599–1660 Diego Velazquez
- 1606–1669 Rembrandt van Rijn
- 1632–1675 Johannes Vermeer
- 1632–1704 John Locke
- 1642–1709 Andrea Pozzo
- 1644–1737 Antonio Stradivari
- 1659–1695 Henry Purcell
- 1685–1750 Johann Sebastian Bach
- 1685–1759 George Frideric Handel
- 1724–1804 Immanuel Kant

Below timeline:
- 1564–1642 Galileo Galilei
- 1577–1640 Peter Paul Rubens
- 1588–1679 Thomas Hobbes
- 1598–1680 Gian Lorenzo Bernini
- 1599–1667 Francesco Borromini
- 1607 Monteverdi's first opera L'Orfeo
- 1632–1687 Jean Baptiste Lully
- 1637 Teatro San Cassiano opened in Venice
- 1643–1715 Louis XIV
- 1655–1731 Bartolomeo Cristofori
- 1678–1741 Antonio Vivaldi
- 1685–1757 Domenico Scarlatti
- 1711–1776 David Hume
- 1732–1806 Jean-Honoré Fragonard

Chapter 8

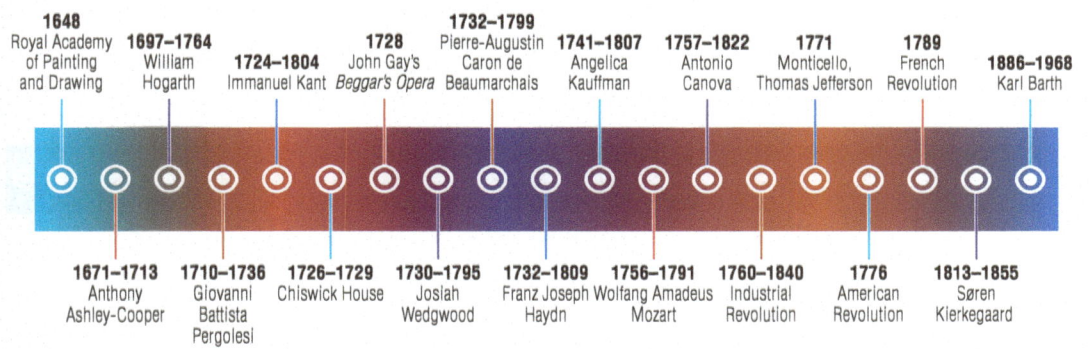

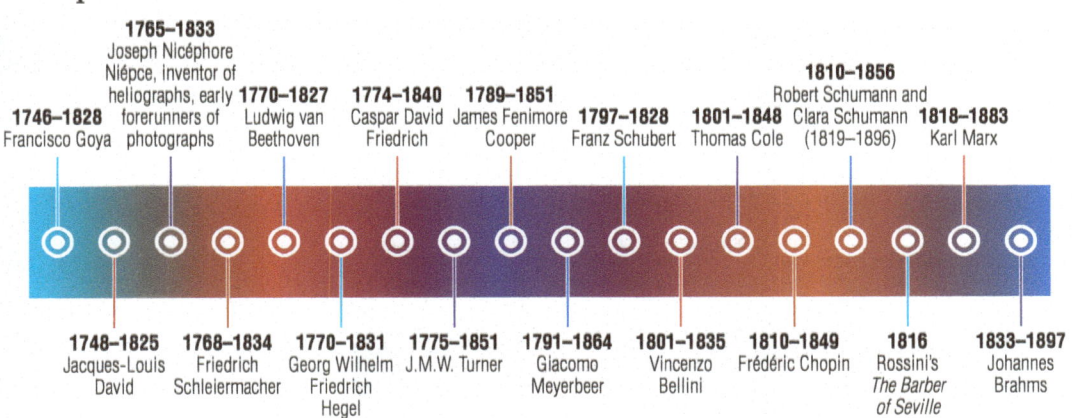

Above timeline:
- 1648 Royal Academy of Painting and Drawing
- 1697–1764 William Hogarth
- 1724–1804 Immanuel Kant
- 1728 John Gay's Beggar's Opera
- 1732–1799 Pierre-Augustin Caron de Beaumarchais
- 1741–1807 Angelica Kauffman
- 1757–1822 Antonio Canova
- 1771 Monticello, Thomas Jefferson
- 1789 French Revolution
- 1886–1968 Karl Barth

Below timeline:
- 1671–1713 Anthony Ashley-Cooper
- 1710–1736 Giovanni Battista Pergolesi
- 1726–1729 Chiswick House
- 1730–1795 Josiah Wedgwood
- 1732–1809 Franz Joseph Haydn
- 1756–1791 Wolfang Amadeus Mozart
- 1760–1840 Industrial Revolution
- 1776 American Revolution
- 1813–1855 Søren Kierkegaard

Chapter 9

Above timeline:
- 1746–1828 Francisco Goya
- 1765–1833 Joseph Nicéphore Niépce, inventor of heliographs, early forerunners of photographs
- 1770–1827 Ludwig van Beethoven
- 1774–1840 Caspar David Friedrich
- 1789–1851 James Fenimore Cooper
- 1797–1828 Franz Schubert
- 1801–1848 Thomas Cole
- 1810–1856 Robert Schumann and Clara Schumann (1819–1896)
- 1818–1883 Karl Marx

Below timeline:
- 1748–1825 Jacques-Louis David
- 1768–1834 Friedrich Schleiermacher
- 1770–1831 Georg Wilhelm Friedrich Hegel
- 1775–1851 J.M.W. Turner
- 1791–1864 Giacomo Meyerbeer
- 1801–1835 Vincenzo Bellini
- 1810–1849 Frédéric Chopin
- 1816 Rossini's *The Barber of Seville*
- 1833–1897 Johannes Brahms

Timelines

Chapter 10

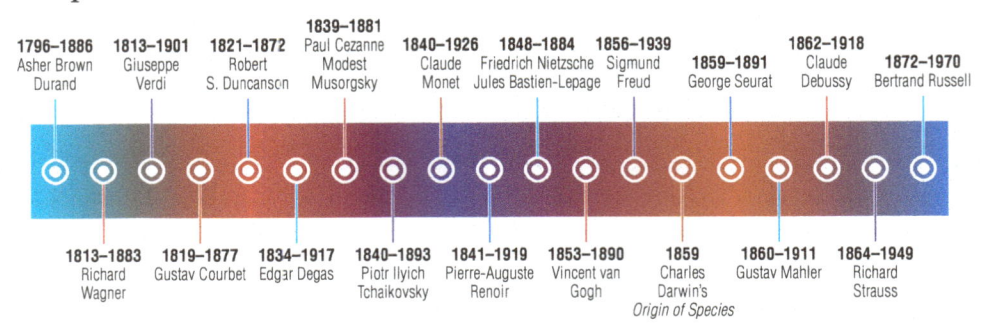

Above timeline (left to right):
- 1796–1886 Asher Brown Durand
- 1813–1901 Giuseppe Verdi
- 1821–1872 Robert S. Duncanson
- 1839–1881 Modest Musorgsky
- 1839–1906 Paul Cezanne
- 1840–1926 Claude Monet
- 1848–1884 Jules Bastien-Lepage
- 1844–1900 Friedrich Nietzsche
- 1856–1939 Sigmund Freud
- 1859–1891 George Seurat
- 1862–1918 Claude Debussy
- 1872–1970 Bertrand Russell

Below timeline (left to right):
- 1813–1883 Richard Wagner
- 1819–1877 Gustav Courbet
- 1834–1917 Edgar Degas
- 1840–1893 Piotr Ilyich Tchaikovsky
- 1841–1919 Pierre-Auguste Renoir
- 1853–1890 Vincent van Gogh
- 1859 Charles Darwin's *Origin of Species*
- 1860–1911 Gustav Mahler
- 1864–1949 Richard Strauss

Chapter 11

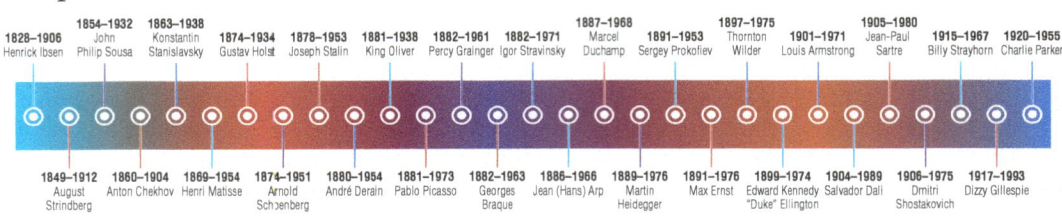

Above timeline (left to right):
- 1828–1906 Henrick Ibsen
- 1854–1932 John Philip Sousa
- 1863–1938 Konstantin Stanislavsky
- 1874–1934 Gustav Holst
- 1878–1953 Joseph Stalin
- 1881–1938 King Oliver
- 1882–1961 Percy Grainger
- 1882–1971 Igor Stravinsky
- 1887–1968 Marcel Duchamp
- 1891–1953 Sergey Prokofiev
- 1897–1975 Thornton Wilder
- 1901–1971 Louis Armstrong
- 1905–1980 Jean-Paul Sartre
- 1915–1967 Billy Strayhorn
- 1920–1955 Charlie Parker

Below timeline (left to right):
- 1849–1912 August Strindberg
- 1860–1904 Anton Chekhov
- 1869–1954 Henri Matisse
- 1874–1951 Arnold Schoenberg
- 1880–1954 André Derain
- 1881–1973 Pablo Picasso
- 1882–1963 Georges Braque
- 1886–1966 Jean (Hans) Arp
- 1889–1976 Martin Heidegger
- 1891–1976 Max Ernst
- 1899–1974 Edward Kennedy "Duke" Ellington
- 1904–1989 Salvador Dalí
- 1906–1975 Dmitri Shostakovich
- 1917–1993 Dizzy Gillespie

Chapter 12

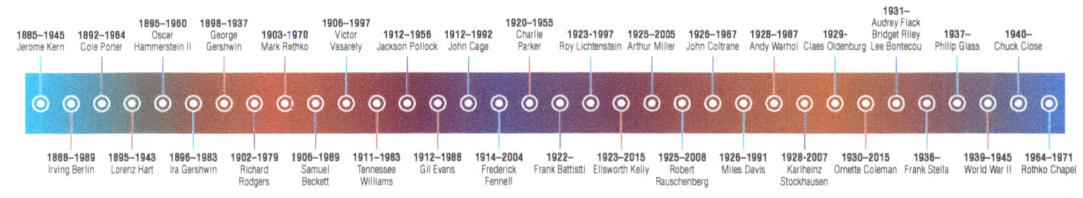

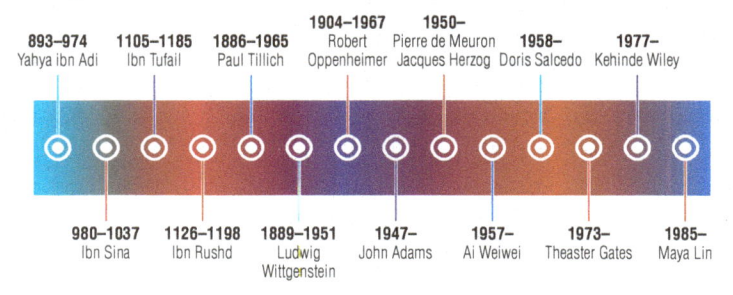

Above timeline (left to right):
- 1885–1945 Jerome Kern
- 1892–1964 Cole Porter
- 1895–1960 Oscar Hammerstein II
- 1898–1937 George Gershwin
- 1903–1970 Mark Rothko
- 1906–1997 Victor Vasarely
- 1912–1956 Jackson Pollock
- 1912–1992 John Cage
- 1920–1955 Charlie Parker
- 1923–1997 Roy Lichtenstein
- 1925–2005 Arthur Miller
- 1926–1967 John Coltrane
- 1928–1987 Andy Warhol
- 1929– Claes Oldenburg
- 1931– Audrey Flack; Bridget Riley; Lee Bontecou
- 1937– Philip Glass
- 1940– Chuck Close

Below timeline (left to right):
- 1888–1989 Irving Berlin
- 1895–1943 Lorenz Hart
- 1896–1983 Ira Gershwin
- 1902–1979 Richard Rodgers
- 1906–1989 Samuel Beckett
- 1911–1983 Tennessee Williams
- 1912–1988 Gil Evans
- 1914–2004 Frederick Fennell
- 1922– Frank Battisti
- 1923–2015 Ellsworth Kelly
- 1925–2008 Robert Rauschenberg
- 1926–1991 Miles Davis
- 1928–2007 Karlheinz Stockhausen
- 1930–2015 Ornette Coleman
- 1936– Frank Stella
- 1939–1945 World War II
- 1964–1971 Rothko Chapel

Chapter 13

Above timeline (left to right):
- 893–974 Yahya ibn Adi
- 1105–1185 Ibn Tufail
- 1886–1965 Paul Tillich
- 1904–1967 Robert Oppenheimer
- 1950– Pierre de Meuron; Jacques Herzog
- 1958– Doris Salcedo
- 1977– Kehinde Wiley

Below timeline (left to right):
- 980–1037 Ibn Sina
- 1126–1198 Ibn Rushd
- 1889–1951 Ludwig Wittgenstein
- 1947– John Adams
- 1957– Ai Weiwei
- 1973– Theaster Gates
- 1985– Maya Lin

Glossary

a cappella: unaccompanied

abstract expressionism: a movement in art that focused on subjective emotional expression and artistic spontaneity

action painting: a method of painting in which an artist drips and splashes layer upon layer of paint onto the canvas until practically every inch has been activated by a dynamic splotch

aesthetics: theory of beauty

affective memory: a term coined by Russian director Stanislavsky to describe an actor's ability to recall past experiences to invoke the same emotions onstage

affects: static emotional states

aleatoric: depending on chance

alla prima: meaning "to the first," the process of completing a whole painting in one session

alto: the lowest female singing voice; also the highest male singing voice in its origin from the Italian word meaning high

anthropomorphic: human-like

antiphonal: a call and response manner between choirs

anti-realism: any style of theatrical production that does not imitate real life

apse: the semicircular architectural element in a basilica

arch: semicircular structure made from a wedge-shaped unit called a voussoir

Archaic period: the Greek historical period between 700 and 480 BCE that described an era of prosperity, much of the imagery created in this era influenced subsequent eras

aria: an elaborate solo song usually within an opera, oratorio, or cantata

Arianism: a fourth century influential heresy denying the divinity of Christ, originated by Alexandrian priest Arius (c. 250-c. 336)

artistic bareness: where the intention of the artist is to convey something significant about humans through nudity and not to attempt to sexualize them in a manner inconsistent with Scriptural commendations concerning sexual relationships

assemblage: also called combines, usually sculptures made up of found objects

atmospheric perspective: the effect of objects or subject matter appearing to lighten in value as they recede in space

atonal: music that does not have a perceptible tonal center

aulos: a front-blown, double-reed, double-pipe (usually) wind instrument popular in ancient Greece and Rome

avant-garde: a term used to describe newfound, often experimental artistic ideas

avant-garde music: music that challenges musical preconceptions

background: in visual imagery, the background is the negative space of the image or the space surrounding the main figure

ballad opera: a play with singing, popular in eighteenth-century England

ballade: a one movement work for solo piano, usually in a lyrical style

bards: traveling musicians and entertainers; as called in England

Baroque Era: period from 1600 to 1750; this was a counterresponse to the Reformation and is defined by its elaborate and dramatic style

barrel vault: the repeated form of an arch to form a ceiling or hallway

basilica: a type of Roman civic building including a rectangular portion ending in a semicircular base, adopted by Christianity as a floor plan for early churches

bas-reliefs: a type of relief with less depth in the faces of the statues when carved proportionately; relief being a type of sculpture that is attached to its original material as a background

bass: the lowest of the four standard singing voices

basso continuo: a continuously sounded bass line, usually requiring two performers. The bass includes a continuously sounded bass line and chords. Associated with the early baroque period

bel canto: Italian style of vocal delivery marked by beautiful singing

Biblical plays: dramatic enactment of the Mass; developed as early as the ninth century as a response to the growing disconnect between church services and congregations who were not only illiterate but also could not understand the classical Latin spoken in Mass

bio-architecture: the design and construction of buildings in an eco-friendly manner and looking to nature's design for inspiration in solving design problems

Black Plague: a global epidemic of the bubonic plague that devastated Europe and Asia in the early 1300s

black-figure technique: the vase painting technique in which the figures are painted in black and the background remains the red color of the clay body

book musical: a contemporary style of musical where the music and lyrics are fully integrated into the story and emerge as a natural continuation of a character's dialogue (the book/script, is also called the libretto)

book-writer/librettist: the one who writes the spoken dialogue in a musical which weaves the story together (the book/script, is also called the libretto)

Broadway theatre: popular productions staged in a theatre within the New York Theatre District and which seats over 500 in the audience (house)

busker: a person who performs music or other entertainment in the street or another public place for monetary donations

Byzantine Empire: the eastern half of the Roman Empire that lasted a thousand years after the Western Roman Empire fell

cabaletta: second part of a nineteenth-century Italian aria

cantata: a medium-length narrative piece of music for voices with instrumental accompaniment, typically with solos, chorus, and orchestra. A chamber cantata often used one soloist and basso continuo on a secular topic. Larger works were often sacred and performed in church buildings

cartoon: to scale preliminary drawings made on paper before being transferred to wall murals or panels

castrato: a male who had been castrated before puberty in order to retain a high voice and develop a powerful vocal range

catacombs: systems of underground tombs

catharsis: release of pent-up feelings

cathedral: large church building in the Middle Ages

chamber music: music for three or more musicians of varying instruments

chiaroscuro: the painterly technique of shading to show three-dimensional form

chorale: a German hymn

chorus: in Ancient Greece, a group of singers and/or dancers who performed in religious ceremonies and dramatic plays

cithara: a large handheld lyre used especially in ancient Greece for festivals and public ceremonies

Classical period: the Greek historical period between 480 and 323 BCE that established the first democracy and marked the zenith of Greek art and philosophy

clavichord: a small, rectangular keyboard instrument that produces a soft sound

clavicytherium: a harpsichord-like instrument that is mounted vertically to save floor space

coda: tail or additional section of music to extend the length of a piece

codex: pages bound in book form

collage: the use of cutout pieces of material, usually paper, that are arranged and glued to a surface to create a work of art

color field painting: paintings that focus on large swaths of color to create their minimalist compositions

Colosseum: a famous Roman amphitheatre built on series of barrel and cross vaults, used for public entertainment

comedy: plays written to amuse and entertain, filled with witty remarks, unusual characters, and strange circumstances that highlighted human frailty and vanity

commedia dell'arte: a form of popular theatre with masked, stock characters in predictable roles

complex rib vault: an intersecting pattern of groin vaults that allowed for high ceilings and the pouring in of sunlight

composer: the one who writes a musical composition

concept musical: a style of musical theatre where the words and music convey a story based on a theme or message, instead of a character-driven plot

concerto: an instrumental ensemble featuring one or more soloists in opposition to a larger ensemble: solo concerto (one soloist playing in opposition to a large ensemble), concerto grosso (small ensemble in opposition to a large ensemble)

consonance: harmonies that sound at rest

consonant: two or more musical tones that are perceived as stable, pleasant, and at rest

contemporary art: art being made in the current moment of time

contrapposto: a common pose for the human figure in the Classical age that depicts the figure with one leg slightly bent, shifting the line of the hips and shoulders to tilt diagonally, creating a natural-looking position

conventions: agreed-upon rules

Corinthian: the most ornate of Greek orders, distinctive in its floral motif at the crown of the column and its wider, more complex base

cornu: a natural horn; an instrument most likely used by the military, showing the pragmatic attitude of the Romans toward music

counterpoint: literally meaning note against note; take a melody and contrast other melodies against it using rules proposed during the Baroque era

Counter-Reformation: a time of resurgence in the Catholic Church as a response to the Protestant Reformation

crescendo: growing gradually louder

cross vault: (also groined), the intersection of two barrel vaults

Crusades: religious wars led by Europeans under the guidance of the new papal monarchy, launched against the rising power of the Islamic Caliphate in Palestine to recover the Holy Land

da capo: typical aria form; *capo* in Italian means "head;" thus, it is a form that requires the singer to return to the "head" or top of the aria to sing the first half of it again

Dadaism: an artistic movement based in absurdism and satire

daguerreotype: an early kind of black-and-white photograph

denouement: the final part of a play or opera when everything is unraveled or resolved

design composition: how formal elements in a visual work are arranged to achieve a specific purpose

development: in sonata form, the middle section explores the musical possibilities of some aspect of the exposition

diminuendo: becoming softer in volume (of sound)

dissonance: harmonies that sound unrestful and needing to move toward a consonance

dissonant: two or more musical tones that are perceived as unstable and unrestful

divas: famous opera singers who made their fortunes on stage; see prima donna

divertissement: a central scene of most acts, was a spectacular display of dance, drama, singing, and set

doctrine of imitation: the Greek idea that music can affect ethos or human behavior

dome: the architectural achievement using the arch rotated in a full circle to create a ceiling in the shape of a hemisphere

Doric: the Greek order most commonly used, defined by its simple, undecorated style

dramatic irony: the idea that the deeds and decisions made in the play have the opposite consequences of the desired effect

duple meter: grouping of notes into measures of two or four beats

early church fathers: those significant Christian theologians and leaders in the first six centuries of the church

earthenware: a type of clay that is fired to relatively low firing temperatures

Edict of Milan: the law in which emperor Constantine legalized Christianity in the Roman Empire

Empire Style: a certain brand of neoclassical art related to the First Empire of France from 1804 to 1814

empiricism: the view that all knowledge is derived from the senses

Enlightenment: reflected a growing dependence on reason rather than emotion; that rationality would bring about a just and equitable society in which ability was more important than birth

epitaph: a short, often witty statement, about a deceased person

Etruscans: a small people group in Northern Italy who subjugated the Romans in the early days of Roman civilization

Eucharist: in which Christians take consecrated bread and wine in commemoration of the Last Supper and Christ's death

exegetical studies: the field that examines the interpretation of Scripture

existentialist philosophy: a belief that one's existence is what he imagines it to be, thus leaving a man to be responsible for his actions and consequences. Believing there is no higher power, existentialists challenge man to derive his own truth rather one handed down to him by authorities or deities

exposition: the first section of sonata form; presents the principal themes and moves from the primary to the secondary key area

facade: the principal front face of a building

feudalism: a system in medieval Europe in which peasants lived on land owned by nobles and paid homage to them through service

figured bass: a bass line for an instrumentalist with numbers written above (or below) the notes; if the numbers notated were 6/4, the musician would play the given note along with a sixth and a fourth above in order to realize the harmony

fine art: the intentional, creative, contemplative expression of an idea and/or value, which frequently says something about humans, the world, and/or God

firing: the ceramic process of bringing clay under very high temperatures to change its composition from soft and malleable to hard and stone-like

Florentine Camerata: groups of scholarly men around 1600 who met in pursuit of knowledge; named for the small private rooms, or chambers, in which they regularly met; one of the big topics of inquiry was the role that music may have played in ancient Greek drama, leading to the development of recitative and early origins of opera

flying buttresses: exterior supports of building in the Gothic style

Folios: the collected, printed, and published works of Shakespeare compiled after his death

foreground: in visual imagery, the foreground is the positive or main figure depicted

foreshortening: creating the illusion of an object receding in space through size and placement

fortepiano: an early form of the modern piano, differing from similar keyboard instruments in that the force of the hand playing altered the volume of the notes played

fourth wall: a mutually agreed upon convention based on an imaginary, invisible wall separating the audience from the stage, through which the audience can see but actors act as if they cannot

French Revolution: the revolutionary upheaval of the French aristocracy in 1789

fresco painting: mural painting that combines pigment with wet lime plaster that when dry, the image becomes embedded in the wall

frescos: murals painted on wet plaster

fugue: a contrapuntal composition where a subject (main theme) is stated in one musical line and then passed to other lines

genre painting: a style of painting depicting scenes from ordinary, everyday life

genre scenes: illustration paintings of everyday popular life

Geometric period: the historical and cultural period of the Greeks between 900 and 700 BCE. The artwork of this time is characterized by its reliance on geometric and abstract patterns

Gesamtkunstwerk: German for total artwork

gesture drawing: quick, experimental sketches that seek to capture the energy of movement

globalization: the process by which different geographical areas and cultures are becoming more interconnected

glossing: comment on a text; addition of a footnote

goliards: wandering (often clerical) students of the twelfth and thirteenth century who wrote satirical literature in Latin

Gothic style: considered new and modern, originally tagged "Gothic" as a derogatory name in its abandonments of classical traditions as the Goths took power; an extreme emphasis on vertical space, articulated by large stained-glass windows, pointed arches, flying buttresses, and thin walls

grattage: the painting technique of scraping paint off an already textured or painted surface

groined: (also cross vault) the intersection of two barrel vaults

ground bass: repeated descending bass pattern

growling: a harsh tone made by a wind instrument by humming or singing into the instrument while playing it. Also, a vocal technique of making guttural sounds while singing

guilds: powerful associations of merchants, bankers, and artisans

hard-edge painting: a style of painting based in geometric swathes of color with abrupt transitions

harpsichord: a keyboard instrument in which the strings are plucked rather than hit by a hammer

Helenistic: Ancient Greek

Hellenistic period: the Greek historical period between 323 and 31 BCE. The period begins with the death of Alexander the Great and ended with the conquering of the Greeks by Rome

Hellenized: to be compelled to live out Greek culture

high relief: a type of relief carving in which the carving stands out strongly against the background

High Renaissance: time period of 1490-1597 that marked the peak flourishing of the Renaissance

history painting: paintings whose subject matter drew from the history, mythology, literature, and Scripture, ranked highest according to prestige and skill in the academy

history play: works dramatizing historical narratives

homophonic texture: displays a prominent melody in the top voice while having the continuation and development of the basso continuo (or supporting harmonies) in the bottom voice

homophony: musical texture in which one main melody is supported by other subordinate voices that move together in the same rhythms and at the same speed

house capacity: the total number of seats a theatre has in its audience

hubris: a tragic pride that ultimately leads to one's downfall

humanism: an intellectual movement originating in the Renaissance, which focused on the retrieval of ideas and values from classical sources

hymn: in Ancient Greece, referred to songs about honoring a god

iambic pentameter: the use of ten syllables per line and syllables alternating between unstressed and stress beats in the pattern of "de/DUM de/DUM de/DUM de/DUM de/DUM"

iconoclasm: the destruction of symbols or representations

iconoclast controversies: disputes during the Reformation on the place of the visual arts in the church

illuminated manuscripts: illumination; handwritten and hand-drawn manuscripts augmented by initials, borders, and miniature drawings

illusionism: a style of painting in which the image is highly accurate and representative of real physical space

impasto: the very thick application of paint to a surface

impresario: opera producer

impressionism: the style of painting that uses general, often loose marks to make the "impression" of details rather than naturalistic ones

indeterminacy: an approach to composing in which the composer leaves part of the performance to chance

installation: a work of art made for a specific site, that immerses the viewer in a three-dimensional space

intaglio: engraved design

interdisciplinary: working across different art media as well as different areas of study

intervals: the distance between any two musical pitches

Ionic: the Greek order distinguished by its scroll motif at its crown and complex fluting in the shaft

jongleurs: traveling musicians and entertainers

jurisprudence: theory of law

keystone: the voussoir at the center of an arch that anchored the support of the shape

kore: a free-standing sculpture of a female figure, typically clothed

kouros, kouroi: a large, free-standing sculpture of a nude male youth

krater: a common ceramic vessel with a large body and wide mouth used for diluting wine with water

laissez-faire: exhibiting a pattern of nonintervention

laments: solo vocal pieces expressing intense grief, often with a repeated descending bass pattern known as a ground bass

Leitmotives: short musical motives that represent a person, idea, thing, or event, and that occur whenever something related to that is on stage

Liberal Arts: the medieval studies comprising the trivium and quadrivium

libretto: the text of an opera or other long vocal work

Lieder: German art songs for solo voice and piano accompaniment

Lindy Hopper: dancers who danced the Lindy Hop, a dance developed in the late 1920s in Harlem's Savoy Ballroom, which became synonymous with the big bands of the swing era

linear perspective: the drawing convention that uses vanishing points, orthogonal lines, and the horizon line to give the illusion of three-dimensionality to two-dimensional art

liturgical drama: play that included monophonic plainchant in Latin, with music serving as an integral part to reinforce the liturgy

liturgical music: worship music in the early Roman Catholic Church standardized by Pope Gregory I, generally called Gregorian chant

low relief: a type of relief carving in which the carving is shallow

lyricist: the one who writes words to a song

madrigal: a popular secular vocal genre mainly during the Renaissance, based on vernacular poetry, and sung by four to six voices, usually a cappella

mannerism: an artistic style at the end of the Renaissance that exaggerated and distorted figures and objects for the sake of expressiveness

mark making: the different lines, marks, patterns, or textures created in drawing

materialism: the philosophy that all there is to life is what can be touched and seen

melismatic: a melodic style with many notes per syllable

metrical psalmody: a style of sacred music limited to regular rhythms and meters with simple tunes written for psalms and no instrumental accompaniment

mimetic: art that imitates reality

minimalism: a movement in art based around grandiose and simplistic figures; a movement in music that uses a small amount of musical material to create longer works

minnesingers: German traveling musicians and entertainers

minor key: a musical key or tonality in the minor mode; a mood of melancholy or pathos

minstrels: traveling musicians and entertainers

miracle plays: dramatizations of the lives and miracles of past saints in the Roman Catholic Church

mixed-media: the use of nontraditional media in a work of art together, such as cardboard, paper, photographs, found objects, paint, etc.

modernism: a twentieth century musical movement that challenged existing musical aesthetics through reorganization and interpretation of melodic, rhythmic, and harmonic concepts

monarchy: ruled by a single king

monody: solo singing accompanied by basso continuo in the early baroque period

monophonic: a single melody with small stepwise movements that connected the tune in a memorable sequence

morality plays: dramatic enactments using allegorical characters usually representing forces of good versus evil, virtue versus vice, or God versus Satan

motet: a polyphonic vocal work that began as a part of chant, and then added lines and words to extend the meaning until it could no longer be considered suitable for sacred use

murals: a large wall painting

music: the art of combining vocal and/or instrumental sounds, organized through time, to produce an intentional human expression

Music of the Spheres: also known as Harmony of the Spheres, a Pythagorean belief that ratios of the arrangement of celestial bodies were analogous to the relationship of musical tones in the diatonic scale

musical neoclassicism: a twentieth-century musical movement that revived musical forms of pre-Romantic eras while using modern tonal language; characterized by a rejection of the overly emotional music of the Romantic composers

musical theatre: theatrical performance that combines spoken dialogue, songs, acting, and dance

mute: a device that changes the timbre or reduces the volume of a musical instrument. For brass instruments, it is a stopper that fits into the bell

mystery plays: a sequence of short plays or scenes that depicted Bible stories or enacted the work of Christ that led to man's salvation

narthex: the entryway of a cathedral

naturalism: an idealized representation of the visual world

neoclassism: the revival of the classical style in arts, architecture, or music, referring to the movement of the eighteenth century

Neo-Platonism: the term given for the school of thought deriving from the work of Plotinus; characterized by the attempt to incorporate Aristotelian philosophy to a Platonic framework

New York Theatre District: the area around Times Square in Manhattan where most Broadway theatres are located (it runs roughly between West 41st and West 54th Streets, and Sixth to Eighth Avenues)

nihilism: the view that life was without intrinsic meaning or value

Northern Renaissance: the experience of new ideas and innovations of northern countries like France, Germany, and England during the same time as the Italian Renaissance

noumena: the realm of things in themselves

oculus: an architectural element of a cut out open circle at the crown of a dome

Off Broadway theatre: less-popular productions staged in a theatre located in relatively close proximity to the New York Theatre District and which seats between 100 and 499 in the audience (house)

Off-Off Broadway theatre: experimental productions staged in nontraditional theatre spaces outside the New York Theatre District and which seat fewer than 100 in its audience (house)

oil paint: pigment suspended in linseed oil

op art: an artistic movement based in optical illusions to challenge the eye

opera: completely sung drama; a dramatic stage work that is entirely sung rather than spoken

opera buffa: comic opera

opera seria: "serious opera," focused on stories from either Greek mythology or Roman history

oral tradition: music taught by hearing and repeating

orant: a praying figure, often seen in early Christian catacomb paintings and sarcophagi reliefs

oratorio: a large-scale musical work for orchestra and voices, typically a narrative on a religious theme, performed without the use of costumes, scenery, or action

orchestra: in Greek theatre, the circular space where chorus and actors would interact; in Ancient Rome, the seating area where senators and other politicians would sit; in music, large instrumental ensemble with a core of stringed instruments

order: the supportive structure of Greek architectural designs defined by its type of column and entablature

organal voice: an added voice to a liturgical chant

organum: an early term found in manuscripts for two or more voices singing different notes together in acceptable intervals

original cast recording: also called OCR, a recording which allows the listener to experience what the musical was like in performance. The show's songs were recorded by the original actors in their roles

orthogonal lines: horizontal parallel lines that appear to converge in vanishing points on the horizon line to the human eye

Palace of Versailles: King Louis XIV's lavish palace that served as the principal royal residence of France from Louis XIV's reign to the French revolution

pantheistic: the view that everything in the universe is God or part of God

Pantheon: a temple built to honor the emperor Hadrian featuring a large dome and oculus

pantomime: a detailed style of movement in which an actor pretends to use something that is not there, such as the simple movement of tossing a ball without using an actual ball

Parthenon: a temple dedicated to the goddess Athena in the Acropolis of Athens

passion: a musical depiction of the story of Christ's crucifixion with orchestra, chorus, and soloists

passion play: a drama focusing on the days leading up to the crucifixion of Christ

pastoral drama: a drama set in the country that focuses on pastoral characters

percussionists: performers on percussion instruments, who produce sound by striking, shaking, scraping, or otherwise manipulating the instrument

perfect 4th: a perfect 4th is an interval the distance of 5 semitones

perfect 5th: a perfect 5th is an interval the distance of 7 semitones

phenomena: the realm of things as they appear to humans

photorealism: an artistic style based in reproducing hyperrealistic depictions akin to a photograph

plainchant: generic term for monophonic medieval church music, often referred to as Gregorian chant

plein-air: painting from life outdoors in a natural setting, often completed in one sitting

point music: music in which each note can be heard as an individual entity

pointillism: the laborious use of individual dotted marks to form the whole of an image

points of imitation: staggered entries of voices in a polyphonic work, all starting with the same recognizable opening notes

polychoral: musical work involving more than one choir

polymath: an individual of varied learning

polyphony: the sounding of two or more melodic lines at the same time

pop art: an artistic movement that did not distinguish between high and low art, often utilizing iconography from popular culture

postimpressionism: a movement that rejected certain limitations of naturalist color of impressionists and emphasized geometric forms and unnaturalistic color

postmodernism: the view that reacted to the Enlightenment by being radically skeptical of all values and any attempt to understand truth

pragmatic: focusing on what works

prepared piano: a piano in which objects such as bolts and felt are placed in the strings in order to create nontraditional sounds

presentational acting: an external (physical) approach to acting that acknowledges an audience is present

prima donna: famous opera singer who made her fortune on stage; see divas

principal voice: the original liturgical chant

printmaking: transferring images from a matrix onto another surface

program symphony: a symphony that the composer associates with a story, a theme, or other extramusical idea

props: an object held or carried by an actor in character, separate from costumes or scenery

quadratura: illusionistic ceiling painting of architectural elements like columns and arches

Quadrivium: consisted of the mathematical arts of arithmetic, geometry, astronomy, and music

Quarto editions: separated, earlier printed editions of Shakespeare's plays, separate from the Folios and smaller in size

radial design: visual symmetry rotating around a central axis

rapture: the intense pleasure or awe one experiences in the presence of something that possesses beauty

readymades: a term for prefabricated or found objects displayed as art

realism: a realistic representation of the visible world; the nineteenth-century movement in art to depict life as it truly was, in representational and mimetic detail

recapitulation: in sonata form, the return to a restatement of the two principal themes in the primary key

recitative: the traditional Greek delivery of actors' powerful speeches and dialogues through a kind of speech-singing

red-figure technique: the vase painting technique in which the background is painted black and the figures remain the red color of the natural clay body

Reformation: a movement that marked the splintering of the Protestant Church from the Catholic Church

relics: sacred earthy objects from Christ's passion and death, like thorns from his crown, wooden shards from the cross, his blood, sweat, and scraps from his burial shroud

reliefs: carved forms attached to a flat base, not fully "in the round" sculpture

reliquaries: containers of metal, enamel, and gems, elevating earthly matter to the holiness of the New Jerusalem

Renaissance: the "rebirth" of the ideas of antiquity in fourteenth- to seventeenth-century Europe, marked by innovations in science, exploration, philosophy, mathematics, and the arts

representational acting: an internal (mental) approach to acting rooted in realism which utilizes the fourth wall

requiem: a mass for the dead, or a funeral mass

responsorial: a call and response manner between soloist and choir

Risorgimento: nineteenth-century political movement that fought for the unification of Italy

rock musical: a style of musical theatre using a rock genre of music and whose themes are often in opposition to someone in authority (government, landlord, etc.) and/or an idea (war, disease, etc.)

Rococo: the late Baroque style most ornamental and theatrical

Romanesque: design style of cathedrals of the Middle Ages that used an adapted floor plan consisting of a narthex, nave, aisle, choir, transept, and ambulatory

Romanticism: the movement in visual art to move toward emotion and revel in nature

rondeau: a memorably simple tune that repeats a two-part melody throughout

rose window: also called wheel window, was a common stained-glass device placed high in a facade

sanctuary: area in a cathedral around an altar

sarcophagi: elaborately sculpted or carved coffins

satirist: one who censures human vices through means of parody or irony, sometimes with the intent to inspire social reform

Scat: the vocalization of syllables in a manner that is similar to what an instrumentalist would play; a musical onomatopoeia

scholastic: related to the system of philosophy and theology taught in Medieval universities

selective realism: a style that only highlights certain thematic elements of a production (scenery, action, language) using realism, but omits others

serial music: music in which the pitch, duration, timbre, and/or dynamics are all determined through rows or other systems to create a composition

sfumato: the painting technique of fading colors gradually into one another to produce hazy forms

Singspiel: literally sing-play; a German form of musical theatre with both singing and spoken dialogue

slip: a mixture of clay and water that when fired turns to a glossy sheen

slip casting: the ceramic production technique in which a specially prepared slip is poured into a mold in order to produce thin-walled object

social contract theory: view that individuals should enter into relationships whereby all parties involved give up certain practices in order to secure certain protections and freedoms for themselves

social practice: art focused on engagement through human interaction and social discourse

sola gratia: Latin for "grace alone"

sonata form: musical form consisting of two melodies or themes (labeled A and B) that are presented in the exposition (changing key for the second theme), a development section that explores the musical possibilities of some aspect of the exposition, and a recapitulation which returns the piece to a restatement of the two themes, but they both remain in the same key

song cycle: a group of songs designated by the composer to be performed at the same time as a set

soprano: the highest of the four standard singing voices

space block planning: architectural planning based on a single geometric unit

Sprechstimme: a vocal method in which the singer sings an approximate pitch, followed by a quick ascent or descent from the original pitch

staccato: short and detached

stele: an upright pillar of stone used in ancient Greece and Rome to mark a grave

stile moderno: New Baroque musical sound that had the text dominate over the music

still lifes: visual studies of inanimate objects

sublime: an almost mystical encounter with nature where the viewer is simultaneously awestruck and humbled

syllabic: a melodic style with one note per syllable

Syncopation: a temporary contradiction of the prevailing meter

tabula rasa: view that a human is born with no innate knowledge and is, thus, a "blank slate"

tempera paint: pigment suspended in egg yolk

tempera panels: gesso covered, engraved, and painted wood

tenebrism: the dramatic use of light as a compositional technique

tenor: a singing voice between baritone and alto or countertenor, the highest of the ordinary adult male range

terraced dynamics: a section of music would be played at a particular volume and immediately change to another

terracotta: figurines that expressed art or religion in Ancient Greece

theatre of the absurd: a theatrical approach born out of existentialism, expressing life as illogical and unreasonable through experimental performance styles

theatrical postmodernism: a style of theatre that arose after the modern era which utilizes a mixture of traditional methods with more experimental ones

theatrical realism: a style of theatrical production that imitates real life through its acting, costumes, and sets

theatricalism: a category of avant-garde theatre employing an exaggerated performance style as to highlight the artifice of a production

theological liberalism: a view that denies the inspiration of Scripture and thereby rejects historically significant doctrines of the Christian faith

tibia: a reed flute-like instrument often associated with religious gatherings in Roman religion

timbre: the distinguishing qualities or properties of a sound

tone poem: a one-movement symphonic work that depicts a specific program, theme, or story

tracery: arched stone latticework bracing the windows

tragedy: plays concerning a main character brought to ruin as a consequence of a tragic flaw that brings his own end

tragicomedy: a hybrid genre of dramatic literature containing elements of comedy and tragedy

transept: bisecting arms on a basilica that create a cross shape

triple meter: grouping of notes into measures of three beats

tritone: an interval the distance of 6 semitones

Trivium: consisted of the language arts of rhetoric, logic, and grammar

tromp l'oeil: meaning "to fool the eye," a style of illusionistic painting

trope: an extension of new words or music to an already established part of the liturgy in the tenth century.

troubadours: traveling musicians and entertainers as called in Southern France

trouvères: traveling musicians and entertainers as called in Northern France

twelve-tone row: Schoenberg's method of musical organization; the row was a preset sequence of the 12 chromatic pitches intended to avoid tonality, but also to give unity to the final composition

tympanum: the semicircular portal above a door

typology: the use of foreshadowing of events in the Old Testament for events in the New Testament

vase paintings: imagery painted on Greek vases, including geometric designs as well narratives of Greek myths

vellum: parchment made from animal skin, bleached white through the preparation process

veristic: a true to life, or realistic, style

vernacular: the common language spoken by the majority of the people, rather than Latin

vielle: medieval fiddle

visual hierarchy: an organization of visual elements to show their importance

voussoir: the wedge-shaped unit that formed the elements of the arch

word painting: musical depiction of a word's meaning

worship wars: the ongoing conflict of musical taste between the church authorities and congregations

zazen: a meditation in which practitioners attempt to silence their ego in order to achieve clear perception of the world around them

Bibliography

Aquinas, Thomas. 2021. "Sancti Thomae de Aquino: Quaestiones disputatae de potentia." Corpus Thomisticum. Fundación Tomás de Aquino." https://www.corpusthomisticum.org/qdp7.html#60200

Aristotle. 1984. "Nichomachean Ethics." In *The Complete Works of Aristotle, 1729-1867*. Vol 1. Translated by I. Bywater, edited by Jonathan Barnes. Princeton: Princeton University Press.

Aristotle. 1984. "Poetics." In *The Complete Works of Aristotle, 2316-2340*. Vol 1. Translated by I. Bywater, edited by Jonathan Barnes. Princeton: Princeton University Press.

Aristotle. 1984. "Politics." In *The Complete Works of Aristotle, 1986-2129*. Vol 1. Translated by I. Bywater, edited by Jonathan Barnes. Princeton: Princeton University Press.

Augustine. 1953. "Of True Religion." In *Augustine: Earlier Writings*, 225-283. Translated by J.H.S. Burleigh. Philadelphia: Westminster Press.

Augustine. 1992. *Confessions*. Translated by Henry Chadwick. Oxford: Oxford University Press.

Avery, Kevin. 2009. "Asher Brown Durand: 1796-1886." https://www.metmuseum.org/toah/hd/dura/hd_dura.htm

Balthrop, David. 2002. *Theatre: Through the Stage Door*. Dubuque, Iowa: Kendall Hunt.

Bearden, Romaire, and H. Henderson. 1992. *A History of African-American Artists: 1792 to the Present*. New York: Pantheon Books.

Bohlman, Philip V. 2011. *Music, Nationalism, and the Making of the New Europe*. New York: Routledge.

Botstein, Leon. 1999. *The Compleat Brahms: A Guide to the Musical Works of Johannes Brahms*. New York: W. W. Norton.

Brockett, Oscar G., and Franklin J. Hildy. 2008. *History of the Theatre*. Boston: Pearson.

Brown, David. 1961. "Balakirev, Tchaikovsky and Nationalism." *Music & Letters* 42, no. 3, 227-41. Accessed April 20, 2021. http://www.jstor.org/stable/731879

Brummel, Kenneth. 2020. "A 'Freeman of Color.'" https://ago.ca/agoinsider/freeman-color

Burkholder, J. Peter, and Claude V. Palisca. 2014. *Norton Anthology of Western Music*. Vol 2. 7th ed. New York: W. W. Norton.

Burkholder, J. Peter, Donald J. Grout, and Claude V. Palisca. 2006. *A History of Western Music*. 7th ed. New York: W. W. Norton.

Burkholder, J. Peter, Donald J. Grout, and Claude V. Palisca. 2019. *A History of Western Music*. 10th ed. New York: W. W. Norton.

Burkholder, J. Peter, Donald J. Grout, and Claude V. Palisca. 2010. *A History of Western Music*. 8th ed. New York: W. W. Norton.

Cleveland Morning Leader. Vol. 15, No. 5. Jan. 7, 1861. "City and News Items," p.1.

Dalferth, Ingolf U. 1988. *Theology and Philosophy*. New York: Blackwell.

Dalferth, Ingolf U. 2009. "God and the Mystery of Words." *Journal of the American Academy of Religion* 60, no. 1, 79-104. https://doi.org/10.1093/jaarel/lx.1.79

Davison, Archibald T., and Willi Apel. 1977. *Historical Anthology of Music*. Vol 1. Rev. ed. Cambridge: Harvard University Press.

Doerries, Bryan. 2021. "You Are Not Alone across Time." Interview by Krista Tippet. On Being with Krista Tippet. The On Being Project. https://onbeing.org/programs/bryan-doerries-you-are-not-alone-across-time/

Durand, Asher Brown. 1855. "Letters on Landscape Painting." *The Crayon* 1, no. 3, 34-35.

Duthuit, Georges. 1950. *The Fauvist Painters*. New York: Wittenborn Schultz.

Edwards, Jonathan. 1989. "The Nature of True Virtue." In *Works of Jonathan Edwards: Ethical Writings*. Vol. 8. Edited by Paul Ramsey. New Haven, CT: Yale University Press.

Ewen, David. 1959. *Complete Book of 20th Century Music*. Englewood Cliffs: Prentice-Hall, Inc.

Fairclough, Pauline. 2019. *Dmitry Shostakovich*. London: Reaktion Books.

Flynn, Thomas R. 2013. The Stanford Encyclopedia of Philosophy. In *Jean-Paul Sartre*, edited by Edward N. Zalta. https://plato.stanford.edu/archives/fall2013/entries/sartre/

Flynn, Thomas R. 2018. *Sartre: A Philosophical Biography*. Cambridge: Cambridge University Press.

Forbes, James. 1824. *An Account of the Life and Writings of James Beattie*. London: W. Baynes and Son.

Fordham, John. 2009. "50 Great Moments in Jazz: The Emergence of Bebop." Music Blog. *The Guardian*, 6 July 2009. https://www.theguardian.com/music/musicblog/2009/jul/06/50-moments-jazz-bebop

Fraser, Neil. 2004. *Theare History Explained*. Wiltshire: The Crowood Press.

Frei, Hans. 1974. *The Eclipse of Biblical Narrative*. New Haven: Yale University Press.

Fuller, Sarah. 1987. *European Musical Heritage 800-1750*. New York: Alfred A. Knopf.

Gann, Kyle. 2010. *No Such Thing As Silence*. New Haven: Yale University Press.

Grant, M.J., and Imke Mische, eds. 2016. *The Musical Legacy of Karlheinz Stockhausen: Looking Back and Forward*. Hofheim, Germany: Wolke Verlag.

Gregory the Great. 1995. "Letter to Mellitus." In *Nicene and Post-Nicene Fathers*, 84-84. Series 2. Vol. 13. Translated by James Barmby. Edited by Philip Schaff and Henry Wace. Peabody: Hendriskcon Publishers.

Hare, John. 2007. *God and Morality*. Malden: Blackwell Publishing.

Hegel, Georg Wilhelm Friedrich. 1975. *Lectures on the Philosophy of World History*. Translated by H.B. Nisbet. Cambridge: Cambridge University Press.

Hegel, Georg Wilhelm Friedrich. 2018. *The Phenomenology of the Spirit*. Translated and Edited by Terry Pinkard. Cambridge: Cambridge University Press.

Heidegger, Martin. 1993. "The Origin of the Work of Art." In *Basic Writings*, 142-212. Revised Ed. New York: HarperCollins Publishers.

Hischak, Thomas. 2006. *Theatre as Human Action*. Lanham: The Scarecrow Press.

Houlgate, Stephen. 2020. "Hegel's Aesthetics." The Stanford Encyclopedia of Philosophy. Edited by Edward N. Zalta. https://plato.stanford.edu/archives/spr2020/entries/hegel-aesthetics/

Hume, David. 2007. *An Enquiry Concerning Human Understanding and Other Writings*. Edited by Stephen Buckle. Cambridge: Cambridge University Press.

Jaquith, Austin K. 2020. "Heldenleben 2020." Unpublished program notes.

Jüngel, Eberhard. 1983. God as the Mystery of the World. Eugene, OR: Wipf & Stock.

Kangas, Ryan R. 2012. "Mourning, Remembrance, and Mahler's 'Resurrection'." *19th-Century Music* 36, no. 1, 58-83. Accessed April 21, 2021. https://doi:10.1525/ncm.2012.36.1.058

Kant, Immanuel. 2000. *Critique of the Power of Judgment*. Translated by Paul Guyer and Eric Matthews. Edited by Paul Guyer. Cambridge: Cambridge University Press, 2000.

Kauffman, David. 2011. "The Theory of Silence." *Musical Offerings* 2, no. 1, 1-9.

Kennedy, Dennis, ed. 2003. *The Oxford Encyclopedia of Theatre and Performance*. 2 V. Oxford: Oxford University Press.

Kerman, Joseph. 1988. *Opera as Drama*. New and Revised Ed. Berkeley: University of California Press.

King, Bruce. 1991. *Contemporary American Theatre*. New York: St. Martin's Press.

Leibowitz, Rene. 1949. *Schoenberg and His School: The Contemporary Stage of the Language of Music*. New York: Philosophical Library.

Lewis, C. S. 2007. *Mere Christianity*. Revised Ed. San Francisco, HarperOne.

Lindbeck, George A. 2009. *The Nature of Doctrine: Religion and Theology in a Postliberal Age*. Louisville: Westminster John Knox Press.

Locke, John. 1892. *Some Thoughts Concerning Education*. Cambridge: At the University Press.

Locke, John. 1996. *An Essay Concerning Human Understanding*. Edited by Kenneth P. Winkler. Cambridge: Hackett Publishing Company.

Lockspeiser, Edward. 1978. *Debussy. V. 1. 1862-1902: His Life and Mind*. United Kingdom: Cambridge University Press.

Luther, Martin. 1965. *Luther's Works. V. 53. Liturgy and Hymns.* Translated by and Edited by Ulrich S. Leupold. Philadelphia: Fortress Press.

Maconie, Robin. 2017. "Saving Faith: Stockhausen and Spirituality." *Tempo* 72, no. 283, 7-20. https://doi.org/10.1017/S0040298217000900.

Malafronte, Allison. n.d. "En Plein Air: Letters on Landscape Painting." Accessed May 14, 2020. https://www.artistsnetwork.com/art-subjects/plein-air/en-plein-air-letters-on-landscape-painting/

Mark, Michael, and Charles Gary. 2007. *History of American Music Education*. 3rd ed. New York: Roman and Littlefield Education.

Marx, Karl. 1970. *Critique of Hegel's 'Philosophy of Right.'* Translated by Annette Jolin and Joseph O'Malley. Cambridge: Cambridge University Press, 1970.

Marx, Steven. 2000. *Shakespeare and the Bible*. New York: Oxford University Press.

Mathiesen, Thomas J. 1999. *Apollo's Lyre: Greek Music and Music Theory in Antiquity and the Middle Ages*. Lincoln: University of Nebraska Press.

McKinnon, James, ed. 1987. *Music in Early Christian Literature*. Cambridge: Cambridge University Press.

Morrison, Simon. 2009. *The People's Artist*. New York: Oxford University Press.

Mortensen, John J. 2020. *The Pianist's Guide to Historic Improvisation*. Oxford: Oxford University Press.

Morton, Brian. 2006. *Shostakovich: His Life and Music*. London: Haus Publishing Limited.

Mueller, Gustav, Jean-Paul Sartre, and Bernard Frechtman. 1949. "What Is Literature?" *Books Abroad* 23, no. 4, 403. https://doi.org/10.2307/40087320.

Musgrave, Michael. 2000. *A Brahms Reader*. New Haven, CT: Yale University Press.

National Gallery of Art. n.d. "Paul Cezanne." Accessed May 14, 2021. https://www.nga.gov/features/slideshows/paul-cezanne.html

Nietzsche, Friedrich. 1993. *The Birth of Tragedy: Out of the Spirit of Music*. Translated by Shaun Whiteside. Edited by Michael Tanner. New York: Penguin Books.

Nietzsche, Friedrich. 2006. *Thus Spoke Zarathustra*. Translated by Adrian Del Caro. Edited by Adrian Del Caro and Robert B. Pippin. Cambridge: Cambridge University Press.

Norwich, Julian of. 2011. *Revelations of Divine Love*. Tr. Grace Warrick. Kindle Edition.

Oxford English Dictionary. 2021. "Amusement." https://www.oed.com/view/Entry/6790?redirectedFrom=amusement#eid

Pastan, Elizabeth. 1997. "The Torture of Saine George Medallion from Chartres Cathedral in Princeton." *Record of the Art Museum of Princeton University* 56, no. 1/2, 11-34.

Pearcey, Nancy. 2010. *Saving Leonardo*. Nashville: B & H Publishing Group.
Peters, Gunter, and Mark Schreiber. 1990. "'How Creation Is Composed': Spirituality in the Music of Karlheinz Stockhausen." *Perspectives of New Music* 37, no. 1, 95-131.
Plato. 1997. "Republic." In *Plato: Complete Works*, 971-1223. Translated by G. M. A. Grube. Revised by C. D. C. Reeve. Edited by John M. Cooper. Cambridge: Hackett Publishing Company.
Pliny the Younger. 2001. *Letters of Pliny*. Project Gutenberg: F. C. T. Boxanquet.
Potter, Pamela M. 1983. "Strauss's 'Friedenstag': A Pacifist Attempt at Political Resistance." *The Musical Quarterly* 69, no. 3, 408-424. Accessed April 18, 2021. http://www.jstor.org/stable/742179
Reich, Nancy B. 1985. *Clara Schumann: The Artist and the Woman*. Ithaca: Cornell University Press.
Robinson, Mark A, ed. 2019. "What Are Broadway, Off-Broadway, Off-Off-Broadway, and the West End?" *Broadway Direct* (July 26, 2019). https://broadwaydirect.com/what-are-broadway-off-broadway-off-off-broadway-and-the-west-end/
Ruskin, Ariane, adapted. 1973. *Seventeenth and Eighteenth-Century Art*. New York: McGraw-Hill.
Salzman, Eric. 2002. *Twentieth-Century Music: An Introduction*. 4th ed. Upper Saddle River: Prentice Hall.
Sartre, Jean-Paul. 1993. *What is Literature?* Translated by Bernard Fretchman. New York: Routledge.
Sartre, Jean-Paul. 2007. *Existentialism is a Humanism*. Translated by Carol Macomber. Edited by John Kulka. New Haven: Yale University Press.
Sayre, Henry M. 2020. *Discovering the Humanities*. 4th ed. Upper Saddle River: Pearson.
Schoenberg, Arnold. 1950. *Style and Idea*. New York: Philosophical Library.
Schrenk, Gottlob. 1964. "Δίκη, Δίκαιος, Δικαιοσύνη, Δικαιόω, Δικαίωμα, Δικαίωσις, Δικαιοκρισία." In *Theological Dictionary of the New Testament*, 174-225. Edited by Gerhard Kittel, Geoffrey W. Bromiley, and Gerhard Friedrich. Grand Rapids: Eerdmans.
Seroff, Victor. 1943. *Dimitri Shostakovich: The Life and Background of a Soviet Composer*. New York: Alfred A. Knopf.
Shakespeare, William, and G. B. Evans. 1974. *The Riverside Shakespeare*. Boston: Houghton Mifflin.
Shakespeare, William. 1960. *King Henry the Fifth*. Folger Library. New York: Simon and Schuster.
Sheppard, Franklin L, and Maltbie D. Babcock. 1986. *The Hymnal for Worship and Celebration*. Ed. Tom Fettke. Waco: Word Music.
Spurling, Hilary. 1998. *The Unknown Matisse: A Life of Henri Matisse*. Berkeley and Los Angeles: University of California Press.

Stiles, Kristine, and Peter Selz, eds. 1996. *Theories and Documents of Contemporary Art: A Sourcebook of Artists' Writings*. Berkeley and Los Angeles: University of California Press.

Stockhausen, Karlheinz. 1989. *Stockhausen on Music*. Compiled by Robin Maconie. New York: Marion Boyars.

Stolba, K. Marie. 1994. *The Development of Western Music: An Anthology*. Madison: Brown & Benchmark.

Stolba, K. Marie. 1997. *The Development of Western Music: A History*. 3rd ed. New York: McGraw-Hill.

Stravinsky, Igor. 1962. *An Autobiography*. New York: W.W. Norton & Company Inc.

Strunk, Oliver. 1988. *Source Readings in Music History*. Rev. ed. Leo Treitler, gen. ed. 7 vols. New York: W. W. Norton.

Taruskin, Richard. 2010. *Music in the Nineteenth Century*. The Oxford History of Western Music. Oxford: Oxford University Press.

Tchaikovsky, Piotr Ilyich. 1981. *Letters to His Family: An Autobiography*. Edited by Percy Marshall Young. Tr. Galina von Meck. New York: Stein and Day.

Thibaudeau, Antoine-Claire. 1827-1828. *Histoire générale de Napoléon Bonaparte: de sa vie privée et publique*. V. 6. Paris: n.p.

Tillich, Paul. 1973. *Systematic Theology*. Vol. 1-3. Chicago: The University of Chicago Press.

Ulrich, Thomas. 2012. *Stockhausen: A Theological Interpretation*. Kurten, Germany: Stockhausen-Stiftung fur Musik.

Van Dycke, Stefania. 2019. "20 Quotes from Claude Monet." December 17, 2019. https://www.denverartmuseum.org/en/blog/20-quotes-claude-monet

Van Gogh, Vincent. 1888. Letter to Theo van Gogh. Written in Arles, 9 September, 1888. Translated by Mrs. Johanna van Gogh-Bonger. Edited by Robert Harrison. number 534. http://www.webexhibits.org/vangogh/letter/18/534.htm

Volkov, Solomon. 2004. *Shostakovich and Stalin*. New York: Alfred A Knopf.

Vonnegut, Kurt. 1988. *Conversations with Kurt Vonnegut*. Edited by William Rodney Allen. Jackson: University Press of Mississippi.

Wagner, Richard. 1964. *Wagner on Music and Drama: A Compendium of Richard Wagner's Prose Works*. Selected and arranged, with an introduction by Albert Goldman and Evert Sprinchorn. Translated by William Ashton Ellis. New York: E. P. Dutton.

Warhol, Andy. 1977. *The Philosophy of Andy Warhol: From A to B and Back Again*. San Diego: Harcourt.

Weiss, Adolph. 1937. *Schoenberg*. Ed. Merle Armitage. New York: Greenwood Press, Publishers.

Whitehead, Alfred North. 1978. Process and Reality. Edited by David Ray Griffin and David W. Sherburne. New York: Free Press.

Wilde, Oscar. n.d. "The Decay of Lying: An Observation." *Intentions*. Transcribed from 1913. Edited by David Price. Project Gutenberg EBook. http://eds.b.ebscohost.com/eds/pdfviewer/pdfviewer?vid=4&sid=36c6f903-99f1-4576-bd0b-a3e750b08334%40sessionmgr103

Wilder, Thornton. 1957. *Our Town: A Play in Three Acts*. New York: Harper & Row.

Wittgenstein, Ludwig. 2009. *Philosophical Investigations*. Translated by G.E.M. Anscombe, P.M.S. Hacker, and Joachim Schulte. Revised 4th Ed. Malden: Wiley-Blackwell.

Wold, Milo Antonio, et al. 1998. *An Outline History of Western Music*. 9th ed. Boston: WCB McGraw-Hill.

Wolterstorff, Nicholas. 1980. *Art in Action*. Grand Rapids: Eerdmans.

Wright, Charles. 2004. "Off-Off-Broadway, Way Back When." TheaterMania. *Theater News* (October 4, 2004). https://www.theatermania.com/new-york-city-theater/news/off-off-broadway-way-back-when_5191.html

Xenophanes of Colophon and Lesher, James H. 2001. *Fragments: a Text and Translation with Commentary*. Translated and Edited by James H. Lesher. Toronto: University of Toronto Press.

Your Dictionary.com. n.d. "Stéphane Mallarmé." Accessed May 19, 2021. https://biography.yourdictionary.com/stephane-mallarme

Zarzeczny, Matthew D. 2013. *Meteors That Enlighten the Earth*. Newcastle upon Tyne: Cambridge Scholars Publishing.

A

Abbey of the Holy Trinity, 99
Abbey Saint-Denis, 100, 102
Absolute Spirit, 230, 231
abstract expressionism, 331–336
action paintings, 332
Adams, John, 383
Adams, Joseph Quincy, 147
The Adventures of Telemachus, 203
Aegean civilizations, 21
Aeschylus, 36
aesthetics, 13
affective memory, 325
Agnus Dei, 87
aleatoric, 350
Alexander, 42
All My Sons, 362
All Shall Be Well, 377, 378
alla prima, 266
Allegory of the Liberal Arts, 138
alto, 140
American Civil War, 261
American landscape painting, 260–262
American voices, 316–317
ancient Greece, 17–39
  art. *See* art, in ancient Greece
  music, 26–35
    musical instruments, 34–35
    myths surrounding, 31–33
    notation, 33–34
    writings about, 30–31
  philosophy, 17–21
  theater, 35–39
    Greek masks, 36
    tragic drama, 36–39
ancient Rome, 41–66
  art, 44–52
    architectural revolution, 48–50
    Etruscans, 45–47
    illusionary wall paintings, 50–52
    portraiture as propaganda, 47–48
  music, 53–62
    music theory, 59–62
    musical activity, 54–58
    musical instruments, 58–59
  theater, 62–66
anthropomorphic, 20
anti-realism, 323, 326–329
antiphonal, 86
Apollo of Veii, 46
Apollonian, 17–18
Apostle Paul, 70–71
"*apotheosis* of theology," 95
The Apotheosis of Thomas Aquinas, 95
Appalachian Spring, 317
apse, 80–81
Aquinas, Thomas, 1, 8, 95–96
arch, 48–50
Archaic period, 22
Archaic smile, 23–24
architectural revolution, 48–50
architectural styles, of Greeks, 25–26
architecture(s)
  Baroque, 163–166
  of renaissance, 128, 129, 133–134
aria, 145, 146
Arianism, 78
Aristophanes, 36
Aristotelian philosophy, 367
Aristotle, 19, 20, 28–29, 37

Armstrong, Louis, 318–323
  New Orleans Jazz in, 319
The Arnolfini Marriage, 129, 132
Arp, Hans, 304, 305
Arp, Jean, 304, 305
Ars subtilior, 114, 115
art(s), 259–275, 298–308, 331–347, 370–379
  ability to interact with, 11–14
  abstract expressionism, 331–336
  American landscape painting, 260–262
  in ancient Greece, 21–26
    architecture, 25–26
    black-figure technique, 23
    contrapposto, 23–24
    Geometric era of, 22
    kouroi, 23–24
    red-figure technique, 23
    vase paintings, 22
  in ancient Rome, 44–52
    architectural revolution, 48–50
    Etruscans, 45–47
    illusionary wall paintings, 50–52
    portraiture as propaganda, 47–48
  art as social practice, 375
  bio-architecture, 370–371
  Christian and, 9–11
  cubism, 301–303
  dada, 303–305
  defined, 3–5
  in early Christian era, 70–82
    holy text, 81–82
    post-Constantine, 75, 77–79
    pre-Constantine, 72–75
    worship, 79–81
  Enlightenment, 197–208
    academy, 200–203
    architecture, 198–200
    artist as satirist, 205, 207–208
    craft and industry, 204–205
    sculpture, 198–200
  environment and ecology, 371–372
  fauvism, 298–300
  gender and sexuality, 376–379
  hard-edge painting, minimalism/op art, 343–347
  in High and Late Middle Ages, 97–108
    cathedrals, 99–100
    entryways, 100–104
    interiors, 104–107
    objects, 107–108
  impressionism, 265–270
  photorealism, 336–339
  pop art, 339–343
  postimpressionism, 270–275
  realism, 262–265
  renaissance, 121–126
    architecture of, 133–134
    mannerism, 134–136
    naturalism and realism, 126–129
    northern renaissance, 129–133
  romanticism
    neoclassical work, 233–236
    romanticism, 236–242
  social activism, 372–375
  surrealism, 305–308
artistic bareness, 14
The Artist's Father Reading His Newspaper, 273, 274
As Vesta Was from Latmos Hill Descending, 144
Ashley-Cooper, Anthony, 194
assemblages, 335
atmospheric perspective, 128
atonal, 311
audio only, 383
Augustine, 44, 78–79, 85, 89
Augustus, Caesar, 47–48
aulos, 28
avant-garde, 327
Ave Maria virgo serena, 140

B
Bach, Johann Sebastian, 175, 178, 179, 180
background, 22
Badge with Saint Leonard, 108–109
ballade (classical music), 249, 250
Ballet Russes, 308–309
bands, 357–359
Banksy art, 297
Baptism, 380
The Barber of Seville (Rossini), 220, 251
bards, 112
Baroque music, 174, 175

Baroque period
  arts, 162–163
    architectures, 163–166
    regions, 166–173
  musics
    composers and forms, 176–181
    instrumental development, 181–184
    stylistic considerations, 174–176
  philosophy of, 159–162
  theatre, 185–186
    Handels operas, 187–189
    opera seria, 186–187
    other languages opera, 189–191
barrel vaults, 50
Barricade in Milan, Porta Tosa, 293
Barth, Karl, 195
bas-reliefs, 36
Basie, Count, 321
basilica, 80
bass, 140
basso continuo, 145
Bastien-Lepage, Jules, 263–265
"Batter My Heart," 383
Battisti, Frank, 358
Beaumarchais, Pierre-Augustin Caron de, 219–220
Beauty and the Beast, 363
Beckett, Samuel, 360, 361
Beggar's Opera, 221, 223
Beijing National Stadium, 371
bel canto singing, 251
Bellini, Vincenzo, 254
Berlin, Irving, 362
Bernini, Gian Lorenzo, 163, 164, 165
Bernstein, Leonard, 317
Bible, 9–10, 34–35
biblical perspective, 228
Biblical plays, 89
Biden, Joe, 274
Billy the Kid, 317
Bingen, 90–91
bio-architecture, 370–371
Birth of the Cool, 354
The Birth of Tragedy, 17, 333
"Black and Tan Fantasy," 321
black-figure technique, 23
Black Plague, 98

Black Square, 13
blank slate. *See* tabula rasa
Blue Poles, 333
Blue Void, 377, 378
Boethius, 59–62
Bonaparte, Napoleon, 235, 236, 253
Bontecou, Lee, 336, 337
book musical, 363
The Book of Job, 386, 387
The Book of Kells, 81–82
book-writer, 363
Borromini, Francesco, 163, 164
Brahms, Johannes, 242, 247–249
Brancacci Chapel, 127
Braque, Georges, 301, 302
Broadway theater, 363
Brunelleschi, Filippo, 126, 127, 133
Bultmann, Rudolf, 297
busker, 212
Butterfly Reliquary, 108
Byzantine Empire, 108

C

Cabaletta, 251
Caesar, Julius, 188
Cage, John, 350, 351
  gives up control, 350–352
Calvin, Jean, 123, 141, 142
Calvinism, 141
Camerata, Florentine, 145
cantata, 116, 181
cappella vocal music, 139–144
Caravaggio, 166–167
Carmina burana, 115–116
Carolingian Renaissance, 97
Carousel, 363
Carracci, Annibale, 167
Carter, Ron, 356
cartoons, 129
castrato, 186
Cat on a Hot Tin Roof, 361
Catacomb of Callixtus, 73
Catacomb of Domitilla, 73
Catacomb of Priscilla, 74
catacombs, 71
Catacombs of Peter and Marcellinus, 75
catharsis, 20

cathedral, 99–100
Catholic Church, 1, 121, 123, 140, 141, 159, 162, 186
Catholicism, 10, 159, 161
Central Committee of the Communist Party, 315
Cézanne, Paul, 273–275
chamber music, 244
Chapel, Rothko, 333, 334
Charlemagne, 94
Charles IV, 235
Chartres Cathedral, 103, 104–105
"Chattanooga Choo Choo," 321
Chavkin, Rachel, 385
Chekhov, Anton, 324
The Cherry Orchard, 324–325
chiaroscuro, 166
Chiswick House (London), 198
Chopin, Frédéric, 7, 249–250
chorale, 142
chorus, 35, 64–65
Christ, 77–78
Christ and the Woman of Samaria, 167
Christian, and arts, 9–11
Christian hymns, 83
Christianity, 228–230, 231, 233, 241
Christians, 1
Christ's serenity, 128
Cinderella, 315, 363
Circle of Animals/Zodiac Heads, 373
cithara, 28
Clair de lune, 12
classical music, 308–317
  cultural influences on, 208–209
  stylistic features of, 209–211
    dance and, 209
Classical period, 22
Cleopatra, 188, 189
Close, Chuck, 338
codex, 82
Cole, Thomas, 227, 228
Coleman, Ornette, 357
Colgrass, Michael, 358
collage, 302
color field paintings, 332
Colosseum, 50
Coltrane, John, 354, 356

comedies, 148, 152–156
A Comedy of Errors, 154–156
commedia dell'arte, 152
communism development, 229
complex rib vault, 99, 100
composers, 362
concept musicals, 363
concertos, 181
Confessions, 85, 89
consonance, 88
consonant, 31
Constellation according to the Laws of Chance, 305
contemporary art, 370
contenance angloise, 136
Contrapposto, 23–24, 128–129
conventions, 162
  of opera seria, 188
Cooper, James Fenimore, 227
Copland, Aaron, 316, 358
Corelli, Arcangelo, 177
Corinthian, 25
cornu, 58–59
Council of Trent, 160, 161
counter-reformation, 160
counterpoint, 174–175
Courbet, Gustave, 263
"Courtesy of the Red, White, and Blue (The Angry American)," 381
COVID-19, 329, 381
Creation of Adam, 122, 136
Credo, 86–87
crescendos, 174, 175
Cristofori, Bartolomeo, 183
cross vault, 50
The Crucible, 362
Crusades, 97–98
cubism, 301–303
Cupid and Psyche, 199, 202
Curiatii of Alba Longa, 235
Cyrus, 43
Cyrus Cylinder, 43

D

da capo, 186
da Vinci, Leonardo, 122, 126, 128, 129, 130, 134, 167

dada, 303–305
Dadaism, 303, 333
daguerreotypes, 337
Daily Cincinnati Gazette, 260
Dali, Salvador, 306
Dance, and classical music, 209
"Dark Ages," 97
Darwin, Charles, 265
"Das Judentum in der Musik," 291
David (Bernini), 163
David, Jacques-Louis, 233–236, 239
David (Michelangelo), 163
David sculpture, 128, 129, 135, 151
Davis, Miles, 354, 355, 356
De institutione musica, 60
de Meuron, Pierre, 371
de Roissy, Pierre, 105
de Valois, Marguerite (Queen), 253
Death of a Salesman, 362
The Death of Klinghoffer, 383
The Death of Marat (David), 233
Debussy, Claude, 12, 285, 286
Degas, Edgar, 268, 270
denouement, 252
"Der Leiermann," 245
Derain, André, 300
des Prez, Josquin, 139
design composition, 203
Deus passus, 380
development, in sonata form, 213
diminuendos, 174, 175
Dionysian, 18
Disputation of the Holy Sacrament, 1, 2
dissonance, 88, 137
dissonant, 31
divas, 186
diversity, 69
divertissement, 189
Doctor Atomic, 383
doctrine of imitation, 30
Doerries, Bryan, 386
A Doll's House, 324
dome, 50
Don Giovanni, 216
Donna Lee, 322
Donne, John, 383
Doric, 25

Doryphoros, 24
Douglass, Frederick, 386
dramatic irony, 37–38
drawing practice, 129
Drying the Sails, 300
Duchamp, Marcel, 304
Dun, Tan, 380
Duncanson, Robert S., 260, 261
Dun's *Water Passion,* 380
duple meter, 140
Durand, Asher Brown, 261, 262
Dürer, Albrecht, 131, 132
Dutch style painting, 169–170

E
early Christian era, music, 82–84
early church fathers, 70
   on music, 84–85
Early New Orleans Jazz/Dixieland
     music, 318
earthenware, 204
Edict of Milan, 71
Edwards, Jonathan, 196
Eibingen Abbey, 90
Ein feste Burg (chorale), 143, 253
Ein Heldenleben, 382
Einstein on the Beach, 353
Elizabeth I of England, 146, 147, 150, 152
Ellington, Duke, 320–321
Empire Style, 235
empiricism, 161
Enlightenment, 193–225, 208
   art, 197–208
     academy, 200–203
     architecture, 198–200
     artist as satirist, 205, 207–208
     craft and industry, 204–205
     sculpture, 198–200
   music, 208–219
     classical. *See* classical music
     Mozart, Wolfgang Amadeus,
       216–219
   philosophy, 193–197
   theatre
     satire and comedy, 219–221
     beyond serious opera, 221–225
Enlightenment movements, 228, 231

entire aria, 383
environment and ecology, 371–372
epitaph, 33
"Epitaph of Seikilos," 33
Erbarme dich, 180
Ernst, Max, 307
Etruscans, 45–47
Eucharist, 108
Euripides, 36
Europe After the Rain, II, 307
European Romanticism, 260
Evans, Gil, 354
exegetical studies, 369
existentialism, 232
existentialist philosophy, 360
exposition, 213
eye music, 113–114

F
Façade, 105
Fanfare for the Common Man, 317
Fantasie impromptu, 7
The Father, 324
fauvism, 298–300
Fennell, Frederick, 358
feudalism, 94
Fifth Symphony, 243
figured bass, 176
fine art, 3
 important components of, 7–9
 reasons for, 5–7
The Firebird, 308, 309
First Suite in E-flat, 322
Five Piano Pieces, 311
Flack, Audrey, 338, 339
Florence Baptistry
 linear perspective of, 127
Florence Cathedral, 125, 133
Floyd, George, 374
flying buttresses, 100
Folds, Ben, 7
Folios, 146
folk art, 6
foreground, 22
foreshortening, 128
Fountain, 304

fourth wall, 325
Fragonard, Jean-Honoré, 173
France, Baroque regions in, 171–173
free-standing sculpture, 128
Frei, Hans, 369
French Grand Opera, 252
French Revolution, 208–209, 233, 235
fresco painting, 1, 2, 105–106
Freud, Sigmund, 230, 306
Friedrich, Caspar David, 240, 260
Fruit Dish, 301
fugue, 178

G
Galerie des Glaces, 172
Galilei, Galileo, 159, 160
Garrett, Kenny, 356
gender and sexuality, 376–379
genre painting, 163
Gentileschi, Artemisia, 168
Geometric period, 22
German literature and theology, 295
German Romanticism to nationalism, 286–287
Gershwin, George, 316
Gershwin, Ira, 362
Gesamtkunstwerk, 287
gesture drawings, 129
Ghosts, 324
Giant Steps, 356
Gillespie, Dizzy, 321
"Gin Lane," 207
Giulio Cesare in Egitto, 188
Glass, Philip, 352–353
global relevance, 379–382
globalization
 art, 370–379
  art as social practice, 375
  bio-architecture, 370–371
  environment and ecology, 371–372
  gender and sexuality, 376–379
  social activism, 372–375
 music, 379–382
  global relevance, 379–382
 philosophy, 367–370
 theatre, 383–387

musical theatre, 385–386
opera, 383–385
resonant across centuries, 386–387
Globe theatre, 147
Gloria, 86–87
Gloria and Chair of Saint Peter, 163, 164
glossing, 90
Gogh, Van, 9
"Golden Age of Opera," 251
goliards, 115
Golijov, Osvaldo, 380
Good Shepherd, 72
Goodman, Benny, 321
Gothic style, 100, 162
Goya, Francisco, 237–238
Grainger, Percy, 322, 323
grattage, 307
The Great Gate of Kiev, 278, 279
Greek masks, 36
Greek philosophy, 368
Gregorian chant, 85–88
Gregory the Great, 69
groined, 50
ground bass, 189
growling, 320
Gubaidulina, Sofia, 380
Gunderson, Lauren, 327
Gutenberg, Johannes, 134

H
Hadestown, 385, 386
Hair, 363
"Hallelujah Chorus," 4
Hammerstein II, Oscar, 362
Hancock, Herbie, 356
Handel, George Frideric, 180
operas, 187–189
Harbison, John, 358
hard-edge painting, 343–347
Harmonics, 60
Hart, Lorenz, 362
Hartmann, Viktor, 277
Hay Making, 263, 264
Haydn, Franz Joseph, 212–216
Hedda Gabler, 324
Hegel, Georg Wilhelm Friedrich, 230–231

Heidegger, Martin, 9, 296, 297
Heldenleben 2020, 382, 383
Hellenistic period, 17, 22
Hellenized, 41
Henry V, of England, 150, 151
Herzog, Jacques, 371
"Hey, Little Songbird," 386
High and Late Middle Ages, 93–118
art, 97–108
cathedrals, 99–100
entryways, 100–104
interiors, 104–107
objects, 107–108
music, 108–114
eye music, 113–114
polyphony, 108, 110–112
secular music and culture, 112–113
philosophy, 93–97
theatre, 114–118
sacred drama, 114–116
secular drama, 116–118
high relief, 75–76
high renaissance, 125, 129
Hildesheim bronze doors, 103
history and historical plays
renaissance, 148, 150–151
A History of African-American Artists:from 1792 to the Present, 260
History of the Christian Church, 83
history painting, 203
Hobbes, Thomas, 162, 166, 167
Hogarth, English William, 205, 207–208
Holland, Dave, 356
Holst, Gustav, 322
Holy Spirit, 2
holy text, 81–82
homophonic texture, 174
homophony, 140, 141
"Horkstow Grange," 323
"Hotter Than That," 319
Houlgate, Stephen, 231
House of the Tragic Poet, 63
house size, 363
hubris, 37
Hudson River School, 260
humanism, 93

Hume, David, 161, 162, 229
100 Years' War in France, 137
hymn, 64–65

I
I-*Ching*, 350
"I Loves You Porgy," 316
iambic pentameter, 147
ibn Adi, Yahya, 368
Ibsen, Henrick, 324
iconoclasm, 123
iconoclast controversies, 10
illuminated manuscripts, 81
illumination, 60–61
illusionary wall paintings, 50–52
illusionism, 126
"Immenso Jehova," 292
impasto, 273
imperialism, 227
impresario, 186
impression, 267
impressionism, 265–270, 285–286
In the Catskills, 261
The Incredulity of Saint Thomas, 166
indeterminacy, 349
indigenous peoples, 228
Industrial Revolution, 209, 233
installations, 371
intaglio, 67–68
interdisciplinary, 370
Interior of St. Bavo's Church, 123–124
International Bach Society, 380
The Interpretation of Dreams, 306
intervals, 31
Into the Woods, 363
Ionic, 25
"It Ain't Necessarily So," 316
Italy, Baroque regions in, 166–167

J
Jackson, Peter, 289
Jaquith, Austin, 382
Jazz music, 318–323, 353–357
Jesus Christ, 197, 233, 242
Johannes Passion, 380
jongleurs, 89, 112
Judith Slaying Holofernes, 168

Jüngel, Eberhard, 12
jurisprudence, 42

K
Kant, Immanuel, 161, 195–197, 229, 231
Kauffman, Angelica, 203
Kaufmann, Phyllis, 386
Kelly, Ellsworth, 344, 345
Kennedy, Edward, 320
Kerman, Joseph, 256
Kern, Jerome, 362
keystone, 50
Kierkegaard, SØren, 195, 231, 232, 239
Kind of Blue, 354, 355, 356
The King and I, 363
King Lear, 148–149
King, Martin Luther Jr., Dr., 386
Klavierstücke XI, 349
Kontra-Punkte, 348
kore, 23–24
kouroi, 23–24
Kreuzspiel, 348
Kyrie Eleison, 86

L
La pasión según San Marcos, 380
Lady Macbeth of Mtsensk, 312, 313
laissez-faire, 43
laments, 189
Landscape Composition: In the Catskills, 262
Landscape with Rainbow, 260, 261, 274
Las Meninas, 168, 169
Last Judgement, west tympanum, 104
The Last of the Mohicans (Cole), 227
The Last Supper, 134, 167
late romantic composers, 280–285
Leatherstocking Tales (Cooper), 227
Leitmotives, 287
Les Fauves, 298
Les Huguenots (Meyerbeer), 252, 253
Letters on Landscape Painting, 261, 262
Lewis, C.S., 11
Liberal Arts, 54
liberal theology, 369
libretto, 186
Lichtenstein, Roy, 340, 341, 342
Lieder, 244

Lin, Maya, 371, 372
Lincolnshire Posy, 323
Lindbeck, Georg, 369
Lindy Hoppers, 321
linear perspective, 126–128
Lingua franca, 321
The Lion King, 363
listening excerpt, 253
Liszt, Franz, 249
The Little Chimney Sweep, 264, 265
A Little Night Music, 363
Liturgical drama, 89
liturgical music, 85
Locke, John, 194, 195
The Lord of the Rings, 289
Louis le Vau, 171–173
Louis XIV, 171, 286
A Love Supreme, 356–357
low art. *See* folk art
low relief, 75–76
Lucas Cranach the Elder, 123
Lully, Jean Baptiste, 182, 189
Luncheon of the Boating Party, 268, 269
Luther, Martin, 10, 97, 123, 124, 142, 143
Lutheranism, 141
lyricists, 362
lyrics, 30
   in translation, 245

M
Madonna and Child, 107, 129
The Magic Flute, 216
Magnus liber organi, 111–112
Mahler, Gustav, 280–281
Mailloux, Cat, 377
Malevich, Kazimir, 13
Mallarmé, Stéphane, 286, 303
Manet, Eduard, 13
Manhattan Project, 383
mannerism, 126, 134–136
Mansart, Jules Hardouin, 172
Marat, Jean-Paul, 233
mark making, 129
The Marriage of Figaro, 216–217, 220
Mars Being Disarmed by Venus (David), 236
Marx, Karl, 229, 330

Masaccio, 127–128
mask decoration in amphitheater, 63
Maslanka, David, 358
Master of the Aeneid, 190
materialism, 265
Matisse, Henri, 298, 299
melismatic, 86
metamodernism, 369
The Metamorphosis of Narcissus, 306, 307
metrical psalmody, 142
Meyerbeer, Giacomo, 252
Michelangelo, 128, 129, 134, 135, 136
A Midsummer Night's Dream, 147
The Mighty Five/The Mighty Handful, 277
Miller, Arthur, 324, 326, 361, 362
Miller, Glenn, 321
mimetic art, 20
minimalism, 343–347
minnesingers, 112, 113
Minority Report (film), 37
minstrels, 112
miracle plays, 114
Miss Julie, 324
Mitchell, Anaïs, 385
mixed-media, 302
modernism, 308
   art, 298–308
      cubism, 301–303
      dada, 303–305
      fauvism, 298–300
      surrealism, 305–308
   music, 308–323
      classical music, 308–317
      jazz, 318–323
   philosophy, 295–298
   theatre, 323–329
      anti-realism, 326–329
      realism, 324–326
Monastery Ruin Eldena (Friedrich), 240
Monet, Claude, 266, 267–269
Monet, Musée Marmottan, 266
Monochord, 31
monody, 145
Monroe, Marilyn, 340
Monteverdi, Claudio, 176, 178
Monteverdi first opera *L'Orfeo*, 185

Monticello, 199
moonlight, 12
morality plays, 90
Mosaic of mask, 64
Moscow Art Theatre in Russia, 325
Moser, Mary, 203, 205
motet, 112
Mozart, Wolfgang Amadeus, 216–219
"Muddle instead of Music," 313
mural paintings, 105–107
murals, 52
music(s), 275–286, 308–323, 347–359, 379–382
  in ancient Greece, 26–35
    musical instruments, 34–35
    myths surrounding, 31–33
    notation, 33–34
    writings about, 30–31
  in ancient Rome, 53–62
    music theory, 59–62
    musical activity, 54–58
    musical instruments, 58–59
  bands, 357–359
  Baroque Era
    composers and forms, 176–181
    instrumental development, 181–184
    stylistic considerations, 174–176
  Cage, John gives up control, 350–352
  cappella vocal, 139–144
  classical music, 308–317
  composers, romantic period
    Brahms, Johannes, 247–249
    Chopin, Frédéric, 249–250
    Schubert, Franz, 244–245
    Schumann, Clara, 246–247
    Schumann, Robert, 246–247
    van Beethoven, Ludwig, 242–243
  early Christian era, 82–88
    church fathers, 84–85
    Gregorian chant, 85–87
    music theory, 87–88
  Enlightenment, 208–219
    classical. *See* classical music
    Mozart, Wolfgang Amadeus, 216–219
  Glass, Philip, 352–353
  global relevance, 379–382
  in High and Late Middle Ages, 108–114
    eye music, 113–114
    polyphony, 108, 110–112
    secular music and culture, 112–113
  impressionism, 285–286
  jazz, 318–323, 353–357
  late romantic composers, 280–285
  nationalism, 275–280
  new aesthetic search, 144–146
  shifting perceptions, 136–139
  Stockhausen controls music, 347–349
Music of the Spheres, 27, 137
music theory, 87–88
musical instruments
  in ancient Greece, 34–35
  in ancient Rome, 58–59
musical neoclassicism, 308
musical theatre, 250, 385–386
musician, defined, 59
musicians, paintings of, 28–29
Musorgsky, Modest, 277
mutes, 320
mystery plays, 114

N
Nabucco, 276, 292
narthex, 100
National Academy of Design, 261
National Broadcasting Company (NBC), 320
National Symphony Orchestra, 7
nationalism, 275–280
naturalism, 126–129, 231
NBC. *See* National Broadcasting Company
Neo-Platonism, 70
neoclassical work, 233–236
neoclassicism, 198
Nero, 57–58
Netherlands
  Baroque regions in, 169–171
New Orleans Colored Waif's Home for Boys, 318
New York Drawing Association, 261
New York's theater district, 363

Nietzsche, Friedrich, 17–18, 21, 230, 333
The Night Café, oil on canvas, 271, 272
nihilism, 297
Nixon in China, 383
Norma (Bellini), 254
northern renaissance, 126, 129–133
Notre Dame Cathedral, 110–111
noumena, 195

O

Oath of the Horatii (David), 235, 237
Obama, Barack, 375
oculus, 50
Odyssey, 31
The Oedipus Project, 387
Oedipus Rex, 36–38, 387
Of Mice and Men, 317
Off-Off Broadway theater, 364
oil painting, 129
Oklahoma!, 363
Old St. Peter's Basilica, 84
Old Testament, 68
Oldenburg, Claes, 342, 343
Oliver, King, 318
op art, 343–347
The Open Window, 299
opera, 146, 211, 221–225, 383–385
  definition of, 185
  Handel, George Frideric, 187–189
  other languages, 189–191
  seria, 186–187
Opera as Drama (Kerman), 255
opera buffa, 224
Oppenheimer, Robert, 383
orant, 72
oratorio, 4
orchestra, 64–65, 182
order, 25
Ordo virtutum, 90, 386
organal voice, 110
organum, 110, 136–137
Origin of Species, 265
Orpheus, 32–33
orthogonal lines, 127, 128
Our Town, 317, 327–328
The Oxford History of Western Music, 287

P

Paintings, of musicians, 28–29
Palace of Versailles, 167, 172
Pange lingua gloriosi, 83
pantheistic, 196
Pantheon, 50, 51
pantomime, 328
Paper Window, 377, 379
Parker, Charlie, 321–322, 356
Parthenon, 26, 27
Passion 2000, 380, 381
passion, Baroque, 179
passion play, 115
pastoral drama, 116
"*Pathetique*," 284
Paul, 33
Pavlova, Anna, 308–309
Pelleas und Melisande, 310
People's Artist award in 1947, 315
percussionists, 380
Perfect Fifth (P5), 88
Perfect Fourth (P4), 88
performers, 59
Persichetti, Vincent, 358
The Persistence of Memory, 306
Peter and the Wolf, 315
Peter, Simon, 151
Petit, Pierre, 288
Petrucci, Octavio, 138, 140
phenomena, 195
philosophy, 41–44, 295–298, 367–370
  in ancient Greece, 17–21
  Enlightenment, 193–197
  in High and Late Middle Ages, 93–97
photorealism, 336–339, 338
Picasso, Pablo, 274, 301, 302, 303
Pictures at an Exhibition, 277
Pierrot lunaire, 311
Pipe, Glass, Bottle of Rum, 303
plainchant, 89
Plato, 19, 20, 30, 42, 122, 126
plein-air, 265
poets, defined, 59
point music, 348
pointillism, 271
points of imitation, 140

Politics, 42
Pollock, Jackson, 332
polychoral, 140, 141
polymath, 122
polyphony, 110
Pompey's theater, 66
pop art, 7, 339–343
Porgy and Bess, 316
Porter, Cole, 362
Portrait of a Man in Red Chalk, 122
Portrait of Modest Musorgsky, 278
portraiture as propaganda, 47–48
post-Constantine, 75, 77–79
    Christ and saints, 77–79
    image and idol, conflict of, 78–79
post-liberal theology, 369
postimpressionism, 270–275
postmodernism, 232, 369
    art, 331–347
        abstract expressionism, 331–336
        hard-edge painting, minimalism/op art, 343–347
        photorealism, 336–339
        pop art, 339–343
    music, 347–359
        bands, 357–359
        Cage, John gives up control, 350–352
        Glass, Philip, 352–353
        jazz, 353–357
        Stockhausen controls music, 347–349
    theater, 359–365
        toward another Broadway, 363–365
        toward selective realism, 361–362
        toward the absurd, 360–361
        toward the musical, 362–363
Pozzo, Andrea, 163, 164, 165
pragmatic, 41
Pravda, 313
pre-Constantine, 72–75
    adapted pagan imagery, 72
    narrative and biblical stories, 72, 74
    stylistic shifts, 74–75
Prélude à "L'après-midi d'un faune," 285, 286
prepared piano, 350
presentational style of acting, 325

Priebe, Rebekah, 152–156
prima donnas, 186
principal voice, 110
printing press, music, 138–140
printmaking, 129, 131
Prizes, Pulitzer, 361
program symphony, 280
Prokofiev, Sergei, 312–316
Prokofiev's Symphony No. 1, 314
props, 328
Psalm, 357
Psaltery, 83
public concerts, rise of, 209–210
Purcell, Henry, 174
Pythagoras, 30, 87

Q
Quadratura, 165
Quadrivium, 54
quarto editions, 146
"Quinten" Quartet, 213
quotes from Shakespeare, 10

R
Radial design, 105
Raphael, 126, 129, 131, 134
rapture, 196
Rauschenberg, Robert, 333, 335, 336
readymades, 304
realism, 126–129, 262–265, 324–326
recapitulation, 213
recitative, 145
red-figure technique, 23
Reed, Alfred, 358
Reformation, 123, 124, 139, 141
regions, Baroque
    France, 171–173
    Italy, 166–167
    Netherlands, 169–171
    Spain, 167–169
relics, 107
reliefs, 75
religion, 230–231
Remus, 44–45
renaissance, 7, 228
    art, 121–126

architecture of, 133–134
mannerism, 134–136
naturalism and realism, 126–129
northern renaissance, 129–133
music
cappella vocal, 139–144
new aesthetic search, 144–146
shifting perceptions, 136–139
philosophy, 124–126
theatre, 146–148
comedies, 152–156
history and historical plays, 148, 150–151
tragedy, 148–149
Renoir, Pierre-Auguste, 268, 269
Rent, 363
representational style of acting, 325
The Republic, 42
Republican Portrait of a Man, 47, 48
requiems, 180
resonant across centuries, 386–387
responsorial, 86
"Resurrection," 280, 281
Rhapsody in Blue, 316
Rhau, Georg, 143
Rihm, Wolfgang, 380
Riley, Bridget, 346
The Ring, 290
The Ring of the Nibelungs, 289
Risorgimento, 275
The Rite of Spring, 309
Robert, J., 384
rock musicals, 363
Rococo style, 173, 198
Rodgers, Richard, 362
Roenne, Henry, 147
Roman Empire. *See* ancient Rome
Romanesque, 99
romanticism
art, 233–242
music, 242–250
philosophy, 227–233
theatre, 250–256
Romeo and Juliet, 315
Romulus, 44–45
rondeau, 113

Rose theatre, 147
rose window, 105
Rossini, Gioachino, 251
Rothko, Mark, 332, 334
Rouen Cathedral, Facade, 269
Rouen Cathedral, West Facade, Sunlight, 268
Royal Academy of Painting, 199, 202
Rubens, Peter Paul, 169
Rumors of War, 375
Rushd, Ibn, 367
Russell, Bertrand, 230

S
Sacred drama, 114–116
Saenredam, Pieter Jansz, 124
Saint Peter's Basilica, 133, 135
saints, 77–78
Salcedo, Doris, 373
San Carlo alle Quattro Fontane Church, 164
sanctuary, 100
Sanctus, 87
Santa Maria del Carmine, 127, 128
sarcophagi, 47
Sarcophagus of the Spouses, 47
Sartre, Jean-Paul, 297
satirist, 205, 207–208
Saving Leonardo, 351
Scarlatti, Domenico, 174
Schaff, Philip, 83
Schleiermacher, Friedrich, 233
Schoenberg, Arnold, 310–311, 347, 348, 350
Schoenberg reorganizes music, 310–312
scholastic, 90
School of Athens, 129, 131
The School of Athens, 2, 3
Schubert, Franz, 242, 244–245
Schuller, Gunther, 358
Schuman, William, 358
Schumann, Clara, 246–248
Schumann, Robert, 246–248
Schütz, Heinrich, 180
Schwantner, Joseph, 358
Scotus, John Duns, 1, 96–97

Scripture, 4–6, 8, 10–13
Scripture teaches, 376
The Sea of Ice (Friedrich), 240, 241
The Seagull, 324
"second Mozart," 242
Second Suite in F, 322
secular drama, 116–118
secular music and culture, 112–113
selective realism, 361
Sellars, Peter, 383
seria, opera, 186–187
serial music, 347
Seurat, Georges, 270–272
sfumato, 167
Shaftsbury, 194
Shakespeare, William
    plays, 146–152
Shaw, Artie, 321
she-wolf, 45, 46
The Sheltered Path, 266, 267
Shibboleth, 374
Shoes (Art), 9
Shostakovich, Dmitri, 312–316
Show Boat, 362
Siegfried, Young, 290
Simple Gifts, 317
Sina, Ibn, 367
Singspiel, 224
Sistine Chapel Ceiling, 122, 127, 136
skepticism, 229
Sketches of Spain, 354
slip, 23
slip casting, 204
Snow Storm: Hannibal Crossing the Alps
    (Turner), 239
social activism, 372–375
social contract theory, 162
social practice, 375–376
social responsibility, 297
Socrates, 19
sola gratia, 97
solo concerto, 210–211
solo sonata, 211
sonata, 213
Sonata in D minor, 174
Sonatas and Interludes, 350

song cycle, 242
songs, 211
Sophocles, 36
soprano, 140
The Sorrows of Telemachus, 203–204
The Sound of Music, 87, 363
Sousa, John Philip, 322
South Pacific, 363
space block planning, 133
Spain
    Baroque regions in, 167–169
spoken drama, 185, 189
Sprechstimme, 311
Springsteen, Bruce, 381, 382
St. Gregory I, 86
St. Mark's Church, 140, 141
St. Peter's Basilica, 163, 164
staccato, 163
staccato style, 163
"Stage Manager," 328
Stalin hampers musical progress,
    312–316
Stalin, Joseph, 312, 315
Stanislavsky, Konstantin, 325
Stella, Frank, 344
stile moderno, 174, 176
Still Life with Dresser, 273, 275
still lifes, 163
Stockhausen controls music, 347–349
Stockhausen, Karlheinz, 347, 349, 350
The Stonebreakers, 263
Stony Island Arts Bank, 375–376
Storytelling after the Storm, 387
Stradivari, Antonio, 183
Strauss, Richard, 282–283
Stravinsky, Igor, 308, 309, 310
Strayhorn, Billy, 320–321
Streetcar Named Desire, 361
Strindberg, August, 324
string quartet, 211
sublime, 238
subvert, 7
"Summertime," 316
Sunday Afternoon on the Island of La
    Grande Jatte, 270–271, 272
sung drama, 185, 188

The Supper at Emmaus, 171
surrealism, 305–308
Swaying Dancer, 268, 270
syllabic, 86
Symphony No. 2 in C minor, 280, 281
Symphony No. 4., 358
Symphony No. 6 in B minor, 284
The Symphony of Psalms, 309, 310
symphony orchestra, 210
Systematic Theology, 369

T

Tabula rasa, 194
Tallis, Thomas, 140
Taruskin, Richard, 287
Tchaikovsky, Piotr Illyich, 283–285
"Teachers of the Church," 1
tempera paint, 125
tempera panels, 107
Temple of Dendur in the Metropolitan Museum of Art, 380
tenebrism, 166–167
tenor, 140
tension, 1
terraced dynamics, 174, 175
terracotta
  amphora, 23
  krater, 22
  lekythos, 23
text in translation, 292
"The Hurdy-Gurdy Man," 245
"The Rising," 381, 382
theater of the absurd, 360
theatre(s), 286, 323–329, 359–363, 383–387
  in Ancient Greeks, 35–39
    Greek masks, 36
    tragic drama, 36–39
  in ancient Rome, 62–66
  anti-realism, 326–329
  Baroque Era, 185–186
    Handels operas, 187–189
    opera seria, 186–187
    other languages opera, 189–191
  early Christian era, 88–91
  Enlightenment
    satire and comedy, 219–221
    beyond serious opera, 221–225
  from German Romanticism to nationalism, 286–287
  in High and Late Middle Ages, 114–118
    sacred drama, 114–116
    secular drama, 116–118
  musical theatre, 385–386
  opera, 383–385
  realism, 324–326
  renaissance, 146–148
    comedies, 152–156
    history and historical plays, 148, 150–151
    tragedy, 148–149
  resonant across centuries, 386–387
  toward another Broadway, 363–365
  toward selective realism, 361–362
  toward the absurd, 360–361
  toward the musical, 362–363
  Verdi, Giuseppe and Opera à la Risorgimento, 291–293
  Wagner, Richard and music drama, 287–291
theatrical postmodernism, 359
theatrical realism, 323
theatricalism, 327
theological liberalism, 232
theory of law. *See* jurisprudence
thespian, 36
Third Earl of Shaftsbury, 194
The Third of May 1808 (Goya), 237, 239
"Three Person'd God," 383, 384
The Three Sisters, 324–325
tibia, 54–55
Ticheli, Frank, 358
Till Eulenspiegel, 282
Tillich, Paul, 369
timbres, 285
Tintoretto, 134
Toccata, 175
Tolkien, J. R. R., 289
tone poem, 382
tone poems, 282
toward another Broadway, 363–365

toward modernism
  art, 259–275
    American landscape painting, 260–262
    impressionism, 265–270
    postimpressionism, 270–275
    realism, 262–265
  music, 275–286
    impressionism, 285–286
    late romantic composers, 280–285
    nationalism, 275–280
  theatre, 286
    from German romanticism to nationalism, 286–287
    Verdi, Giuseppe and Opera à la Risorgimento, 291–293
    Wagner, Richard and music drama, 287–291
toward selective realism, 361–362
toward the absurd, 360–361
toward the musical, 362–363
tracery, 105
tragedy, 148–149
tragic drama, 36–39
tragicomedy, 325
transept, 99
The Tribute Money, 127
triple meter, 141
tritone, 88
The Triumph of St. Ignatius, 163, 164
triumphalism, 231
Trivium, 54
tromp l'oeil ("to fool the eye"), 52
trope, 89
troubadours, 89, 112
trouvères, 112
Trumpet Concerto, 215
Tufail, Ibn, 367
Turner, J. M. W., 239, 240, 260
twelve-tone row, 311
tympanum, 104
typology, 74

U

Uncle Vanya, 324
Untitled, 304, 305
Utrecht Psalter, 81

V

"Va, pensiero," 292
van Beethoven, Ludwig, 242–243
van Eyck, Jan, 129, 132
van Gogh, Vincent, 271–273
van Rijn, Rembrandt, 170
van Zandt, Steven, 382
Vasarely, Victor, 344, 345
vase paintings, 22
Velazquez, Diego, 168
vellum, 82
Verdi, Giuseppe, 276
  and Opera à la Risorgimento, 291–293
veristic, 47
Vermeer, Johannes, 169
vielle, 113
A View from the Bridge, 362
The Village Voice, 364
virtual tour, 48
visual hierarchy, 75
"Viva Verdi," 276, 277
Vivaldi, Antonio, 174, 181, 182
von Bingen, Hildegard, 386
von Goethe, Johann Wolfgang, 287
voussoir, 50

W

Wagner, Richard, 276, 287–291
Wagner, Richard and music drama, 287–291
Waiting for Godot, 360, 361
Walkin', 354
Walt Disney Corporation, 363
Wang Chen, 134
Warhol, Andy, 339, 340, 341
Washington, George, 199–201
Water Passion after St. Matthew, 380
Wedgwood, Josiah, 204
Weelkes, Thomas, 144
Weiwei, Ai, 372, 373
Wheat Field with Cypresses, 273
Whitehead, Alfred North, 19
Wild Beasts, 298
Wilder, Thornton, 327, 328
Wiley, Kehinde, 374
Williams, Tennessee, 361

Wilson, Robert, 353
Winterreise album (Schubert), 244–245
Wittgenstein, Ludwig, 369
Wolterstorff, Nicholas, 13
Woman Writing, 302
word painting, 144
World War I, 362
World War II, 360, 383
worship, early Christian, 79–81
worship wars, 111

Y
Y2K, 379, 381
Young, Lester, 322

Z
Zazen, 351
Zoom, 387
Zwingli, Ulrich, 123